THE COMPLETE
HOME DECORATOR

1000 DESIGN IDEAS FOR THE HOME

THE COMPLETE HOME DECORATOR

1000 DESIGN IDEAS FOR THE HOME

STEWART WALTON

RIZZOLI
NEW YORK

INTRODUCTION

The COMPLETE HOME DECORATOR has been designed to provide a wonderful source of ideas and inspiration, combined with a goldmine of practical advice. Armed with this book, you should be able to effect a complete transformation of your home, if that is what you desire — or, on a more modest level, give a new look to one particular room. At the very least, it will enable you to accentuate the best features of your home and to disguise the worst.

I have worked on this book with a team of contributors, all well known in their fields. Together, we have tried to cater to every taste, budget and level of expertise, giving hard, practical information in easy-to-follow steps, special techniques in boxes, and styling tips in the outside margin of the pages. Certainly, there will be something new for everyone to try, no matter how experienced.

The main thing I hope you will learn from this book is the fun and the satisfaction that can be had from design and decorating. Be brave, be adventurous, and you may surprise yourself with what you achieve — remember that most mistakes can easily be put right. Try color combinations that you have shied away from in the past; put together different textures. If you have always chosen cool colors and a modern feel, decorate one small room in a warm, rich style to see whether you enjoy it. Buy a small artifact or accessory you really like, even though you cannot think of a place for it, and make a feature out of your favorite objects. The important thing to remember is that you will be happiest in a home that truly reflects your own personality.

Stewart Walton

THE CONTRIBUTORS

Jill Blake, who wrote *The Rooms,* is a highly acclaimed journalist who has written about interiors for many successful magazines. She is the author or co-author of a number of books including *The Book of House Style* and *Furnishing Details*. She has worked as a color consultant for a number of companies including Berger Paints and is a senior lecturer at a London interior design college. **Barbara Chandler**, who wrote *Architectural Style*, has been writing on interior design and furnishing for nearly thirty years. She contributes regularly to *Ideal Home* magazine and *The London Evening Standard*, and has also written for the *Daily Telegraph* and *The Sunday Times*. The author of several books, she also broadcasts on radio and television. She is a consultant and teacher with the Regent Academy interior design college. **Jennifer Jones** is the author of *Finishing Touches*. She is a freelance editor and writer, specializing in the areas of interior design, crafts, gardening, and cooking. Over the years she has worked with a wide variety of authors, including Rosie Fisher on *Decorating Children's Rooms*, Patricia Seligman on *Painting Murals,* and Jane Churchill on *The Collins Book of Soft Furnishings*. **Mike Lawrence**, who wrote the *Decorating* chapter, has been writing about woodworking for over twenty years, contributing regular articles to all the major do-it-yourself magazines. He has also written or contributed to over forty books, edited three major do-it-yourself publications, and has spent seven years answering questions on local radio. **Maggie Stevenson** wrote the *Soft Furnishings* chapter; she has spent several years as Home Editor of *Woman and Home* magazine, developing their coverage of crafts and home furnishings. Now a freelance journalist, she contributes regularly to *Family Circle, Homes and Ideas*, and to a range of women's magazines. She is the author of *Kitchen and Bathroom Ideas*.

CONTENTS

Architectural Style 6

The Rooms 34

Decorating 82

Soft Furnishings 156

Finishing Touches 222

ARCHITECTURAL STYLE

MANY OF TODAY'S DESIGNS FOR THE HOME draw on what has gone before: a glance at any manufacturer's current wallpaper and fabric collections will reveal influences as diverse as Gothic, Neoclassical, and Art Nouveau. Understanding such visual references is rewarding in itself, but in recent years it has gained a new significance, due to the vogue for restoring properties to their original style. Each major period of architecture had its own way of using materials, space, and proportion. Knowing something about them is essential if you are decorating an older house or apartment.

A home need not be particularly historical or especially grand to be considered worthy of being lovingly restored to its original style. Many modest houses of the 1920s and 1930s, subsequently "modernized" in the 1950s or 1960s, can gain considerable appeal by being returned to a look that is more suited to the age in which they were built. The scope of the restoration can range from the simple matter of choosing appropriate color schemes for paintwork and patterns for curtains, to the more extensive replacement of architectural features such as dado and picture rails, doors and door hardware, and windows. In more markedly "period" properties, restoration may involve reinstalling fireplaces, replacing cornices and moldings, and removing double-glazing in favor of old-style sashes and casements. Where time and money are limited, it is enough to reflect the general look of an original period in your decorating style, and this can be achieved in quite simple ways, as the following pages show.

LEFT: THE WILDER EXCESSES OF ART NOUVEAU TURNED THE FACADES OF THE MOST ADVENTUROUS NINETEENTH-CENTURY BUILDINGS INTO CURVACEOUS COMPOSITIONS OF COLORED PANELS AND TWISTED IRONWORK. YOU CAN SEE THIS TODAY IN CITIES SUCH AS VIENNA AND BARCELONA. THE FACADE ON THE LEFT CREATED IN THE 1980S IN VIENNA BY ARTIST FRIEDENSREICH HUNDERTWASSER, IS CLEARLY INFLUENCED BY ART NOUVEAU.

RIGHT: THESE DECORATIVE PLASTERWORK CORBELS ARE A CLASSICALLY INSPIRED DETAIL ON AN EIGHTEENTH-CENTURY HOUSE.

EARLY STYLES

THE FIRST EXAMPLES OF WHAT CAN BE CALLED ARCHITECTURE date from the rise of early civilizations in the Middle East (c. 3000–1200 B.C.). Their walled cities were built with ziggurats (tiered towers topped by a temple), an idea that was continued by the Ancient Egyptians with their pyramids, tombs and temples. But it was the Ancient Greeks who developed architecture into an art form: their classical principles, forms and ornament – later modified by the Romans – left a legacy which has influenced all of western architecture. The building styles of Greece and Rome have inspired countless styles of architecture and interior design all over the world. Greek Classicism would be revived in many forms for centuries to come, while the Roman introduction of the vault led to the Gothic style of architecture, seen at its peak in many cathedrals of Europe.

THE RUINS OF THIS PERFECT LITTLE GREEK TEMPLE DISPLAY THE ESSENCE OF GREEK ARCHITECTURAL INSPIRATION: SIMPLE LINES, PERFECT PROPORTIONS AND THE BUILDING'S HARMONY WITH ITS SURROUNDINGS.

THE CLASSICAL TRADITION

The importance of Ancient Greek classical architecture, which reached its peak in the mid-fifth century B.C., lay not in its diversity or complexity of form, but in its simplicity: the basic constructions used columns as vertical supports for horizontal beams or blocks of stone or marble. The great achievement of the Greeks was to show how beauty can be achieved by careful attention to line and proportion. They demonstrated how a building can be a harmonious work of art in its own right, rather than just a basic shelter from the elements or a place of worship or trade. Important Greek structures such as temples were always considered in relation to the landscape and were sited where they had plenty of surrounding space. The most famous example of Greek architecture is the Parthenon.

The Romans (500 B.C.–A.D. 300) adopted Greek design traditions, but were the first to use brick and cement to build new elements such as the dome, arch and vault, which enabled buildings to be constructed with four or five floors, rather than the usual Greek one or two. The result was impressive architectural showpieces such as the Colosseum and Pantheon in Rome and aqueducts, such as the one found in the French city of Nimes. Under the Romans, the classical style became more florid and ornate; this influenced future "Classical" revivals.

CLASSICISM IN THE RENAISSANCE

Classical forms in architecture were largely abandoned during the Middle Ages, but were rediscovered during the Renaissance, which reached its architectural peak in sixteenth-century Italy, spreading out from there through the rest of Europe. In this revival, the Roman version of the Classical Orders (rules of proportion and decoration for the columns and beams of buildings) was adopted as the main framework for design. The subsequent classical revival of the later eighteenth century found Greek forms in favor, while the nineteenth century drew freely from classical sources and experimented with proportion and detail.

GOTHIC STYLE

Gothic architecture, current in Europe between the late twelfth century and the middle of the sixteenth century, perfected vaulting, buttressing and the pointed arch, which eliminated thick, load-bearing walls and allowed buildings to be built higher than ever before.

At its most sublime in the many cathedrals still standing today all over Europe, Gothic architecture showed how buildings can express the spiritual aspirations of mankind. The style began in France, with the Abbey of St. Denis (1144) near Paris, followed by the cathedral of Notre Dame. The cathedrals of Reims (1211) and Chartres (1260) were the culmination of the style. Many centuries later, these buildings still capture the excitement of large, soaring volumes of space.

Gothic buildings, built principally in stone in various textures and colors, were illuminated by natural light flooding in through tiers of windows. The interplay of light and shadow framed by arches became an important element of the design as their decoration became increasingly ornamental, with flowing stone tracery.

THE ELEGANT POINTED GOTHIC ARCH HAS INFLUENCED THE ARCHITECTURE, FURNITURE, AND EVEN WALLPAPER AND FABRIC PATTERNS OF NUMEROUS "REVIVALS". HERE IT SHAPES THE TOP OF A SIMPLE WHITE WINDOW WHOSE QUATREFOIL, TREFOIL AND SIMPLE GLAZING BARS RE-INTERPRET THE MAGNIFICENT STAINED GLASS OF MEDIEVAL CATHEDRALS. NOTE HOW THE VALANCE FOLLOWS THE WINDOW CURVES.

ABOVE: THE WORK OF THE GREAT EIGHTEENTH-CENTURY BRITISH CLASSICAL ARCHITECT AND INTERIOR DESIGNER, ROBERT ADAM, IS STILL SEEN IN MANY GRAND HOUSES TODAY. TYPICAL "HALLMARKS" INCLUDE PALE PASTEL WALLS COMBINED WITH WHITE MOLDINGS AND CLASSICAL DECORATIVE MOTIFS SUCH AS SWAGS, PALM LEAVES, URNS, BASKETS OF FRUIT AND DRAPED CLASSICAL FIGURES.

THE SEVENTEENTH CENTURY

THIS SPLENDID ITALIAN FACADE IS TYPICALLY BAROQUE. ARCHES, PILLARS, BALUSTERS AND STEPS ARE PILED HIGH IN A MAJESTIC SYMMETRY WHICH IS AT THE SAME TIME DRAMATIC AND EXUBERANT.

THE MAIN ARCHITECTURAL MOVEMENT OF THE SEVENTEENTH CENTURY was the Baroque, in which the classical forms of the Renaissance were used freely to create an opulent style characterized by a liberal use of curves and extravagant decoration. Although the style originated in Italy at the beginning of the century, it would eventually become more predominant in France during the reign of the "Sun King", Louis XIV, the driving force behind the magnificent Palace of Versailles.

The seventeenth century saw many changes in interior design and furnishing. Although still magnificently decorated, houses by the end of the century were becoming, first and foremost, homes for people to live in, comfort and practicality came increasingly to the fore.

ITALIAN BAROQUE

The Baroque began in Italy as a papal style which filtered through from Rome and the Vatican to other cities and then to the palaces of great families such as the Medicis. Very much a public style rather than an intimate setting for private life, it provided a lavish background for the elegant social gatherings of the rich. Indeed, private rooms of the period were often shabby and poorly decorated by comparison.

The two great Italian architects of the Baroque were Bernini (1598–1680), famous today for his Roman fountains, and Borromini (1599–1667), who was chiefly responsible for transforming Rome into a Baroque city. They, and later architects of the Baroque throughout Europe, continued to use the Classical Orders for both construction and decoration, but were not restrained by purist classical disciplines. The Baroque approach was freewheeling and ornate, with a series of curves boldly linking floor, walls and ceilings to give interiors a feeling of vitality, movement and drama.

Furnishings were now considered as part of the overall effect. For the first time on any scale, furniture, including chairs, small tables, and beds, was designed for specific rooms, along with fitted mirrors, carved, gilded, and painted paneling, paintings in ornate wooden or plaster frames, and painted ceilings and walls. The Baroque style piled decoration on decoration, with elaborate frescoes, paintings and sculptures filling every gap between elaborate pillars and entablatures, to be echoed by the curves of vaulted frescoed ceilings. The interior still worked as a whole, however, due to a mastery of proportion and balance.

FRANCE

The French developed their own variation of Baroque: a sophisticated and luxurious form of Classicism, which only later became more ornate. A strong advocate of the style was the prolific architect Francois Mansart, whose first private house commission was in Paris in 1598. He relied on the pure beauty of classical features for his numerous interiors, and he and his contemporaries also took great pains to plan buildings carefully, arranging staircases, public galleries, and private suites in a new and original fashion, and inventing oval and octagonal shapes for rooms.

With the architect Charles Le Brun, "Classical Baroque" reached its peak. He created the "Louis XIV style", which found its ultimate expression in the fabulous apartments of the Palace of Versailles (1671–1681). Louis XIV himself was keenly involved in furnishing his palace and set up the Gobelin workshops specifically to embellish the royal residences. Colored marble for floors and walls, patterned bottle-green and crimson velvets, fountains, vaulted ceilings, *trompe l'oeil* murals, ornately framed pictures, walls of mirrors, gold-threaded tapestries and solid silver furniture all combined to create interiors of unparalleled wealth and glamour. With his meticulous attention to every furnishing detail, Le Brun could be regarded as the world's first all-round professional interior decorator.

ENGLAND

Baroque went to England, too, as seen in the great pillars and domes of Christopher Wren's St. Paul's Cathedral. Other English architects took up the theme, including Hawksmoor and Sir John Vanbrugh, who collaborated on the theatrical design of Blenheim Palace. English Baroque never attained the grandeur of its continental equivalents, but the style flourished in plasterwork and wood carving.

ABOVE: THE EXPOSED WOODEN BEAMS OF WOODENFRAMED HOUSES, FOUND IN MANY PARTS OF NORTHERN EUROPE, CREATE AN ATTRACTIVE ARCHITECTURAL STYLE, ECHOED INSIDE BY EXPOSED CEILING RAFTERS, PLANKED WOODEN FLOORS AND ROUGH-CAST, WHITEWASHED WALLS.

RIGHT: MARBLE WAS A MATERIAL MUCH BELOVED BY BAROQUE ARCHITECTS, PARTICULARLY IN ITALY WHERE A VARIETY OF BEAUTIFUL COLORS AND TEXTURES WAS IN PLENTIFUL SUPPLY, TO BE USED FOR COLUMNS, ARCHES AND WALLS, AS WELL AS FOR INTRICATE FLOOR MOSAICS, AS ILLUSTRATED HERE.

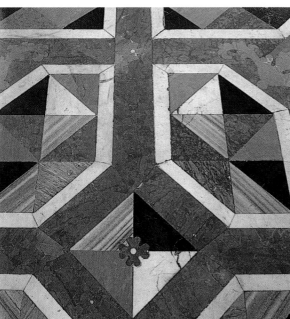

SEVENTEENTH-CENTURY STYLING IDEAS

WOODEN SHUTTERS ARE AN ANCIENT FORM OF WINDOW DRESSING AND WERE WIDELY USED IN THE SEVENTEENTH CENTURY. IN NORTHERN EUROPE, IT WAS THE FASHION TO SET THEM INSIDE WINDOWS TO KEEP WARMTH IN AND LIGHT OUT, BUT IN THE MEDITERRANEAN, EXTERNAL SLATTED SHUTTERS THEN, AS NOW, DECORATED THE OUTSIDES OF BUILDINGS, PROVIDING PRIVACY AND SECURITY WHEN CLOSED, BESIDES WARMTH IN WINTER AND SHADE IN SUMMER.

Wood paneling was popular for interiors, either in its natural form – made from oak, chestnut or walnut – or painted in white, pale green or pale blue. Wool tapestries were used to decorate the walls, although in later years this combination of wood and wall-hangings was replaced by wall and ceiling paints, with many walls painted to imitate grand and intricate materials like marble, tortoiseshell and lapis lazuli.

Floors were usually scrubbed wooden planks, often covered with rush matting. Parquet flooring also came into vogue; in France, it tended to be lozenge-shaped, and covered with Persian, Turkish or Savonnerie carpet squares, while in Germany and Scandinavia, rich, inlaid wooden floors were often covered with straw for protection. The main ground floor rooms of grand Dutch houses were, by contrast, paved with black and white marble tiles.

Windows with wooden glazing bars were now a great improvement over leaded lights; sliding sash windows were in use in Paris by 1640. Shutters took various forms; in the Netherlands the top of the window was left unshuttered. Most windows did not have curtains at first, but toward the end of the century curtains were hung in pairs, with the rods and rings disguised by a valance. Curtain fabric often matched that used for wallhangings and upholstery.

Mirrors and candles Although large sheets of mirror glass were not made until late in the century, rooms were often hung with groups of smaller mirrors to create a feeling of light and space. Candles were used liberally: their holders took many forms, including floor-standing candelabras, wall sconces, and low-hung chandeliers. Grand candlesticks were brass and humbler varieties of pewter, with silver candlesticks increasingly popular toward the end of the period.

Furniture In most countries oak was used to make robust carved furniture in upright, rectangular shapes, although toward the end of the century, walnut, often with marquetry inlay, became fashionable in grander homes. Tall Baroque chairs had scrolled or barley-twist legs, carved tops, and caned or velvet-covered seats. Louis XIV carved and gilded furniture in heavy, ponderous shapes was popular all over Europe.

ABOVE: THIS FINE WALL DETAIL FROM AN ITALIAN DUCAL PALACE ILLUSTRATES THE SEVENTEENTH-CENTURY PRACTICE OF USING PAINT TO IMITATE GRAND MATERIALS WORKED INTO INTRICATE PATTERNS, SUCH AS INLAYS OF MARBLE AND OTHER PRECIOUS STONES. THIS IS A TREND THAT CONTINUES TODAY, WITH THE FASHION FOR SPECIAL PAINT EFFECTS.

RIGHT: SEVENTEENTH-CENTURY BEDROOMS WERE CHILLY, DRAFTY ROOMS, AND THICK BED CURTAINS WERE SUSPENDED FROM TWO POSTS AT THE FOOT AND A HEAVY HEADBOARD AT THE TOP, TO CREATE A PRIVATE, COZY FABRIC-LINED BOX. TODAY, DECORATIVE POSTS, ORIGINAL OR REPRODUCTION, WILL ADD STYLE TO BEDROOMS, WITH OR WITHOUT FABRIC HANGINGS.

RECREATING THE STYLE

For walls, oak paneling could be used with wool tapestries or damask hangings, as could a marbled paint effect or one of the wallpapers based on authentic seventeenth-century fabric patterns. Oriental wallpapers, panels or screens would be appropriate.

Authentic curtaining can be re-created with silk festoons drawn up and down with cords, or Venetian blinds with wooden slats. Suitable fabrics include printed Jacobean designs on heavy cottons and linens, "flamestick" bargello patterns in weaves or prints, embroidered crewelwork fabrics, and faded colors for velvets and silks. Use silk, damask, and moiré for a French Baroque style and delicately patterned Indian-style calico "chintzes" for a less formal look.

Floors Parquet and other types of wooden flooring are readily available. Use them plain or covered with Indian or Persian rugs. Alternatively, you could sand and seal existing wooden floorboards and cover them with natural flooring. There are many varieties of black and white vinyl flooring which will imitate the look of marble very successfully.

Furniture Original seventeenth-century furniture is very expensive, but reproductions are plentiful. Popular English and American choices are the refectory table with a planked top above an ornamental frieze, with chunky legs linked by stretchers at the bottom; gate-leg tables; chests of drawers; and extending drawleaf tables. Simple chairs with turned legs and rush seats, or tall chairs with caned backs and upholstered seats would be suitable for everyday use, with fully upholstered armchairs for the bedroom, with its four-poster bed.

THE EIGHTEENTH CENTURY

THE EIGHTEENTH CENTURY saw two important architectural movements: Rococo, a style that was characterized by its light elegance, and Palladianism, based on the work of the sixteenth-century Venetian architect, Andrea Palladio, whose interpretations of Roman classical architecture had a profound effect throughout Europe. Palladianism took root firmly in England, where it formed the basis of the Georgian style, later extending its influence to America. In the mid-eighteenth century, Palladianism made way for Neo-classicism, a term used to describe a variety of international styles which in practice differed widely. All, however, shared the aim of imitating or at least evoking the art of the ancient world, whether Greek, Roman, or a mixture of the two.

ROCOCO

Rococo (from the French *rocaille*, meaning rockwork, and *coquille*, meaning shell) began in France as a reaction against the excesses of the final high phase of Louis XIV Baroque. With this new style, classical formality was replaced by intimacy, elegance and convenience, as seen in Mansart's Chateau du Val near Paris, built in 1674 with small rooms in a one-story pavilion. Gradually, the new style – nicknamed "anti-Baroque" – was taken up for all important buildings in France, spreading finally to the Palace of Versailles in 1735. Rococo reached its peak during the reign of Louis XV and spread from France to most European countries, except for England, where Palladianism had a firm hold.

IN THE EARLY NINETEENTH CENTURY, FASHIONABLE AMERICA ADOPTED NEOCLASSICISM WITH ENTHUSIASM. THE RESULT WAS LIGHT, GRACEFUL INTERIORS WITH PALE PAINTED OR PAPERED WALLS, AND SIMPLE MOLDINGS FOR PLASTER AND WOODWORK. THE SIMPLE SWATHES OF FABRIC THAT TOP THE WINDOWS HERE TYPIFY A DESIRE FOR ELEGANCE AND PROPORTION.

HARKING BACK TO CLASSICAL ROMAN ARCHITECTURE, THE PALLADIAN IDEAL WAS A CAREFULLY ORDERED, RESTRAINED AND REGULAR SYMMETRY FOR ARCHES, COLUMNS AND PEDIMENTS WHICH EXTENDED TO EVERY DETAIL OF A BUILDING, AS IN THE DOOR PANELS AND GLAZING BARS SEEN HERE.

PALLADIANISM

During the reign of Queen Anne in England at the beginning of the eighteenth century, furnishings were elegant and delicate. Simple styles were carried out with first-class workmanship and materials. Cabriole legs and claw feet featured on chairs, sofas and tables, and a wide range of new types of furniture was designed, including, for the first time, tables made specially for the dining room. The Queen Anne style was also taken up enthusiastically in America, where it was to last longer than in England. Regional styles varied, with different woods favored by different parts of the country: mahogany and walnut in Rhode Island, cherrywood in Connecticut, and maple and ash in the Hudson Valley. New York stayed faithful to its Dutch heritage: hand-painted Delft tiles were often used for fireplaces, and furniture was painted in Dutch style.

During the English Georgian Age, which began with the accession of King George I to the throne in 1714, the Queen Anne style was replaced by Palladianism – largely due to the influence of architects such as the Earl of Burlington who, in 1715, returned from his travels in Italy with a collection of Andrea Palladio's drawings. These he reproduced in the form of Palladian buildings such as Chiswick House in west London, built to hold his collection of art and sculpture. Its style, reminiscent of a Greek temple, was widely adopted elsewhere.

The years from 1720 to 1760 saw the introduction of many typically rectangular Palladian-style country houses. Exteriors were restrained, symmetrical and correct, with banks of sash windows broken only by a central portico and pediment, and topped by a parapet. Interiors, by contrast, were often ornate affairs of gilt, marble, mirrors and large-scale decorative furniture. In towns, too, the terraces built in the streets and squares of fashionable English spa towns such as Tunbridge Wells and Bath echoed the proportions and details of Palladian villas. Many American eighteenth-century buildings reflect the simple, classical forms of Palladian ideals. The earliest is Drayton Hall, near Charleston (1738–1742). with a chimney piece in the hall based on a design by Inigo Jones.

Andrea Palladio and Inigo Jones

ANDREA PALLADIO (1508--1580) was an Italian architect whose work and widely translated books were influential in many countries, in his own lifetime and beyond. Using his studies of classical Roman architecture, Palladio perfected a style of carefully ordered symmetry for the steps, columns, pediments, arches and domes of his domestic buildings, generally known as villas. The most famous example is the Villa Capra (the Rotunda) near Vicenza.

INIGO JONES (1573--1652) was greatly influenced by Palladio; indeed, he was the first English architect to adopt the pure classical forms of the Renaissance. Unfortunately, few of his buildings remain. Of those that do, the most famous are the Banqueting House in Whitehall, London (1619--1622), and the Queen's House in Greenwich (1616--1635).

MID-EIGHTEENTH TO MID-NINETEENTH CENTURIES

In England, Neoclassicism reached its peak in the interior design of Robert Adam (1728-1792) and the architecture of John Nash (1752-1835), London's most inspired town planner who popularized the fashion for sweeping crescents of pillared stucco-fronted houses.

NEOCLASSICISM

This was the first truly international style, spreading from France, England, Italy, Spain, Germany, Russia, Sweden, and Denmark over to America, where it was adopted with particular fervor after independence.

Eighteenth-century France: a reaction against Rococo In France in the second half of the eighteenth century, Neoclassicism started as a reaction against the curvy excesses of Rococo (now considered "ridiculous" and "depraved"), resulting in a new popularity for rectilinear doors, windows, paneling, and mirrors, combined with columns and friezes. Wreaths, ribbons, swags, laurels, acanthus and trophies became popular decorative motifs. Louis XV's first architect at Versailles, Gabriel (1698 -1782), created small rooms of great elegance and restraint, with plain white ceilings and walls in white, pastel green or pale grey. Elegant marble mantelpieces were surmounted by large mirrors.

Eighteenth-century England: the Adam style The famous firm of the four Adam Brothers worked in Britain in the second half of the eighteenth century. After a three-year Grand Tour of Europe, Robert Adam returned to England in 1758 and set up practice with his brother, James, intent on introducing elements of French Neoclassicism to the predominantly "Roman" Palladian style. Robert soon became the most dominant and fashionable of the brothers. His style was light and elegant, adapting classical proportions and decoration to create rooms with "movement" (his declared aim) and expressed in such buildings as Syon House and Osterley House, near London. He was adept at remodeling the interiors of older buildings to suit commissions.

The Adam style embraced not only the proportions of a room but every aspect of its furniture and furnishings, for Robert Adam the architect was also an interior decorator *par excellence*. He is best remembered for his fireplaces and his paneled ceilings, intricately adorned with delicate plasterwork and painted insets.

Regency England: Greek revival Toward the end of the eighteenth century, many architects began to look

beyond the buildings of Rome back to the purity of Ancient Greece. The result was a plainer, more severe style of classical building, with shorter, stockier columns supporting weightier entablatures. Houses became more intimate and informal. Smaller, lighter rooms featured walls in clear, pale colors, topped by a narrow frieze, and plain, lower ceilings with, perhaps, a central garland from which hung a chandelier. Furniture became more solid, with the emphasis on form.

Nineteenth-century France: the Empire style French interiors of the early nineteenth century were triumphal in spirit, reflecting the victories of Emperor Napoleon. The classical influence remained strong: furniture was decorated with gilt and ormolu. Lustrous colored silks in sunny yellow, brilliant green, crimson or royal blue

THE EMPIRE STYLE OWES ITS NAME AND INFLUENCES TO THE EARLY NINETEENTH-CENTURY VICTORIES OF THE FRENCH EMPEROR NAPOLEON. STRONG, CLEAR COLORS WERE POPULAR FOR WALLS, AS WERE CLASSICAL MOTIFS SUCH AS THE GARLANDS HERE, WHOSE SPIRIT IS ECHOED IN THE LYRE LAMP BASE. FURNITURE, PLAIN AND HEAVY BUT WELL PROPORTIONED, WAS TYPICALLY MADE FROM BEAUTIFULLY FIGURED WOODS, AND THE MATCHING PICTURE FRAMES, WITH THEIR CORNER SQUARES OF DARK VENEER, ARE A CHARACTERISTIC DETAIL.

were draped or pleated across walls and ceilings to create the atmosphere of a grand military tent. As Napoleon conquered Egypt, so the sphinx, obelisk and winged lion joined other popular decorative motifs and were used, for example, for chair arms and table legs.

Nineteenth-century Germany and Austria: Biedermeier In Germany and Austria, nineteenth-century middle-class homes retained a Classical influence, while rejecting the often over-blown grandeur of French Empire. "Papa Biedermeier" (from *bieder*, meaning plain, and Meier, a common German surname) was an early nineteenth-century cartoon character whose name was adopted for a simple, pleasant way of furnishing, which was above all comfortable and homey. Walnut or fruitwood furniture, placed on parquet or varnished boards, was kept

at eye level, and pictures in simple molded frames were hung in rows. Wallpaper or fabric in small flowers or fine striped patterns were popular for walls, and pale curtains hung from brass rods were supplemented by shades fitted close to the window.

Neoclassicism in America An early example of the Greek revival in America is Latrobe's Doric Bank of Pennsylvania (1799–1801). Neoclassicism was popular throughout the 1820s and 1830s in many state capitals and for Washington's government buildings. It was also used for a number of fine private houses in New York and New England. Staircases became graceful, light and curved, with slender, elegant rails, and wooden paneling was replaced with painted, papered or fabric-covered walls and plaster cornices.

THE EMPIRE STYLE DREW HEAVILY ON CLASSICAL MOTIFS, AS DOES THIS MODERN FABRIC, WITH ITS CAREFUL DRAWINGS OF URNS, COLUMNS AND ROMAN BUSTS. GREEK KEY-PATTERN BRAID ON THE YELLOW UPHOLSTERY (YELLOW OR GOLD WAS AN EMPIRE FAVORITE) CLEVERLY UNDERSCORES THE CLASSICAL THEME.

EIGHTEENTH-CENTURY STYLING IDEAS

"PLAIN AND SIMPLE" WAS THE SHAKER WAY OF LIFE AND IS THE ESSENCE OF AMERICAN COUNTRY STYLE, TYPIFIED HERE BY THE SIMPLE, FUNCTIONAL LINES OF THE BUILT-IN STORAGE AND PLAIN PANELED DOOR IN UNADORNED GOLDEN WOODS, AND BY THE UNCARPETED, DARK-STAINED, PLANKED WOODEN FLOOR.

Wood paneling was popular early in the century for its attractive appearance and warmth. Plain pine was painted in a dark shade or grained to imitate a more decorative wood. Wall paneling was divided horizontally into three areas (dado, infill, and cornice) and often incorporated columns, arched niches, cupboards and fireplaces.

Walls Paint was used increasingly by now. Early English Georgian colors were strong and dark, although the paler colors introduced by Robert Adam (pink, blue, grey, and the celebrated "Adam green") and used as a background for white plasterwork moldings such as festoons and swags, baskets of fruit, draped classical figures and winged griffons, became ever more popular. Many Georgian town house walls had distemper backgrounds which were "scumbled" with oil paints to create a marbled or grained effect. In grander houses, fabric wallcoverings were favored in the early part of the century, although in later years printed wallpapers were used for smaller rooms: flock papers imitating Italian cut velvets appeared in around 1730, and luxury papers, with Oriental scenes of flowering shrubs and exotic birds in rich colors, were imported from China. In America, stenciling was a favored form of decoration from the second half of the century.

Windows Finely proportioned rooms were lit by large sash windows which were either shuttered or covered with festoon hangings in fabrics ranging from silks and brocades to plainer cotton prints. This century saw the flourishing of English-produced chintz: patterns of exotic flowers, fruits and winding stems derived from old Indian chintzes and from Chinese hand-painted wallpapers. In France, Toile de Jouy fabrics – attractive all-over pastoral scenes printed in a single color on a white or cream ground – were first produced in 1760. An eighteenth-century fashion matched curtains to fabric wallcoverings; a little later, fabrics, wallpapers and upholstery were matched.

Floors Parquet flooring continued its popularity in France. In England, plain oak-boarded floors were favored, but by the 1750s, fitted carpets with narrow widths sewn together, edged with a border, were in use.

MULTIPANED, BEAUTIFULLY PROPORTIONED SASH WINDOWS ARE A GEORGIAN FEATURE TO BE TREASURED. USE SIMPLE RODS AND RINGS TO SUSPEND FULL-LENGTH CURTAINS OF PLAIN COTTON FABRIC TO OFFSET THEIR CLASSIC SIMPLICITY.

RECREATING THE STYLE

Paneling effects *for walls and ceilings can be created with applied moldings, or even wallpaper borders. Modern* **trompe l'oeil** *printed paper decorations can be pasted straight onto walls to create the effect of classical pillars, niches and balustrades or maybe lighter, more delicate designs such as garlands, ribbons, tassels and bows. You could simply break up a wall horizontally with a deep molded wooden dado at chair height and add a deep wallpaper border at the top to create a frieze, then fill in the spaces with broken-color paint effects such as dragging, sponging or rag-rolling.*

Dark paint colors *such as browns, muddy olive greens, greys and off-white will successfully reproduce the interior of an early Georgian room; latex paint washes in pale shades of green, blue, pink and grey combined with white woodwork and moldings will recreate the feel of an Adam-style room. Marbled or distressed latex paint effects would also be appropriate for the period.*

Floors *can range from bare boards – stained and perhaps protected with a polyurethane seal – to parquet flooring arranged in a geometric pattern, or vinyl floor tiles resembling marble and stone effects. A large carpet square with painted or stained surrounding floorboards would also be suitable for this era.*

Windows *that are large and sash-style can be shuttered or dressed with shades, curtains or festoon hangings (a single piece of fabric drawn up to a valance by cords and pulleys). For a Neoclassical look, use a pelmet board of carved and gilded wood. For a Georgian style, hang full-length curtains from brass rods and rings, or top pairs of curtains with elaborate swags and tails. Authentic-style fabrics include damasks and velvets or coarser block-printed cottons, chintz and Toile de Jouy; the latter are often available in matching papers and fabrics to help create the coordinated fashion of the period. Self-colored woven damask is a suitable choice for a matching look that includes upholstery.*

Finishing touches *should include large mirrors to reflect light and increase the apparent size of a room. Ideally, these should have scallop and shell designs or classical motifs on the frames. A mirror placed over a fireplace or between a pair of windows will look particularly authentic.*

Lighting *should be subtle and subdued. Candles should be used with Georgian-style candlesticks, made of silver, walnut or mahogany. Alternatively, use candelabra on a dining-room table or in front of a mirror, where the light will be magnified. For an eighteenth-century period effect, do not use electric chandeliers ,as their light will be too bright.*

THE NINETEENTH CENTURY

CLUTTER AND WARMTH WERE CHARACTERISTICS OF VICTORIAN ROOMS THAT ARE EASY TO RECREATE TODAY, WITH A MIXTURE OF RICH, RED PATTERNS FOR WALLS, PLUMP UPHOLSTERY AND CARPET. EVERY SPARE SURFACE HERE — FROM HEARTH TO MANTELPIECE TO CABINET TOP — IS CRAMMED WITH ORNAMENTS AND OBJECTS.

THE NINETEENTH CENTURY was a time of constant change in interior design. Neoclassicism was replaced by a freer and less formal approach, in which architects and interior designers plundered history with energy and enthusiasm for design ideas. Queen Victoria built Osborne House on the Isle of Wight as a Tuscan villa, but favored a Scottish baronial style for Balmoral in Scotland; Napoleon III chose Gothic for Pierrefonds, but Baroque for the Louvre. An explosion of mass-production made such "styles", formerly the prerogative of the rich, readily available to the ordinary home-owner, albeit often misinterpreted. Among the wealth of historical design movements serving as inspiration during this age of "historicism" a few proved to be most popular.

Chinoiserie European interpretations of Chinese art first appeared during the seventeenth century and became very fashionable in interiors toward the late eighteenth and early nineteenth centuries. Design themes such as pagodas, dragons, and lotus flowers were used for ornate stucco and wood carving, wall-paper, furniture (as in "Chinese Chippendale"), tex-tiles and porcelain. For authenticity, a great deal of merchandise was imported from the Far East.

Chinoiserie became the inspiration for decorating whole rooms and was particularly fashionable for ladies' bedrooms. The most famous example is the Royal Pavilion in Brighton, England (built 1815-1820). By now, the style had become rather heavy compared to earlier versions, which are more fanciful and delicate. Chinoiserie spread to America by 1760; it was used for the dining room of Gunston Hall, Virginia.

Gothick and the Gothic revivals "Gothick" describes the revival of curvaceous, romantic medieval styles which took place at the end of the eighteenth century as an

alternative to the more restrictive, formal semi-circles and straight lines of Palladian Classicism. Horace Walpole's Strawberry Hill Gothick, used for his villa in Twickenham near London, for example, was a fanciful interpretation of pointed arches, vaulted ceilings, slender piers and trefoiled tracery windows.

A number of other English architects adopted this style for its romantic and picturesque effect. Although the shapes and the forms harked back to Gothic architecture, the proportions and atmosphere were very different from those of the great medieval cathedrals; instead of substantial stone piers, for example, cast iron was used for slender columns, and plaster ribs decorated the vaulted ceilings. This all changed in the 1840s, when the Gothic revival became more seriously based on archeological study, and iron and plaster were rejected in favor of a return to stone. The most outstanding example is London's Houses of Parliament, rebuilt by Sir Charles Barry and A.W. Pugin in "Perpendicular Gothic" style after a fire in 1834. High Victorian Gothic flourished in Britain between 1855 and 1885 and was used for city halls,

hotels, universities and schools, country houses, and even railroad stations. However, the use of mass production meant that these imitation Gothic edifices lacked the spirit and grace of the original medieval buildings, becoming hard and repetitive.

Victorian eclecticism The Victorian age was the age of eclecticisim, in which British middle-class homes mixed historical styles indiscriminately, adding a profusion of pattern and rich colors for walls, and heavy drapes for curtains. Furniture was crammed into every corner; chairs and sofas were now well-sprung, richly padded and often deeply buttoned. The walls were covered with pictures and miniatures, and bric-a-brac (ceramic vases and figures, domed glass cases, shell-covered boxes, lamps and souvenirs) was strewn over every available surface.

The explosion of mass-manufacturing techniques was celebrated in "The Great Exhibition of the Works of Industry of All Nations" of 1851, which was housed in a specially erected glass and metal "crystal palace" in London's Hyde Park. Mass production

ABOVE LEFT: DEEP CHINESE RED WAS POPULAR TOWARD THE END OF THE EIGHTEENTH AND BEGINNING OF THE NINETEENTH CENTURIES, WHEN THE FASHION FOR CHINOISERIE INFLUENCED EVEN FURNITURE DESIGNERS SUCH AS THOMAS CHIPPENDALE. TODAY IT CAN STILL (EASILY AND INEXPENSIVELY) MAKE A BLEAK ROOM INTIMATE, LESSEN THE EFFECT OF HIGH CEILINGS, AND PROVIDE A FITTING BACKGROUND FOR PRINTS AND PICTURES.

ABOVE RIGHT: RICH COLORS TEAMED WITH GOLD AND FEATURING HERALDIC MOTIFS SUCH AS THE LION RAMPANT AND FLEUR DE LYS WERE A FEATURE OF THE NINETEENTH-CENTURY GOTHIC REVIVAL. THE POINTED ARCH BECAME POPULAR FOR ARCHITECTURAL DETAILS AS WELL AS FOR FURNITURE.

THE ARTS AND CRAFTS MOVEMENT OF THE LATE NINETEENTH CENTURY DECLARED WAR ON VICTORIAN CLAUSTROPHOBIC CLUTTER AND GARISH COLORS. THE RESULT WAS A SIMPLE STYLE FOR INTERIORS AND FURNISHINGS, WHICH STILL LOOKS SINGULARLY MODERN TODAY.

brought decorative home furnishing within the reach of many more people, and life certainly became more comfortable and convenient for many. Unfortunately, however, novelty often triumphed over beauty. There was little true innovation of style, which still relied on a medley of shapes and motifs from the past.

The Arts and Crafts movement As mass production increased, a protest movement emerged. The textile designer William Morris (1834–1896) – who referred to the exhibits of the Great Crystal Palace Exhibition as "tons and tons of unutterable rubbish" – became the leading light of a group of architects and artists who, appalled by the decline in taste, declared war on Victorian claustrophobic clutter. Their aim was a

revival of hand crafts, and the result was a simple domestic style for interiors and furnishings, wellsuited to middle-class needs. The Red House, built for Morris in Bexleyheath near London in 1859, was the starting point for the new style.

Morris and Company, founded in 1861, produced furniture, carpets, wallpapers and textiles, all made by traditional methods to the highest possible standards, while retaining their simplicity. Morris's famous golden rule was: "Have nothing in your houses that you do not know to be useful, or believe to be beautiful." Rooms in the style of Morris were carefully designed in a dignified, rather somber style, with an attendant loss of comfort. Furniture for everyday use was simple and plainly made by hand; typical examples were the unpolished oak settle and the rush-seated chair. By the end of the century, the movement was taken up enthusiastically in America, where it was called the "Craftsman style" and adopted by the designer Gustav Stickley.

The Queen Anne revival Distinctive features of the Queen Anne revival style, popular in England from around 1860, were white-painted sash windows, curly gables, pretty balconies and molded brickwork and terracotta, as taken up by the architect Norman Shaw for his "garden suburb" of Bedford Park in west London. From the 1870s on, the Queen Anne style became popular in America, where wood was used extensively for shingle cladding, verandas, and decorative facade details.

Art Nouveau The sinuous style of Art Nouveau, which developed out of the Arts and Crafts Movement, had its origins in book illustration, glassware, textiles and furniture. Its distinctive curvaceous motifs were based on undulating plant forms, flowing hair, moving waves and flames; its sources can be traced back to the asymmetry of Rococo in the early eighteenth century. Complete facades and interiors were created around a complex interaction of organic shapes and wavy lines. The name by which the style became known came from a Paris shop which opened in 1895, La Maison de l'Art Nouveau, which aimed to sell original "modern" merchandise.

Art Nouveau spread throughout Europe. In Brussels, Victor Horta (1861–1947) created some of Europe's most celebrated Art Nouveau interiors, especially notable for their twisted, tendril-like ironwork. Horta designed everything himself, from door handles to

stained glass, which he used not only for windows and door panels, but also for whole ceilings. In France the movement was called "le style Guimard" after the architect Henri Guimard (1867–1942), who designed the famous Paris Metro entrances. In Spain, Antoni Gaudi (1852–1926) took the style to bizarre limits for his buildings in and around Barcelona. In England, Liberty's Regent Street store produced wallpaper and textiles in the new "modern style".

However, it was the Scottish architect Charles Rennie Mackintosh (1868–1928) who developed a restrained and refined British version of Art Nouveau, distinctive for its elongated forms and pastel colors. Mackintosh rooms were designed around grid patterns, dominated by slightly curving verticals and ending in stylized petal shapes, offset by occasional shallow curves. These patterns were also expressed in furniture (both freestanding and built-in), in surface decoration, in textiles, and in metal fittings. Characteristically, windows and doors were unframed and recessed into walls to emphasize the room's solidity and mass. The overall effect was angular and sparse, rather than curvilinear and excessive.

The restrained, upright lines of Mackintosh were influenced by the Austrian Secessionstil, the Secession group of artists in Vienna – Otto Wagner, Joseph Olbrich, and Joseph Hoffmann. They rejected the twisting excesses of the Belgians and French in favor of a more austere style, influenced by the glittering jewel-like paintings of Gustav Klimt (1862–1918).

TOP LEFT: THE TURN-OF-THE-CENTURY STYLE OF ART NOUVEAU FEATURED DISTINCTIVE CURVED MOTIFS BASED ON UNDULATING PLANT FORMS. ITS INFLUENCE EXTENDED WIDELY FROM ARCHITECTURAL DETAILS, SUCH AS THE MAJOLICA ON THIS VIENNESE FACADE, TO INTERIOR FEATURES LIKE DOOR KNOBS AND FINGER PLATES.

TOP RIGHT: NEAT, NARROW GEOMETRY IS A CHARACTERISTIC OF THE PARTICULAR STYLE OF ART NOUVEAU CREATED BY THE SCOTTISH ARCHITECT CHARLES RENNIE MACKINTOSH AND HIS WIFE, MARGARET.

NINETEENTH-CENTURY STYLING IDEAS

A NINETEENTH-CENTURY SLIM BRASS POLE AND RINGS IS STILL AN EFFECTIVE WAY TO HANG CURTAINS TODAY, PARTICULARLY FOR SOFT, HEAVY FABRICS WITH GOOD DRAPE. TO MAKE A SMALL WINDOW MORE IMPORTANT, HANG A ROD WELL ABOVE IT, EXTEND IT GENEROUSLY ON EACH SIDE, AND TAKE CURTAINS TO THE FLOOR.

At the beginning of the century, houses were light in atmosphere and color: light, bright yellow, green and scarlet were popular, set against striped or sprigged, pale-colored curtains of linen, silk or chintz, looped back to let more light through large windows.

English Regency furniture used low horizontal lines for simple, solid shapes with gentle curves and a restrained use of reeding and fluting. A typical feature was the sweeping curve of the distinctive saber leg. Egyptian motifs, such as lotus leaves, winged disks, and sphinxes, were a characteristic feature.

The French Empire style used fabric with abandon, filling rooms with "tumbling drapery". Beds and windows were heavily draped, and even chair legs and backs were festooned. Fabrics were used for tented ceilings, or pleated or gathered across walls.

The cluttered Victorian style (or lack of style, as it has been called) of the later part of the century had sitting rooms crammed with furniture and favorite ornaments, including pictures and souvenirs. Patterns for carpet, upholstery and walls might all be different. For the first time, color schemes and design styles varied from room to room. Indeed, after the middle of the century, the rooms within one house might feature a number of totally different styles: Gothic or Tudor, perhaps, for dining rooms and libraries, and Rococo Revival for more feminine drawing rooms and boudoirs.

Stenciling was used in repeating patterns for borders and corner ornaments for walls and ceilings, although papered walls were to become increasingly popular. A manufacturing method for continuous rolls of wallpaper was patented in the early nineteenth century, and mass production began in the 1840s. The quality ranged from simple patterns on plain paper, through shiny satin papers to elaborate flocks and printed pictorials, at which the French excelled.

In the Victorian Age, walls were considered as three separate elements: floor to dado or chair rail; dado to picture rail or architrave level; architrave to ceiling level, including the cornice. The dado formed an important horizontal division around the lower half of a room and was often decorated with an embossed wallpaper that imitated plasterwork, painted in a dark color and varnished. Above the dado itself, a richly patterned, dark wallpaper provided the background for a mass of gilt-framed pictures and mirrors. White ceilings went out of fashion, dark colors being considered cozier and more practical, disguising marks made by the fumes from gas and oil-lamps.

Flooring for halls and porches consisted mainly of encaustic tiles, in which different colored clays are inlaid to form a pattern. The Arts and Crafts movement favored stained floors of natural oak.However, by the middle of the nineteenth century, power looms were mass-producing multicolored, patterned Axminster carpets, which the newly affluent middle classes could now afford.

Windows Shades – usually highly ornamental, with painted or printed designs or woven patterns – were popular, but curtains, at this time, really came into their own. The new Jacquard looms mass-produced richly colored and textured furnishing damasks and brocades. Textiles were used with enthusiasm, not only for draperies, but also for fringed, braided, and tasseled hangings for every flat surface, from large writing surfaces and pianos to small occasional tables. Fabrics were reduced in bedrooms, however, as new ideas about hygiene demanded free circulation of air. Uncurtained brass and iron bedsteads became popular.

Furniture The Victorians perfected the art of producing comfortable furniture, concentrating on upholstered seats. Sofas and easy chairs were fully sprung and padded, with buttoning to hold fillings in place, as seen in the "chesterfield" sofa. Rounded backs were curved to continue as arms; a typical shape is the balloon-back dining chair, with curved back and padded seat. The "parlour suite" – forerunner of the three-piece suite – also made its first appearance.

An alternative to "cozy clutter" was provided by the baronial Gothic Revival look, featuring stained glass, oak linenfold paneling, and wallpapers in dark, gilded patterns with touches of bright contrast. Richly stained "Jacobethan" furniture was paneled and heavily carved.

William Morris left a rich legacy of graceful curvy wallpaper and fabric designs of flowers, fruits and animals, block-printed in flat, dull colors based on natural vegetable dyes. For an Arts and Crafts look, use painted tongue-and-grooved boarding to shoulder height, and finish with a rack to display a collection of different plates.

RECREATING THE STYLE

In view of the many different styles available during this period, you need to decide whether to adhere to a particular look, such as Empire, Regency, Victorian or Gothic Revival, or opt for a mix of styles with sympathetic themes.

Walls *Regency-style walls should carry friezes with classical motifs such as urns or Empire-style swags and baskets of fruit. For a Victorian look, a cornice in low plaster relief and a ceiling rose with a floral or leaf design would look appropriate. A dado is optional, though there should, ideally, be a picture rail about three-quarters the height of the ceiling to break up the expanse of the wall.*

Paint colors *will vary, depending on the style being emulated. Rich crimsons and browns were favored during the Victorian Age, while the Arts and Crafts movement favored lighter, more natural schemes. For this look, woodwork should be painted in cream colors, and walls in a contrast of, say, deep blue and brown, or gold and green. For an Edwardian feel, use white and pastel shades, with white or cream paint for interior woodwork and combinations of soft pinks and blues, with a white or grey background for walls.*

Floors *Tiled floors are appropriate for hard-wearing areas such as porches, hallways and kitchens; there are now authentic-looking reproductions of encaustic tiles. For other rooms, stained wooden floors and wall-to-wall fitted carpets are equally acceptable. Victorian-style bedrooms can be left uncarpeted.*

Curtains *should be used in abundance, even around doors, if wished. For an authentic Victorian look, they should be dark, fringed or tasseled, and topped with an elaborate valance. This main set of curtains should cover a second set of "subsidiary" curtains, made of lace or gauze.*

Accessories *can be used in plenty to create an authentic Victorian feel. The multipaneled folding screen was a Victorian notion that is still useful for adding mystery and atmosphere to the corner of a room. Other favorites, easily copied today, are houseplants massed together on ornamental stands; ferns were a great favorite. Tall palms and shiny-leaved aspidistras were placed in individual jardinieres to serve as a focal point for the room.*

THE TWENTIETH CENTURY

THIS HAS BEEN A CENTURY OF RAPID CHANGE, accelerated by two world wars and huge advances in technology. Two hundred years ago, style took decades to creep around Europe and across the ocean to the New World. Today, the media broadcast changes of fashion around the world within days; consequently, fashions come and go in decorating almost as easily as in clothes. Since people cannot afford to change their furnishings and decoration every decade, styles inevitably overlap, often within the same home.

THE MODERN MOVEMENT

A reaction against excessive ornament in the early 1900s prompted some European designers toward a style of architecture that emphasized space, proportion and smooth surfaces. In France, the Modern Movement was spearheaded by Le Corbusier (1887–1965), whose *Vers une Architecture* was published in English in 1927, outlining his "Five Points for a New Architecture": *piloti*; horizontal windows; a free plan; free facades; flat roofs.

In the United States, Frank Lloyd Wright (1867–1959) developed the simple horizontal lines and low spreading rooms of an architecture that aimed to develop "from within outwards, in harmony with the conditions of its being". His famous prairie houses around Chicago were startlingly bare, combining exposed internal brickwork with carefully chosen woods; the effect was uncluttered, yet welcoming.

The Bauhaus The Bauhaus design school, founded in Weimar, Germany, in 1919, was a powerful expression of Modern Movement ideals. The aim of its leader, Walter Gropius (1883–1969), was to link together all training in art, architecture and design. The resulting architecture was flat-roofed and box-like, broken by the bold upright and horizontal lines of large metal-framed windows to let in lots of light.

Modernity, efficiency and hygiene were the essence of the new style. White was the preferred color for walls which, shorn of traditional baseboards and picture rails, became smooth and blank. Doors abandoned traditional paneled forms and were faced with single sheets of painted plywood. Streamlining was further achieved with an abundance of built-in furniture for living rooms, kitchens and bedrooms. Furniture and furnishings received the same minimal treatment; the tubular metal furniture of designers such as Marcel Breuer is an essential component in recreating the purity of the original Modern Movement.

THE TWENTIETH-CENTURY SCANDINAVIAN LOOK IS A SUBTLE BLEND OF FOLK AND COUNTRY, USING BLONDE NATURAL WOODS, SIMPLE SHAPES, AND COOL BLUES AND GREENS FOR A RUSTIC EFFECT.

De Stijl In Holland, the Dutch group De Stijl ("The Style", named after an avant-garde magazine of the same name) was equally dedicated to breaking with past forms to take design forward into the twentieth century. Its leader, Gerrit Rietveld (1888-1964), was a "constructivist" who based his designs on abstract rectangular forms in the primary colors red, blue and yellow. His most famous building, the Schroeder House in Utrecht, used clean-cut, slab-like surfaces without any moldings for walls and ceilings, with continuous horizontal strips of metal-framed windows.

Art Deco Running counter to the austerity of the Modern Movement was the glamorous style of Art Deco, which took its name from the Exposition des Art Decoratifs held in Paris in 1925 and became fashionable in Europe and America during the 1920s and 1930s. Above all, the new style was geometric. Circles and semi-circles, triangles, octagons and cubes were used as patterns on carpets, rugs, wallpapers, tiles and fabrics, as well as in shapes for tableware, furniture and headboards, fireplaces and mirrors, along with the new electric heaters, light fixtures and radios. Typical motifs featured sunrises, stylized trees and flowers, fans, fountains and graceful animal forms, in particular deer, while inspiration also came from the ancient world of the Aztecs (as in the stepped "ziggurat" temple shape) and the Egyptians (after Tutankhamen's tomb was opened in 1922).

This essentially exotic style was most suitable for luxury hotels, bars and restaurants, trans-Atlantic liners, theaters and film sets. Designers expressed the smooth, curved shapes of Deco artefacts in a wide variety of materials, creating opulence with blonde woods (walnut, light oak, sycamore), leather, marble and glass. Chrome was used for all kinds of household furnishings and fixtures, and variety was created with new plastics such as Bakelite, also hard and shiny. This rich mix of materials was set against backgrounds of off-white, cream and beige, with fabrics of peach and eau-de-nil. Splashes of orange, emerald, cornflower blue and vermilion were inspired by the flamboyant costumes designed for Diaghilev's pre-war Paris ballets.

In the United States, the movement was called streamlining, and the fluid, rounded corners of railroad engines and cars were repeated in household objects such as refrigerators and vacuum cleaners, as well as multistoried public buildings. On both sides of the Atlantic, sleek, streamlined forms prevailed.

THIS DINING ROOM HAS ALL THE HALLMARKS OF ART DECO STYLE: THE WALNUT DINING TABLE AND CHAIRS, WITH THEIR "ZIGGURAT"-INSPIRED LEGS, THE SHAPE OF THE MATCHING GLASS-FRONTED DISPLAY CABINET WITH ITS CURVED ENDS AND TOPPED WITH A RECLINING-FIGURE ORNAMENT, AND THE DESIGN OF THE WALL MIRROR AND THE GLASS AND CHROME LIGHT FIXTURE. THE WALLS AND THE PARQUET FLOOR CREATE A NEUTRAL BACKGROUND FOR THIS STYLISH INTERIOR.

CONTEMPORARY STYLES

World War II abruptly put a halt to most developments in design and architecture, although plywood technology forged forward under the impetus of airplane design. But in 1951, the Festival of Britain celebrated the end of the immediate post-war austerity, and the style that emerged for the 1950s and 1960s was light, bright, and "contemporary". The exhibition was visited by eight million people, and it had an enormous impact on style. Concrete, glass and steel were subsequently used for buildings such as the Royal Festival Hall, which still stands on the south bank of the River Thames in London today.

On view in the Dome of Discovery were ball-and-rod models of molecules. These inspired designs for chairs and coffee tables with angular steel-tube feet tipped with small beads of bright plastic. The shape was also taken up for magazine and record racks, clocks and light fixtures, and reflected in spindly graphics for fabric, wallpaper and china patterns.

Although decor remained simple and rather stark (no picture rails and only sill-length curtains and narrow baseboards), color and comfort were creeping back in modern versions of wing chairs, standard lamps, and cozy rugs and cushions. A fitted carpet became the new luxury. New technologies were used to make curved chairs in molded plywood and countertops in plastic laminate. One or two walls might be papered in a fashionable abstract pattern and others painted plain. Yellow and grey was a popular color combination.

High-Tech High-Tech is an approach to architecture rather than a specific style. It was developed in the main by English architects of the 1970s, such as Richard Rogers and Norman Foster, whose buildings deliberately expose their engineering and technology to dramatic effect. Thus you can see metal frameworks and services such as pipes, ducts and elevators through or in front of a smooth impervious "skin", which is often glass. Famous examples include Foster's Sainsbury Centre for the University of Norwich (1977) and Rogers' Pompidou Centre in Paris, of the same year.

High-Tech architecture inspired some interiors that were almost brutal in their lack of subterfuge. Pipes, ducts and fixtures for heating and sanitation were all deliberately exposed, and industrial or commercial materials such as studded rubber flooring, factory shelving or office chairs found their way into homes.

BELOW: MODERN INTERIORS DEPEND FOR THEIR EFFECT MORE ON SPACE AND LIGHT THAN ON COLOR AND PATTERN, WHICH ARE DELIBERATELY UNDERSTATED. NATURAL MATERIALS SUCH AS THIS SLATE FLOOR ARE REVERED FOR THEIR TEXTURE AND BEAUTY. NO ATTEMPT IS MADE TO HIDE THE BONES OF THE BUILDING, SUCH AS THE ELECTRICAL TRUNKING AND SUPPORTS FOR THE LIGHTS IN THIS ROOM.

RIGHT: THE "CONTEMPORARY" STYLE OF THE 1950S AND 1960S WAS LIGHT, ANGULAR AND BRIGHT. NOTE THE SPIKY METAL FEET OF THE TABLE AND CHAIRS AND THE VIVID COLOR OF THE BACKGROUND WALL WITH ITS GEOMETRIC YELLOW FLASH MOTIF. NEW MATERIALS ARE IN EVIDENCE IN THE MOLDED CHAIRS AND THE MELAMINE-TOPPED TABLE.

TWENTIETH-CENTURY STYLING IDEAS

THE CLEAR LIGHT OF THE SOUTH REVEALS THE BEAUTIFUL NATURAL TEXTURES OF THE BRICK-ARCHED WINDOWS AND THE EXPOSED STONE WALLS. WHEN BRINGING THIS LOOK TO NORTHERN CLIMES, ADD PLENTY OF NATURAL WOOD AND USE IT WITH WARM TERRACOTTAS AND CREAMS.

Twentieth-century interior design makes a distinction between "integrated" and "superimposed" design. Integrated design is the province of the architect, whose choice of forms and texture is to a great extent intended to be a permanent part of the room. In the words of the architect, Frank Lloyd Wright: "It is impossible to consider the building as one thing and its furnishings another." Superimposed design is the work of the interior designer or the home owner. Here, interiors are flexible and easily altered (with the use of wallpaper, fabric and paint), according to the changing dictates of furnishing fashions.

Over the years, plainer treatments have come to be adopted for interiors. To some extent, this has simply mirrored the natural development of exterior design into simpler, more rational styles. Yet the reasons have often been as much economic as aesthetic: pressures on building space and budgets have resulted in smaller, lower rooms which require careful planning to fulfill a wide range of family needs.

A simple room without architectural details such as moldings, ornaments, and panels is cheaper to build: the flush door, for example, has become common-place. Modern rooms have been reduced to the flat horizontals of floors and ceilings and the uninterrupted vertical planes of walls. Baseboards have become a narrow strip; dado and picture rails have disappeared, along with the frieze and the cornice. This is true as much for rooms in converted or modernized older buildings as for those in newly built developments.

Yet the modern style of neutral colors, simple shapes, and hard materials has never really appealed to mass taste in any country. Faced with the typical twentieth-century "box", home owners have developed ways of adding color and ornament by using deep tones of latex paint, co-ordinating collections of wallpapers and fabrics, textured or patterned carpets, and lavish curtain treatments.

Room planning and even the very design of houses themselves has been shaped by the technologies of modern life: the telephone, the television, the hi-fi, the refrigerator, and the microwave, all twentieth-century inventions. Lighting, both natural and artificial, has become an important way of adding atmosphere to modern rooms, while functional lighting is now a carefully controlled discipline. Built-in kitchens, too, are a modern phenomenon. As early as 1922, Marcel Breuer of the Bauhaus designed the first built-in kitchen, with everything carefully hidden behind uniform cupboard doors.

The twentieth century has excelled at discovering new materials for the home: plastics are used for everything from telephones and flooring to window frames; synthetic fibers are used for carpets, curtains and bed and table linens. New materials can make a statement in their own right: the exciting shape of a molded plastic chair, for example, or the smooth curve of a stainless steel sink. Or they can achieve a successful imitation of natural materials – velvet, say, or stone. The recent proliferation of synthetics has focused attention on the beauty of natural materials such as wood, wool and silk. The "natural look" has in fact been one of the most important design influences in the last decade of the twentieth century.

THE FRIENDLY, INFORMAL LOOK OF THE COUNTRY COTTAGE IS UNIVERSALLY LOVED. USE IT, AS HERE, FOR LOW-CEILINGED ROOMS WITHOUT ELABORATE ARCHITECTURAL DETAILS. BRING THE OUTSIDE IN WITH PATTERNED FLOWERS FOR CURTAIN FABRICS AND REAL ONES SPILLING OUT OF JUGS AND BOWLS ON TABLE AND WINDOWSILL. BOTH FURNITURE AND FLOOR FINISH ARE SIMPLE.

THE NATURAL TEXTURES AND SIMPLE PLANES OF THIS HARMONIOUS ROOM ARE ESSENTIALLY JAPANESE, WITH AN EMPHASIS ON MINIMALISM AND FREEDOM FROM CLUTTER. AN ATMOSPHERIC DETAIL IS THE SHOJI SCREEN, WITH ITS DISCIPLINED SQUARES OF TRANSLUCENT PAPER FILTERING AND SOFTENING THE LIGHT.

A CHOICE OF STYLE

As the twentieth century draws to a close, freedom of style is as current for decorating as it is for dress. You can take your pick from a wide variety of "looks".

English country house Evolved over many centuries, this is a style that today inspires decorators all over Europe and in the United States. Its emphasis is on informal grandeur and comfort, the aim to create a warm and welcoming ambience. The English country-house style is best suited to large rooms: period features such as molded window and door frames fit in

well, as does a traditional fireplace and mantelpiece. If it is not practical to burn a real fire, consider installing gas logs or coals in a traditional grate.

Patterns are mainly floral, large in scale, and based on a rich treasure house of archive designs from the eighteenth and nineteenth centuries. Reproduced for wallpapers and matching chintz fabrics, they can be used for windows, upholstery and slipcovers, bedspreads and valances. A typical color scheme is pink, with white or cream and touches of green, but schemes may be based around yellow and blue or shades of old gold and brown. Colors should look muted, or even faded, rather than brilliant and new. Darker, rich glowing woods are suitable for furniture in period styles; painted furniture also works well.

Windows are given great importance. Fabric is used generously for full-length curtains, which can be ruffled, fringed or trimmed with braid, and looped back with bows or tassels. Floors should be warm and soft: a fitted carpet is ideal, perhaps in a plain shade with the addition of patterned rugs.

Country cottage This look is as likely to be found in a town kitchen as in a rural parlor; it works best in small, low-ceilinged rooms without elaborate architectural details such as ceiling roses or cornices. Attics, with sloping ceilings and interesting alcoves, are ideal. The country-cottage style favors stained or natural wood, used for simple pieces of furniture and for floors whose boards are sanded smooth and then stained or varnished. Wood might also be found in panels for walls, wooden beams for ceilings, and, in a kitchen, for units and worktops. Wooden furniture, floors or walls can be given a white pickled finish, or a pale wash of color, and "distressed" to look old.

Most natural materials, such as wood, stone, slate, rush, cane, wool and cotton fit in well. Avoid using modern materials such as smoked glass or chromed steel, or those with grand associations, such as marble, silk and brocades. Suitable upholstery fabrics include burlap, gingham and lightweight cottons with floral prints on a cream or white ground, teamed perhaps with white or cream cotton lace. Add a touch of patchwork for throw pillows or bedspreads.

Walls can be simply painted white or cream in flat latex, or you could use a paper with a small all-over pattern. Against this muted background, you might add clear colors such as delphinium blue, leaf green or peony pink: the colors found in a summer flower bed are a good guide.

Oriental The Oriental style is exquisite, minimalist and free from clutter. The few objects used, whether functional or decorative, are placed with great care, with a studied avoidance of symmetry.

Interiors and exteriors are linked with sliding walls to afford delightful outdoor views, and maximum use is made of natural light, softly filtered through *shoji* paper screens. The Japanese sleep on their sweet-smelling, springy matted *tatami* floors, and during the day roll up their cotton futon mattresses and store them away. Larger rooms can be subdivided into separate bedrooms in an instant with sliding screens.

For a Western adaptation of this look, use white and cream natural fabrics, with touches of black and scarlet, and green plants. Have cotton futons on wooden bases which turn into seats by day. Add beautiful screens, floor cushions, and low tables with porcelain and rich red and black lacquerware.

American country The early American colonists carried the folk arts of their countries in Europe across the Atlantic where they blended to become the unsophisticated style of American country. Informal and essentially unpretentious, the American country look, typified by Shaker furniture, Amish quilts, rag rugs and stencils, is popular worldwide. "Whatever is fashioned, let it be plain and simple and for the good," said Mother Ann Lee of the Shaker sect.

Carpenters and cabinet-makers were influenced by English and Dutch provincial furniture, but often had to work in rough woods, which they painted to look grander. Chunky cupboards and chests, rush-seated chairs, settles and rockers, all fit into the American country idiom. Colors are subdued, confined to vegetable hues for rough, home-spun fabrics and earth pigments for "buttermilk" paints. The early settlers created their own patterned designs using stencils. These dense flat paints are still available and can be used for furniture and woodwork, to contrast with creamy walls, perhaps outlined with a pretty stencil.

Splashes of brilliance come from patchwork and rugs, originally made from scraps of carefully hoarded fabrics. "Rags" for rugs can be hooked into a burlap backing (early settlers would have used a sack), or plaited into strips curled into circular or oval shapes.

Minimalist Favored by architects and designers, the Minimalist look is a legacy of the pre-war Modern movement. It is intentionally bare and free from clutter; "Less is more," said Minimalist architect Mies van der

Rohe. Minimalist rooms are severe and rectilinear, furnished with hard materials – natural, such as wood, leather, and stone, or man-made, such as linoleum, plastic, and chromed steel. The impact of the room comes from the appeal of these materials and their delineation of space. The Minimalist style does not like pattern and favors "non-colors" of black, white, cream, oatmeal and grey. Soft surfaces such as carpets are avoided in favor of ceramic or vinyl tiles. Curtains are replaced at the windows by simple shades or slatted blinds. Meticulous planning conceals the clutter of everyday living as far as humanly possible.

THE FOLK ART OF EARLY EUROPEAN SETTLERS HAS RESULTED IN THE LOOK WE TODAY CALL AMERICAN COUNTRY, EXEMPLIFIED HERE BY THE RUSTIC CHAIR AND OTHER FURNITURE, THE RAG RUGS, BED QUILTS, PLANKED FLOOR, BEAMED CEILING, AND THE GENERAL AIR OF SIMPLICITY AND INFORMALITY.

THE ROOMS

All interior decoration should begin with the room itself and the way you intend to use it. Everybody can learn to be their own interior designer: to design their own home to suit their own lifestyle, preferences and family needs. Good design is simply about creating a comfortable, workable interior which is pleasant to live in and in which each room is planned so that it suits the purpose for which it is intended. Planning how to use the space is an integral part of the design process and should be the first step you take, long before you think about color schemes, fabrics or furniture. The basic shape and size of a room, as well as its aspect and the amount of natural daylight it receives, will influence your choice of colors and furnishings. If a room has any distinctive features, these can be the inspiration which serves as a starting-off point for your scheme; they may dictate whether you choose a specific period look. Any other stylistic aspects should be taken into account — they can either be emphasized and enhanced or camouflaged and disguised, but they should never be ignored.

LEFT: ROOMS MUST ABOVE ALL BE PLANNED WITH THEIR USE IN MIND. IN THIS MODERN LIVING ROOM, THE EMPHASIS IS ON COMFORT AND RELAXATION, WITH THE SOFA AND GENEROUS ARMCHAIRS TAKING PROMINENCE. DISPLAY SHELVES AND A LOW CABINET HAVE BEEN CREATED IN A NATURAL ALCOVE, AND THE TALL SIDEBOARD HAS BEEN PAINTED TO BLEND IN WITH THE WALLS AND NOT LOOK TOO DOMINATING. FLOOR-TO-CEILING CURTAINS AND PALE FLOORING HELP TO MAKE THE ROOM APPEAR TALLER. THE HONEY-COLORED VARNISHED FLOORBOARDS AND SISAL CARPET OFFER NO COMPETITION TO THE FRESH COLOR SCHEME OF BLUE AND CREAMY YELLOW.

RIGHT: BABIES' AND CHILDREN'S ROOMS SHOULD NOT BE OVER-DESIGNED, SINCE THEIR TOYS AND EQUIPMENT WILL ALWAYS PROVIDE ENOUGH DETAIL AND COLOR. HERE, A CHILD'S ROOM IS PERSONALIZED BY STENCILING REPEATING ANIMAL MOTIFS ON THE WOODEN PANELING TO MATCH THOSE STENCILED ON THE WHITE COTTON CURTAINS WITH FABRIC PAINTS.

ROOM PLANNING

BEFORE YOU START TO THINK ABOUT ROOM STYLING, color schemes, home furnishings or floor and wall treatments, you should work out a basic plan of the whole house, even though you may be intending to design and decorate one room at a time. Any major structural changes, involving walls being knocked down or built, as well as the installation of plumbing, heating and lighting, must be considered at the outset so that it can be carried out before any redecoration takes place.

MAKING A PLAN

A room should be always planned according to its main use, so that the furniture, equipment and any appliances fit comfortably into the space available, allowing people to walk around the room, to open doors and drawers, and to use the equipment and furniture efficiently. Once the positions of these are established, the lighting, sockets, plumbing and any other services can be organized in relation to them (you will need to consult a qualified electrician or plumber to carry out this work).

The best way to work out how everything will fit in is to measure the room and make a scale plan of it, using squared graph paper. Take accurate dimensions, remembering to indicate any alcoves, projections or awkward angles, and convert them to the scale you are using; it is usual to work to a scale of 1:25 or 1:50. Use a retractable steel tape to measure as fabric ones stretch in use.

It is helpful to draw wall elevations as well as a floor plan, so draw these to scale in the same way, indicating structural features such as doors, windows, fireplaces and walls accurately. Plot the positions of existing radiators, light fixtures, any electrical points and plumbing pipes and show which way the doors open. This will help you to judge how furniture will fit into the room – whether pieces can go under window sills and shelves, in alcoves and so on – and to decide where to position any new wall lights. The dimensions of windows will help you to work out the best style of curtain or blind and to calculate the quantities of fabric and wallcovering needed.

Cut templates to the shape of each item of furniture or equipment, reduced to the scale of the floor plan. You can measure existing items at home, new ones in the shop, or work to dimensions quoted in catalogs. Move the templates around on the plan until you are satisfied with their position; once you have worked out

PLANNING THE BEST USE OF THE SPACE IS EVEN MORE IMPORTANT IN DUAL-PURPOSE ROOMS. IN THIS KITCHEN, WHICH DOUBLES AS A DINING ROOM, THERE IS JUST ENOUGH CIRCULATION SPACE LEFT ON EACH SIDE OF THE TABLE WITH THE CHAIRS IN PLACE.

the best arrangement for the room, draw around, or stick down, the cut-outs on your plan.

CHOOSING A SCHEME

All rooms have three major surfaces – the floor, the walls and the ceiling. They may have other dominant elements, such as the units and work surfaces in the kitchen; the upholstery on sofas and chairs in the living room; the bedcovers in the bedroom; sanitary-ware in the bathroom. Window treatments may also be an important feature of each room.

The scale of pattern and the strength of color of any fabrics, wallcoverings or flooring you choose must always relate to the surface area on which they will be used. Bold designs and strong colors look best on wide expanses of wall, large floor areas, generous sofas and chairs, and at opulent windows, while petite patterns and paler colors are more suited to restricted floor and wall areas, short, sill-length curtains and blinds, or for upholstering small pieces of furniture.

Take your room plan with you when you go to see what is available. No scheme can work around vague ideas: it can only be implemented with actual fabrics, wallcoverings, paint, flooring, light fixtures and accessories. As your thoughts begin to firm up, ask for some samples of fabric, floor tiles, carpet and wallcoverings; bring these home and look at them under both natural daylight and artificial light. Always try to obtain larger samples, rather than snippets, especially of anything that has a large pattern; it is often possible to borrow a length of fabric, a large piece of carpet, a wallpaper book or a mini-curtain from suppliers and keep them for a few days, on a sale-or-return basis, before ordering the materials. You can buy a small tester can of paint for walls or stains for floors: paint this onto a piece of lining paper, hardboard or wood. If testers are not available, buy just a small quantity to try out.

Look at all these samples in position – floorcovering on the floor, curtain fabric against the light, gathered up in your hand as it will be seen when made up, upholstery fabric draped over a sofa or chair. With patterns that travel across the width of a wallcovering or fabric, try to see at least two widths side by side to get the full effect: some small designs and pale colors tend to fade into insignificance when used in bulk. Leave your samples in the room for a few days, perhaps clipping them to a color board, and look at them at various times of day. Once you are happy with your scheme, use the scale plan to work out quantities required and to order the materials.

ORDER OR WORK

If you are having a lot of work done, it helps to make a timetable. The structural work should be done first: this includes electrical work and plumbing, as well as any heavy building work. If you are dealing with the whole house, try to plan the work so that you start at the top and work down, and work from the back to the front. The preparation work for decoration should be done next. Any new solid floors should be laid so that the decorating, tiling and so on can be completed. If you are building in any furniture or storage which is to be painted, install this between undercoating and top-coating the other woodwork in the room, so that it can be treated at the same time. Once carpets are laid and curtains and blinds hung, you will have the fun of adding the room's accessories and finishing touches.

THIS FORMAL SITTING ROOM HAS BEEN PLANNED ON SYMMETRICAL LINES, WITH IDENTICAL SOFAS ON EACH SIDE OF THE WINDOW. THE OPULENT WINDOW DRESSING IS VERY MUCH IN KEEPING WITH THE MARBLE-PANEL WALLS, STUDIOUSLY CREATED BY EXPERTLY APPLIED SPECIAL PAINT EFFECTS. RICH FABRICS AND WARM COLORS, WITH THE DEEP MAHOGANY PARQUET FLOOR, SET THE MOOD OF THE ROOM PERFECTLY.

PLANNING YOUR KITCHEN

THIS GALLEY-STYLE KITCHEN IS AN EXCELLENT EXAMPLE OF A WELL-PLANNED NARROW SPACE IN WHICH THE BLACK AND WHITE COLOR SCHEME KEEPS THE EFFECT CLEAN AND SIMPLE. THE CHECKED FLOOR TILES HELP TO WIDEN THE AREA VISUALLY, WHILE THE VERTICALLY STRIPED BLIND ADDS INTEREST AND AN ILLUSION OF HEIGHT AT THE NARROW END OF THE ROOM. THE USE OF CEILING-RECESSED DOWNLIGHTERS AND STRIP LIGHTS UNDER WALL-MOUNTED CUPBOARDS ILLUMINATES ALL AREAS SUCCESSFULLY.

WHATEVER ITS SIZE OR SHAPE, your kitchen should be planned in such a way that it can be used to its full potential. It must allow for efficient and economical movement when you are preparing food, cooking, serving and washing; it should include adequate and practical storage space and incorporate appliances tailored to suit your needs; it must provide adequate lighting, heating and ventilation and have practical, easy-to-clean work surfaces and floors. This means positioning units and equipment in a layout that entails the least walking between sink, oven units and the food-preparation / storage area and refrigerator. The line drawn between the three areas of this layout is called the work triangle. The work triangle should have sides of not less than 10 feet (3 meters) , so the cook is not cramped into a corner, and not more than 20 feet (6 meters), so that every task does not involve a hike. There should be no doors to break up the sides of the triangle.

Layouts

THE WAY YOU ARRANGE THE BASIC LAYOUT will largely depend on the size and shape of your kitchen - and this will dictate how the work triangle fits in.

In a small space you may end up with all the essential items grouped along one wall, called a single-line layout (often used if the cooking area is to be hidden behind closed doors).

SEPARATE ZONES

If the kitchen is large enough, it should also be "zoned" or partially divided off into separate areas for working, eating and utility.

The working zone includes work surfaces for the preparation of food; a storage area for dry, canned and perishable goods; the stove (oven and burners) and refrigerator; storage for cooking pots, pans and *batterie de cuisine;* a serving area; and a place to wash the dishes. This zone will contain the work triangle.

An eating area will depend on the amount of space available – in a large, streamlined kitchen, the dining section might be separate, possibly divided from the working area by units incorporating a worktop for serving food. In a more informal and possibly unfitted kitchen, a large table with a scrubbed top could serve for both preparation and eating. A breakfast bar with stools is an alternative, or a small, circular space-saving table with folding chairs; the table itself could even fold down, or might be hung on a wall when not in use.

A utility area should include the washing machine and dryer, ironing equipment and storage for cleaning materials. If there is plenty of space, it might also house an extra sink, drainer, long-term storage of dry goods and freezer.

BEGIN AT THE BEGINNING

Before you can figure out how to zone your areas and fit in the work triangle to best advantage, you will need to do some homework. Sit down and list all the existing features or aspects which you like – and dislike – about your current kitchen, if necessary turning this into a family conference. Then add to the list all that you would like to have in your kitchen. Think about the type of cooking you do, or propose to do, and try to plan exactly what you want in your working zone – microwave; freestanding stove or built-in oven and separate burners; 'fridge/freezer; dishwasher. Aim to have a heatproof surface next to any cooking appliances on which to stand hot pans.

The next step is to visit showrooms and collect catalogs and literature so that you form a more precise idea of what you want and have at your fingertips all the vital statistics of cabinets, stoves, appliances and equipment. You can then see exactly what you can – and cannot – accommodate in the space available by measuring up, making a scale plan, and seeing what might go where. It is a good idea to do this, even if you intend to call in built-in furniture experts or specialist kitchen planners. At this stage you should include any non-essential items of equipment, units or appliances which you might install at a future date, such as a dishwasher. It is better to plan, and leave space for, these items and to get any electrical work and plumbing done at the outset, when the majority of the structural work is being done.

BUILT-IN OR NOT?

A fundamental decision at this early stage is whether to go for a built-in style of kitchen or not. Kitchens have for a long time been streamlined and fully built-in, with matching prefabricated units, but there is a growing trend toward the "unfitted" kitchen, where

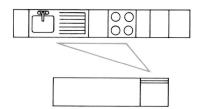

In a long, narrow kitchen, the galley-style (as in a ship) may work best .

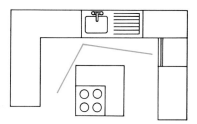

An island layout allows the food preparation surface and stove top to be centrally positioned, with sink and units ranged around the outside walls.

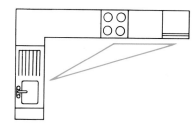

Larger or squarish rooms can accommodate an L-shaped layout, which allows cabinets and equipment to be placed along two sides of the room, or a U-shape, where they are wrapped around three walls.

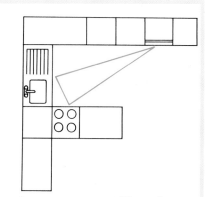

In a generous space, this can be expanded into an F-shape, providing space for a separate dining area.

SAFETY FIRST

☛ **Keep sharp implements and knives on a special magnetic rack, or in an enclosed knife block - never leave them jumbled up in the bottom of a kitchen drawer.**

☛ **Do not site the burners under a window where curtains could catch fire, or where you have to lean across to open the window.**

☛ **Never position the stove next to a door, where pan handles could be knocked as the door opens.**

☛ **Do not place sink and stove opposite each other in a confined space; and do not have a door which crosses the route from the sink to the stove.**

☛ **Wall-hung cupboards should not be mounted too low on the wall. Always place them above a unit, table or appliance to avoid banged heads or people walking into them.**

☛ **Never allow electric cords to trail across, or be close to, the sink.**

☛ **Choose a slip-proof floor and make sure it is anchored down around the room's perimeter, especially in front of sinks, appliances and doorways.**

☛ **Sharp, square corners on units/work surfaces can cause bruises, so look for rounded corners on post-formed worktops.**

☛ **Despite good modern insulation, try not to place the stove or oven and fridge next to each other.**

☛ **If there are young children in the family, use a guardrail to protect the top of the stove and prevent pans from being pulled over. Consider retractable curly cords for hot appliances; never have trailing tablecloths; use special shuttered or dummy plugs to protect sockets.**

☛ **Keep a first aid kit handy for burns, cuts and scalds.**

THE NOSTALGIC, OLD-FASHIONED LOOK OF THIS ROOM HAS ALL THE ELEMENTS OF A TRADITIONALLY UNFITTED, ALMOST SPARTAN KITCHEN. THE CONCRETE FLOOR HAS BEEN HAND-PAINTED IN A REPEATING STENCILED DESIGN IN EARTH COLORS WHICH ECHO THE WARMTH OF THE CREAM-PAINTED WALLS.

separate (and sometimes disparate) pieces of freestanding furniture are used. Pine is a favorite wood, but specialist painted finishes can also help to enhance the style. Where a built-in kitchen is space-saving and looks uncluttered, an unfitted kitchen creates a more comfortable and cozy atmosphere and is also more flexible, since the furniture can be changed occasionally. The unfitted style works best in a well-used, informal kitchen which is the center of family activity; you need to have at least a medium-sized room for this style of kitchen. It may well have an old-fashioned range as its hub and is best decorated in "country" style. Furniture may include a display hutch, storage and pantry, a portable butcher's block, a large, centrally positioned table, a deep sink with a separate drainer – and even a wooden settle or rocking chair if there is space. Accessories in keeping with this style may include a traditional wooden plate rack as well as a ceiling-mounted air dryer on a pulley.

THE THIRD DIMENSION?

Scale plans work on the horizontal plane and will enable you to see what will fit in where, in terms of the floor space. But you will also need to think three-dimensionally, to make the most of the space above eye-level for wall-mounted shelves and cupboards; to ensure units and appliances will fit under window sills; and to allow for any beams or changes in level. In order to work out a practical solution on this plane, you may have to draw out elevations – this is simply a drawing to scale of a wall, showing all the important structural features like doors, windows, fireplaces, pipes, and electrical fixtures in the exact position they occupy on the wall. You can use this to see how your units and appliances will fit in – and to show you exactly where you need to site the plumbing and electrical points. It is also a good way of testing out a proposed window treatment. Remember to allow space for heating, in the form of a radiator or an independent or freestanding heater.

KITCHEN SCHEMES

THE KITCHEN CAN HAVE AS MANY DIFFERENT MOODS, and be styled in as many different ways, as any other room in the house. But whether you prefer a traditional heart-of-the-home ambience, or a modern control-room image, the kitchen must be organized carefully so that it is safe, hygienic and well lit, with all surfaces made from durable and easy-care materials.

PRACTICAL CONSIDERATIONS

The basic plan and the choice of cupboards, equipment and appliances, as well as the colors, patterns and textures used, will all depend on the way you and your family use the kitchen, and the type of cooking you do. Circumstances alter: cooking for two may change to providing meals for a growing family in a surprisingly short time. The space available and the size of your budget will of course also dictate what you can and cannot do. And you will need to look at the overall style of your existing kitchen and the usefulness of any built-in features before deciding whether to retain and enhance these, or reject and remove them – or simply to camouflage them.

The amount of natural daylight the kitchen receives and at which part of the day, and the question of ventilation or condensation are further important considerations. Having insufficient daylight might be improved by installing a larger window or mullioned door. Ventilation and condensation problems could be dealt with by putting in an efficient exhaust fan or air conditioning; by enlarging the heating system; and/or by providing a moisture-proof layer in construction. Structural issues like these, as well as installing lighting and any re-plumbing, will have to be resolved at the outset; they may involve consulting a specialist.

STYLISH SURFACES

Once you have assessed the situation, listing faults and problems as well as good features and advantages, and have worked out your "master plan", you can start to think about style and color schemes and to select surface treatments for worktops, walls and floors. It is important to have practical surfaces in the kitchen; they should be fully washable (scrubbable in some cases), but they need not be harsh and clinical and can still have great style.

IN THIS UNFITTED COUNTRY-STYLE KITCHEN, THE SIMPLE STAINLESS STEEL SINK IS SET INTO A WORKTOP AND DRAINING BOARD MADE FROM OLD WOOD TREATED WITH SEVERAL COATS OF VARNISH TO MAKE IT STAIN RESISTANT AND EASY TO CLEAN. THE HANGING RAIL ABOVE THE STOVE PROVIDES EXCELLENT STORAGE FOR KITCHEN UTENSILS AND EQUIPMENT.

Cupboard units and work surfaces are largely a matter of personal taste, as well as cost, and will also depend on the overall style chosen for your kitchen. Whether you select a warm wood or a shiny laminate, check that doors and drawers are easy to open, with no awkward finger-pinching catches or handles, and that they are easy to clean, inside as well as out.

Worktops will need to be appropriate for the type of units they link and for the type of cooking you do; a regular pastry-maker may want a marble slab set into part of the work surface, for example. Choose hygienic worktops without seams so they are easy to clean. The most conventional solution is post-formed laminate with rounded edges, but you should also look at some of the more unusual options, such as ceramic tiles, granite, marble, or a resin-based product like Corian, which can be molded into a continuous surface, to include the sink. Some of these materials are heavy, so if you are thinking of putting them on top of existing cupboards, the frames may have to be strengthened. For tiled worktops use special grouting which is impervious to acids and cooking liquids, to ensure they are hygienic to use.

Sinks do not have to be sited in the conventional place under a window (although this does make for easy plumbing); indeed, if you also have a dishwasher and therefore spend less time at the sink, you may consider it a waste of a prime site and may wish to have your food preparation area under the window instead. Nor do sinks have to be stainless steel, especially as this material does not fit in with every scheme. Enameled bowls and drainers come in a wide range of styles, shapes and colors, including some cunning corner models. The old-fashioned Belfast or butler's sink is much deeper and is more practical if you grow your own vegetables, or do a lot of flower arranging. With a wall-mounted wooden plate rack to drain above, the practical planning of a bygone age comes into its own.

The floor will have to withstand food spills and splashes from hot fat, as well as the tramp of dirty feet, so a washable material is essential; but it must also be non-slip, so check how any proposed floorcovering performs when wet. If you are lucky enough to have original flagstones, do not take them up but restore and seal them instead. Quarry or ceramic tiles are hardwearing and easy to keep clean, but these permanent materials are hard on the feet, and anything dropped on them may shatter. They can be softened with mats in areas away from the sink or stove.

If you prefer something a little more "bouncy" underfoot, look at cushioned vinyls, vinyl tiles, cork tiles (which must be properly sealed, as cork swells and pushes up when wet), linoleum (which can be cut and inlaid in interesting patterns). Rubber is making a comeback as a material for kitchen floors, but avoid the studded variety, as food spills are not easy to clean out of the indentations. There are also special bonded kitchen carpets and carpet tiles (not always practical around the sink and stove, however); tiles are more sensible as they can be taken up and washed if necessary, changed around to even out wear, or replaced individually. Tiles permit interesting designs to be created at relatively little cost.

Walls also need to be splashproof and washable. They can be part-tiled around the stove, sink and above the work surfaces, though all-tiled kitchen walls can look rather institutional. Other treatments include washable vinyl wallcoverings (washable wallpaper is unsuitable as it is only spongeable); wood cladding (seal it properly with varnish after painting or staining); and specially formulated kitchen and bathroom paint. Gloss paint, normally used for woodwork and radiators, can attract condensation, but an eggshell finish (oil-based but matte) is suitable. Sometimes a combination of different wall treatments is the best option, provided they are selected from a co-ordinated range, or chosen from the same color palette for a harmonious effect. You can buy ceramic tiles as well as vinyl wallcoverings and paint in co-ordinated ranges.

Window treatments should always be practical. Short, crisply gathered curtains in a washable fabric and wipeable shade or tailored Roman blinds all provide night-time privacy without cutting out any daylight. Slatted Venetian blinds look appropriate in a modern kitchen though they can be difficult to clean: the vertical type are more practical than the horizontal. Flapping curtains over the sink or stove are a safety hazard, while Austrian shades look silly in a kitchen, and their deep folds collect dirt and condensation.

STYLING IDEAS

☛ *If you inherit a kitchen you cannot afford to change, imprint your personality on it through the use of inexpensive accessories and accents – a new window blind; new door handles or knobs; cooking implements hung from a chain; a display of china on a shelf.*

☛ *If you have tiled worktops, use grouting which is impervious to acids and cooking liquids: this ensures they are hygienic.*

☛ *Tiled wall areas can be totally transformed by altering the color of the grouting between the tiles. Use a bright primary, a deep tone, or pick a color to link with a pattern on the tiles. Colored grouting is readily available from do-it-yourself outlets, or make your own by adding poster color/acrylic paint to standard white.*

☛ *Give your kitchen a new lease on life by changing the door and drawer fronts. Buy them ready-made (if a standard size will fit your cupboards) or have them made to measure (make sure they are strong enough to take the weight); or use a special self-adhesive material – some are ready-cut to size, or they can be cut from a roll.*

☛ *Cover poor-quality kitchen walls (or badly crazed tiles) with tongue-and-groove boarding. Install it by means of battens screwed to the wall (do not remove old tiles), and secret nailing. Paint or stain, then seal it with polyurethane varnish.*

☛ *Hide clutter on open shelves with a pull-down shade.*

☛ *If you want a streamlined look, hide the refrigerator, freezer and dishwasher behind integrated doors to match the rest of the kitchen.*

RIGHT: THIS DUAL-PURPOSE KITCHEN IS SIMPLE YET STYLISH. THE LIGHT CREAM PAINTWORK BRINGS MAXIMUM LIGHT TO WHAT COULD BE A DARK CORNER OF THE ROOM. THE CIRCULAR TABLE MAKES THE MOST OF THE SPACE IN THE BAY; A CRISP TABLE DRESSING SETS THE SCENE.

FAR RIGHT: THIS STREAMLINED ARRANGEMENT MAKES MAXIMUM USE OF A CENTRAL PENINSULAR UNIT, HOUSING THE SINK AND THE DISHWASHER, TO DIVIDE COOKING AND EATING AREAS. STAINLESS STEEL, USED FOR ALL SURFACES AND UNITS, INCLUDING THE STOVE, IS AN APPROPRIATE MATERIAL FOR THIS ULTRA-MODERN KITCHEN. RECESSED DOWNLIGHTERS ABOVE THE "ISLAND" UNIT PROVIDE A DISCREET FORM OF LIGHTING.

STYLING IDEAS

☛ *If your kitchen is the heart of the home, keep the family bulletin board here – use it to note dates and appointments; keep shopping lists and cleaning tickets. Leave space for drawings by budding family artists.*

☛ *Lay tiles on the kitchen floor in an interesting pattern – to outline the units or dining area; create stripes widthwise across the floor; or use a diamond or triangular effect from corner to corner. Similar effects can be achieved with wall tiles.*

☛ *Try to provide a cozy place to sit if the kitchen is large enough, by means of a rocking, cane, or rush-seated chair; a bench furnished with squab cushions; or an ottoman with a padded lift-up top.*

☛ *Choose practical styles of window treatment, without frills or flounces to dip into the sink or brush across worktops: blinds are a wise option in a kitchen.*

Color schemes can be relaxing or stimulating, and again will need to relate to the overall style. In general you should avoid strong colors and clashing, or busy, patterns on worktops or small wall areas. In a kitchen that gets warm (temperatures can be fairly high with the stoves, washing machine and dryer all sited in the room), a cool scheme based on blues, greys or greens can be enjoyable to live with – you can always spice it up with interesting accents and accessories. A more neutral scheme will work well in a country-style kitchen, perhaps using shades of cream or buttermilk on the walls and natural-colored cork tiles on the floor. For a dark room, pastel shades or ice-cream colors – lemon sorbet, sugar-pink, pistachio, frosted lime, apricot or peach – will add light and subtlety. Red is a difficult color for the main wall surface in a kitchen as it can alter the appearance of food (meat will look undercooked, for example, if it reflects the red). However, it makes a cheerful addition to the scheme when used as an accent color, for instance, on the door fronts of cupboards or for seat covers, curtains or blind, and a tablecloth.

LIGHTING AND ELECTRICS

Electrical wiring and outlets need to be positioned close to the stove, refrigerator, dishwasher and any electrical appliances and equipment (see Planning Your Kitchen, page 38). Always allow for twice as many sockets as you think you will need; install double sockets for maximum efficiency.

Aim for clear task lighting over the stove, oven, sink and all work surfaces, to illuminate them clearly without glare or dazzle. This can be provided by either strip lights concealed behind wall-mounted cup-

boards, downlighters sunk into the ceiling, or spotlights mounted on track; a central fluorescent strip can be too harsh in a kitchen. Light the insides of any deep cupboards and larders, preferably by means of a light which comes on as you open the door. The kitchen table may be lit in a similar way to the diningroom table; you should have this on a separate circuit from the rest of the lighting so that lights for the working end of the kitchen can be turned off or dimmed while you are eating. (For more on kitchen lighting, see page 228).

LIVING ROOMS

THE LIVING ROOM OFTEN HAS TO BE THE MOST VERSATILE room in the home and, depending on its use or uses, can be designed, furnished and decorated in a variety of different ways, according to family requirements and lifestyle. It may be a formal room, for adult relaxation and entertaining only, or a busy center of activity, with the television, music center, piano, computer, and children's toys and games all competing for space and attention. Some living rooms have to be dual- or multi-purpose, combining study and home office facilities with family activities – or need to convert from being a daytime playroom to becoming an evening dining room and study. Furniture, storage, lighting and materials will have to be carefully selected to suit the room's purpose and function, as well as helping to set a style.

PRACTICAL PLANNING

Most living rooms, especially the multi-functional ones, suffer from lack of space, so before going any further you need to sit down and list all the activities which are likely to take place in the room. Think ahead to any probable changes in the family situation, such as children or teenagers going away to school or college; the arrival of a new baby; an elderly relative coming to stay; a new job requiring an amount of business entertaining, or working from home part-time, creating the need for a study area.

Try to be objective: look at the whole area with fresh eyes, considering the size, shape, orientation and architectural style of the room and the amount of natural daylight it receives. Assess the existing furniture and storage and decide how comfortable and how efficient they are. Work out what must be replaced or renewed; bear in mind how much you can afford, which means having a realistic budget at the outset. Decide where to put the television if you will watch it in the living room, and a record player or music center. Not only will this affect the placing of seating, but it will also effect the provision of electric points and the cable or aerial connection.

You will then have to measure accurately and prepare a plan (see page 36), using templates to fit in the furniture on paper first. Allow for the opening and closing of doors and drawers and avoid placing units, cupboards and sideboards too close to other pieces of furniture which will make using them difficult. Allow enough space to walk around the room comfortably and to clean it easily. Do not position upholstered furniture too close to a fire, where it could get scorched.

This master plan will help you to see what you can – and cannot – get into the room. If you find that the

THIS COOL, NEUTRAL SCHEME IN A CONTINENTAL FARMHOUSE RELIES ON FORM AND TEXTURES TO PROVIDE VISUAL INTEREST. THE BRICK FLOOR AND BLEACHED WOOD OF THE CEILING BEAMS AND DOOR LINTEL HAVE AN INHERENT NATURAL BEAUTY, WHILE THE LOOSE-COVERED ARMCHAIRS AND THE HONEY-COLORED STONE JARS HAVE A PLEASING FORM. THE ROOM'S ATMOSPHERE IS COOL, RELAXED AND INVITING FOR SUMMER; WARMER TOUCHES COULD BE ADDED FOR WINTER.

outsize sofa or grand piano you had in mind will not fit, you know you must compromise with two smaller sofas, a selection of differently shaped chairs or modular seating, and with an upright piano. You can use the plan to help you balance your budget by using differently colored templates – one color for essential items, another for possibles and a third for any later luxuries, so you can see at a glance what to buy first.

SELECTING A SCHEME

Start by creating an interesting framework for the room, choosing the wall, floor and window treatments carefully, to give a relaxing atmosphere, but without being bland or boring. In a well-used room, such surfaces, as well as the upholstery, will have to be selected for their hardwearing and easy-care qualities; the furniture will have to be functional, as well as comfortable, and a suitable scale for the size of the room – large, tall items in spacious rooms and lower,

neat pieces for smaller spaces. A specific period style can be elegant, especially if it emphasizes the architectural character of the property, but too rigid a treatment, with all pieces matching, can end up looking like a furniture showroom!

The floor Try to begin here, since the floor is a dominant feature in a living room. It gets the most wear and tear in a family living room and is likely to have to last through several changes of decorating scheme, so it needs to be extremely hardwearing. Besides this, the floor relates to all the other surfaces: walls butt up to it, baseboards surround it, curtain fabrics touch it, and both upholstered seating and other items of furniture stand on it. A bold pattern, or a strong color on the floor will tend to be overpowering, but a very pale color, or a fragile texture will be impractical in a family living room, so a balance must be sought.

THE ATMOSPHERE OF THIS COUNTRY-STYLE LIVING ROOM IS CREATED THROUGH THE USE OF TRADITIONAL FURNITURE, FLORAL CHINTZ FABRICS AND A SOFT COLOR SCHEME OF NEUTRALS AND PALE BLUE.

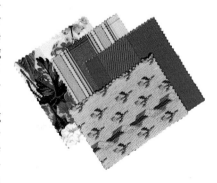

STYLING IDEAS

○ *Change the living room with the season, by switching colors, soft furnishings, accessories and the arrangement of the furniture. Place the seating to face the garden during the summer and group it around the fireplace in winter; hang patterned cotton or chintz curtains in summer, replacing them with heavier velvet or tweed in the autumn; cover the sofas and chairs with paler slipcovers during the summer; add cool-colored accessories in summer and warm ones in winter.*

○ *Turn a sunny bay window into a mini-conservatory: fit double-glazing, install cane chairs and a glass-topped cane table; mass plants on it and light from below with an uplighter; hang trailing plants above the table, and stand potted palms in cache-pots or an aspidistra on a stand.*

○ *Mix and match the styles of upholstered furniture for interest and a more at-home look: combine a Knowle settee with two cane-framed bergère chairs, or a Chesterfield sofa with a bentwood rocking chair and two wing armchairs, for example.*

○ *To make a long, narrow living room look wider, "zone" it into areas: position two sofas facing each other across a coffee table at right angles to a long wall; back one with a sofa-table or sideboard, facing the dining area.*

○ *In a square sitting room, arrange the seating in an L or U shape, more conducive to conversation.*

○ *To draw attention to sitting room windows, dress them with opulent treatments, colored to contrast with the surrounding wall area; to "fade" them into the background, choose simple blinds or curtains to match the wall color.*

If you intend to carpet, choose as good a quality as you can afford, with a hard-twist, velvet or close, looped pile; long, luxurious piles are a better choice for floors which take less punishment. A mid-tone color and/or a simple pattern will be easier to live with and more practical, unless you want to give the room a period look with a carpet in an authentic design. However there are many other options, from stripped, sanded and sealed or stained, stenciled or painted floorboards; special wood treatments like parquet, woodstrip or wood-block; sealed cork tiles; linoleum (which can be laid in interesting patterns); and sea-grass, sisal or rush matting. All these floorings can be adequately softened with a rug in the main sitting area, placed in front of sofas or chairs; make sure these will not slip or creep by fixing a non-slip adhesive underlay to the rug.

The ceiling is frequently ignored as an element in the decorative scheme and often painted safe white, but it can equally be treated as an important feature either by painting it an exciting color, with any cornice, covings and ceiling roses and moldings picked out to contrast, or by giving it a beamed treatment. Either of

THIS MODERN INTERIOR RELIES ON THE USE OF COLOR FOR DRAMATIC IMPACT, WITH THE COMFORTABLE ORANGE ARMCHAIRS AS A COUNTERPOINT TO THE BLACK AND WHITE CHECK-EFFECT RUG. THE COFFEE TABLE AND ACCESSORIES SUCH AS THE VASES PROVIDE A CURVING CONTRAST OF FORM TO THE STRAIGHT LINES OF THE ROOM'S ARCHITECTURE AND THE OTHER FURNITURE IT CONTAINS.

these ideas will depend on the height of the room, since they will make a ceiling look lower, especially if you echo the ceiling color on the floor. If you want to "raise the roof" a little, color the ceiling the same, or a few tones paler than, the walls or the background color to any wallcovering.

The walls Living room walls can take up a large area: they are in effect a total blank canvas on which to work some innovative effects, and there are many possibilities; however, bear in mind that too bold a treatment will not be very restful. Tall, wide areas of wall can be reduced in apparent height by using a dividing dado rail, picture rail and frieze to create horizontal lines; lower, narrow wall areas can be visually expanded by vertical treatments, such as wide stripes

○ *In a dual-purpose living/dining room, define the different areas with a change in floor treatment use wood, vinyl, cork or linoleum for an easy-care dining area and add carpet, sisal, rush matting or an ethnic rug in the sitting room.*

○ *Use vertical Venetian blinds to divide living and dining areas – lighter than doors, they take up less space.*

○ *To make a small living room look larger, paint the baseboards the same color as the floor, cover upholstered furniture to match the carpet and use flexible unit seating which can be moved around easily.*

○ *If the living room is low, throw light up onto the ceiling using wall-mounted uplighters or wall lights: do not position them too high up on the wall, because they will scorch the ceiling.*

○ *Draw attention to a handsome fireplace by painting the surrounding area to contrast. Conceal an ugly one by coloring the chimney breast to match.*

○ *Hide unsightly radiators behind casing or radiator covers made of trellis or mesh; for a quick and easy camouflage, paint them to match the surrounding wall area.*

○ *Use antique textiles for accessories such as cushions, table covers or throws. Fragile pieces can be mounted on a net backing and framed as a picture, or placed under a glass table top.*

○ *Smarten up a shabby armchair with an attractive afghan or shawl, or totally engulf it by tieing it up in a large piece of sheeting or fabric.*

○ *"Pattern" a plain wall with an eye-catching group of pictures or prints of different shapes and sizes.*

or a paneled effect. Sometimes plain walls provide a perfect foil for a special collection of pictures, prints or wallhangings which will add visual interest and a personal finishing touch for the room.

Most walls will not be an uninterrupted, flat expanse, but are more likely to have projections, recesses, alcoves or niches, or be broken up by fireplaces, windows, doors, built-in cupboards or shelves. While these can add character to the room, they may look rather scattered. You will have to decide whether to try to unify everything by coloring the additions to tone in with their surroundings, creating an impression of space, or to treat them differently so they are emphasized and enhanced.

In this inviting Edwardian living room the areas are carefully "zoned" to divide the sitting from the dining space. The L-shaped seating arrangement grouped around the fire is backed by a circular table used for display. Window treatments are minimal — sheer blinds and shutters — so the window's shape can be appreciated. The stripped wooden floor and wall treatments are neutral surfaces, with color provided in accents and accessories, giving greater decorating flexibility. The alcove on one side of the marble fireplace, with its ornate wooden surround, houses the bookshelves.

Seating arrangements

LIVING ROOM SEATING should be arranged to be conducive to conversation and so the sitters can relate to each other. They may want to warm themselves at an open fire, watch television or listen to music in comfort in the winter and to face the garden in summer.

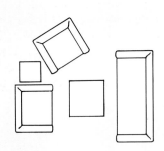

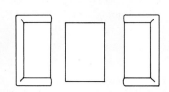

Two sofas, or sofas and chairs, can be placed facing each other across a coffee table.

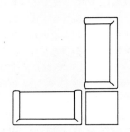

An L-shaped arrangement can be fitted into a corner, or can act as a divider in a multi-purpose room.

Two- or three-seater sofas can provide seating, or use a mixture of sofas and chairs – a three-seater can be tight squeeze for three adults! There are several possible arrangements, depending on the size and shape of your room. The first two will work in a fairly small space, or at one end of a dual-purpose living room.

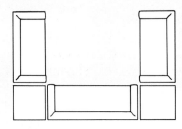

A U-shaped arrangement is more comfortable and gives greater freedom of access but takes up more space.

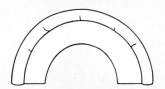

In some rooms, curved seating units can add visual interest by introducing a contrast in form, but these can waste space and do not always fit happily into a square or rectangular room.

The windows are an integral part of the architecture of the room. You should draw attention to them if they are pleasing, either by dressing them simply so their basic shape and style can be appreciated, or by using an extravagant treatment to contrast with the surrounding wall area. If they are unattractive, and especially if there are several differently shaped windows on one wall, you may prefer to unify them with a single treatment, or dress them using simple blinds or curtains to match the wall color, so they fade into the background. Alternatively, if you have an ugly view or undistinguished windows, you may prefer to use a very opulent window dressing to create a focal point in the room and mask what lies beyond.

CHOOSING FURNITURE

Upholstered furniture is an important and dominant feature in a living room. If you are buying it new, there are several criteria to apply. It has to be selected for comfort (always try sitting on it before you buy); safety of fillings and fabric (check the flammability of these); ease of cleaning and care. Shape, size and scale are also important considerations. Large sofas or seating units in a variety of interesting shapes and contrasting textures, especially those upholstered in a bold design or a strong color, will add an extra dimension to a large living room. But they can be too dominant in a small one, where it is better to use simpler forms of seating, with plainish covers. Stripes and checks can create a neutral background, while giving sufficient interest, and they can be mixed successfully with plains, floral and geometric patterns.

If you want to unify several different pieces of upholstered furniture which you already have, cover them in the same fabric or choose a co-ordinated fabric range, perhaps using a plain fabric for a sofa and a matching stripe for two or three chairs, piping the plain item with the striped fabric and vice versa. One or two other items, such as a stool or an occasional chair, could be covered in checks or a floral pattern from the same color palette, possibly piped in the plain fabric to give definition and to outline the form of the furniture. Tailored or close-fitting covers will work best on furniture with curves, but square or rectangular shapes can have slipcovers, which can be more easily removed for laundering or dry cleaning – or renewed when you want a change.

Living rooms also have to accommodate furniture other than upholstered seating. They are often the place where television is watched and music played, so shelves or a table will need to be provided. The living room may also have to house the dining table and chairs and provide storage for bottles, glasses and the dinner service, as well as for books, videos, tapes, CDs, records, games and children's toys – and possibly much more if the room is truly multi-functional. As with any other room, you need to figure out exactly what you want to store and the most useful, space-saving and visually acceptable means of storing it (see Storage, page 233).

Whether you choose to have mainly built-in shelves and cupboards, possibly decorated to match the room, or freestanding pieces – or even a mixture of both – is largely a matter of personal taste, but it will also depend on the size and style of the room, and the space available. It makes sense to use alcoves, for example, for built-in shelves and cupboards unless you plan to have a large, single piece of furniture set back into them. Some occasional items of furniture – tables, desks, small cupboards, sideboards and bookcases – can all add character and an individual touch to a room, and should be chosen for their intrinsic interest, provided they are in keeping with the style or period of the living room. Avoid using all-matching items from the same manufacturer, in the same finish. Wood can be successfully mixed with cane and metal items, for example, and wooden furniture does not all have to be made in the same timber, such as pine or oak, provided there is no clash of color. Some woods are reddish, others yellowish, some pinkish, and these all blend well together; other woods tend toward being greenish or brownish, others blackish or greyish and these are better not mixed with the warmer tones. A painted or lacquered piece of furniture can often provide a link between several different items.

THE BEST LIGHTING

Good illumination is essential in the living room and this may entail using several different types of lighting. Most seating areas need some general background lighting, in the form of a ceiling or wall lights, as well as special task lighting, provided by table or standard lamps, and possibly some display or accent lighting to draw attention to a feature such as a picture or a collection displayed on shelves. Dining areas within a dual-purpose living room need light over the dining table in order to see to serve the food.

Once you have made your master plan, and know where the furniture is to be positioned, you can use it to work out the lighting, so that fittings and fixtures relate to the various parts of the room. Install several different circuits so that you can "fade out" one part of the room when not in use, and try to connect at least one circuit to a dimmer switch so you can adjust the light level. To allow for flexibility, plan to include some table and standard lamps and uplighters which can be easily moved around – this will mean installing plenty of socket outlets.

ACCESSORIES

There are many finishing touches which can be used to enhance the living room scheme and to give it character. The use of some sharp color or textural contrast will help to brighten a bland or very neutral scheme; softer tones and textures can calm down a stimulating scheme or provide a necessary link between contrasting colors and patterns.

Cushions of different shapes, sizes, colors, patterns and textures can be piled onto sofas, chairs and window seats to add contrast or to link several different upholstered items together. You might repeat the curtain fabric on another surface. Always buy a little extra curtain, upholstery or cover fabric for cushions, and keep an eye open for bargain remnants, as well as for antique and unusual textiles in specialist shops or rummage sales. Other fabric accessories include covers for occasional tables, throws or draped shawls. In their colors, patterns or texture, they should relate to the overall mood of the living room and the basic style selected for its decoration, furniture and furnishings.

Collections of glass, china or other ornaments, small pieces of statuary or sculpture, books, pictures and prints are all interesting and colorful finishing touches; screens, small stools, fenders and other accoutrements for a fireplace provide less familiar ones. In many living rooms, dried and fresh flowers and the grouping of plants are all an integral part of the overall theme. Select these for contrast in form (for example, feathery, variegated and glossy leaves) and light them well.

STYLING IDEAS

❍ *In a living room scheme based on neutral colors, use textural contrast to add interest and spike it with bright, contrasting accents in accessories.*

❍ *Consider size and scale: use bold patterns and bright colors on large surfaces, small-scale patterns and pale colors on small areas.*

❍ *To create a country feel in the living room of a town apartment, choose a fresh decorating scheme based on greens, sunny yellow and sky blue; use floral chintz fabrics and accessorize freely with lots of house plants.*

❍ *Make the most of the chimney recesses by using them for built-in shelves and storage or for freestanding furniture.*

❍ *Hide away the hi fi or television by housing it in a cupboard or unit, on a slide-out or revolving shelf.*

❍ *Let your color scheme create an ethnic mood, keeping the furnishings simple. Bright blues, yellow and white suggest a Mediterranean feel, while rich earth colors such as browns and terracotta, might be the base of an African theme. Buy fabric, cushions, ornaments and other decorative accessories from stores which sell imported goods, for an authentic result.*

DINING ROOMS

A DINING ROOM USED TO BE THE HUB OF THE HOME — A SEPARATE ROOM, set aside for the enjoyment of food, wine and good conversation. But a conventional dining room is almost a thing of the past, and nowadays a dining area is more likely to be part of the kitchen or living room, or even sited in the hall. If you do have an individual room, it may have to work hard as a multi-purpose area, serving as a playroom/ study/music room as well as a dining area, or even doubling up as a guest room. Some houses have a conservatory built on, which serves as a dining room, too.

CHOOSING A THEME

The style of a dining room, like that of the kitchen, may well depend on the type of food you serve and the entertaining you do. If you are a creative cook, who enjoys feeding friends and family, an upretentious country-style room could work well, with a vast stripped pine table, a decorative hutch and a cheerful fireplace, decorated in spring-like colors, with flowery chintz fabrics. If formal entertaining is part of your lifestyle and you have an older property, you may wish to decorate the dining room with a specific period flavor, such as Victorian or Edwardian. Other alternative styles include sleek Scandinavian, French Empire, Colonial, Conservatory (lots of cane and greenery) or Mediterranean, where materials and vivid colors could suggest dining *al fresco*. Whichever style you choose, the dining area should be as inviting as possible. Color, decorate and furnish it to create a feeling of warmth and intimacy, to encourage family and guests to linger over the enjoyment of a meal.

PLANNING AND FURNISHING

Dining rooms have to serve a purpose, so there must be ample space to walk around the table, serve guests and open doors and drawers without knocking into the backs of chairs. So when you work out a room plan, remember to allow for "traffic flow" (see page 36). Chairs should be comfortable, and must fit around the table, allowing plenty of space for diners'

A SMALL DINING ROOM IS BROUGHT ,TO LIFE BY THE FRESH, CHEERFUL COLOR SCHEME, ECHOED IN THE DECKLE-EDGED TABLECLOTH AND THE TABLE SETTINGS. THE CANE EASY CHAIR AND FOLDING "GARDEN" DINING CHAIRS ALL CONTRIBUTE TO THE OUTDOOR AL FRESCO IMAGE.

knees and elbows. A circular table is often a wise choice, especially if the room is small, as round tables take up less space than square or rectangular ones; they can often be fitted with an extra leaf or two which will expand the table to a larger, oval shape. This will mean buying extra chairs, so you must have space to store them elsewhere in the house when not grouped around the table. If you have very little space, consider a folding or trestle table, which can be dual-purpose, and folded away when not in use.

In a larger dining room, several tables might provide a more flexible arrangement – these can be pushed up together for a large party or buffet; separated into smaller individual ones on less formal occasions; or used to provide extra serving space. Another alternative is to use a table on a firm pedestal base and have an extra, larger top (a circular one is often the best shape) cut from blockboard or plywood to place on top and cover with a cloth to increase the table size when necessary; bear in mind that you will need somewhere to store this top when not in use.

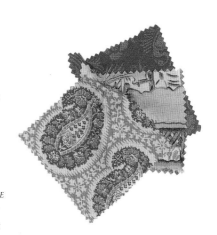

BELOW LEFT: A TRADITIONAL DINING ROOM SETTING IN A PERIOD HOUSE HAS AN ELEGANT BUT INVITING FEEL. THE COLORWASHED WALLS IN RICH INDIAN RED CREATE AN INTIMATE ATMOSPHERE, APPROPRIATE TO A DINING ROOM; THIS IS OFFSET BY THE CRISP WHITE NAPERY AND CHAIR COVERS. THE STRIPED, HEAVY CURTAINS, WITH ITALIAN STRINGING, ENHANCE AND SOFTEN THE SHAPE OF THE TALL SASH WINDOWS.

BELOW RIGHT: A SIMPLE, BISTRO-STYLE EATING AREA IN A KITCHEN HAS A CHEERFUL COLOR SCHEME WHICH MAKES FOR A WELCOMING AMBIENCE. THE ORIGINAL AND EYE-CATCHING LIGHT FIXTURE FOCUSES ATTENTION ON THE DINING TABLE. A SLIDING PARTITION BEHIND THE DINING AREA MEANS THE KITCHEN UNITS CAN BE SCREENED OFF WHEN REQUIRED.

STYLING IDEAS

✎ *Decorate dining rooms in warm, appetite-inducing colors - red is particularly effective in all its tints, tones and shades, ranging from deep wine to crushed strawberry and terracotta.*

✎ *If the dining area is part of the living room, link the schemes visually by making a tablecloth and/or napkins to match the curtains and cushions.*

✎ *Pick restrained patterns - bold geometrics and over-abundant florals can be distracting.*

✎ *Avoid too many light-reflecting surfaces and textures: dining rooms should be cozy and intimate.*

✎ *Set a pretty table with linen and napkins colored to echo the design on the dinner service.*

✎ *Add a touch of sunshine to a dark dining room with clear yellow walls and deep gold flooring, teamed with sky blue.*

✎ *Create a focal point with a display of china or colorful glass in an alcove, either in a special cabinet or on shelves - and illuminate it well.*

✎ *Use mirrors to reflect flickering candlelight.*

✎ *Change your table settings to suit the type of meal being served. Use white double-damask cloth, sparkling crystal and gleaming silver for a formal dinner party, a cheerful red-checked gingham cloth and studio pottery for a bistro-style supper and primary colored "disposables" for a children's tea party.*

✎ *Create Christmas cheer with a red and green scheme, trimmed with tartan bows, and sparkled with frosty white or silver.*

A PLACE FOR EVERYTHING

Dining room storage may well have to be tailored to accommodate all the occasional items of china and linen that you wish to store, since it is often more practical to keep the best glass, silver, dinner service and table linens in the dining room, where they will be needed for setting a stylish table. This will mean working out exactly what you need to store and measuring it all – a pile of dinner plates can be surprisingly tall and very heavy, and a meat dish much wider than you realized – to make sure it will all fit into any proposed units, cupboards or cabinets. You will need a suitable heat- and scratchproof surface from which to serve food, which may have to incorporate a plate/food warmer, especially if the dining room is some distance from the kitchen. This could form the top of, and be an integral part of, the storage system.

SELECTING SURFACES

A dining room floor can soon become scruffy, especially if there are young children in the family, so this may not be the best place to have a fitted carpet; certainly a pale, delicate color should be avoided. A harder, more easily cleaned flooring could be introduced – wood, cork, linoleum, ceramic or quarry tiles, vinyl tiles or sheet vinyl – but make sure that any of these are properly sealed. Hard surfaces can be softened with a carpet, rug or natural matting such as rush or seagrass, but make sure these will not slip; use a non-slip adhesive underlay if necessary.

Upholstery needs to be hardwearing and easy to clean; treat any pale-colored or fragile fabrics with a spray-on finish to make them spill- and stain-resistant. Chairs with tie-on or slip-on covers are easily removed for laundering or dry-cleaning.

Decorate the walls so they can be washed or wiped down – especially at the back of any serving area. Options include washable vinyl wallcoverings, washable wallpapers (which in reality are only wipeable) and paint in a variety of finishes. Paint can be applied over a textured wallcovering, or become a decorative feature in its own right if you choose to use a painting technique such as marbling, dragging, sponging, stenciling (see page 104).

Opulent window dressings may be chosen for a dining room, since it is often used in the evenings, and an attractively styled window treatment adds warmth and intimacy to the scheme. But remember that very heavy fabric will pick up and harbor food smells – velvet, for example, would not be a wise choice.

THE RICH COLORS OF THIS DINING ROOM - GOLDEN YELLOW WALLS AND DARK, KELIM-PATTERNED FABRIC FOR THE DRAPED CURTAIN - ECHO THE MELLOW COLOR OF THE WOODEN FLOOR AND POLISHED MAHOGANY DINING TABLE. THE BOTANICAL PRINTS ON THE WALLS LEAD THE EYE THROUGH INTO THE GARDEN. BENCHES FOR SEATING MAKE GOOD USE OF THE RESTRICTED WIDTH AND ALLOW FOR MOVEMENT AROUND THE TABLE. THE HEAVY CURTAIN CAN BE DROPPED FOR EVENING DINING, MAKING THE ROOM EVEN MORE INTIMATE.

LIGHTING

Good lighting is particularly important in a dining room and should above all be subtle; it must light the table clearly, but without glare, and should never shine into the diners' eyes. A lamp on a rise-and-fall chain which pulls down centrally over the table, or strategically placed ceiling-recessed downlighters focused on the table, will create an intimate ambience and give good light. Chandeliers may give added sparkle, but they can be too harsh a light source, so fit them with a dimmer switch and hang them high enough to prevent dazzling people around the table.

Candlelight is the most flattering light of all, but keep the flame above, or below, eye level when guests are seated, and always provide additional lighting to illuminate any serving area (individual table lamps, wall lights or uplighters are all possible options). Display lighting in storage units, or as an integral part of a shelving system, can provide a warm background glow. Have different types of lighting on separate circuits, especially in a dual-purpose room, so that you can dim one area if necessary.

STYLING IDEAS

✎ In a traditional setting, put up a Delft rack (a wide shelf at picture rail height) and use it to display plates, cups and bowls.

✎ Fruit and flowers are favorite dining room motifs; have borders or cornices depicting swags of vine leaves, bunches of grapes or sharply defined citrus fruit.

✎ Use the pineapple, symbol of hospitality, on curtain fabric, in borders or as a stencil motif.

✎ If the ceiling is tall, paint it a rich, warm color and echo this on the floor. Avoid pendant lights and, as an alternative, provide pools of light from table lamps and low-level wall lights.

✎ In a small, square dining room, use pale colors for the walls and windows and take the wall treatment up onto the ceiling.

✎ Light a feathery plant dramatically, so the shadow outline is thrown on to the wall and ceiling.

✎ Create an al fresco mood with cane or metal dining furniture; make a screen from garden trellis and combine it with plants.

✎ Dining rooms should be comfortably warm but not too hot: a gas-log-flame fire set into an elegant fireplace will give a cheerful background glow.

✎ Disguise an old dining table or a temporary trestle table with a floor-length fabric "skirt". Make it from new sheeting or an old sheet (this is extra wide so needs no seams) and dye it or batik it, paint it with fabric paint or stencil on a pattern.

HALL, STAIRS AND LANDINGS

IN DECORATING, AS IN ALL THINGS, FIRST impressions are important, so the hall – the area of the home usually seen first – should be warm, welcoming and at the same time give an intriguing glimpse of what is to come in the surrounding rooms.

MAKING AN ENTRANCE

Many halls are scarcely larger than a corridor and few are big enough to hold much furniture, so in theory they should be easy to plan and design. And as most halls are used merely as a route to other rooms, and not actually lived in (apart from those large enough to double as a dining hall or study area), decorating schemes can be bold, stimulating and dramatic, rather than bland and relaxing.

Wherever possible, space should be made in the hall for at least a chair and a table, or a desk, to accommodate the clutter of daily life – keys, letters, packages, shopping, library books, message pads, homework, sports gear and dog chains – which usually collect in this central clearing house. Try to provide a place to hang visitors' coats and umbrellas, too. If the area is very narrow, install a bench or wall-mounted shelf instead of a larger piece of furniture. An old-fashioned hall stand would combine coat-hanging facilities with a shelf, a drawer for small items, a mirror and an umbrella stand. It can be painted to fade into the background or decorated so that it stands out. You could have a modern equivalent built in by a carpenter.

In a very long, corridor-like hall, a pair of matching tables, chests or cupboards with mirrors or a pier glass above, could provide practical storage, at the same time creating an illusion of greater space, width and light. You can play other *trompe l'oeil* (eye-

THIS IMAGINATIVE BUDGET DECORATING SCHEME USES WARM COLORS TO MAKE THE MOST OF A BOX-LIKE HALL. THE WOODEN STAIRS, HANDRAIL AND BANISTERS HAVE BEEN STAINED AND WIPED, SO THE GRAIN OF THE WOOD STILL SHOWS THROUGH. THEY ECHO THE COLORS USED IN THE DIAMOND-PATTERNED, ROUGH-PLASTERED WALLS.

THIS LONG, NARROW ENTRANCE HALL IS MADE TO LOOK WIDER THROUGH THE USE OF THE CHECKERBOARD VINYL-TILED FLOOR AND THE MIRROR ABOVE THE BOXED-IN RADIATOR. ALTHOUGH THE HALL IS NOT WIDE ENOUGH FOR A TABLE, THE RADIATOR TREATMENT PROVIDES A SURFACE ON WHICH TO STAND THE LAMPS AND DECORATIVE PIECES AS WELL AS THE ESSENTIALS SUCH AS LETTERS AND KEYS. THE IMPRESSION OF SPACE IS ALSO ENHANCED BY THE REMOVAL OF PART OF THE DINING-ROOM WALL – A CURTAIN CAN BE CLOSED AT NIGHT FOR GREATER PRIVACY AND TO CUT OUT DRAFTS. THE WHITE DADO RAIL, CORNICE AND CORBELS CONTRAST WITH THE WARM APRICOT WALLS.

MAXIMUM USE IS MADE OF A HIGH WALL ON ONE SIDE OF THE STAIRS TO DISPLAY AN EYE-CATCHING ARRANGEMENT OF PICTURES AND PRINTS, GUIDING THE VIEW THROUGH TO THE GALLERIED LANDING. THE OFF-WHITE COLOR SCHEME CREATES AN IMPRESSION OF SPACE AND PREVENTS ANY CLASH WITH SCHEMES IN THE ROOMS LEADING OFF. THE STAIR CARPET, IN A DARKER SHADE, IS HARDWEARING, AND ITS SUBDUED PATTERN DOES NOT SHOW EVERY SPECK OF DIRT.

deceiving) tricks with mirrors, light-reflecting textures, and monochromatic color schemes, to help increase the apparent size. If the hall is high and narrow, paint the ceiling in a rich tone and use the same color, or tonal value, on the floor. Pick out any cornice or coving as a contrast, and paint the frieze (the area above the picture rail) the same color as the ceiling. Give the walls a "split" treatment, with panels or a dado rail, decorating the area below differently from the wall above. If the walls have no horizontal divisions, you may wish to install a dado rail or a cornice using wooden molding or plasterboard panels. Otherwise, you could simply use a border or hang a wallcovering with a definite horizontal pattern.

SELECTING MATERIALS

Use warm, inviting colors such as rich terracotta, deep Indian red or muted rose in larger halls and pale peach, dusky apricot or pastel pink in smaller spaces. Or suggest a sense of continual sunshine with yellows and burnished gold, contrasted with sparkling white. Inviting textures, such as a deep-pile oatmeal carpet or a flocked wallpaper, will add to the welcoming atmosphere, whereas luxurious ones will create a mood of opulence, for example through gilt mirrors or picture frames. White walls look cold for a hall.

Choose materials that will withstand wear and tear, and be as easy to clean as possible, since this is the area of the home with constant through traffic, and in some houses everything from the buggy to the trash-can may have to be brought in through the main entrance. Hall and stairwell walls (especially at the lower level, which suffers the majority of the knocks and bumps) should be both tough and washable. Practical options include a textured wallcovering, painted in a fairly dark color with an eggshell finish; a washable vinyl wallcovering; a sponged, marbled, dragged or ragged paint finish; or a tiled dado area. Doors into and leading off the hall also take their toll of sticky fingermarks, so a natural wood finish, properly sealed with polyurethane varnish; or a serviceable color of paint are much more practical than white, cream or magnolia.

Hall floors suffer from the daily tramp of feet, and mud, grit and snow can all be walked into the hall. So choose a tough, easy-to-clean surface, and protect it by installing a good-quality doormat set into a well just inside the front door; have one outside too, if practical. If you are going to carpet the hallway, continuing up the stairs and onto the landing, choose as

STYLING IDEAS

❍ *To create a spacious impression in a small property (essential in two or three-roomed apartments, bungalows and small houses), let the hall scheme "flow" into the rooms leading off by laying the same flooring throughout, or at least use the same color on all the floorcoverings.*

❍ *In a narrow, tunnel-like hall: mount mirrors or mirrored panels on one wall; paint each door a different color (to link with colors in the wallcovering); use a dramatic treatment on the wall or door opposite the front door.*

❍ *Paint the baseboard to match the floor to make a hall seem larger and wider.*

❍ *Use warm, welcoming colors on the main surfaces – floor, walls and ceiling – and add a few sharp, cool contrasts in accessories.*

❍ *If it suits the style of the property (and the ceiling is fairly tall), create a dado rail from beading and fix it to the wall about 3 feet (1 meter) above the floor; decorate the area below with a heavily-textured wallcovering and paint it with a washable finish; use lighter-weight paper to cover the wall above.*

❍ *For a less permanent version of the above treatment, divide the lower and upper wall area with a border at the same height and use different, but co-ordinating wallcoverings above and below it.*

❍ *If you do not have space for a conventional coat rack or stand, install a discreet strip of Shaker-style wooden pegs to hang up guests' coats and umbrellas. Ideally these should be at picture-rail height for continuity, but if this is too high, mount them at a suitable lower height.*

good a quality as you can afford, in a wool and nylon mixture with a hard-twist or looped pile. A mid-tone, possibly incorporating a small pattern, is serviceable.

It is not mandatory to carpet the hall or the stairs. You can lay ceramic tiles – the traditional flooring in Victorian and Edwardian houses; sealed cork tiles; studded rubber (if it suits the style of the property); vinyl in sheet or tile form; linoleum, which can be inlaid to create interesting patterns (or combine tiles with sheet material). Other possible floor treatments include sisal, coir, coconut and rush matting or sea-grass matting, but these tend to be too slippery for use on stairs. The stairs themselves could be left uncovered and simply sanded and sealed, but this can be noisy underfoot and is not practical in a house with elderly occupants or young children. Otherwise, lay a hardwearing carpet (to co-ordinate with your washable hall flooring) on the stairs and up onto the landing. Stair carpets should be non-slip (so some looped piles are not suitable) and must be firmly anchored to prevent accidents. One practical treatment is to use a stair runner up the center of the stairway (leaving the edges uncovered), fixed with special clips or stair rods. This allows the carpet to be moved up and down the stairs fairly easily to even out wear.

VISUAL LINKS
Try to link the decorating scheme so it flows up onto the landing and through into the rooms leading off it. Co-ordinate the colors or pick patterns which can be echoed in a different scale or used on alternative surfaces in another room. Look at companion groups of fabrics, borders and wallcoverings to help you mix and match schemes in an interesting way. A similar colored flooring throughout will help give enough of a visual link – you could use a patterned carpet in the hall and on the stairs, for example, and pick a different color from the design for a plain flooring in each of the other rooms. You will need to use threshold strips across the doorways where the two areas of carpet seam; this not only covers the seam but visually separates non-matching carpets. Wooden strips can be painted to match the color of one of the carpets.

LIGHTING
Hall and stairs often lack natural daylight. Choose window treatments like sheers, lace panels, slatted blinds or plantation shutters to diffuse the light; or hang curtains or blinds which will not obscure the windows during the daytime. If a landing window or a

AN L-SHAPED WINDOWLESS "CORRIDOR" HALL IN AN APARTMENT IS GIVEN VISUAL INTEREST THROUGH THE MARBLED DADO TREATMENT, REDUCING THE APPARENT HEIGHT OF THE HALL, AND THE BLACK-MARBLED BASEBOARDS. DISCREETLY STRIPED WALLPAPER ABOVE THE DADO AND A PALE WOODSTRIP FLOOR BOTH REINFORCE THE HALL'S ELEGANT ATMOSPHERE. THE SLIM CONSOLE TABLE TAKES UP VERY LITTLE ROOM BUT PROVIDES ESSENTIAL STORAGE AND DISPLAY SPACE; CLEVER LIGHTING FOCUSES ATTENTION ON THE ORIGINAL WAY OF HANGING AND DISPLAYING THE FOUR CO-ORDINATING PRINTS ABOVE.

glazed fanlight or door incorporates stained glass, leave it uncovered so you can appreciate the glowing colors – this might provide the starting point for your overall scheme.

Artificial lighting should give good background illumination and light the treads of the stairs clearly for safety, as well as lighting any irregularities like small steps or changes in floor level. Use accent or display lighting to highlight any special features, and to throw light up onto the ceiling if you want to make it look taller. Lights on stair walls should never be positioned so they shine into people's eyes as they ascend or descend the staircase; organize the lighting circuit so that it is dual-switched from both hall and landing, allowing the lights to be turned off at either level.

FINISHING TOUCHES
Hall and stair walls are often an ideal place to display a collection of prints, pictures or photographs; colored mounts, chosen to echo a color scheme used elsewhere, can help with visual links. Decorative display shelving, Delft racks, alcoves and niches all add character and interest. In some halls, landings or corridors there is ample space for bookshelves or low-level bookcases. Plants also have a role in furnishing halls or landings; a deep window reveal could be turned into a miniature conservatory, for example; always light plants well for maximum impact.

STYLING IDEAS

❍ **Add interest to a landing window with a blind patterned with a view. or install glass shelves across the window and use them to display a collection of colorful glass objects.**

❍ **If the front door lets in drafts, cover it with a heavy curtain mounted on the back of the door with a special porti`ere rod, which rises and falls as the door opens and closes.**

❍ **Make sure that stair carpets are safe and firmly anchored and that the lighting will illuminate the edge of the treads clearly.**

❍ **Light the front door and house number or name so it can be seen from outside; have hall and landing lights dual-switched so they can be controlled from both up and downstairs.**

❍ **Make maximum use of the understairs area: depending on the space, this can be converted to streamlined storage; opened up to make a study corner; or even used to house a shower cabinet.**

BATHROOMS

WHETHER YOU ARE DESIGNING A BATHROOM FROM SCRATCH, or revamping an existing one, it will have to be planned as thoroughly as the kitchen, partly because of plumbing considerations. The layout, equipment, materials and surfaces will need to be considered carefully, especially if the room is to be shared by several different generations, and even more so if it is the only bathroom in the house or apartment. Space permitting, you might also want to create a dual-purpose bathroom — a bathroom/dressing room can be a practical option, and in some homes it is possible to combine utility room facilities (built-in washing machine and drying cupboard) with bathing, provided the electric power supply can be separated safely; fitness fanatics may want a work-out area, including space for an exercise bike, or a sauna.

Start by assessing the daily situation in your household. Think about the way you and your family use the bathroom – is there a time of day when everybody wants to be in it at the same time, for example? This could be solved by installing double basins in a counter top, with cupboards below, if there is space, but it might not be practical if the only toilet in the house is in the bathroom. For this reason, never be tempted to take down a wall between bathtub and toilet if it is the only W.C. in the house.

A shower is wonderful for a quick freshen-up or to hose down muddy children, besides using far less water than a bath. But do not be tempted to totally

remove a bath in favor of a shower – try to combine them for the best of both worlds. If there is no space for a separate shower, consider installing a shower-bath, which has a totally flat, non-slip "shower tray" at one end, or a small ship's bath – this takes up about half the space of a conventional bathtub and has a restricted seat or "shelf" to sit on; a shower can be fitted above either of these.

You might wish to look at the possibility of siting a shower somewhere else such as in the bedroom (see page 64): electric pumps and instantaneous water heating make this feasible, as you do not need to worry about water pressure, or having to have the water tank higher up than the shower head. But you do need to think about the capacity of the hot water system if you are extending the bathroom facilities in any way, either putting in a much larger bath, adding a shower which is to be connected to the main water system, or possibly adding a second bathroom by converting a bedroom or other spare room. Will the

existing boiler and hot water tank be able to provide enough hot water to cope? Consult a plumber to help you decide. If you are considering installing an extra-large bathtub or laying new ceramic or marble flooring, you will also need to think about the increase in weight – a large cast-iron bath filled with water and people can be very heavy, and it may be necessary to have the floor and joists strengthened.

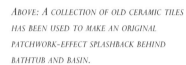

ABOVE: A COLLECTION OF OLD CERAMIC TILES HAS BEEN USED TO MAKE AN ORIGINAL PATCHWORK-EFFECT SPLASHBACK BEHIND BATHTUB AND BASIN.

FAR LEFT: IN THIS SPACIOUS BATHROOM, THE COOL BLUE COLOR SCHEME IS WARMED UP WITH THE RICH WOOD OF THE ARTS & CRAFTS FURNITURE, THE TERRACOTTA AND GOLD IN THE SHADE AND THE SUBTLE ORANGE-SPONGED WALLS. THE TOP TWO ROWS OF TILES ARE LAID DIAGONALLY, TO CREATE A SERRATED-EDGE BORDER TO THE TILED AREA.

LEFT: THIS HARMONIOUS TREATMENT RELIES ON MATCHING PANELING FOR THE BATH SIDES, THE DADO AND THE SHOWER SCREEN. THE WINDOW FRAME AND BUILT-IN CUPBOARD ARE PAINTED IN THE SAME COLOR FOR TOTAL HARMONY, WHILE THE WALLS ARE SIMPLY A PALER SHADE. THE VENETIAN BLIND ALLOWS THE VIEW TO BE ENJOYED IN THE DAY BUT CAN TOTALLY OBLITERATE IT FOR NIGHT-TIME PRIVACY.

STYLING IDEAS

✔ **Paint existing tiles with special tile or deck paint to change the wall color or spray-paint a stenciled design across them for interest.**

✔ **To make changes inexpensively, stencil a matching pattern on the bath panel and across any bathroom furniture.**

✔ **To make the bathroom look larger, increase the apparent floor size by covering or coloring the bath panel to match the floor.**

✔ **If you have a washable cotton rug on the floor, make sure it is not too large to go into your washing machine: on a large floor, two medium-sized rugs are more practical than a large one.**

✔ **Use special de-mist mirrors in bathrooms (some cabinets with mirrored doors have heating elements). If you opt for mirror tiles, make sure they are mounted on a perfectly flat surface, or you will get a distorted image. Glue them to a board panel and then mount this on the wall if necessary.**

✔ **Cover up existing tiles with new ones; there is no need to strip the others off the wall as long as you use the universal type with some chamfered edges. Wood-cladding is another suitable cover-up: seal it properly against splashing.**

✔ **If you want pretty fabric shower curtains, perhaps to co-ordinate with the window treatment, make a second-layer curtain of transparent plastic and mount it inside the main curtains with special curtain-lining tape. This allows the two layers to be separated when the shower is in use and for washing/drying.**

✔ **Give plain towels an individual touch by adding lace or other trimming; add appliquéed shapes along a plain border.**

THE WOODEN TONGUE-AND-GROOVED PANELING IN THIS WELL-PLANNED SMALL BATHROOM HAS BEEN PAINTED WITH AN OIL-BASED PAINT, SO THAT SPLASHES CAN EASILY BE WIPED OFF. THE LIGHT, WARM, CREAM COLOR SCHEME MAKES THE ROOM LOOK MORE SPACIOUS; IT RELIES ON ACCESSORIES SUCH AS THE RAG RUG AND THE PRETTY, SCALLOPED-EDGE SHADE TO ADD IMPACT.

When deciding on a model of bathtub, think ahead and consider the practical aspects of bathing children (you need to be able to bend over the bath easily) and possibly the ease of getting in and out of the bathtub when joints become stiff and when handles and faucets are difficult to operate. There are many ergonomically-designed bathroom groups, faucets and accessories, which are specifically designed for use by the very young, the disabled or the elderly – and which also have stylish good looks. Decide what other facilities you need in addition to the bathtub, shower and wash basin: a bidet; a sauna; a whirlpool bath? If you wish to install one, make sure you buy a safe model and that it is installed by an expert; do not be persuaded to convert an existing bathtub, as this could turn out to be both unsafe and unhygienic.

When deciding on a color for the bathroom suite, do not be tempted by the latest fashion trend. Choose a color you can live with through several changes of decorating scheme, and one which is easy to clean. Black, dark blue or burgundy bathtubs and basins are impossible to keep looking pristine; it is better to choose middle or pastel tones, or simply white, around which is easy to make the changes.

Lighting in the bathroom needs to be safe, so fixtures should be fully enclosed; they should provide a clear, direct light so that you can see when bathing, showering or shaving, and so that any mirror is well lit, without glare or dazzle. It is also pleasant to have a soft background glow, rather than bright directional light, when you have a relaxing soak in the bath, so consider installing several different circuits (see page 224). Any switches should be the pull-cord type, or positioned outside the bathroom door.

THIS TOTALLY MODERN, STREAMLINED BATHROOM BRINGS DRAMA TO THE ROOM ITSELF, WITH ITS ELEGANT SHUTTERED WINDOW. THE STAINLESS STEEL-CLAD BATH AND LAVATORY ARE SEPARATED BY A CURVED SCREEN COVERED IN SMALL BLACK MOSAIC TILES. THE LARGE MIRROR GIVES AN IMPRESSION OF GREATER SPACE, WHILE BRINGING MORE LIGHT INTO THE ROOM. THE RADIATOR BENEATH THE WINDOW DOUBLES AS A TOWEL ROD.

FEASIBILITY STUDY

Once you have decided what you want, you can search for suitable equipment in bathroom specialist showrooms and building supply outlets, or simply send off for catalogs. Then measure the space, make a scale plan and use the template method to see whether the proposed equipment will fit in (see page 36). Mark on your plan the existing positions of water inflow and waste outflow: changing these can be costly, and you may prefer to site the new bathtub and basin in the same position as the old to avoid too much upheaval and expense. Call in a qualified plumber and an electrician, discuss your plans with them and ask them to estimate for the work; it is always wise to have estimates from two or three people for any one job. Ask about the time it will take, as well as cost, since you do not want to be without the bathroom or toilet for more than a day or two. The bathroom or built-in furniture specialists whose show-rooms you visited will also do an estimate for you.

SURFACES AND MATERIALS

The main surfaces should be as practical as possible – waterproof, easy-to-clean and accident-proof.

The floor should be splashproof, so consider ceramic tiles, pre-sealed cork tiles; vinyl or linoleum, or you can show off existing floorboards, provided they are properly waterproofed; any of these can be softened by a non-slip, washable cotton rug. You can also use bathroom carpet or carpet tiles: make sure neither is too firmly anchored down, in case they need to be taken up for drying should flooding occur; however, they should not be loose laid in case of accidents.

The walls can be tiled, part-tiled or painted with a special bathroom paint, or with eggshell or a silk or flat latex; they may be covered with wood cladding; or you may prefer to use a vinyl wallcovering. The bathroom ceiling can be given an interesting treatment, since you look up at it when lying in the bath.

Bathroom windows are usually small and may have obscured or opaque glass panes: remember that these can be seen through at night when the lights are on, as can sheer or lace coverings. Stained or etched glass panels can add interest to a bathroom window, but will need obscuring at night unless the window is not overlooked. Keep the window dressing simple, and relate the scale of any pattern on blinds or curtains to the size of the window.

THEMES AND SCHEMES

When choosing a color scheme for your bathroom, consider the color of the porcelain fixtures first. You can then select the rest of the scheme to either co-ordinate or to contrast. If it contrasts, the room will seem smaller, whereas if the overall effect is harmonious, using different values of one color, it will appear larger. Since bathrooms tend to be small, pale, cool colors will help to enlarge it, but they can look rather chilly. If you choose pale, or subtle colors from the warmer side of the spectrum – pinks, rose, soft yellows, gold, apricot, peach, cream, soft terra-cotta – the room will appear larger, without being too cold. If your porcelain is white, of course, you have considerable leeway.

Light-reflecting textures – shiny faucets, silky wall-coverings, shiny paint, glazed chintz and ceramic tiles – will all create an impression of space, as will strate-gically-placed mirrors or panels of mirror tiles. These can look rather busy and distracting, however, if they are not tempered with some softer textural contrast. Warm or light-diffusing textures will help to take the chill off a bathroom; these are found in long-pile rugs; deep-piled towels; cane screening; baskets filled with soaps; lace, muslin or sheer drapes; fine-slatted Venetian blinds. Plants, particularly those with varie-gated and feathery foliage, will soften any hard edges; choose those which love a steamy atmosphere.

HEATING SYSTEMS

The bathroom should always be adequately ventilated and warmed to avoid condensation. Heat can be supplied by a radiator/towel rail combined, which is part of the central heating system, or by one of the more modern ladder-style radiators, which can also be used as a towel warmer. These may be positioned high up on a wall, or used as a divider where it would be impossible to site a conventional radiator. It is wise to have bathroom radiators on steam systems put on "gravity feed" which means it will automatical-ly come on when the boiler is working and so will heat the room and towels in summer, even when the main central heating system is switched off.

If you prefer more instant heating, there are various wall-mounted heaters available, including some which are combined with a light; these must, of course, be safe for bathroom use, correctly installed and sited sufficiently high up. There are also oil-filled radiator/towel rails available which warm up when plugged into the power circuit.

BEDROOMS

BEDROOMS ARE THE MOST INDIVIDUAL AND PERSONAL ROOMS IN THE HOME; whether they belong to adults, adolescents or children, they should reflect the personality of their owners. A bedroom may have to be a shared space or a dual-purpose one (study / office, dressing room / bedroom, playroom / nursery, guest room), and these will require especially careful planning and scheming. As bedrooms usually receive less wear and tear than the more "public" areas of a home, decorating materials can be paler, more delicate and more luxurious than family living rooms, though dual-purpose and children's rooms will of course require hardwearing, preferably washable surfaces.

WHERE TO START?

Besides being the room in which you sleep, most bedrooms are used for storing personal effects, from clothes and accessories to luggage, sport and hobby equipment, toys and games, and, if they are to be dual-purpose, television and a computer. So the starting point could well be the essential items of furniture for storage, which can be either fully fitted (built-in) or a selection of freestanding items – or a mixture of both. Ideally this storage should be planned from the inside out, by measuring all that needs to be accommodated and then planning the necessary hanging, shelf and drawer space (this is covered in more detail under A Place for Everything, page 230). The materials and finish used will also help to set the style of the room, which can be echoed and enhanced in the treatment of the walls, window and bed.

CHOOSING A BED

While storage furniture may be essential to the bedroom, the bed is all-important! The bed should above all be comfortable: the firmness of the mattress can be chosen to suit the sleeper, but in the case of children's beds, it should be firm enough to support young bones. If a sofa bed is being considered for a dual-purpose room, the "fold-down-slab" type may be adequate for occasional guests, but not for sleeping on every night. In this case, a quality mattress, which folds back into the base of the sofa on a firm, folding frame, or a futon, are better options.

It is always wise to test a bed before you buy it, which means going to a reputable store or bedding supplier, taking off your shoes and trying out a few different makes and types of mattress. Lie full-length on the bed, with a normal complement of pillows, and stay there for a few minutes. If the bed is to be used by somebody else, take them with you to test it, and if it is to be a shared double bed, both partners should lie on it together. Beds can be ordered with a different firmness of spring on each side, or it is possible to have a zip-and-link system, comprising two bases and mattresses which can be either divided and used as single beds, or pushed and linked together to

form a double bed. This is often a wise choice for a spare room; you should test guests beds for comfort too. Never buy a second-hand mattress since it could have a different "sleep pattern" from yours, or be unhygienic. But there is no reason why you should not buy an old bed frame, base or bedstead, provided you test for metal fatigue or inspect it carefully for woodworm before purchasing.

SIZING UP

The size of the bed will need to relate to the shape of the room and the space available, as well as to the style you want to achieve. A four-poster bed may well suit a room with country-house styling, but would be impractical in a cottage with low ceilings, where a similar effect could be created with curtains hung on the headboard wall. A brass bedstead or simple iron trundle bed will be in keeping with a Victorian house; a circular or heart-shaped divan with luxurious padded and buttoned headboard can suggest Thirties Hollywood; and for an elegant French Empire look, use a *bateau-lit,* a shaped wooden bedstead, with a sheer drape suspended from a coronet above. Neat divans with tailored covers, functional futons and minimalist metal-framed beds relate better to a contemporary style of room.

The best way of planning the room, and working out what type of bed will best fit in, is to measure up and make a scale plan (see page 36). Remember, when doing the calculations, that beds also have to be pulled out for cleaning underneath, and that you need enough room to move around them for bed-making. If space is short and you need only occasional extra sleeping facilities, there are various types of stacking beds (where a second or third bed pulls out from underneath) worth considering, as well as bunks which sub-divide and beds which will fold up inside cupboards, chairs or tables.

If you opt for an unusual shape, or an extra-large queen- or king-sized bed (which may be necessary if the sleeper is unusually tall or heavy), bear in mind that the bedding will also have to be larger, or shaped to fit it. This may involve buying larger blankets, quilts and sheets; add this extra cost into your calculations.

In a shared space, you may want to try to divide the room, which can be done in various ways, although long-term partitions can spoil a room's proportions, and cut the light considerably from one section. Semi-permanent solutions, which might only be used at night, include vertical Venetian blinds as well

STYLING IDEAS

❖ *Create an unusual ceiling, since you notice it more when lying in bed: paint it a rich color or use an interesting texture; tent the ceiling with fabric; use a cloudscape effect in paper or paint; or speckle it with cut-out stars.*

❖ *In a small bedroom, hang a full-length mirror securely on the back of the door (you may need to strengthen the hinges).*

❖ *To create an instant sofa in a guest room make a tailored cover for the divan, with matching bolster cushions each end, or suspend squab cushions on a wall-mounted pole to form a comfortable "back" to lean against.*

❖ *Make the bed the focal point with an overhead fabric treatment : use a canopy to suspend romantic floor-length drapes, or create a half-tester effect with curtains mounted on double-valance track (see page 174).*

❖ *If space is restricted, use the bed base to provide storage: buy a bed with pull-out drawers, or perhaps use stacking baskets or drawers on castors beneath the bed frame, and conceal them under a fabric valance.*

❖ *Fill the recesses on each side of a chimney breast in an older-style property with built-in cupboards: you need a minimum depth of 53cm (21in). If you are working to a tight budget, install shelves and a portable clothes rod in the recess and cover them with a curtain or pull-down blind.*

❖ *In a child's room, use a special "dim-out" shade to persuade a child to sleep through short summer nights.*

❖ *Use an enclosed shade for any pendant light fixture so that you do not see the bulb when lying in bed.*

STYLING IDEAS

❖ **Light the inside of any cupboards or wardrobes:** switches mounted on the door jamb will turn the light on and off as the door opens.

❖ **Outline the shape of the bedhead or headboard** with a border or stenciled pattern on the wall behind the bed.

❖ **Smother the bed with lots of different-shaped, colored and textured cushions** for a luxurious effect; or create a softer layered-look with quilts, coverlets, throws, shawls and lace.

❖ **An ottoman with padded lift-up top** placed at the foot of the bed will provide storage space, as well as somewhere to sit or to put the television set for bedtime viewing.

❖ **If bedroom and bathroom are connected,** decorate so that the scheme flows through from one area to another.

❖ **In a large bedroom, make a private corner:** have an occasional table beside an easy chair or chaise longue, or install a desk for paperwork and diary writing.

❖ **Create a cozy bed-in-a-cupboard** – place a single bed parallel to an unbroken wall; install wardrobe cupboards at head and foot and link them across the top with smaller wall-mounted ones; suspend a simple curtain under these to close across at night.

❖ **For total co-ordination, make curtains** for any glass cupboard doors to match the window drapes and the bed treatment.

THE CUSTOM-MADE OVERHEAD CANOPY FOR THIS DAYBED IN AN EMPIRE-STYLE BEDROOM CREATES A LUXURIOUS EFFECT. THE COLORS OF THE FABRIC ARE ECHOED IN THE RICH COLOR OF THE WALLS AND THE CONTRASTING BASEBOARDS, WINDOW FRAMES AND CORNICE.

as curtains, folding louvered doors and portable screens. The arrangement of furniture can help to divide the room, using bunks, beds, wardrobes, chests of drawers, cupboards, desks or dressers to separate the areas. These may be incorporated with roller shades which can then be pulled down to close a gap above lower items of furniture. In children's and teenage rooms, brightly colored metal or wooden "scaffolding" systems can define a territory without cutting out too much light.

CALLING IN THE EXPERTS

When you have a rough idea of what you want and have made a few calculations, you may decide to have a bedroom made to measure, in which case, as with the kitchen, a specialist will visit your home and help to plan and style the room from scratch. Initially you can usually see examples of built-in bedrooms in the showroom or catalog, or they will have a portfolio of design ideas to show you. There will be a choice of finishes and styles, from wooden and painted to laminate-finish furniture, and various types of folding, slid-

ing or space-saving doors on closets; bear in mind that mirrored doors can help to create an illusion of space in a small room.

Once your requirements have been discussed, a scale plan will be prepared, including suggestions for the cupboard interiors; a complete range of pull-out drawers and racks, sliding or fixed rails, adjustable shelves, shoe racks or built-in linen boxes can also be provided. Built-in-bedroom companies usually have a team who will supply and install the bedroom. Some come fully finished, while others are completed on site; some suppliers will provide primed furniture which you, or a decorator, can paint after installation. Many of the smaller local suppliers will install and decorate, as well as suggesting and/or supplying, a total scheme complete with floorcovering, bed dressings and curtains.

A BUILT-IN RUN OF CLOSETS ALONG ONE WALL MAKES THE BEST USE OF LIMITED SPACE IN THIS SMALL ATTIC BEDROOM. PLANTATION SHUTTERS AT THE DORMER WINDOW ARE PAINTED THE SAME COLOR AS THE WALLS AND CUPBOARDS TO CREATE A STREAMLINED LOOK AND A FEELING OF SPACE.

THE OPULENT TREATMENT OF THE FOUR-POSTER BED IS ECHOED IN THE
WINDOW DRESSINGS AND CHAIR COVERS IN THIS ALL WHITE-AND-CREAM
BEDROOM, DESIGNED FOR PEACE AND RELAXATION.

CREATING THE LOOK

If you are putting together your own decorating plan, including window and bed treatments, always remember that the bed is usually the most important thing in the room – in a small bedroom, it can easily take up most of the space! Because it is so integral to the scheme, the bedding, covers and any over-bed drapes should be considered at the outset and not purchased afterward as accessories. If you do not want the bed to assume massive proportions, dress it to blend in with the surroundings, with bedding in the same shade as the floor and walls. To make it stand out, dress the bed to contrast, using an opulent fabric treatment such as a four-poster with tented ceiling and curtains. Or the bed could be topped with a tailored or loose slipcover, or a patchwork quilt.

Color schemes in a main bedroom should be chosen to create a relaxing atmosphere, while in teenagers' and children's rooms, they can be brighter and more stimulating. If the bedroom lacks light or tends to be cool, brighten it up with warm colors such as yellows, golds, pinks, peach or apricot. Use pale or middle tones for the main surfaces, such as the walls, then add some definition or contrast in accents and accessories – sharp jade or turquoise with the above colors, for example. If you wish to create an impression of space, choose colors from the cooler side of the spectrum – blues, lavenders and silver greens – and warm them up with splashes of terracotta, Indian red, fuchsia pink or raspberry. Natural or neutral colors will help to achieve a restful atmosphere, though the greyed neutrals can be somewhat cold, so you would need to add a few warm touches. Many of the cream and beige-based neutrals will give a feeling of warmth and intimacy, while being quietly relaxing.

Busy designs and glossy textures will be distracting, so aim to balance patterned and plain surfaces carefully, and offset a shiny surface with softer, matte, shaggy, velvety and light-diffusing ones. Bedrooms do need some sharp, textural contrast: try combining cane, lace and brass with rich mahogany for a period look and open-weave sheers, tweed, burlap and lacquered furniture for a more modern idiom.

Bedroom lighting usually needs to be as flexible as it does in the living room: a general background glow is necessary in order to see to move about and get dressed on dark mornings, but specific task lighting will also be required for a dresser mirror or to read in bed. You might consider installing several different lighting circuits (see page 224).

ROOMS TO GROW UP IN

PLANNING, DECORATING AND FURNISHING A BEDROOM FOR A CHILD can be fun — but full of pitfalls! If you design it before the baby is born, you may well be over-sentimental, and opt for lots of fussy, frilly furnishings and appealing nursery characters on everything. In any case, it simply is not economically viable to buy furniture to suit one age group only, except perhaps for the initial nursery stage. Pint-sized furniture is quickly outgrown, so plan a room which can "grow up" with the child, using a line of units or different freestanding pieces painted the same color to unify them, which can be added to over the years. If you are designing a room for an older child, try to involve him or her in choosing the color scheme and fabrics, but keep a final right of veto against current fads and fashions whose appeal may rapidly pall.

It is a good idea to discuss your proposed budget with an older child and to distinguish between those items which will have to last through several changes of scheme (flooring and some furniture, for example), and the elements which are relatively easy and inexpensive to alter, such as a blind or curtains, a duvet cover, a frieze or a set of prints.

THE SIX MAIN STAGES

The Nursery: The needs of a small baby, in room terms, are comparatively simple: somewhere to sleep, to have a diaper changed and a wash and brush up, and perhaps take a bath; somewhere for the mother or carer to sit comfortably while nursing or feeding ; and a place to store small garments, toiletries and toys. The secret of success is to keep it simple, so use pretty pastels and provide design interest in a mural, or in fabrics and a nursery frieze. Make sure you include a low-wattage night light for feeding or changing at night and for the baby's sense of security.

The Toddler's Playroom: Storage requirements are basically the same at this stage except that extra space is needed to store large toys and early books. The crib may well be exchanged for a junior bed or bunks; an adjustable bed, which can be extended as the child grows up, is the most practical proposition. Space and yet more space is required for making a mess, for constructing things, and for playing imaginative games, alone or with small friends. This may be the place for a play house, an indoor trampoline or jungle gym; it is also the place for a wall-mounted blackboard, scribbling space and a bulletin board. The need is for practical, washable surfaces everywhere, and the best decorating scheme will use bright primary colors.

CHEERFUL COLORS AND AN INTERESTING PATTERN MIX PROVIDE A STIMULATING SCHEME FOR A TODDLER'S ROOM. FREESTANDING, MOVEABLE FURNITURE ALLOWS PLENTY OF ADAPTABLE FLOOR SPACE FOR DIFFERENT PLAY ACTIVITIES. THE NEUTRAL, TEXTURED CARPET AND THE SIMPLE CURTAINS ON POLES ARE EASY, PRACTICAL SOLUTIONS; BRIGHT ACCESSORIES FOR THE ROOM INCLUDE KITES AND HANGING MOBILES.

The School Room: Early school years bring another change and a desk or large work/play surface will become essential. The bed may be changed for a divan, and space will be needed for books and games. More sophisticated clothes storage will be necessary if the child is to be encouraged to be neat and to take a pride in his or her things. Surfaces will still have to be both practical and washable. An interest in various hobbies – sport, music, dancing, skating, mountain biking or horse riding – may develop at this stage, and the equipment will require specific storage. These interests may be reflected as motifs in the room decor, such as a thematic stenciled frieze around the walls.

The Pre-teen Pad: This is the age of constant change: interests will come and go, and many will be a nine-day wonder. A computer, snooker table, complicated train or car layout, individual television set and music center may all be requested as an interest in technology grows. But facilities for quiet study may also be necessary. The pre-teen bedroom is also essentially somewhere private – a place into which to invite friends, but probably off limits for the family. Exactly what can, and cannot, be fitted in will depend on space and budget, but if a sofa bed or floor cushions, folding or stacking chairs or an occasional table can be accommodated, any of these will create a feeling of independence. Color schemes and styling may become a little more sophisticated at this stage – but remember that spills will still occur.

The Teenage Den: This extension of the previous stage may be a good time to encourage the teenager to plan, choose materials for and actually decorate (under supervision) their own room – or at least to make or adapt some items to give their room a distinct personality. Entertaining friends in their own room will help them to grow up gracefully; snack-preparation facilities might be added, but the teenager will still require space to study, indulge hobbies, listen to or play music and have friends to stay overnight. It may be possible to create a split-level storage and sleeping/sitting system, to make the best use of the available space.

The Collegiate Space: Before the fledgling leaves the nest, he or she may go to college – away from home for part of the year – or may alternatively be out at work all day. Independent young people will definitely

want privacy in the holidays, or at night, which will mean converting the room into a "bedsitting" room. If possible, install a wash basin and built-in closets and cupboards (perhaps fitting the wash basin inside a cupboard); try to provide some modest cooking facilities, too. Aim to zone, or divide the room into sections in some way, so that sleeping, sitting and eating areas are defined. If study facilities are still required, these will need to be in a quiet and well-lit corner, with adequate storage for reference books. A system of sliding oriental screens can work well in some rooms. The decorating scheme will have to be fairly simple to avoid an over-crowded look, but at this stage the style of the room and its furniture and furnishings will be a very personal choice.

A PRETTY SCHEME FOR A YOUNG GIRL'S BEDROOM USES PASTEL SHADES OF PINK AND BLUE. THE SOFTLY COLORWASHED WALLS ARE HIGHLIGHTED BY A STENCILED FRIEZE ALONG THE TOP; A CO-ORDINATED REPEATING MOTIF OUTLINES THE CURVED CAST-IRON BEDSTEAD.

WHOLE HOUSE RETHINK

The expanding needs of a growing family may lead to a total reconsideration of how the property is used. While the main bedroom is usually the largest, and may start off as the parents' room, it may later have to be turned over to the siblings to share, in which case some form of division may be necessary (see page 65). In a conventional house, a smaller room could become a bedroom/playroom, with a larger room, perhaps the living room, used as a family living room, and there is no reason why the largest upstairs bedroom should not at some point become an adult living room. It is always essential to be flexible in a family situation, which is never static for long.

IN THIS SMALL STUDY-BEDROOM, THE BATEAU LIT STYLE BED DOUBLES AS A SOFA IN THE DAY, AND THE DESK TOP AND DECORATIVE SHELVES ARE BUILT INTO A NATURAL RECESS. THE STREAMLINED WINDOW TREATMENT OF A WHITE WINDOW SHADE IS SOFTENED BY A LACY-FABRIC SWAG ABOVE IT, WHICH SERVES AS A DECORATIVE VALANCE.

STYLING IDEAS

❏ **Use an old trolley, painted to match the room, for nursery toiletries; convert it to practical large-toy storage at toddler stage; use it for a music-system/computer in the teenage years.**

❏ **A baby-changing table can be created by linking two waist-high units or cupboards with a continuous countertop, leaving a "kneehole" in between: later, it can convert to a play surface, a desk and finally a dresser.**

❏ **Children are fickle and their fashions change quickly: so use nursery and television character designs and patterns sparingly. They are best confined to surfaces which are easy to change, such as duvet covers, lampshades and accessories; or you could glue a border on a plain-painted wall surface or use a fabric border to trim curtains at valance and hem.**

❏ **In a bedroom doubling as a playroom, a train/car layout could be mounted on a large piece of chipboard which can be raised toward the ceiling and lowered at playtime on a pulley; or hinge it back against a wall. Make sure either system is safe.**

❏ **Cabin-style beds do not always have to be nautical in theme; they can incorporate toy storage, a miniature theatre, a dolls' house or bookshelves in the base.**

❏ **In a teenage room, industrial slotted-angle shelving or scaffolding can be painted a bright primary color to become storage, a desk or a music center .**

ONE-ROOM LIVING

STUDENT AND TEENAGE ROOMS MAY END UP BEING multi-functional, but some first homes and studio apartments, however well appointed, are also in effect one large room which has to provide the space and facilities in which to sit, sleep, relax, work, eat and entertain, as well as to store everything neatly. In some cases, the room has also to contain a cooking and food preparation area, and possibly even a shower and washbasin.

THE MINIMALIST DECOR AND NEUTRAL COLOR SCHEME OF THIS JAPANESE-INSPIRED ROOM KEEPS IT UNCLUTTERED. A LOW PARTITION, INCORPORATING A STORAGE SHELF, SEPARATES THE SLEEPING AREA FROM THE COOKING SECTION OF THE ROOM. BOOKSHELVES EXTEND TO CEILING HEIGHT FROM THE WARM-COLORED WOODBLOCK FLOOR.

Multi-purpose rooms need planning carefully to obtain maximum use from the available space and to fit everything in comfortably, while also allowing adequate circulation space. This means room to move around, to get in and out of bed or open up a folding table or folding bed, to sit comfortably at a desk or table, to open cupboard doors and drawers – and to do all this safely, without crashing into something else. You will need to make a master plan to help you sort out the space (see below).

It is practical to try and zone the different areas, without creating actual physical barriers which would take up too much space. However, sometimes furniture can be placed at right angles to a main wall to make a division, or a clothes cupboard placed beside the entrance door to create a small vestibule. In tall rooms, it may be possible to divide the space horizontally, and install a bed on a platform, with storage/study space underneath.

MAKING A MASTER PLAN

First think about all the activities which will take place in the room, and consider all that you will need to store. You will want to have some items continually to hand, while others can go into longer-term storage at the back of, or on top of, the cupboards. It is often practical to line one or two adjacent walls with storage furniture, and possibly with cooking facilities; tables, desks or other work surfaces might be part of this run and can be made to fold down or pull out. If space is very short, a bed can be made to fold away into one of the cupboards.

Start by dividing the room broadly into distinct areas.
The cooking and eating area is best kept separate if at all possible, and might even be concealed behind sliding doors or screens when not being used. Adequate storage for food and cooking implements will be essential, as will some form of efficient ventilation if the whole room is not to smell of stale food. A table (to seat four) for dining can also be used for food preparation provided the surface is suitable, and it can also double up as a desk or other work surface; if space is very tight, it could be a folding table. Other alternatives include pull-out or drop-down tables, but these need to be specially built in.
The washing area might be provided by a separate basin and shower, but in some rooms, when space and

plumbing facilities are restricted, the washbasin and sink may have to double up. In this case, keep a separate bowl to use in the sink for personal washing.

The seating area should provide somewhere comfortable on which to relax; ideally it should not contain the bed, as flopping down on a bed will ruin the springs. Seating can take the form of a conventional sofa, a sofa bed, low unit seating (very flexible) or floor cushions, although in a room with restricted space one comfortable chair may have to suffice. If the bed has to be used as seating, make sure that it is a firm-edged divan and base and make a washable, tailored cover for it.

The sleeping area should not be too "bedroomy" so avoid frills, flounces and padded headboards. Try to site the bed away from drafts and not too close to a stove. If you plan to use a futon or sofa bed for both sitting and sleeping on, always store away any bedding during the day. Remember to test the bed for comfort in terms of both sleeping and sitting before you buy: a firm base is essen-

A SERIES OF CLEVER DECORATIVE SOLUTIONS MAXIMIZES THE SPACE IN THIS MULTI-FUNCTIONAL ROOM. THE WALLS AND FLOORING ARE IN PALE, NEUTRAL TONES, WHILE PATTERNED CUSHIONS AND A FLOOR RUG ADD INTERESTING TEXTURES AND COLOUR. THE BED, WITH BUILT-IN STORAGE TO ONE SIDE OF IT, CAN BE SCREENED OFF WITH A CURTAIN. THE FOLDING CHAIRS CAN BE SIMPLY STACKED AWAY WHEN NOT IN USE.

tial if you use a sofa bed for both purposes. It should be easy to open out and fold up: measure it in both open and closed positions. Other alternatives include beds which fold away or which convert to chairs.

The storage area will look neater if it is unified, whether built-in or freestanding. Look for adjustable shelving, wire baskets, and other practical interior fittings to maximize space. Open shelving can appear more spacious than closed cupboards; mirror panels or doors create an illusion of space; and louvered doors look lighter than solid ones. Open shelving and hanging space can sometimes be hidden behind co-ordinating blinds or curtains.

THIS AREA IS CLEVERLY PLANNED AND ZONED TO PROVIDE EATING, SITTING, WORKING AND SLEEPING FACILITIES. THE RELAXING NEUTRAL COLOR SCHEME IS LIVENED UP BY THE BRIGHT KELIM ON THE FLOOR AND BY THE BEAMED CEILING; THE WHOLE EFFECT IS COMFORTABLE WITHOUT BEING CRAMPED.

WALLS AND WINDOWS

The main surfaces need to be hardwearing and easy to clean. Keep bold patterns to a minimum, as they can be annoying after a time. Use mainly solid colors and interesting textures; provide pattern in accessories such as pictures, posters and other wallhangings, as well as rugs on the floor. Keep to a simple color scheme: monochromatic, natural/neutral and adjacent colors are least intrusive, so choose pale to mid-tone values of one color, then liven them up with contrasting accents. Most of the walls are likely to be covered with storage or to have something hanging on them, so use a simple paint finish or wallcovering. Windows may be curtained or can have a more tailored treatment, using either Roman or slatted blinds.

ATTICS AND STUDIOS

TRADITIONALLY, A STUDIO WAS SITED IMMEDIATELY UNDER A SLOPING ROOF, with a large rooflight, or a dormer window in the gable end, originally to provide an artist with a clear north light, as well as attractive sloping ceilings and possibly exposed beams, girders or rafters. Nowadays this type of room is more likely to be found in a warehouse conversion, or when a large period property is converted into apartments. Such rooms have a definite character of their own and when they are being planned and decorated, their distinctive architectural features should not only be taken into consideration – they should be emphasized and enhanced.

A studio or attic room is often required to be multi-functional – to provide for sitting, sleeping, eating, relaxing and entertaining – so many of the comments on planning areas for one-room living will apply here (see page 72).

You will need to do some detailed calculations in order to work out a practical plan (see page 36), and it will have to be based on the vertical as well as the horizontal plane, since sloping ceilings and other structural features of unusual height can make the conventional placing of furniture and storage virtually impossible. You may need to think in terms of built-in furniture and some special made-to-measure designs.

BUILDING CONTROLS

If you are converting an attic for separate use, you may well find you have to conform to building regulations (official approval of each stage of a conversion), and you should check this out thoroughly with your planning authorities before going ahead. Ideally, such apartments should have a separate entrance, though they may have to be reached via the main building. They should be a private entity, with a proper (lockable) entrance door. And heating, cooling and lighting should be provided individually, on a different circuit and meter from the rest of the house.

MAXIMUM LIGHT IS LET INTO THIS ATTIC CONVERSION THROUGH HUGE, SLOPING DOUBLE-GLAZED WINDOWS. USED AS A STUDIO-SITTING ROOM, IT IS REACHED BY A GALLERIED SPIRAL STAIRCASE; SLIDING PATIO DOORS LEAD OUT ONTO A ROOF TERRACE. A NAUTICAL THEME IS SUGGESTED BY THE PAINTED BOARDING ON THE SLOPING WALLS AND CEILING; IT IS PAINTED WHITE TO KEEP THE IMPRESSION OF LIGHT AND SPACE. BUILT-IN SHELVING MAKES THE BEST USE OF THE AVAILABLE SPACE WHERE THERE IS RESTRICTED HEADROOM.

STYLING IDEAS

○ *If access to the attic is restricted, plan to buy flat-pack furniture which can be taken up in pieces and assembled in the room – or have special items built on site.*

○ *Attic windows often slope, and can be difficult to dress. Skylights may be fitted with special shades or Venetian blinds which do not flop forward because they have several "stopping" positions. If installing new skylights, order them double-glazed with a shade layered between the two panes of glass.*

○ *Dormer windows can have sill-length curtains suspended from a hinged track, which folds back into the angle of the wall/window during the day. Full-length curtains can be slotted behind a pole hung across the angle of the sloping roof and the wall.*

○ *Small attic windows can cause a loss of natural light, so decorate in pale, sunshine colors such as yellow, peach and apricot; use light-reflecting textures; make use of mirrors to reflect daylight.*

○ *To make sloping ceilings look taller, decorate them to match the walls, using paint, a textured wall-covering or small-print wallpaper (the design of a paper must be non-directional; otherwise, it will be impossible to match up the pattern where the ceiling and wall join).*

○ *To emphasize sloping ceilings and walls, color them to contrast or outline the slope/angle with a border design.*

Space under the roof can become intolerably hot in summer, as well as chillingly cold in winter, so try to insulate the area immediately under the roof; insulating material can be placed behind plasterboarding or wood paneling or can go at the back of built-in furniture. Apart from adequate insulation, the area should be well heated (and cooled), and well ventilated. Noise can be a problem, both from below (noise rises like hot air), as well as from the occupants of the apartment and from any plumbing and water tanks sited in the roof space. To insulate against noise, put insulating material around the floor joists between the attic floor and the ceiling of the room below, and select a sound-absorbing floor covering such as long-pile carpet or carpet tiles on a good quality underlay.

Safety is an important consideration, too. If an attic is being converted in a duplex or row-house property, the party wall must be fireproofed. If there is an outside staircase or fire escape, the access must be clear and not obstructed in any way from the inside. If there is no escape route, a strong rope ladder should be kept handy, with firm hooks in a practical position for anchoring it. Install a fire alarm in the ceiling outside the apartment and have a fire extinguisher or fire blanket readily accessible inside.

AESTHETIC CONSIDERATIONS

Color schemes can be chosen to be flexible, so they are neither too hot in summer nor too cold in winter. A natural, neutral or fairly pale scheme for the main surfaces can have warm accents added in the window treatments and accessories in winter, which can be changed for cooler ones in summer; this is a fairly inexpensive way of bringing about a total change of mood and scene. Do not choose too pale a scheme, however, as large, sloping walls and ceiling areas can cause glare, with the light bouncing off them. Since this type of space is often cold-looking because of the direct light, you would do better to consider pale values of the slightly warmer colors and neutrals. Try to introduce some brighter contrasts if the outlook will be permanently grey. Aim to have color flowing throughout the whole apartment; use a continuous floor covering, with the separate areas defined by rugs, or use different wall, ceiling and woodwork treatments for different areas.

IN THIS COZY SITTING ROOM CREATED IN A ROOF SPACE, THE SLOPING WALLS AND CEILING ADD TO THE CHARM. DECORATING THE WALLS IN A SOFT, CREAMY NEUTRAL SHADE LINKS THEM WITH THE UPHOLSTERED CHAIR, SOFA AND CARPET FOR AN IMPRESSION OF UNCLUTTERED SPACE.

ADDING AN EXTRA ROOM

IMPROVING YOUR HOME BY ADDING AN EXTRA ROOM, rather than going through the upheaval of moving, can be an attractive proposition, especially if you are running out of space. A conservatory, today still seen as a status symbol, much as it was in the turn-of-the-century era, is an addition which will provide a pleasant dual-purpose room. Or you might prefer to add an extension at the back of the house to enlarge the kitchen and living area, or to provide a new kitchen, a utility area, a separate dining room or a playroom. Smaller additions can include building a porch on the front or back door (to prevent drafts); glazing a balcony to make a lean-to greenhouse, or adding a mini-conservatory to either the back or side of the property.

Another possibility is to convert an integral garage into a habitable room (which might entail building a separate garage or carport on the side of the house), or in some cases it is feasible to build another room on top of a flat-roofed garage, with access from an existing internal stairway. There may also be convertible space above your head or below your feet – attics can be altered and roofs opened up to provide extra living space; basements and cellars can be dampproofed and converted into workshops, playrooms, dens or utility rooms.

PRACTICAL CONSIDERATIONS

Before you rush to prepare plans, bear in mind that in some places the addition of an extra room may require planning permission if the extension will increase the cubic capacity of the house by more than the agreed 'permitted development' size, or will alter the look of the property from and to the outside. You could pay a visit to the planning department of your city or town to discuss the project – or ask an architect, surveyor, or, in the case of a conservatory, a conservatory specialist for advice. Even if you do not need permission, any extension will probably still have to conform to the building regulations (to ensure it is built to certain standards and will be safe in use), so it may be inspected, and approved, at various stages of construction; it is advisable to check this before going ahead. Think carefully about the ease of access from and to the existing building. Ideally, there should not be any change in floor level, and the new space should link visually with the original. Consider the use of a proposed attic conversion – you will not want hefty teenagers thumping around overhead at night, and the elderly may find steep stairs a problem. Basements require safe access and quick exit facilities, in case of fire.

THE BLUE AND WHITE COLOR SCHEME OF THIS LUXURIOUS CONSERVATORY IS COOL AND RESTFUL, AND WORKS WELL WITH THE SEALED BRICK FLOOR. THE WEALTH OF GREENERY GIVES AN OUTDOOR FEEL TO THE ROOM, WITH CLIMBING PLANTS TRAINED UP THE GLAZING BARS OF THE PITCHED ROOF. MAKE SURE THAT ANY FABRICS USED FOR SEATING AND FOR CUSHIONS ARE FADE- AND ROT-PROOF, AS THEY WILL INEVITABLY BE EXPOSED TO STRONG, BRIGHT SUNLIGHT.

THIS GLAZED EXTENSION TO THE HOUSE PROVIDES A MINI-GREENHOUSE FOR GROWING PLANTS ON SLATS AND IN POTS ON THE FLOOR. THE WHITE-PAINTED WALLS REFLECT LIGHT, AND TOMATOES AND TENDER PLANTS BENEFIT FROM THE WARMTH CREATED.

CONSERVATORIES: HOTHOUSE OR SUNROOM?

If you opt for a conservatory, decide exactly to what use you intend to put it. If it is to be planted with exotic flora and foliage, you will need to pay great attention to heating, ventilation, sun screening and watering facilities – and you may not be able to use it additionally as a dining room or extension to a kitchen. On the other hand, if its main purpose is a sitting area, it can be designed to link with the patio or garden; if it is to be a poolhouse or work-out area, safety glazing which can be screened off for privacy is essential. However you intend to use a conservatory, it should always be fitted with primary double-glazing (the two panes of glass sandwiched together before being put into the frame), or it will be too cold in winter and impossibly hot in summer, however efficient the heating or cooling systems are. If a sophisticated heat control system is required, some of the windows can be programmed to open and close as the temperature inside the conservatory rises and falls.

The glass will also need screening from sun in summer and frost in winter, especially if there are to be lots of plants. There are many interior blinds designed for the purpose, from simple rattan screens to sleek slatted blinds and softer sheers; select a type to suit the design of your conservatory and the proposed decorating style. You can also have an exterior system that works on a solar "eye", which will open, close and angle the blinds automatically as the sun moves around; they will also provide almost total security when closed. Make sure the blinds can be operated by hand as well, so you can open them at night if required.

There are many conservatory specialists who will design, build, furnish, light and decorate a conservatory for you, including applying for any planning permission. You can also buy ready-made conservatory sections to be bolted together by a builder on site. If the conservatory is to be planted, this should be done before the final decorating and integration with the rest of the property, especially if it involves carrying soil, rocks and large plants through the house.

MAIN SURFACES

The exterior walls of a conservatory are usually very small or nonexistent, as they are mainly glass, but when a conservatory is built onto the exterior house structure, the original house wall will become a major feature. Brick and stone left unpainted can provide an attractive texture, or if you wish to paint it, use masonry paint. Wood paneling is a pleasing alternative, either in natural (sealed) form or painted; if you want to soften a harsh finish, mount wooden garden trellis on the wall and train climbing plants to cover it.

Flooring will have to be both hardwearing and easy to clean, as feet will tramp in straight from the outside. It should also be non-slip and impervious to damp if there are many plants to be watered. You might wish to achieve a visual link with the garden and patio outside, in which case stone slabs, bricktiles can be considered. If you opt for ceramic tiles, make sure that they are frost-proof, as a fully-glazed room can become very cold in a hard winter, and a sudden shaft of sunlight could cause non-frostproof tiles to crack. Sealed cork tiles, good quality linoleum and strong, rigid vinyl tiles are possible alternatives, any of which can be softened with non-slip rugs in a sitting or dining area.

A CEILING FAN, WOODEN SLATTED BLINDS AND RATTAN FURNITURE LEND A "RETURN TO THE RAJ" TROPICAL THEME TO THIS CONSERVATORY. THE VENETIAN BLINDS CAN BE ADJUSTED TO SHIELD THE GLARE OF THE SUN OR TO LET IN MAXIMUM LIGHT ON DARK DAYS; THEY ARE SUPPLEMENTED BY SPLIT-CANE FOLDING BLINDS TO ENSURE THAT THE CONSERVATORY IS STILL COMFORTABLE TO SIT IN DURING THE HEIGHT OF SUMMER. THE TILED FLOOR AND THE UNPAINTED WALLS OF HONEY-COLORED STONE LINK NICELY WITH THE ADJOINING TERRACE.

STYLING IDEAS

✳ **Furniture for a conservatory can be of the outdoor garden type, in cast iron, wood or plastic.**

✳ **Rattan, wicker, bamboo and cane look fitting if you want a colonial image. But more conventional dining and sitting room furniture can be used if you want the conservatory for summer relaxing and entertaining.**

✳ **Loose slipcovers are more practical on upholstered furniture than tight-fitting ones.**

✳ **The colors and patterns used in a conservatory can be brighter and bolder than in a more formal environment, but avoid tones which will cause glare in strong sunshine.**

✳ **Create an Oriental or Indian theme with futon, floor cushions, sparse storage furniture, lacquered items, rattan blinds and ceiling fan.**

✳ **Reserve an area to display a special collection – group of straw hats; stuffed birds in cages; mounted butterflies and moths; shopping, picnic and bicycle baskets; colorful gourds; unglazed terracotta pots and bowls.**

✳ **Hang baskets filled with plants and flowers from brackets or trellis on the original house wall. Hang a wicker or metal bird cage, or wire kitchen baskets, from the beams and fill them with feathery trailing plants.**

✳ **On a practical note, install adequate electrical plugs, lighting and watering facilities; provide somewhere to store the barbecue and the outdoor furniture in wet weather.**

STUDIES AND WORKROOMS

UNLESS YOU WORK FROM HOME AND HAVE SET ASIDE A ROOM to be used as an office, a retreat from the rest of the family (in the form of a book-lined study or a well-equipped workroom or hobby area) may seem an impossible ideal, because of lack of space or funds. But it is essential in most homes to try and create a quiet corner in which to study and read, to deal with household accounts, to write letters, to sew, to quilt, to knit, to make model airplanes or pursue other hobbies.

Very often a study area has to fit into one end of the main living room, or be tucked away in a corner of the landing or hall (sometimes the understairs area converts well to this purpose). It may have to double up with a dining room or guest room, or be part of the main bedroom. However small, this section of a room should be tranquil, well lit for study/reading purposes and should ideally be decorated in such a way that it is conducive to concentration. If the quiet area is at one end of an otherwise busy family sitting room, some form of semi-permanent screening (folding doors or a decorative portable screen), or a change in level or at least in the type of flooring will help to separate the area visually.

Storage will be crucial for all the materials, books, files and other equipment you need to have on hand. Purpose-built cupboards, desks and drawers may help to solve a clutter problem, but books, which are decorative in their own right, can be housed on open shelves or in bookcases, where they will help achieve the atmosphere of a study/library in that section of the room. Dark, rich colors make a good background for books, so a deepening of the color scheme at one end of the room will help to define the study area.

TAILOR MADE

If you are lucky enough to be able to plan a study or workroom from scratch, first think about its main purpose and decide on priorities. Will there be a lot of noise (music, instruments, machinery, typewriters, hammering) which will disturb the rest of the household? If so, install some sound insulation and do not site the room over, or next to, a space where children sleep. If there are likely to be strong smells from varnish, paint or glue, provide adequate ventilation. Allow for plenty of electrical circuits – both for power and light – and plan task lighting to be as flexible as

MAXIMUM USE IS MADE OF THE SPACE IN A MODERN HALL TO FIT A DESK NEATLY INTO A DRAFT-FREE CORNER UNDER THE GALLERIED STAIRS. IT RECEIVES AMPLE NATURAL LIGHT FROM THE LANDING WINDOW, MAKING IT AN IDEAL PLACE FOR READING OR LETTER-WRITING. A BRIGHT KELIM ON THE FLOOR HELPS TO DELINEATE THIS AREA.

possible. Always install twice as many sockets as you first thought of, sited in relation to the position of the desk, drawing board, work bench or other equipment. Will you need a water supply and sink? If so, organize this at the outset.

Specialized storage may well be essential, for tools and other equipment; remember the golden rule and measure everything you need to store, then plan cupboards, shelves and drawers from the inside out (see page 230). Plan for twice as much storage as you think you need and allow for some flexibility, with adjustable shelves and interior fixtures for cupboards.

Surfaces should be as practical as possible, depending on the activities which are to take place: hard, scrubbable flooring which is impervious to spills may be essential, but even in a room mainly used for dressmaking, you will need to be able to see and sweep up pins, threads and snippets of fabric. The walls may also need to be washable, which means paint or ceramic tiles.

Color schemes are largely a matter of personal taste and will also depend on the size of the room, its orientation and the atmosphere you want to create. While bright, stimulating color schemes may be appropriate for creating modern music or for design work, they are not conducive to writing or quiet study; here, softer neutrals or warm mid-tones work better. Avoid colors which cause glare (bright yellow, orange, brilliant white), and shiny textures, especially with a computer screen in the room – but do not go to the other extreme and create a dark or gloomy mood.

THE HOME OFFICE

If you work from home, the way the room is planned will depend on the nature of your business, and whether clients, patients or customers will be visiting you. In the latter case, a separate entrance, or at least a practical hall treatment, is necessary. It may also be essential to keep the rest of the family at bay: a lockable door is a wise precaution if there is a risk of inquisitive small fingers spoiling immaculately prepared work. Requirements for essential services will vary, in terms of telecommunications, fax, computer terminals and photocopiers. Even if you start off as a one-person band, you may eventually need space for extra staff and should plan for some flexibility. If the family is out at work or school all day, it makes sense to have a separate heating system for the office.

A WARM, INVITING STUDY AREA HAS BEEN CREATED IN PART OF THIS LIVING ROOM, VISUALLY SEPARATED BY A CHANGE OF FLOOR COVERING. A DESK LAMP GIVES EXTRA ILLUMINATION IN THE EVENINGS.

STYLING IDEAS

❖ *In a restricted space use a folding trestle table or architect's drawing board as a work surface.*

❖ *Make maximum use of the backs of cupboard doors to store small sewing and hobby items; install racks/doweling for thread spools, small cans of paint or tools.*

❖ *Use a segmented filing drawer to store paper and knitting patterns.*

❖ *Build a cupboard to fill one wall of a sewing room and install a drop-down ironing board behind one of the doors. A sewing or knitting machine can stand inside on a pull-out top or workbench.*

❖ *Build adjustable shelving into a recess above desk or workbench – position these high enough so that you do not knock your head if you stand up in a hurry!*

❖ *In a dual-purpose area, use a wheeled trolley for a computer, typewriter or other small, easily portable equipment.*

❖ *A filing cabinet which has to be sited in a dual-purpose room can be hidden under a fabric "skirt" to coordinate with upholstery or blinds.*

❖ *Fit a worktop into a bay window; support it on filing cabinets, drawers or units, leaving a kneehole between and have the top cut to follow the shape of the bay. If necessary, support the span on a wall-mounted bracket.*

❖ *In a high-ceilinged, traditionally styled living room, create a study corner by siting a freestanding bureau-bookcase in one fireplace recess; match it with built-in shelves in the opposite recess.*

❖ *Always try to have spare work space on each side of the typewriter or keyboard for books, notes or print-outs.*

Decorating

Interior decorating is by far the most popular do-it-yourself activity, and the reason is obvious. It costs a small fortune to employ a professional decorator these days, and since modern decorating materials are now so easy to use, there is nothing to prevent the avid homeowner from attempting it.

It is not only the money-saving aspect that matters: many people positively enjoy decorating their own homes and the rewards are great. The least appealing aspect is the preparatory work that has to be done before decorating can begin. It is tempting to try skimping on this, but in the long run, thorough preparation is the secret of decorating success. This chapter covers using paint, wallcoverings, wall and floor tiles as well as other floor coverings to decorate your home. Along with information to help you choose and use the various materials, you will also find everything you need to know about that vital preparation work. Throughout the chapter there are practical tips and styling ideas to help you achieve a professional-looking finish. But first there is some advice on choosing a color scheme.

This flagstone-floored hall, suffused with sunshine, creates a welcoming impression on entering the house. The yellow walls are given a decorative treatment with a hand-stenciled frieze running along the top and bottom of the walls and framing the open doorways. The lighter-painted ceiling enhances the airy, spacious feel of the room.

This painted cupboard is in keeping with its period, but serves as inspiration for bringing life to contemporary furniture by hand painting it to match a particular color scheme.

UNDERSTANDING COLOR

CHOOSING A NEW COLOR SCHEME when you are redecorating a room can be one of the most challenging decisions you have to make. Successful color planning comes easily to a fortunate few, rather like good dress sense, but for the majority it poses questions they would rather duck: why else do paint manufacturers sell so much white and cream paint? However, producing a color scheme that works, and is pleasant to live with, need not be difficult if you understand the way colors work — both in isolation and in harmony or contrast with each other. And if you still doubt your ability to color-scheme your home yourself, do not be afraid to borrow ideas from the professional and the successful. Every room set shown in books and magazines devoted to interior design — and in wallpaper pattern books, too — is the handiwork of either a skilled interior designer or a gifted amateur. If you like the end result, either use it as inspiration for devising your own scheme, or simply copy it in your home.

THE ROUGH PLASTERED WALLS HAVE BEEN GIVEN A LIGHT WASH OF COLOR WHICH BRINGS A TRANSLUCENT QUALITY TO THEM WHILE EMPHASIZING THE SIMPLICITY OF THE DECORATIVE TREATMENT. THE DIFFERENT EARTH COLORS USED ARE APPROPRIATELY OFFSET BY THE FLAGSTONE FLOOR AND THE HEAVY WOODEN DOORS.

USING HARMONY AND CONTRAST

A harmonious color scheme is restful on the eye and offers a visual solution to the problem of bringing together the disparate features of a room, including the walls, floor covering, window dressings and the various items of furniture. A contrasting scheme stimulates the eye, with the use of color contrast highlighting the individual features of a room, whereas a harmonious scheme would blend them into the background. Harmonious schemes work best in rooms where you spend a lot of time relaxing – living rooms and bedrooms, for example. Schemes with a lot of contrast are best saved for other rooms or areas of the home which are more functional or where you pass through, such as halls and landings, the kitchen and the bathroom. Children's or teenage rooms might successfully use contrasting color schemes.

As with all things carried to extremes, you can overdo the harmony and contrast in your color scheming. Too much contrast looks restless and constantly jars the vision, while too much color harmony simply looks monotonous. The ideal color scheme is essentially harmonious, created using colors from one segment of the color wheel as its main theme, but which has ele-ments of contrast – in accessories, for example – to brighten things up.

USING PATTERN

Mixing pattern with plain color can help to create the balance so essential in a color scheme. Hanging patterned curtains against a painted wall or laying a patterned rug on a plain carpet are two obvious examples. The patterned element can be in colors that either harmonize or contrast with the background color, according to the visual effect you want to achieve. You can even mix pattern with pattern, such as cushions on a sofa, provided there is a link through color.

COLOR INTENSITY

The value, or saturation, of color is reduced as adjacent colors on the color wheel are intermixed. The pure primary colors have the highest color intensity, and the more intense the color, the more sparingly it should be used; a bright blue room would be visually quite overwhelming. The secondary and tertiary colors on the color wheel are each made up from just the three primary colors, used in varying proportions. Color intensity lessens with each intermixing.

What's in a color?

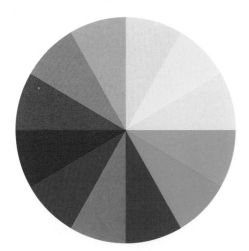

AN IMPORTANT BASIC PRINCIPLE is that all colors are a mixture of just three basic colors: blue, red and yellow. These are known as the primary colors, and they can be intermixed ad infinitum to produce every color under the sun. You will have an idea of the principle if you look at the picture on the page opposite under a strong magnifying glass; you will see that it is made up of tiny red, yellow and blue

dots, with the addition of black. The mingling of different strengths of these four dots creates all the various intermediate colors in the picture.

The basis of color selection is a visual device called the color wheel. Imagine a circle divided into three equal segments, each occupied by one of the primary colors. If adjacent primary colors are mixed and the results are placed between each primary color pair, there will now be six equal segments on the wheel: red, orange, yellow, green, blue and violet. Orange, green and violet are known as the secondary colors. By repeating the mixing of adjacent colors, we create twelve segments with six new colors – red-orange, orange-yellow, yellow-green, green-blue, blue-violet and violet-red. These are called the tertiary colors. The complete twelve-section wheel provides an invaluable tool for color-planning.

Types of color

COLORS WORK IN A VARIETY of different ways. For a start, those in the sector of the wheel from yellow through the reds and around to violet are referred to as advancing colors, because they make a surface

decorated in this color appear to advance toward the viewer. In a room, this creates an effect that is warm and inviting, but one which makes the room seem smaller, too. The colors in the other sector of the wheel are receding colors and have the opposite effect to the advancing colors; they appear to recede into the distance and make a room seem large, cool and spacious.

Next, colors can be in harmony or in contrast with other colors. Colors in adjacent segments of the wheel, or in the same part of it, appear to go well together and will not clash when both are used in a color scheme. Those on diametrically opposite sides of the wheel contrast strongly with each other, and are (rather confusingly) said to be complementary colors. They add spice to color schemes, preventing them from appearing bland to the eye. Red and green are the most obvious example of complementary colors; used together in their pure form, they would produce a disturbing effect on the eye, but a rich red or a terracotta pink next to a dark olive green could work very well.

There is another way of reducing the intensity of a color. The addition of the so-called neutral tones – white, black and the various shades of grey resulting from mixing white and black together in different proportions – allows you to produce lighter or darker and therefore less intense, or less pure, shades of each color. These neutral tones can be, and are, also used on their own, especially white which gives a sense of spaciousness and light, and is the perfect companion for areas of strong color or pattern. Grey shades of the secondary and tertiary colors are also useful for softening the intensity of color schemes. Finally, black adds drama, but should not be used to excess, for obvious reasons.

TONAL VALUES

The tone of a color refers to how light or dark it is, which depends on how much black and white are mixed into it. The wide choice of off-white paint colors for decorating (such as magnolia, ivory, apricot white, apple white and so on) is evidence of the range of tonal values there are. Successful color schemes depend as much on their tonal relationship as on the actual hues you choose to put together. It is generally a good idea to use two colors of the same tonal value in a room decorating scheme, with emphatically darker or lighter toned colors reserved for accessories or for smaller areas.

The way color is applied, as well as the choice of colors, significantly affects the look of a room. The use of special paint effects, such as stippling or rag rolling, depend on overlaying a second color over a base color, and this introduces a further spectrum of nuances and subtle effects. The variations made possible by the juxtaposition of the colors chosen and their intensity, their luminosity and the way one color absorbs or reflects the other, are limitless. The use of broken color in these special effects may create an illusion of depth and a more atmospheric feel than the use of flat, uniform color, and this can enhance the features of a room as well as its furnishings. However, you need to have developed an eye for color and a reasonably steady hand in order to achieve the lightness of touch that produces good results and the best way to perfect these is to experiment, using different color combinations, on scraps of plain wallpaper.

USING COLOR EFFECTS

Always let color be your servant, not your master, when devising color schemes for your home. After all, if you

do not like the effect you have created, you can always change something (or everything!) in order to redress the balance.

As we have seen, colors – used alone or in combination – create a variety of overall visual effects in a room. The warm colors such as reds and oranges, the colors of fire, make a room seem cozy and inviting, while the yellows evoke sunshine and brightness and are ideal for rooms with poor natural light. Cold colors, containing blue, create a cool, airy feel in their lighter tones. Greens bring the outdoors indoors, giving a room a light, restful atmosphere that is ideal for workrooms such as kitchens and also for recreational areas such as a conservatory. Blues themselves are cooler still than greens; while giving a feeling of spaciousness to a room, they need sunlight to bring them to life and should be avoided in north-facing rooms. The last color segment, the violets, are rich and sumptuous, but should be used sparingly for best effect.

ABOVE: SINCE A BEDROOM IS AN ENTIRELY PERSONAL SPACE, THIS IS A GOOD ROOM IN WHICH TO EXPRESS A JOY IN COLOR AND EXPERIMENT WITH COMBINATIONS AND EFFECTS WHICH NOT EVERYONE WOULD FIND RESTFUL. WHILE SEVERAL DIFFERENT COLORS HAVE BEEN USED IN THIS CONTRASTING SCHEME, THEIR SIMILAR TONAL VALUES GIVE THE FINISHED RESULT A DEGREE OF UNITY.

RIGHT: THE UPHOLSTERY OF THE CHAIRS WAS THE STARTING POINT FOR THIS EXCITING, HARMONIOUS COLOR SCHEME. THE LIGHT AND DARKER SHADES OF BRICK-ORANGE TO TERRACOTTA-BROWN HAVE BEEN SPECIALLY MIXED TO MATCH THE COLORS OF THE FABRIC AS CLOSELY AS POSSIBLE. THE NATURAL SISAL FLOORCOVERING IS A PERFECT FOIL FOR THE RICH, WARM COLORS USED ON THE WALLS.

Reducing the color intensity by intermixing produces color schemes that can be either delicate and pretty (the pinks and lilacs are good examples) or homey and subdued (the creams and browns). Elements of contrast used in a subtle way work especially well with these shades.

PLAYING COLOR TRICKS

Apart from giving a room a particular mood, color can also be used to deceive the eye by playing a range of clever decorating tricks. One of the simplest examples of this is the use of a darker color on the ceiling than on the walls of a room, to make it appear lower than it really is. This works especially well in high rooms with a picture rail; carrying the dark color down the walls as far as the rail makes the effect even more potent. If the ceiling has any decorative features such as a coving or a ceiling rose, picking these out in a lighter color will draw attention to them and bring them closer to the eye. Simply reverse the procedure, especially by painting the ceiling white, to make a low-ceilinged room appear higher.

The same trick can be employed to make one wall of a room advance or recede, so helping to alter its apparent proportions. It is a useful way of adding interest to square and otherwise featureless rooms.

Pattern can be used to deceive the eye, too. Wallcoverings with a strong vertical element in their design – stripes are the obvious example – make a wall appear taller and narrower, while those with a horizontal bias achieve the opposite effect, making the wall seem lower but wider.

Small pattern motifs on wallcoverings make a wall seem to recede from the eye, while large ones make it appear to advance toward you. You can use strong pattern, like strong color, to make one wall of the room the focus of attention. Covering the end wall of a long corridor with a strongly patterned wallpaper will bring it closer and will thereby distract the eye from the long side walls.

SOLVING PROBLEMS WITH COLOR

Color can help you to resolve all sorts of decorating problems. A common dilemma is what to do with ugly features such as surface-mounted pipework and central heating radiators; painting them the same color as the room walls will help to blend them into the background. You can also make a prominent chimney breast, pier or lintel recede by decorating it in the same way as the wall or ceiling surfaces flanking it.

Rooms with sloping ceilings are another problem area, since deciding whether the slope is wall or ceiling can be tricky. One simple solution is to paint the whole room in a single color and to use a frieze to create a false ceiling line. Another is to use a wallcovering with a small, non-directional motif and a free pattern match to decorate both walls and ceilings. If you wish to use wallpaper with a stronger pattern, confine it to the vertical end walls of the room to avoid potential problems with pattern matching.

STRIPES HAVE THE EFFECT OF MAKING A LOW-CEILINGED ROOM APPEAR TALLER; PAINTING THE CEILING WHITE, IN CONTRAST TO THE DARKER WALLS, REINFORCES THE ILLUSION. THIS BOLD COLOR SCHEME WORKS BY KEEPING TO THE THREE DOMINANT HUES IN THE WALLCOVERING AND CURTAIN FABRIC — ECHOING THE RED IN THE CARPET, FOR EXAMPLE, AND USING A MORE INTENSE SHADE OF BLUE IN THE SOFA.

COLORWASHED YELLOW WALLS BRING SUNSHINE TO AN OTHERWISE DARK BEDROOM. THE OVERLAYING OF SEVERAL LAYERS OF PAINT IN THIS TECHNIQUE GIVES GREATER DEPTH TO THE COLOR AND MORE CHARACTER TO THE ROOM. THE COOLER "GREY" SHADE OF GREEN USED FOR THE CARPET AND THE SHUTTERS IS MORE NEUTRAL, ALLOWING THE YELLOW TO SHINE OUT; THE GREEN IS REPEATED, ALONG WITH A GREY-WHITE AND OTHER MUTED COLORS, IN ALL THE ACCESSORIES, BRINGING CONTINUITY TO THE ROOM SCHEME.

COLOR MIXING TIPS

○ **Forget color swatch cards and experiment with your own color mixing for more exciting results. Always start with a very limited palette and see how many different nuances of color you can achieve.**

○ **As a starting point, simply add a tint to a pot of white latex. The color can consist of anything, provided it is water-soluble: another latex, colored ink, artist's stainers, gouache (opaque water-colors) or even food or fabric dye.**

○ **For mixing with solvent-based (gloss) paint, use only an oil-based pigmented product: another gloss paint, eggshell, undercoat, artist's oils. Never mix oil and water.**

○ **For an experiment that is more ambitious, mix two complementary colors (opposites on the color wheel) with varying amounts of white to give a family of related shades, from palest pastels to deep, sludgy tones, all of which will work together and could form the basis of an interesting decorating scheme.**

○ **Add white to lighten a color and its complementary to darken: black only makes a color dirty and dull, deadening its luminous quality.**

○ **Some colors reflect more light and therefore have more luminosity: whites, creams, yellows and pale reds reflect the light and bounce it from one wall to another, making a small room look more spacious.**

○ **Dark reds, greens and blues absorb light and make a room appear smaller than it is; these colors are best for large, light rooms with high ceilings.**

TYPES OF PAINT

PAINT IS THE MOST VERSATILE HOME DECORATING MATERIAL — it is easy to put on, looks good, wears well and can be overpainted quickly for a change of color scheme, besides which, it is relatively inexpensive.

ALL TYPES OF PAINT consist of solid particles of pigment, which give the paint its color, carried in a liquid binder that bonds the pigment to the surface once the paint has been applied. To enable you to spread the paint easily, pigment and binder are either suspended in water as droplets or dissolved in a petroleum-based solvent. This distinction gives us the two well-known paint types, latex and solvent-based paint, formerly known as oil paint. Traditionally, water-based paints are used on walls and ceilings and on outside masonry, while solvent-based types are used on wood and metal. However, there is a movement away from the use of volatile solvents in paint for health and environmental reasons, and water-based finishes for wood and metal are becoming increasingly popular since advancements in paint technology have improved both their performance and their durability.

WATER-BASED PAINT: KEY FACTS

❍ When you apply water-based paint, the water evaporates and allows the binder to form a continuous film on the surface you are decorating. It dries very quickly and does not have the strong smell associated with solvent-based paints.
❍ Vinyl latex paint for walls and ceilings is available with a flat finish (**2, 6, 9, 14**) or satin finish (**7**). Water-based acrylic paints for wood (**12**) usually dry to a satin finish rather than a high gloss. The terms vinyl and

acrylic simply refer to the type of synthetic resin used as the binder and film-former in a paint or varnish.
❍ Latex paint does not need an undercoat; on bare plaster, thinning the first coat with water makes it easier to apply. Water-based acrylic paints need a primer.
❍ Non-drip latex paint contains additives that help to prevent runs and drips and also allow you to apply a thicker film and so achieve better coverage. You can apply both types with a brush, a roller or a paint pad.
❍ So-called solid latex paint is thicker still, and is intended mainly for use on ceilings. It is sold pre-packed in a rectangular tray and is designed to be put on with a roller.
❍ Textured latex paint is a thickened paint used for creating three-dimensional effects on walls and ceilings, using special rollers and other texturing tools.
❍ Latex paint for exterior masonry is available in smooth (**4**) or textured (**5**) forms. Both contain fungicides (to discourage mold growth) and fillers that help them to bridge small cracks.
❍ You can clean painting equipment with water unless the paint has set really hard, when a special brush cleaner may be needed.

SOLVENT-BASED PAINT: KEY FACTS

❍ This paint dries as the solvent evaporates, giving the product its characteristic smell. It takes longer to dry than latex paint, but the resulting film is generally tougher.

❍ Solvent-based paints need both a primer and an undercoat (**10**) on bare wood and metal, although self-undercoating or one-coat gloss (**1**) will need a primer only.
❍ Non-drip types (**8**) offer easier application and better coverage than runny types. Both are generally applied with a brush, but a paint pad or roller can be used.
❍ The finish may be a high gloss or a satin finish, also known as eggshell. (**3**). The former is marginally more hardwearing, but it can magnify any surface blemishes.
❍ You usually need turpentine, paraffin or a commercial brush cleaner to clean painting equipment. Some paints contain special additives that allow cleaning with hot, soapy water, provided the paint has not set hard.

OTHER PAINTING MATERIALS
Primers (**6**) are the first coat of a paint system. Their job is to provide a good bond to the surface, a sound base for the undercoat and, on metal, to help stop the surface from corroding. Traditional wood and metal primers are solvent-based, but water-based formulations are now available. Combined primer-undercoats help speed up the painting process by cutting out one stage of a traditional three-coat system.
Artist's colors can be used to tint white paint if you want to create a unique color. Use oil colors with solvent-based paint and acrylic colors, or even watercolors, to tint latex paint.

Glazes (sometimes called scumble glazes) are transparent or semi-transparent materials applied over previously painted surfaces to give a special broken-color effect such as stippling, rag-rolling or dragging. They are solvent-based and are thinned if necessary with mineral spirits.

Varnish (**13**) is a clear finish used mainly on wood to expose its grain and enhance its natural appearance; it is essentially paint without the pigment. Most varnishes are solvent-based, but quick-drying water-based acrylic varnishes are becoming more widely available. The finish may be satin or a high gloss. Apart from products giving a clear film, there are also varnishes incorporating a small amount of dye which color the wood without obscuring the grain. These seal the wood, too, but if you want a stronger colored effect, you can use a wood dye first, followed by clear varnish as the protective surface film.

Lacquers are clear or colored coatings used on both wood and metal. They are based on a cellulose derivative in a volatile solvent, and dry to give a hard, glossy finish.

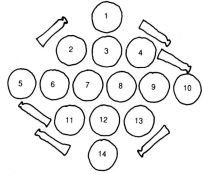

PAINTING EQUIPMENT

IT IS IMPORTANT TO ASSEMBLE THE CORRECT TOOLS before you begin any painting job. Buy the best quality you can afford and the most practical size for the task at hand: you may well need a range of sizes. It is usual to paint woodwork with a brush, while walls and ceilings can be painted by brush, pad or roller, depending on the surface and on your inclination. Take good care of your painting tools: wash brushes, rollers and pads thoroughly in the appropriate solvent for the paint used. Allow them to dry properly, then wrap them in newspaper or foil and secure with an elastic band to store.

(Top shelf hanging on wall)

Paintbrushes The bristle is the most important part: its quality, length and thickness determine how well it will hold paint when you load the brush, and how smoothly it will apply paint to the surface. Boar bristle is best; some cheaper brushes use synthetic materials which now perform as well as bristle with water-based paints. The length and quantity of the bristles govern the brush's performance and price. Cheap brushes have short bristles and not many of them. More expensive ones have thick, plentiful bristles, long enough to bend easily as the brush is drawn across the surface. The bristles are usually cut to a slight bevel across their ends.

Paintbrushes come in a wide range of sizes, from ½in (12mm) across up to 8in (200mm). Sizes over 4in (100mm) are for walls and ceilings.

Cutting-in brush Its bristles cut at an angle make it easier to apply paint up to an edge, such as around the glazing bars of a window.

Masking tape Helps to achieve straight lines and to protect the glass when painting around windows.

(Top shelf)

Artist's brushes Invaluable for special paint effects and painting furniture and tiles. It is a good idea to have several, in a range of sizes.

Radiator brush, Hockey brush Used to apply paint to surfaces that cannot be reached with a conventional brush, such as behind radiators. Its long wire handle can be bent so the bristles can be drawn at the correct angle.

Sandpaper Sheets of sandpaper from fine to coarse are used wrapped around wooden blocks to roughen a previously painted surface.

Paint shield Hold it so that its edge marks the line up to which you wish to paint; useful for moldings.

Stenciling brush Consists of a clump of bristles held in a steel ferrule attached to a rounded handle; used to apply paint to a background through a stencil for a soft effect.

Stippling brush Has a bed of fine bristles cut off square, so that when the brush hits the paint surface, all the bristles make contact with it. Removes some of the top coat of paint to create a textured, "stippled" effect.

(*Bottom shelf hanging on wall*)
Scrapers (Strippers) A general-purpose tool, used to remove paint, varnish and old wallcoverings. It looks like a putty knife in shape and size, but has a much stiffer blade. Blade widths range from about 1in (25mm) up to 6in (150mm). The smaller sizes are used on narrow surfaces such as window and door frames.

(*Bottom shelf*)
Paint pads These have a piece of short-pile fabric stuck to a foam backing, attached to a backing plate and handle and are an alternative to the paintbrush for applying paint and varnish. Paint pads come in many shapes and sizes, mostly rectangular. Sizes range from around 2½ x 2in (62 x 50mm) for general-purpose work up to 6 x 4in (150 x 100mm) for fast application to walls and ceilings. Smaller "toothbrush" pads deal with painting around windows and cutting in at the edges of painted areas. There are also wheeled paint pads for painting along the angle between wall and ceiling or wall and baseboard.

Paint rollers A hollow cylinder covered with a sleeve of natural or synthetic fiber. It is slipped onto an open wire cage mounted on an axle to which a handle is attached, allowing the sleeve to be driven back and forth across the surface. Fibers include mohair, lambswool, sheepskin and synthetic fibers, but the pile length is more important. Short-pile sleeves such as mohair and wool are best on smooth surfaces like wood and bare plaster; use longer pile types on textured surfaces such as relief wallcoverings and mortar rendering, where the longer fibers help force the paint into the recesses. Sleeves of expanded plastic foam are set directly on the axle of the roller handle, rather than on a cage. They are the cheapest type of sleeve to buy, but the least satisfactory to use.

Rollers are sized according to the length of the sleeve; you can also buy mini rollers of 3in (75mm) for small areas or special effects. Sleeves of one brand may not fit cages of another.

Roller tray Sold in widths to match available roller sizes. Plastic trays are preferable to metal ones, since they are easier to clean and do not rust.

Paint bucket A container with a hoop handle used to carry a small amount of paint to the work area. A typical bucket holds up to a quart (litre) of paint, but is usually used only about half full. Plastic buckets are easier to clean than metal ones, which also tend to rust if scratched. They are also lighter to hold for long periods.

Molding scrapers A special stripping tool used to remove paint and varnish from intricate moldings and awkward corners. There are three blade patterns – pear-shaped, triangular and combination: the last has straight, convex and concave curved edges to cope with a range of surface detail.

Dragging combs In a range of sizes for creating dragged paint effects.

Stiff, long-bristled paintbrush Used for dragging large expanses of wall.

Sea sponge Natural product used for all sponged paint effects.

PREPARATION FOR PAINTING

MODERN PAINTS DO THEIR JOB extremely well, thanks to the continuing advances in paint technology. However, they cannot perform miracles and will give of their best only if the surfaces to which they are applied have been properly prepared first.

Bare wood

SAND THE SURFACE of the wood with sandpaper, using medium and then fine grades to remove any blemishes. Finish with flour-grade sandpaper, working in the direction of the grain.

IF THERE ARE ANY DENTS or splits in the wood, fill them with cellulose filler and then sand the surface smooth when the putty has dried. Use wood stopper in a color that matches the wood if you intend to use varnish rather than paint.

Painted or varnished wood

WASH THE SURFACE WITH a solution of sugar soap or strong detergent to remove from it all dirt, grease and fingermarks. Rinse with clean water afterward.

IF THE SURFACE is in good condition, flatten the gloss finish by rubbing it with fine wet-and-dry abrasive paper, used wet. Rinse again with clean water and allow the surface to dry.

IF THE SURFACE IS CHIPPED, touch in the defects with paint (or with primer if bare wood is exposed) to restore the surface paint to a uniform level.

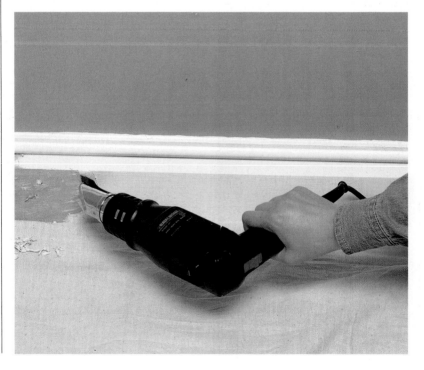

IF THE SURFACE IS IN EXTREMELY POOR condition, with large-scale chipping, flaking or blistering of the paint, strip it off completely using a hot air gun or chemical paint stripper. Use the former on large flat surfaces and the latter on intricate moldings, or if you intend to redecorate with varnish rather than paint.

If you are using a hot air gun, take great care. Play the airstream back and forth over the paint until it bubbles up. Then scrape it off and deposit the scrapings in a heatproof container such as an old can. Use a flat scraper on smooth surfaces, a shavehook to strip moldings and architraves. Remove remaining traces of old paint from the wood surface using fine sandpaper.

Bare plaster or plasterboard

WHEN USING A CHEMICAL stripper, start by reading the manufacturer's instructions carefully. Then apply the stripper to the surface using an old paintbrush and leave it to work for the recommended time. Scrape off the paint as described above, depositing the scrapings safely, and apply more stripper if necessary to remove multiple coats of paint or to strip stubborn areas. When you have removed all the paint, rinse the surface with water or mineral spirits as required by the instructions; do this very thoroughly, or any traces of stripper that remain will attack the new finish. Finally flatten the wood grain with a fine grade of sandpaper if you rinsed it with water.

ON NEWLY PLASTERED SURFACES, remove any nibs of plaster with abrasive paper. Treat any exposed plasterboard nails with a metal primer. Then apply either a commercial plaster primer or a coat of latex paint, thinned slightly with water.

ON STRIPPED WALLS OR CEILINGS that were previously decorated with a wallcovering, wash the surface thoroughly with water to remove paste residues. Then fill any cracks, dents and other surface defects with putty, leaving the material standing out slightly so you can sand it flush once the putty has hardened. Use a flexible decorator's mastic to fill cracks in wall/ceiling angles and where the plaster meets woodwork, such as baseboards or window frames.

Painted wallcoverings

WASH THE SURFACE AS FOR painted plaster, and seal in any serious discoloration with a stain block. Glue down any raised seams or tears by brushing on a little wallpaper adhesive. Slit raised bubbles with a sharp knife, brush paste inside them and press them firmly back against the plaster.

TIPS

❍ *Use a long-handled crevice brush or a specially adapted crevice roller when you are painting behind radiators and pipework.*

❍ *When painting cornices or ceiling roses, always use a water-based latex paint. Make sure that intricate moldings do not get clogged with paint by applying it in thin coats with a narrow 1in (25mm) brush.*

Painted plaster

WASH THE SURFACE WITH a solution of sugar soap or strong detergent to remove dirt, grease and fingermarks. Rinse it off with clean water and leave to dry, ready for repainting. If the surface is marked by water stains (caused by plumbing leaks, for example) or by cigarette smoke, treat it with a stain block to seal in the stain and prevent it from penetrating the new coat of paint.

BASIC PAINTING TECHNIQUES

YOU CAN APPLY PAINT IN ONE OF FOUR WAYS: with a brush, a roller, a pad or with paint-spraying equipment in the form of a spray gun or an aerosol paint can. Each requires a different technique, which may also vary according to the surface you are decorating.

PAINT GIVES A FINISH THAT IS BOTH PRACTICAL AND RESTFUL FOR THIS STYLISH EATING AREA WITHIN A KITCHEN. EGGSHELL, A FLAT-FINISH SOLVENT-BASED PAINT, HAS BEEN USED ON THE WOOD PANELING AND THE CORNER CUPBOARD, WHILE LATEX PAINT HAS BEEN APPLIED TO THE PLASTERED WALLS. CAREFUL PREPARATION OF THE SURFACES IS AMPLY REWARDED BY THE PROFESSIONAL-LOOKING PAINT FINISH ACHIEVED.

Using a paintbrush

BEGIN BY MAKING SURE THAT THE brush is free from dust and from loose bristles. Flick it back and forth several times across the palm of your hand. Open the can of paint, after dusting its lid, and stir it if any liquid has separated out on the surface of the paint; cut around and carefully remove any skin that has formed on the surface if the tin is part-used.

You can use paint straight from a new can, but with part-used cans it is better to strain some into a paint bucket first, since the paint may be contaminated with bits of hardened paint skin and also with loose bristles and dust from any previous jobs.

Load the brush by dipping it into the paint to a depth of about half the bristle length and remove the excess paint by pulling the bristles across the edge of the can.

APPLY THE PAINT TO THE SURFACE in a series of parallel bands until little more is being released by the bristles. Then blend the bands together with shorter transverse strokes, and finish off with lighter strokes, running parallel with the original bands.

Reload the brush and repeat the operation on the adjacent area, blending the wet edges of the two areas together. Continue until the surface is completely painted.

Using a paint roller

SELECT THE CORRECT SLEEVE for the surface you are decorating and the paint you are applying (see page 92), then fit it onto your roller cage. Unless you are using solid latex paint with its own roller tray, pour some paint into your tray (via a strainer if it is from a part-used can). Fill it to a depth of about ¾in (20mm).

Run the roller down the slope of the tray into the paint, then roll it up and down the slope a few times in order to distribute the paint evenly over the roller. When using solid latex, run the roller back and forth a few times over the surface of the paint.

APPLY THE PAINT by running the roller over the surface you are decorating, first in one direction and then at right angles to guarantee even coverage. When little more paint is being transferred to the wall, recharge the roller and repeat the operation on an adjacent area, blending the two together carefully. Continue until the entire surface is covered.

A roller will not paint right up to internal angles; stop painting about 1in (25mm) from the angle, and complete the job using a paintbrush.

Quick and Easy Stripes

YOU CAN ADAPT A LARGE sponge roller with the use of string to make it an effective tool for creating stripes. Tie a length of string tightly around the middle and two more lengths ⅜in (10mm) on each side of it, then a further piece of string at each end of the roller. Water down the latex paint until it is the consistency of heavy cream; use the adapted roller to create a series of soft-edged dual stripes.

Using a paint pad

POUR OR STRAIN SOME PAINT into the tray; load the pad by dipping it into the paint to the depth of the pile. If the tray has a loading roller, run a large pad across it to distribute the paint and squeeze out the excess.

DRAW THE PAD ACROSS THE SURFACE to spread the paint, working first in one direction and then at right angles to ensure good coverage. Reload the pad and repeat the operation. Use a small wand pad to paint narrow surfaces and to touch in parts missed by a larger pad.

If you are using an edging pad with guide wheels to paint up to an internal angle, press the guide wheels firmly against the surface not being painted as you move the pad along.

Spraying paint

IF YOU ARE USING A SPRAY GUN, follow the maker's instructions for loading the paint container and selecting the appropriate nozzle. If you are using an aerosol paint, shake the can well. With either, point the nozzle at the surface you are painting and start the paint flowing. As it emerges, move the gun or can from side to side, keeping it the same distance from the wall rather than swinging your arm in an arc. When one band is covered, move to the next area and blend the two together.

Instant Tile Effect

USE A 3IN (75MM) MINI-ROLLER to create a tiled effect for the walls of your bathroom or kitchen. Simply load it with paint and work from left to right, painting rows of squares and leaving a small, even gap between each block of colour. The irregular edges add to the hand-made tile illusion.

Achieving straight edges

ONCE YOU HAVE MASTERED the basics, painting is child's play. The only remotely difficult part is getting a neat straight edge at the perimeter of whatever you are decorating. For example, when painting window frames, the paint film should extend over the putty (both inside and out) and onto the glass by about ⅛in (3mm); the idea is to seal the junction between putty and glass so that rain outside or condensation indoors cannot run down between the two and cause the frames to rot. But glazing bars are awkward to paint and getting a straight edge on the glass face is hard to do freehand. The end result is often wobbly edges that look very amateurish.

Similar problems arise when you are painting walls and ceilings a different color, painting baseboards, or if you want each side of a door to match the color scheme of the room it faces. Here you do at least have a sharp angle between the surfaces – an internal one between walls and ceilings, moldings or baseboards, an external one on door edges – but it can still be difficult to achieve a perfectly straight paint line.

The last decorating area where you might want neat straight lines is where you are being creative, when painting bands of contrasting colors on walls, for example. Here, too, a steady hand alone may not produce perfect results.

Painting baseboards

MASK THE SEAM BETWEEN baseboards and walls by applying masking tape to the wall surface before you start painting. If you are painting them before hanging wallcoverings, masking will not be necessary, however; simply take the paint onto the wall surface by about ½in (12mm) so that any uneven trimming of the wallcovering will not leave bare wall visible.

Use masking tape along the angle between baseboard and floor, too, if you have a hard floor covering like vinyl, cork or woodblock. With carpet, it is better to use a paint shield to hold the fibers away from the baseboard as you paint it. Move it along as you complete each section. Strips of thin cardboard tucked under the baseboard will serve just as well; leave it in position until you have finished, to stop the fibers from getting stuck to the wet paint.

Painting stripes

USE MASKING TAPE to help you achieve straight-edged bands of color. Stick it into position with one edge along the boundary line where one color will finish, then paint up to that line, allowing the paint to overlap onto the face of the tape. When the paint is dry, simply peel the tape off to leave a perfectly straight edge. When you want to butt a second color neatly up to the edge of the first, stick some tape along the edge of the area you have just painted, once it is hard-dry, and repeat the process. Always make sure the tape is pressed down well onto the surface it is masking, or paint will tend to creep under the edge; running over the tape with a seam roller before you start painting will help with this.

Painting window frames

WASH THE PAINTWORK thoroughly, scrubbing out any black mold around the edges with a small toothbrush, and apply a fungicide, or household bleach diluted 1:4 with water, to kill any remaining spores. Then sand the surface lightly with fine wet-and-dry abrasive paper, used wet, to provide a key for the new paint film. Wipe down the surfaces again to remove the paint slurry that results, rinse off with clean water and leave to dry. Finally, clean the windows; paint does not stick well to dirty glass.

Cut a strip of masking tape a fraction longer than the width of the pane, and stick it to the glass parallel with the top edge, 1/16 – ⅛in (2-3mm) from the angle. Press it down firmly by hand, and use a craft knife to cut the ends of the length so they finish ⅛in (3mm) in from the sides of the pane. Then peel back one end of the tape by about 1½in (40mm).

Apply the second length of tape to the side edge of the pane, overlapping it onto the stuck-down end of the first length. Press down and trim as before. Then apply the third length along the bottom edge of the pane, so one end overlaps the end of the second length; trim.

Finally, stick the fourth length in place, trim as before, and stick the peeled-back end of the first length over the stuck-down end of the final one. Applying the tape in this sequence makes it much easier to strip off after painting.

Painting casement windows

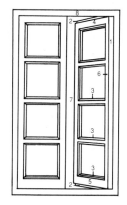

PAINT THE RABBETS FIRST, then the glazing bars and finally the frame. Start early in the morning so they are dry enough to close by night.

Painting sash windows

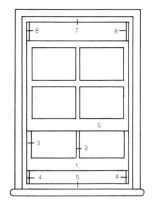

WITH THE OUTER SASH LOWERED, paint as much of it as possible, as well as the bottom edge of the inner sash and the top of the pulley stiles. When dry, raise the outer sash and lower the inner to paint the rest of the window. Avoid getting paint on the sash cords; if you do, they will stiffen and crack.

CHECK THAT ALL THE TAPE EDGES are firmly stuck to the glass; then start painting, using either a narrow 1in (25mm) ordinary brush or a cutting-in brush. Tackle each masked edge first, then paint the rest of the glazing bar or frame next to it, before moving on to the next section. Do not apply the paint too thickly or you will get unsightly runs. Follow the correct sequence for painting sash and casement windows, shown left.

Leave the paint until it is touch-dry, then use the tip of your craft knife to lift one corner of the square of masking tape carefully, so you do not mar the still-soft paint. Once you have raised it enough, take hold of it and peel the tape away by pulling the corner toward the center of the pane. As you reach the second and third corners, the overlaps you carefully formed earlier will lift the next length cleanly away; just reverse the direction of pull so you are always pulling the tape at an angle toward the center of the window pane.

Painting doors

IF YOU ARE PAINTING THE TWO sides of a door in different colors, you will be faced with two long edges where the color changes. The convention is to paint the opening edge of the door (the one nearest the handle) the same color as the door face that opens into the room, and the hinged edge to match the door's other face. This ensures that when the door is open, the visible edge and face match in each room.

Start by wedging the door open and removing the hardware. Then clean the existing paintwork as for windows – that is, wash down, sand lightly, rinse and allow to dry. There is no need to mask an external angle such as the edge of the door before you start painting; the sharp angle itself acts as a guide provided you apply the paint correctly.

Painting paneled doors

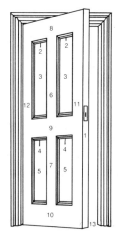

PAINT A PANELED DOOR and its frame in the sequence shown, using a 1in (25mm) brush for moldings and narrow edges and a 2in (50mm) brush for the rest.

PAINT ONE EDGE OF THE DOOR FIRST, then its matching face. Always draw the brush across the surface toward the edge, using very little pressure as the bristles reach it. Then allow them to run off the edge, and lay off the paint in the usual way, with a final light brush stroke parallel with the edge. If you draw a loaded brush across the corner, you will "scrape" a thick layer of paint off the bristles, and the result will be unsightly runs and a build-up of paint which may ultimately cause the door to bind in its frame.

Wait until the first color is touch-dry before painting the other face and edge. Keep pets and children away until the paint is dry. Then replace the door hardware, but leave the door ajar overnight so there is no risk of any tacky spots sticking to the frame. For paneled doors, follow the painting sequence shown left, following the grain of the wood.

TOOLS FOR STRAIGHT EDGES

❍ *A cutting-in brush is a slim paintbrush with the bristles cut across at an angle. You use it by drawing the edge of the brush with the longer bristles along an internal angle. However, it still relies on your having a steady hand to achieve good results.*

❍ *A paint shield is a metal or plastic plate which masks the surface you want to protect and gives a straight edge against which to paint. It takes practice to achieve good results, since it is all too easy to get paint on the edge or underside of the shield and smear it inadvertently on the wall. The shield is most useful for jobs like painting baseboards; it will hold the carpet away from the baseboards while you apply the paint.*

❍ *A special paint pad with guide wheels is designed for painting along internal angles. For straight edges, the surface the wheels run against must be true; if not, the paint line will follow its contours and may end up looking wavy.*

❍ *Masking tape, a paper tape with a low-tack adhesive on the back, is the most versatile assistant of all. Never leave the tape on too long, or try to remove it too soon: wait until the paint is touch-dry, then peel it off by pulling the tape away from the painted area in a continuous motion. If you need to mask over a freshly painted surface, leave it until it is hard-dry (overnight for gloss, four hours for latex) before applying the tape.*

ACCESS EQUIPMENT

PROPER ACCESS EQUIPMENT is essential for many decorating jobs since most accidents happen when people fall off something makeshift while trying to gain height. The equipment must be used properly, too; there are many other falls from ladders and steps that are incorrectly set up or used in a careless manner.

IT IS IMPORTANT TO SET YOURSELF UP WITH GOOD ACCESS WHEN PAINTING THE LONG DROP INVOLVED IN STAIRCASES AND HIGH CEILINGS. NARROW-BASE TOWERS ARE THE BEST SOLUTION FOR CONFINED AREAS SUCH AS A STAIRWELL. TO PAINT THE STAIR WALLS, YOU NEED STEPLADDERS WHICH CAN BE SET IN AN OFFSET MODE, WITH ONE FOOT SECURELY ON EACH STAIR.

STEPLADDERS

EVERYONE IS FAMILIAR WITH THE traditional wooden stepladder; its top platform falling into place as the ladder opens out is the perfect place to stand a paint can. You can still buy wooden steps, but their place has largely been taken by lightweight aluminum step-ladders, which need no maintenance – they will not rust or splinter as wood does. Most still have a folding top platform, and many also have a guardrail at the top so you can stand on the platform in relative safety. When choosing a stepladder, remember that wide treads are kinder to the feet than narrow ones.

COMBINATION STEPLADDERS

IF YOU NEED A STEPLADDER FOR everyday use and a short ladder only once in a while, consider a combination ladder. The basic design is a straight ladder which hinges to form a stepladder. Ingenious locks keep the structure rigid in whatever mode is selected; one that can be particularly useful is the offset mode, allowing the steps to be used safely on a staircase. Most combination ladders are aluminum, but you can also buy tubular steel models with wide wooden treads. Both will reach to about 10ft (3m) when used as a ladder.

TRESTLES AND STAGING

DECORATING FROM A STEPLADDER has drawbacks. Your reach is limited, so you have to keep climbing down and repositioning the steps with a paint can in one hand and a brush in the other. And even with wide treads, your feet begin to ache after a while. The alternative solution is to use a pair of traditional trestles with staging boards between them to provide a wide, level working platform. These look at first glance just like wide steps with widely-spaced treads, but the cross-rails are actually staggered on alternate sides of the trestle to allow the staging to be raised or lowered in around 10in (250mm) stages. They come in several sizes, but a pair about 6ft (1.8m) high will cope with all interior decorating, in conjunction with a length of 18in (460mm) wide staging. It will probably be best to rent trestles and staging boards when you need them, rather than buy your own and have to store them.

EXTENSION LADDERS

For easy access to heights above about 13ft (4m), there is really no substitute for the extension ladder. A two-part ladder will be adequate for most two-story houses, but there is much to be said for having a three-section ladder. It takes up less storage space, feels more rigid when extended than a two-section ladder and provides extra versatility, in the form of a short single ladder plus a two-section ladder, when the components are separated.

Traditional wooden extension ladders are still widely available, with either wooden or aluminum rungs, and have one major advantage over their all-aluminum relatives: your hands do not freeze when you climb them in cold weather. However, they tend to be heavier to carry around and to erect, and they must be stored under cover if they are to remain free of rot.

SCAFFOLDING

For decorating out of doors you may prefer using an access tower to a ladder. This structure slots together to provide a large, stable working platform at whatever level you need, with a safety handrail all around.

The basic component is an H-shaped frame made of galvanized steel or aluminum alloy; the components are slotted together in alternating parallel pairs until the required working height is reached. Diagonal braces stiffen the structure at intervals, while square feet spread the load at ground level. The feet can be adjusted to level the tower, and can be replaced by lockable castors to make a mobile tower. Platform boards and toe rails are fitted at the working level to complete the tower.

Most domestic scaffolding is about 4ft 3in (1.3m) square, and can be built up in increments of 2ft (0.6m) to a maximum height of 16ft (4.8m), which gives a working height of about 22ft (6.5m) from the platform – enough for most two-story homes. You can also get narrow-base towers measuring 4ft 3in x 2ft (1.3 x 0.6m) which are absolutely ideal for working in restricted spaces such as stairwells. It will generally be most economical to rent scaffolding as and when you need it.

EXTERIOR DECORATING

KEEPING THE EXTERIOR OF YOUR HOUSE or apartment looking fresh and in good condition is for most people a regular home maintenance project. It is also a job that can be a complete failure if not done properly and with the right materials. Before you get out your ladders and paintbrushes, it pays to do a brief survey of the various surfaces that make up the exterior of your house. There will be masonry and woodwork, some metal, perhaps even plastic, and each requires a different approach. What needs to be done will also depend on whether the surface has already been decorated, and if so, what condition it is in.

MASONRY

Brickwork If the walls of your house are of what is called fair-faced brickwork, count yourself lucky. They were built to show off the color and texture of the bricks, and do not need any decorating at all. In fact, painting brickwork is a bad idea; once done, it is extremely expensive and almost impossible to remove, and it ruins the character of the house. If the brickwork has become porous and protection against the elements is needed, other means of waterproofing are available, without changing its looks. And if the brickwork is just dirty, cleaning is infinitely preferable.

Of course, if your house has already been painted, you are stuck with it (unless you are prepared to go to the considerable expense of having it removed by sand-blasting) and you will simply have to repaint it from time to time to keep it looking good.

Stonework Some stone, like brickwork, should never be painted. However, in many areas, there is a strong tradition for painting stone buildings – either in white or with a color wash – while in industrial towns stonework was often painted to combat smoke and pollution. If your home has painted stonework, that is probably the way it is meant to look, and you can repaint it with a clear conscience.

Rendered walls The idea of covering brick and stone walls with a layer of rendering is nothing new – it has been done for centuries, for two main reasons. The first is to improve the weather resistance of the wall, especially where the local stone is porous and local bricks of poor quality. The second is to change the house's appearance, perhaps so far as to imitate other materials, as in rendering that is ruled off to resemble ashlar stonework, for example. Whatever the reason, rendering, with the exception of pebbledashing, was always intended to be painted.

MASONRY PAINT CAN BE APPLIED TO RENDERED WALLS BY BRUSH, ROLLER OR SPRAY GUN. IT IS AVAILABLE IN A MODEST CHOICE OF COLORS. WOODEN SHUTTERS WILL NEED PAINTING EVERY OTHER YEAR TO KEEP THEM LOOKING GOOD.

Pebbledash is the odd man out. It became popular during the building boom of the 1920s and 1930s, as an easy cover-up for the poor workmanship of unskilled bricklayers, and the intention was to let the colors of the pebbles provide the decoration. As time went by, however, the surface got drab and dirty, and people started painting it to cheer it up. Only recently pebbledashed walls should be left untreated.

Preparing masonry Whatever your walls are built from, you should approach the job of painting them in much the same way. The first thing to establish is how porous the surface is, by splashing some water on and seeing whether it runs off or soaks in. Next, see whether the surface is firm or dusty, by brushing your hand against it. Third, look for signs of mold growth – a green or black discoloration of the surface, most common on sheltered north-facing walls.

Start by tackling the mold, applying a fungicidal wash over the affected areas. This kills the spores and helps discourage others from growing. Use a branded product or household bleach diluted 1:3 with water.

If the surface seems porous, you need to seal the surface, using a multi-purpose primer on unpainted brick, stone, rendering and concrete. On new rendering, which is highly alkaline in nature, switch to an alkali-resistant primer. On previously painted surfaces, no primer is needed unless the old paint is unsound, when a multi-purpose primer should again be used.

If the wall is chalky to the touch, treat it with a stabilizing primer. This binds together the surface particles and provides a firm base for subsequent painting, besides reducing the porosity of the wall surface.

Painting masonry There are four choices when it comes to painting your walls – cement paint, exterior-grade latex, textured latex (all are water-based) or solvent-based masonry paint.

Cement paint is a powder which you mix with water and put on with a brush (which must be of synthetic fiber: cement ruins bristles) or a roller. It is cheap and reasonably durable, but can become chalky with age and comes in a limited range of pastel colors only. Use it if your walls have been cement-painted in the past, or you want a cheap cover-up for new rendering.

Exterior-grade latex paints, formulated for outdoor use, usually have a fungicide added to discourage mold growth. They will generally last between four and seven years, and their smooth surface tends to look brighter for longer than that of their textured cousins.

IT IS WORTH PAINTING A HOUSE WITH WOODEN FASCIAS OR BARGEBOARDS WITH MICROPOROUS PAINT SO THAT FUTURE REDECORATION CAN BE KEPT TO A MINIMUM. THESE PAINTS ALLOW WATER VAPOR TO EVAPORATE, AVOIDING CRACKING AND BLISTERING. PROVIDED TWO COATS ARE APPLIED TO BARE WOOD IN THE FIRST INSTANCE, THEY WILL LAST FOR FOUR TO FIVE YEARS BEFORE A FRESH TOPCOAT OF PAINT IS NEEDED.

Textured latex has added fillers – chopped fibers or mineral particles – which are intended to help the paint bridge hairline cracks. They are usually brushed or rolled on; you can spray them on with special equipment, but the fillers make it difficult to keep the gun's nozzle clear of blockages. Their life expectancy is similar to that of ordinary exterior latex, although the textured surface tends to harbor dirt more readily; the color range is more restricted, too.

Solvent-based masonry paint is a dying breed in the do-it-yourself paint market. The reasons are probably a combination of relatively high price, anxiety about the health risks of paint solvents, and the fact that the paint has to be cleaned from painting equipment with mineral spirits rather than water. However, the smooth eggshell surface texture is hardwearing, making it an ideal choice for houses in polluted areas as it holds dirt less readily than textured types.

Spray-painting rendered walls

IF YOUR HOUSE WALLS have a deeply textured rendered or pebbledashed finish, it can be very time-consuming brushing paint into the relief surface. Consider renting paint-spraying equipment so that you can spray the paint on instead. The time spent masking doors, windows and downspouts will be far outweighed by the time saved on the actual painting – and the finish will be more even, too.

WOODWORK

Almost every home has some exterior woodwork. Wooden windows and door frames are more common than any other type, and you are likely also to have wooden soffits, fascias and bargeboards along the roof edges. You may even have areas of wood cladding on part or all of your exterior walls. The way you decorate them is very much the same in every case.

Wood can be left bare but this is unusual except where durable woods such as oak or cedar have been used, since the wood will quickly rot. Exterior wood can be colored with special preservative stains, which leave the wood grain visible while keeping rot at bay. It can be given a traditional paint or varnish treatment, but both methods rely on forming a waterproof surface skin, which soon deteriorates and lets in water if it cracks, causing rot to develop. Finally, it can be treated with one of the "breathing" or microporous paints or varnishes, which allow water vapor to evaporate through the surface layer without causing the cracking common with traditional paints and varnishes.

Painting woodwork If you plan to use a traditional paint system on new exterior woodwork, treat any visible knots with a coat of knotting to stop resin from seeping out and marring the finish. Then apply a primer – either an ordinary wood primer or an acrylic primer on softwood, and an aluminum wood primer on hardwood – followed by one or two undercoats and one topcoat of gloss paint. With non-drip gloss paints, leave out the undercoats and apply two topcoats instead.

If you are repainting sound painted woodwork, simply apply one more topcoat over the existing surface after cleaning and sanding it lightly. Touch in any bare wood with primer first, and fill cracks and holes with a flexible exterior-grade putty.

Microporous paints avoid cracking and blistering, but must be applied to bare wood if they are to perform properly. However, once they have been applied, future redecoration chores are kept to a minimum. All that is needed is a wash and the application of a fresh coat of paint every four to five years. The usual system is two coats, applied directly to the wood, although some systems have a special basecoat which is applied first.

Varnishing woodwork The traditional equivalent of the three-layer paint system is three or four coats of varnish, with the first coat thinned on new wood. For exterior use, gloss varnish – either an alkyd or polyurethane type – should always be chosen for durability. However, varnishes suffer from the same problems as paint films, and transparent microporous versions have now been developed to overcome them. These work in the same way as microporous paints, with two coats being applied directly to the bare wood or over a basecoat, depending on the brand. Some are clear, others are pigmented to make your wood look like mahogany, teak or dark oak.

Staining wood Preservative stains are a less expensive alternative to microporous and traditional varnishes for exterior woodwork. They penetrate the wood to give protection against rot, coloring it in the process if they are pigmented, and contain water-repellent additives to keep water out. They are the ideal low-cost treatment for wooden cladding and outbuildings.

METALWORK

Modern homes have very little in the way of exterior metalwork; rainwater systems are now usually made of plastic, and any metal window frames are likely to be aluminum. However, in older homes galvanized steel windows and cast iron rainwater goods are fairly common, and both need painting to keep them in good condition. The enemy of both is rust, which will attack unpainted metal over time, as surely as rot will attack unprotected wood.

As with woodwork, there is both a traditional and a modern approach to painting metal. The traditional method is to apply primer, undercoat and topcoat, while the modern solution is a one-coat treatment that even kills rust. The secret of success with metal lies in choosing the right primer. Ideally, you need a calcium plumbate primer for iron and steel (including galvanized surfaces), and a zinc phosphate or zinc chromate primer for aluminum and other non-ferrous metals. However, there are now universal primers available which are formulated to cope with all surfaces, and have the advantage of being quicker-drying, too. The primer coat is followed by undercoats and a topcoat if you are using liquid gloss, or just two topcoats with non-drip gloss paint.

The one-coat treatment involves applying one thick coat of a specially formulated rust-inhibiting paint directly to the metal surface, where it neutralizes any existing rust and primes the surface. It can also be applied over existing paint, so future maintenance is greatly reduced.

RENOVATING EXTERIOR WOODWORK

Sand the old paintwork with wet-and-dry abrasive paper until it is smooth. Apply primer to any bare wood.

Scrape out any cracked and chipped old putty with a triangular scraper.

Apply new putty with a narrow scraper or a putty knife. Allow to dry out.

Protect the glass with masking tape. Take the paint over the putty and about ⅛in (3mm) onto the face of the glass.

SEE ALSO:

PAINTING EQUIPMENT	92
PREPARATION FOR PAINTING	94
ACCESS EQUIPMENT	100

SPECIAL PAINT EFFECTS

PAINT EFFECTS FALL INTO TWO CATEGORIES - broken color and imitation. In the first category, various techniques are used to apply a second color over a basecoat so the base color still shows through. In the second, paint is used to give a surface the appearance of another material, such as marble or exotic wood veneers. Experiment on some scrap material first to assess the finished result, and perhaps modify the depth of color or the strength of the applied effect.

THE OPULENCE OF THIS LIVING ROOM RELIES TO A LARGE EXTENT ON THE USE OF COLOR, A RICH RED, AND THE PAINT EFFECTS CREATED. MARBLED PANELS SUPERIMPOSED ON THE WALLS OF FLAT COLOR ARE USED TO DISPLAY PICTURES AND MIRRORS. THE DEEP MARBLED BASEBOARDS ARE BALANCED BY A HAND-PAINTED FRIEZE RUNNING AROUND THE TOP OF THE WALL.

Surface preparation

IF THE SURFACE IS NEW and has no finish on it, simply sand it down carefully. On walls, apply a diluted coat of latex paint to act as a primer, followed by a full-strength coat in your chosen base color. On wood, apply a wood primer and an undercoat, as if you were building up a traditional paint system. If the surface is already painted or varnished and the finish is sound, just sand it lightly to improve the adhesion of the paint and attend to any surface blemishes.

Mixing your own colors

IF YOU ARE UNABLE TO OBTAIN PAINT in a particular shade, mix your own by adding universal stainers or artist's oil or acrylic paint colors to ordinary white paint. Add the stainers little by little, mixing them thoroughly after each color addition. A paint paddle, driven by a variable-speed power drill, will ensure quick and even mixing.

Stippling

STIPPLING INVOLVES BRUSHING a second color out over the basecoat and then using a special brush to stipple this second coat, to allow the basecoat to show through. It works best with water-based latex paint. As the stippling brush creates the stippled effect by removing some of the topcoat, you need to brush this paint out onto some scrap paper as you work, to stop the paint you pick up from clogging the bristles.

APPLY THE BASECOAT TO THE SURFACE and allow it to dry thoroughly, then brush the topcoat over it. While this is wet, use the brush with a dabbing motion to stipple the surface of the wet film so the base color just shows through. Make sure the bristles hit the wall squarely to avoid smudging the effect. Work across the surface in bands, overlapping the blows slightly for an even finish.

Sponging

SPONGING INVOLVES APPLYING splodges of the second color over a plain basecoat to create a pleasing random color effect. You can add a third or fourth color to the surface if you wish, to give a more multicolored finish. Sponging is usually done by using latex paint on walls; on wood, it is best to use eggshell paint for the basecoat, thinned slightly for the topcoat. The only equipment needed is a bowl and a small piece of natural marine (not synthetic) sponge.

Apply the basecoat evenly to the surface, using a paintbrush, roller or pad, and let it dry thoroughly. Meanwhile, soak the sponge in water so it swells to its full size.

Pour some of your topcoat paint into the bowl, and thin it slightly with mineral spirits if using eggshell, or with water if you are working with latex. Use one part thinner to nine parts paint.

SQUEEZE THE SPONGE OUT WELL and dab it lightly into the thinned paint. Then test the effect you will get on the wall by dabbing the sponge onto some clean scrap paper (lining paper or the back of old wallpaper is ideal). Experiment with varying amounts of paint and different degrees of hand pressure until you get the result you want.

START SPONGING AT ONE EDGE of the area you are decorating and work over the whole surface, dabbing on paint lightly but evenly and refilling the sponge as necessary. If you do not achieve a completely even effect at the first attempt, let the paint dry, then sponge on some more paint over the "thin" areas. Do not try to add more paint over areas that are still wet; you will simply smudge the first coat and destroy the effect.

Rag-rolling

RAG-ROLLING MEANS EXACTLY what its name suggests – rolling a bunched-up rag back and forth over the wet topcoat to create a broken-color effect. It is best to use clean, lint-free cotton rags for this technique, cut into 12in (300mm) squares. Keep a good supply, since they soon get soaked in paint and become less effective at creating the pattern.

Soak the rags in mineral spirits before starting work, then squeeze them out well to help stop them from clogging with paint.

APPLY THE TOPCOAT TO AN AREA of the surface you are decorating, about 2ft (600mm) wide. Then bunch up the rag and dab it across the wet paint surface (or form it into a twisted sausage shape and use the palm of your hand to roll it across the surface to create a broad, blurry band). Keep changing direction and re-folding the rag as you work to ensure that your pattern is not too repetitive. Wipe your hands frequently on an old towel or fabric apron. Repeat the process for the next area, discarding the rags as they become saturated with paint.

Ragging-on

RAGGING-ON USES A SIMILAR technique to sponging, the difference being that a small piece of bunched-up cloth is used to apply the topcoat instead of a sponge. You can vary the effect by using different rag textures or altering the way you bunch up the rag which will affect the pattern you "print". Ragging gives a more definite pattern than sponging and can even create the look of damask. As with sponging, it is worth experimenting with some of these variations before starting decorating in earnest.

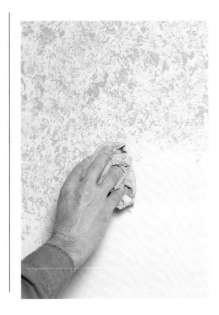

APPLY THE PLAIN BASECOAT AS FOR SPONGING. Dip your bunched-up rag into the topcoat paint and dab it onto the wall with a light touch. Do not try to put more paint onto areas that seem to have insufficient color. Let them dry before dabbing on more second color where it is needed to get an even overall effect. Thinning the topcoat will make the ragged-on color look less defined.

Frottage

THIS TECHNIQUE IS A DEVELOPMENT of ragging which produces a more unpredictable, irregular effect. Sheets of newspaper are placed flat against the surface of the wall while the topcoat is still wet and rubbed around with the palms of the hand. Where the topcoat of paint was applied most thickly, splodged effects will occur, and the basecoat color will show through irregularly over the whole surface, producing an effect rich in texture and variety. It works best with water-based paints; since newspaper is very absorbent, a lot of oil-based paint would be needed.

OTHER RAGGING IDEAS

○ *Ragging gives a good finish for large areas of wall such as halls and staircases. It is effective confined to softer colors, particularly when interesting pastels are ragged over an off-white ground such as a warm cream or a slightly greenish/grey "dirty" white. Darker, rich-looking colors such as deep ocher or terracotta will give a suggestion of sophistication and luxury.*

○ *Bag-graining is a variation on the ragging technique for creating a texture similar in appearance to a rag-rolled one. It is done by dabbing the wet topcoat with a plastic bag tightly packed with crumpled-up rags, so you can cover a larger area at one time.*

○ *Brush the well-thinned topcoat on over your basecoat, one area at a time. Then press the bag lightly onto the wet paint film, overlapping successive dabs slightly to create an even finish that allows the basecoat to show through. Wipe excess paint off the bag from time to time as you work.*

BRUSH ON THE TOPCOAT of paint quite liberally, one area at a time. While the paint is still wet, lay a sheet of newspaper against the surface and rub it around smoothly, varying the pressure from your hands.

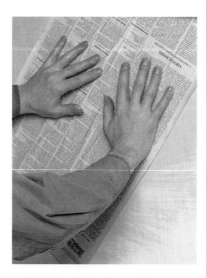

PEEL THE NEWSPAPER OFF THE WALL gently. Any unsuccessful patches can be touched in and rubbed again. Use a fresh sheet of newspaper for each section of wall.

Colorwashing

THIS IS A LOOSE, FLEXIBLE TECHNIQUE which gives a subtle, dappled watery effect, with a varying intensity of luminous color. It is a good finish for walls that are in a poor condition, merging in any imperfections so they become a part of the finished effect. It is delicate enough to make a suitable background for stenciling or other additional decoration.

The colorwash can be an oil glaze, tinted with universal stainers or artist's oil colors, and thinned to a watery consistency with mineral spirits, used over a base color of eggshell (a matte oil-based paint). Or you can use thinned latex paint over a latex basecoat; it is usual to thin down the colorwash about 1:9 with water, to give the right translucent consistency.

After applying the basecoat and leaving it to dry, cover the floor with a waterproof sheet, as some of the thinned colorwash will inevitably run down the walls.

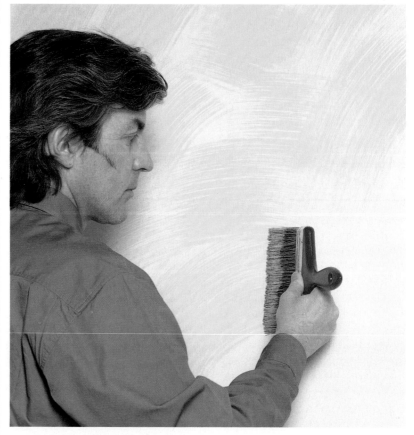

APPLY THE THINNED COAT OF LATEX or tinted glaze to the wall, using a wide, soft paintbrush. Brush it out loosely and irregularly in a crosswise direction; this will counteract the tendency of the thin colorwash to run down the walls. Avoid heavy brushmarks and hard edges, and leave a proportion of the basecoat uncovered.

LEAVE THIS COAT TO DRY overnight, then repeat the process, brushing over most of the bare patches and some of the first coat of color with the next coat. The wall will probably look a mess after the first coat, but the second gives the color a luminous quality, making the walls come alive.

Dragging

THIS EFFECT INVOLVES DRAGGING the bristles of a dry, long-bristled paintbrush over the wet topcoat to produce regular, parallel lines of the second color on the surface of the basecoat. If ordinary paint is used for the topcoat, the brushing action merely spreads it out as if you were trying to apply an even coat of paint, so you need a special product called scumble glaze (see page 91). This is a transparent or white medium which you color with paint stainers or artist's oil paints to achieve the color you want. Scumble glaze is very slow drying and remains in the raised lines formed by the dry brush strokes. You need a steady hand and a light touch to get good, uniform results.

THIN THE GLAZE with an equal amount of mineral spirits in a paint bucket. Mix a small quantity of paint stainer or artist's oil paint with a little glaze and add this to the thinned scumble in your bucket, stirring it in thoroughly. Test the color, and add a little more stainer if necessary to get the shade you want for the topcoat.

WHEN YOU ARE HAPPY with the color, use a paintbrush to apply the glaze over your basecoat, working parallel to the direction in which you will apply the dragging strokes.

WITH YOUR DRY DRAGGING BRUSH, create a series of parallel lines in the topcoat. Wipe the brush regularly with a dry cloth to stop it from becoming clogged with paint as you work.

PAINT EFFECT TIPS

○ *If you are a beginner, keep the topcoat (of any broken color effect) close in tone and color to that of the basecoat. Any mistakes, smudges and areas of uneven coverage will then be less apparent.*

○ *It saves time and money if you can work with an existing background: if your walls are a boring neutral shade or an unattractively vivid tone, modify them with a quick colorwash. You could tone down a too-bright yellow, for example, with loosely applied strokes of a very dilute red or white. Thin water-based paint with water and oil-based paints with mineral spirits until they are a thin, creamy consistency.*

○ *Gouache, a water-based pigment, comes in a range of strong pastel colors and mixes easily with latex, giving greater opacity than ordinary watercolors. It is perfect for colorwashing when the paint is thinned with water.*

○ *If you want to give your walls the patina associated with age, make a virtue of any imperfections: do not fill all the cracks and blemishes before applying paint. Wash them with several related earth tones for a finish of character and depth.*

○ *Try vinegar-graining wooden shelves or cheap knock-down furniture for a more sophisticated look. Paint the surface with a coat of flat latex paint and leave to dry. Mix 2 tablespoons of white vinegar with half a teaspoon of sugar and add powdered color until the glaze runs freely. Brush this on to the surface, then distress it with a rolled-out piece of modeling clay or putty. Vary the direction to change the pattern; wipe off excess from time to time with paper towels.*

Graining

THIS TECHNIQUE is used to make bland, pale woods look like more exotic hardwoods, and was very popular from Victorian times into the 1930s. It is a technique where practice makes perfect, and it is extremely rewarding to master. As with dragging, you will get the best results by using scumble glaze rather than paint or stains.

Start by applying a basecoat of eggshell paint to the surface and let this dry. The color depends on the type of wood you are imitating: use a pale yellow for light oak, a deep red-brown for mahogany.

COLOR YOUR SCUMBLE to a darker shade with stainers or artist's oil paints, and brush it on, dragging the brush down the surface to form broad stripes. You can then soften these by drawing a dry, soft-bristled brush along the grain lines.

ON LIGHT BACKGROUNDS, an alternative to this technique is to grain the wood overall, then to wipe off the scumble where you want the area of heart-graining to be and to paint in the heart grain using a fine artist's paintbrush. Use ragged strokes to imitate natural grain patterns, and again soften the effect with a dry brush. Add knots if you want them by applying a little scumble to the end of your finger and "twisting" it onto the wood surface. Finish off by applying two coats of clear varnish over the graining to seal in the color.

As an alternative to using brushes to create the grain effect, you can buy special graining tools which do the job more quickly and easily. Apply the glaze as before, then pull the tool through the glaze to form the desired grain pattern. To create a heart grain effect, start with the tool on its far edge and roll it onto the edge closest to you as you draw it across the surface. Use the comb side of the tool to create areas of straight graining.

Marbling

THE SIMPLEST METHOD for creating a realistic marble effect on furniture, fireplaces and other surfaces is known as splatter-effect marbling. The tinted glaze for the marble colors should be made up from 1 part linseed oil, 3 parts mineral spirits, a drop of liquid driers, and whatever color artist's oil paint you choose.

APPLY THE BASECOAT in a fairly neutral tone, then roughly brush on the first marble color, using a small paintbrush; aim to leave areas of the basecoat showing through.

REPEAT THE PROCESS with the second marbling color, which is usually a slightly darker shade of the first one, again using random brush strokes to build up an authentic pattern.

SOFTEN THE OUTLINE OF THE BRUSH strokes by dabbing the wet paint film with a bunched-up rag or piece of natural sponge. Then "spatter" on a third (and even a fourth) color from a small artist's brush, by drawing a finger across the lightly loaded bristles to flick speckles of paint onto the surface.

FINALLY, SPLATTER ON UNDILUTED mineral spirits to open up patches of the base color and create an overall random "splotched" effect. Then add veins in white, using a very fine brush rolled over the surface of the wet glaze.

FINISH OFF BY DABBING the surface with a piece of natural sponge moistened with mineral spirits, to blur the outlines of the color and soften the overall appearance. Protect the surface with two coats of clear varnish once it has dried.

A SUBTLE COMBINATION OF COLORS PRODUCES A NATURAL-LOOKING MARBLE EFFECT IN A COOL HALL. THE MARBLING IS TAKEN OVER THE BASEBOARD AND A DADO "RAIL" CREATED USING A DARKER SHADE OF PAINT.

STENCILING

STENCILING DIFFERS FROM OTHER SPECIAL PAINT EFFECTS in that it produces a specific repeated design rather than a random one. The paint is applied to the wall through the cut-out portions of a mask called a stencil, using a special stenciling brush. A wide range of pre-cut stencils is available from decorating suppliers and craft shops, or you can make your own from stencil blanks using a craft knife or sharp scalpel on a cutting board to cut out the design.

SCALLOP SHELLS, WITH THEIR SEGMENTED STRUCTURE, MAKE AN IDEAL STENCIL MOTIF FOR THIS DADO-LEVEL FRIEZE. THEY HAVE BEEN SPRAYED ON FOR A SMOOTH, EVEN FINISH, THE COLOR DEEPENING AT THE TOP, TO MATCH THE ELEGANCE OF THIS STYLISH BATHROOM.

Cutting stencils

If you cannot find any ready-made stencils you like, or you want to copy a unique motif from a tile or a furnishing fabric used in the room, you can cut your own stencils instead. For this, you will have to buy special stiff oiled stencil board from a craft shop; you will also need some tracing paper for transferring your motif to the stencil, as well as some carbon paper and a sharp craft knife.

Start by tracing the motif. Then tape the tracing paper to the stencil board with a sheet of carbon paper in between, and draw over the tracing with a ballpoint pen. Then break down your finished stencil design to incorporate bridges, the uncut areas linking the open areas, to prevent the stencil from collapsing; make sure your design has enough bridges to hold it together. (A broken bridge can always be repaired by using masking tape on each side.)

Transfer the stencil to a cutting board and carefully cut out the design using a scalpel or craft knife. Always cut towards you; at corners, turn the stencil, not the knife. Do not necessarily attempt to cut out every smallest element of the design and cut out small areas before larger ones, or you will weaken the stencil and make it difficult to use. You can always touch in small details freehand with an artist's paintbrush once the basic stenciling is complete.

If your stencil design involves more than one color, cut separate stencil cards for each color; make sure they will line up by laying them over each other and punching through with a nail to give registration marks at each corner.

An alternative to stencil board is to use transparent acetate, which makes registration marks unnecessary; simply line it up with the previous design. Acetate lasts longer and wipes clean, but is more expensive and can be fiddly to use.

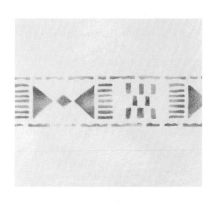

Stenciling a border

Apply the base color to the surface you are decorating and allow it to dry, then pour some paint – latex is ideal – onto a flat board and dip the tips of the brush bristles into it. Then dab the brush on scrap paper to remove any excess paint, to ensure that it will apply the color evenly.

Hold the stencil flat against the wall or anchor it in place with masking tape. Dab paint into the cut-out portions with the brush held at right angles to the surface. Paint the edges of each area first, then fill in the middle. Reload the brush as necessary to achieve the depth of color you want.

PEEL AWAY THE STENCIL carefully and wipe off any paint that has seeped onto the reverse side of it. For a repeat motif, reposition the stencil and paint through it again.

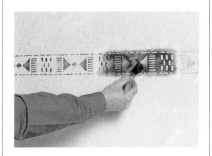

CLEAN ANY PAINT OFF the front of the stencil once the design is completed.

Stenciling wooden floors

Give a stripped softwood floor an individual touch by stenciling a pattern on it. Seal the floor surface first with clear varnish, then stencil on your chosen design, using the same basic technique as for stenciling walls. You can use paint or, for a softer effect which allows the grain of the wood to show through, use colored wood stains. Finish by applying an extra coat of sealer over the stenciled design.

STENCILING IDEAS

❍ *Stenciled borders or friezes can stand in for architectural detail where this is absent. Position them where natural breaks occur: between ceiling and wall, at picture-rail height, at dado height or at baseboard level.*

❍ *A frieze of stenciled motifs along the top of a wall can bring decoration to a room lacking a cornice; one at the bottom can compensate for the absence of a baseboard.*

❍ *A dado created by stenciling a pattern around the walls, one-third of the way up from the floor, will visually balance the expanse of wall above it.*

❍ *Stenciled features can be used to liven up drawer fronts, cupboard doors, chair backs and headboards. Traditional folk-inspired motifs include flowers, hearts and stars as well as naive animals and birds.*

❍ *Suitable stencil themes for more classical rooms include wreaths, scrolls and traditional fleur-de-lys.*

❍ *A wide range of paints can be used for stenciling. Acrylic (water-based) or Japan (oil-based) paints are fast-drying and can be used for woodwork or furniture. Use latex paint for walls.*

❍ *Spray painting (using a can of car paint) is a faster alternative but does not have the hand-painted effect achieved with a brush.*

PAINTING FURNITURE

A PAINTED FINISH IS AN EXCELLENT WAY OF COVERING UP THE WEAR AND TEAR suffered by everyday furniture and of giving old or second-hand pieces a new lease of life. Larger pieces of furniture, such as blanket chests, are sometimes decoratively painted with motifs inspired by traditional folk art. Hand painting a particular motif or theme on to a child's chair, applying a stenciled design to the front of kitchen cupboards, or using one of the many suitable paint effects, such as marbling, dragging or wood graining, on a chest of drawers, can give freestanding or built-in furniture a unique look.

A CUSTOMIZED "HIPPO" CHEST IN A CHILD'S ROOM HAS BEEN PAINTED TO MATCH THE SPIRIT OF THE WOODPECKER MURAL BEHIND IT. AFTER PREPARING THE WOOD, THE DESIGN CAN BE PAINTED FREEHAND USING EITHER ACRYLIC PAINTS OR ORDINARY LATEX PAINT AND THEN FINISHED WITH TWO COATS OF MATTE VARNISH.

Preparation

If you are planning to repaint furniture that already has a painted finish, treat it in the same way as you would any other woodwork in the house (see page 94) in terms of preparation. Inspect the condition of the existing paint, looking for chips and other blemishes. If the surface is basically sound, it will need nothing more than a good wash to remove dirt and grease, a light sanding with wet-and-dry abrasive paper to key the paint surface, and possibly some local filling in places, to make it ready for a fresh coat of paint. But if the existing paintwork is in poor condition – extensively chipped, and possibly worn through to bare wood in places – it will be better to strip off the old paint using a paint stripper or a hot air gun and start again.

Wood with a varnished finish can be treated in the same way as painted furniture, but check first whether a wax finish has been applied over the varnish, by seeing if you can scrape the polish off with a fingernail. If wax has been applied, you will need to strip it off with fine steel wool dipped in

(see page 94)

Antique paint finishes

Giving furniture an antique appearance with paints and stains is part of the furniture finisher's skills. Two popular techniques are liming (best used on open-grained woods such as oak) and pickling (used on pine).

LIMING involves brushing a runny mixture of slaked garden lime and water on to bare wood, after opening up the grain with a wire brush. Leave it to dry, then sand the surface and finish it with a matte varnish or French polish.

PICKLING involves brushing nitric acid (available from a pharmacy: use diluted with 8 parts water) on to the bare wood and leaving it to dry, then treating the wood with a dilute solution of bichromate of potash, finishing with light sanding.

mineral spirits, wiping it down with a clean spirit-soaked cloth. You can then paint directly over the stripped and keyed varnish.

Applying the paint

Remove all decorative hardware such as door or drawer handles before you start, and always try to work in a dust-free environment. If possible, raise the piece of furniture above your work surface by driving nails or screws into the underside, so that you can paint the legs and side panels right down to ground level. Always take special care not to allow paint to build up on edges or within moldings as you work: bear in mind that two thin coats will look much better and give a tougher finish than one thick coat.

The best paint to use on pieces of furniture is a flat, oil-based paint: tinting a flat white to the shade required using artist's oil colors will give the most subtle effect. Being soft-textured, it will need several coats of matte varnish to make it durable in use. Rub down lightly with fine sandpaper in between coats of varnish.

Alternatively, use latex or acrylic paint: these are faster drying. Flat latex paint is the most suitable for a simple, rustic overall finish, and acrylic paint for any decorative painting on top. Cover this with two coats of clear matte varnish to retain the non-shiny finish. A glossy finish usually looks inappropriate, especially on old pieces of furniture.

Cheap cover-up

PHOTOCOPIED SHEETS OF NEWSPAPER or music – or even comics, menus, old deeds, playbills or graphic motifs – can be used to create all-over decoration for furniture or walls. They can be enlarged or reduced to make a more abstract design. Do not use actual sheets of newspaper as they are too absorbent. Apply *wallpaper paste to each sheet, glue it in position and brush out any air bubbles with a sponge or paintbrush. When dry, apply a thin coat of water-based varnish. If you want an antique appearance, use tinted varnish and put it on unevenly with a medium-sized brush. Apply a second coat when the first is dry if the result is too light.*

SEE ALSO:

PAINTING EQUIPMENT	92
PREPARATION FOR PAINTING	94
UNDERSTANDING COLOR	84

STYLING IDEAS

❍ *To get inspiration for painted furniture, look at the colors and patterns on old English cottage furniture, which was often painted chalky blue or bottle green. For a more folk-art idiom, look at the rich reds and greens of Scandinavian furniture, the bold stenciled designs of American country furniture, or the vivid cobalt and turquoise blues of Mediterranean-style furniture and furnishings.*

❍ *Aged or distressed finishes are softer than sparkling fresh paint and go better with certain styles of room scheme. Experiment with layers of different washes or glazes to build up the richness and depth of color which are associated with the mellowed appearance time bestows on furniture.*

❍ *Most modern furniture painters now use water-based latex instead of oil-based gloss or eggshell paints for an all-over painted surface. It is easy to use, fast drying, covers well and provides a good surface for subsequent decoration. Its final appearance is closer to the matte look of old painted pieces.*

❍ *For instant decoration, "gilding" can be drawn in using metallic felt-tip pens.*

TYPES OF WALLCOVERING

THERE IS MORE TO CHOOSING WALLCOVERINGS than meets the eye. Whether you want a wallpaper with an attractive pattern, one that will hide the lumps and bumps on your walls or bring your room a touch of something exotic, you have many different products to choose from. This section explains them all and tells you the best way of hanging each type. Wallcoverings come in rolls of varying lengths and widths; buy all rolls from the same batch to ensure that colors match.

WALLPAPERS

All wallpaper has a printed color on the surface, which may be flat or embossed. It is available in several weights and a huge choice of designs, including paint-effect look-alikes. Wallpaper is the least expensive type of patterned wallcovering, except when hand-printed. However, it is not washable or stain-resistant, so should not be used in areas subject to heavy wear or to moisture. Hang it with an ordinary paste, mixed to a consistency to match the weight of the paper .

Washable wallpaper (**15**) This has a transparent protective plastic film on the surface, which makes it resistant to stains and relatively easy to wash if marked. Some types are ready-pasted; otherwise, hang it with a medium-duty paste containing a fungicide.

Hand-printed wallpapers (**13**) These are printed by hand rather than machine, making them considerably more expensive. Designs are applied either by block printing or screen printing, and the end result has a delicacy ordinary printing can seldom match. They are generally available only from specialist suppliers, and the edges may have to be trimmed before hanging. Leave hanging to a professional, so he or she can pay for any mistakes!

Lining paper (**14**) This plain, porous wallpaper is used to provide a smooth surface of uniform porosity on walls and ceilings, ready for subsequent paperhanging. It can be overpainted, but ordinary lining paper produces a rather hairy surface finish. However, there is a special extra-white grade intended to be used when a smooth painted finish is required and the wall surface is not good enough for direct painting. Hang lining paper with an ordinary paste, and leave it to dry out for 48 hours before overpainting it.

Ready-pasted wallcoverings These have a coating of dried crystalline paste on the back which is activated by water, avoiding the messy and time-consuming process of brushing on liquid paste. Their main disadvantage is that the thin coating of paste can dry out too soon when hanging lengths which involve a lot of fiddly cutting. Most ready-pasted wallcoverings are washables or vinyls.

Hang them by immersing the cut length in a trough of cold water placed against the baseboard next to the hanging position. Roll the length up loosely, top outermost, so you can draw it out of the trough and place it straight onto the wall, allowing surface water to run back into the trough.

Vinyl wallcoverings (**9**) These hardwearing wallcoverings consist of a layer of polyvinyl chloride (vinyl) onto which the printed design is fused, and a paper backing that is pasted in the usual way (unless it is a ready-pasted type). The vinyl surface can be cleaned vigorously to remove stains and marks without fear of damaging the pattern. They are easy to strip, since the vinyl layer can simply be peeled off dry from the paper backing.

Vinyl wallcoverings can be hung with either a medium or heavy-duty paste containing a fungicide. Any unavoidable overlaps can simply be stuck down with special overlap adhesive.

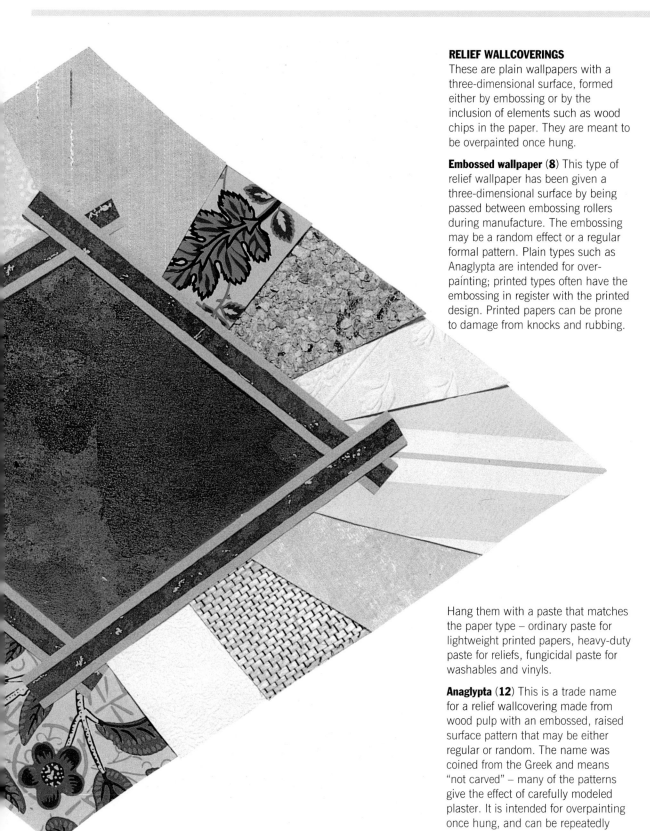

RELIEF WALLCOVERINGS

These are plain wallpapers with a three-dimensional surface, formed either by embossing or by the inclusion of elements such as wood chips in the paper. They are meant to be overpainted once hung.

Embossed wallpaper (8) This type of relief wallpaper has been given a three-dimensional surface by being passed between embossing rollers during manufacture. The embossing may be a random effect or a regular formal pattern. Plain types such as Anaglypta are intended for over-painting; printed types often have the embossing in register with the printed design. Printed papers can be prone to damage from knocks and rubbing.

Hang them with a paste that matches the paper type – ordinary paste for lightweight printed papers, heavy-duty paste for reliefs, fungicidal paste for washables and vinyls.

Anaglypta (12) This is a trade name for a relief wallcovering made from wood pulp with an embossed, raised surface pattern that may be either regular or random. The name was coined from the Greek and means "not carved" – many of the patterns give the effect of carefully modeled plaster. It is intended for overpainting once hung, and can be repeatedly redecorated by painting it with latex paint. It is particularly good at hiding cracks and uneven surfaces, and is therefore used on ceilings as well as on walls.

Hang it with a heavy-duty paste, allowing each length to soak for a while (check the precise time with the instructions) to eliminate bubbling and pattern-matching difficulties during hanging. Take care not to flatten the embossing as you handle each length and brush it into place; avoid seam rollers at all costs. Allow the paste to dry for 48 hours before overpainting.

One version of Anaglypta is made from cotton fibers rather than wood pulp, so it is much stronger and can carry more pronounced embossing. Anaglypta is also available with a solid vinyl surface layer which carries the relief pattern, and is paper-backed for ease of hanging and stripping. It is therefore less prone to surface damage than its embossed relatives. Hang vinyl Anaglypta with a heavy-duty paste containing a fungicide.

Lincrusta (3) This relief wallcovering is made from a mixture of linseed oil and fillers, hardened rather like putty and formed into a thin sheet material. It is available in a range of embossed decorative effects unmatched by other relief wallcoverings. It is generally overpainted with gloss or eggshell paint and can also be given a variety of interesting broken paint finishes. It is a hardwearing wallcovering, but is not easy to remove once hung. It may have to be ordered from a specialist.

Hang it with special Lincrusta adhesive, after soaking the back of each length with warm water. Rub lengths down into place with a felt roller, and trim edges and seams with a sharp knife and a straight edge.

Woodchip wallpaper This thick, pulpy wallpaper contains small chips of wood which give it a surface texture resembling coarse oatmeal. Several grades are available, ranging from fine to coarse in texture. It hides cracks and other surface blemishes and is meant to be overpainted once hung. Hang it with a heavy-duty paste, and allow it to dry for 48 hours.

FABRIC WALLCOVERINGS

These are made by bonding plain or patterned fabrics to a paper backing for ease of hanging. Burlap is the most common and the cheapest type (see below), but a number of more expensive fabrics, such as silk **(5)**, linen and felt, are available. Except for burlap, most are too expensive to use for anything other than small areas. They have to be edge-trimmed after hanging, and need to be handled carefully. They come in a range of widths, and are sold by length.

Hang them with a stiff ready-mixed tub paste, keeping this off the face of the wallcovering. If you have to overlap and trim joints, place a narrow length of lining paper beneath the overlap to keep paste off the surface of the length just hung, and cut through all three layers with a sharp knife and straight edge. Then remove the lining paper and the trimmings and brush the seams down carefully.

Burlap (10) This coarse fabric wallcovering is usually sold paper-backed. A natural oatmeal color is widely available, but it also comes in a range of dyed shades. These may fade in sunny rooms, however, and it is important to check for any shade variations between rolls before hanging begins. Burlap is usually sold in complete rolls or by length; check the roll length if you want large quantities. Hang burlap with an ordinary heavy-duty paste. If the roll edges are ragged, overlap adjoining lengths slightly and trim through the overlap (see above).

Cork (2) This exotic (and expensive) wallcovering is made by bonding thin veneers of cork to a paper backing; the cork may be stained or overprinted. Being rather fragile, it is best restricted to display areas. It is usually bought by length. Hang it with

a special tub paste, taking care not to get any of the paste on the face of your wallcovering.

Grasscloth (11) This luxury wallcovering consists of strands of dried natural grasses bonded to a paper backing. It is expensive and very fragile so is best restricted to display areas. It is sold by length, usually from rolls 915mm (3ft) wide. Hang it with a ready-mixed tub paste. Handle it carefully as you brush each length into place: use the brush with vertical downward strokes only, to avoid loosening any strands.

Flock wallcoverings (16) These have a surface pattern consisting of areas of raised-pile wool, silk or synthetic fibers which have been bonded to the paper backing. Ordinary flock wallcoverings are expensive and extremely delicate, but modern vinyl flocks have the pile areas fused into the vinyl surface and are tough enough to withstand regular washing. Hang ordinary flocks with a heavy-duty paste and vinyl flocks with a stiff paste containing a fungicide; always keep your paperhanging brush scrupulously clean.

Foil wallcoverings (center) These consist of a metallized plastic film on a paper backing; they are often over-printed with patterns. The surface is resistant to moisture, though it is generally less hardwearing than a vinyl wallcovering. Since some foils conduct electricity, the wallcovering should be hung with care behind light switches and electrical outlets. Hang foils with a paste containing a fungicide.

Within the many different categories of wallcovering that now exist (shown and described on the previous pages), there is a wide range of exciting designs and textures available, some of which are shown on the left. The scale of the pattern on printed wallpapers varies significantly and should generally be in keeping with the proportions of the room in which the paper is used. The depth of pattern repeat is something to be borne in mind when calculating the quantities required (see page 125).

Left-hand column, from top:
Metal effect mesh vinyl, made of vinyl and with a rubbery texture; suede-effect wallcovering; anodized copper-effect wallpaper; foliage and trellis design; large-scale printed wallpaper with leaf design.

Middle column:
Paisley-design miniprint; distressed effect wallpaper; classic stripes; muted trellis-design miniprint; traditional chintz design.

Right-hand column:
Copy of an original 18th-century English wallpaper; modern design inspired by chinoiserie; repeating stars motif; design inspired by toile de Jouy, a fabric popular in France in the 18th century; small repeating acorn motif.

Edged border based on twisted ribbon design.

WALLPAPER PASTES

Wallpaper paste combines immediate adhesion with good "slip", allowing the length of wallpaper to be moved slightly for alignment and any pattern matching. Most are either starch or cellulose-based and they come in powder or ready-mixed form. Packet pastes are sold in quantities that will hang a stated number of standard-sized rolls. As a rough guide, 1 quart (litre) of paste will cover between one and a half and two rolls. Ready-mixed pastes come in 1- or 2-quart (litre) tubs.

Lightweight pastes will hang most plain papers, but heavier-duty types are necessary for thicker relief or embossed papers. Paste containing a fungicide must be used with all washable and vinyl wallcoverings. Ready-mixed tub pastes are recommended for most fabric wallcoverings. Pastes can also be used to "size" freshly plastered walls. They are made up into a thinner paste for this purpose; the correct dilution is given on the packet.

PAPERHANGING TOOLS

THE TOOLS AND EQUIPMENT YOU WILL NEED FOR HANGING WALLCOVERINGS are few and inexpensive, but they will greatly facilitate what can otherwise be a tricky operation. You can always improvise some items: a pasting bucket and brush need not be bought specially; a clean household bucket and an old paintbrush will suffice. But a paperhanging brush and long-handled scissors are indispensable. A pasting table can be any surface that is long enough and sufficiently steady, but in fact the purpose-made pasting tables are both economical to buy and, being of the folding type, take up very little space when not in use. Small, specialist tools such as a plumb bob and line and a seam roller are invaluable for helping you to achieve a professional-looking result.

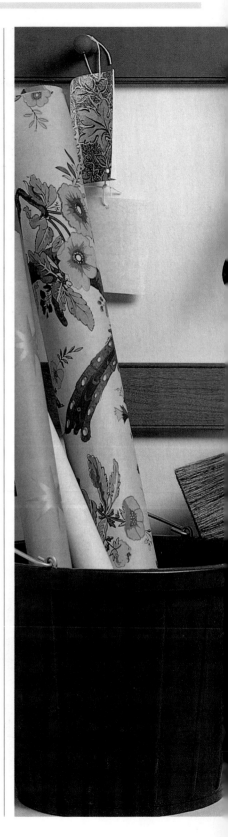

ON THE TABLE:

A pasting table is a lightweight folding table used to support cut lengths of wallcovering while they are being pasted. The top is in two halves, hinged along the center line. It measures 6ft (1.8m) long when open, and is 22in (560mm) wide – just wider than most rolls of wallpaper.

A pasting bucket is wider than a normal bucket and made of heavy-duty plastic. Tie a length of string across the bucket between the handle anchors to act as a brush rest and a scraper for removing excess paste from the pasting brush.

A pencil and tape measure are needed for measuring and marking lengths of wallcovering prior to pasting and hanging them. A tape measure that can be locked in the extended position when measuring lengths is ideal.

A chalk line is useful for marking guidelines on walls and ceilings. The small drum contains a length of fine thread and a reservoir of colored chalk. As the line is drawn out, it is coated with chalk; you hook the free end over a pin at one end of the line you wish to mark, draw the thread taut at the other end, and then use

your free hand to pull the thread away from the surface slightly. When you release it, it snaps back and leaves a neat, straight chalked line. A side handle is used to re-wind the thread.

A carpenter's level is used to check that friezes and borders are straight.

A steam stripper is an electrically-powered machine designed to speed up the stripping of wallcoverings that are difficult to strip by conventional means – notably washable papers and relief and other types that have been overpainted. It consists of a boiler, a connecting hose and a steaming plate with a handle attached. When the water is heated to boiling point, the steam passes up the hose to emerge through dozens of tiny holes in the underside of the steaming plate. The plate is pressed against the wallpaper, forcing the steam into it and softening the paste behind, allowing it to be stripped off readily. Once one area has been steamed, the plate is moved to an adjacent section while the first is being scraped.

Steam strippers are expensive and are generally rented rather than bought. An alternative for small-scale use is this miniaturized version that closely resembles a steam iron.

FIRST ROW OF HOOKS:

A paperhanging brush is a wide, long-bristled brush with a short, stubby handle, used to smooth wallcoverings onto the wall surface as they are being hung. Common widths range from 7in (190mm) up to 10in (250mm).There are two main reasons for using a brush: it follows the contours of the surface with ease, ensuring a good bond, and it eliminates any hand contact with the wallpaper, which could transfer paste from the back of the paper, staining it. It is vital that the brush is kept dry in use; if any paste is picked up by the bristles, they should be washed and dried immediately.

A stripping knife is used to strip old wallcoverings from the surface of walls and ceilings. It resembles a filling knife in shape and size, but has a much stiffer blade. Stripping knives have blade widths ranging from about 1in (25mm) up to 6in (150mm).

A seam roller is a small hardwood or plastic wheel about 1in (25mm) wide, running on an axle attached to a handle. It is used when hanging smooth wallcoverings to ensure that the seams between lengths are thoroughly stuck down.

TOP ROW OF HOOKS:

Paperhanging scissors are long-bladed scissors, used both for cutting lengths of wallcovering before pasting and for trimming the top and bottom of each length once hung. The curved tips of the blades are also used to press the ends of the length into the angle between wall and ceiling, baseboard or door frame, so marking the cutting line. The long blades make it easier to achieve a straight cut; sizes range up to 12in (300mm) overall.

A serrated scraper is a stripping knife with small teeth along the end of the steel blade. It is used to break up the surface of washable or painted wallpapers during stripping: the teeth score the water-repellant coating or the paint film, allowing water to penetrate and soften the paste behind.

A plumb bob and line is a device used to make sure that lengths of wallcovering are hung to a true vertical. The plumb bob itself is a cylindrical weight, usually made of brass, to which a length of string is attached. To use it, the end of the string is pinned to the wall surface at ceiling level, and the bob is allowed to hang to just above floor level. When the bob comes to rest, the string line marks a true vertical. A pencil and straight edge are then used to draw a visible guideline on the wall, following the plumb line.

A pasting brush is very similar to an ordinary 4in (100mm) wide paintbrush. It is used to apply paste evenly from the bucket to the cut lengths of wallpaper.

WALL PREPARATION

MODERN WALLCOVERINGS ARE VERY GOOD AT THEIR JOB, provided the surface to which they are applied is sound. What you need to do depends on the present state of your wall surfaces. You may, for example, be faced with decorating bare walls in a new house or in a recently completed home extension. You may also reveal bare plaster by stripping off existing decorations. Plaster or plasterboard that has been painted with latex or gloss paint needs very little preparation and offers a perfect surface for any type of wallcovering. Beware of old distemper, however, which you may find beneath old wallcoverings: it is very difficult to decorate over successfully. Old wallpaper must always be stripped off; you simply cannot trust it to stay put underneath new wallcoverings. This tedious job can be dramatically speeded up with a steam stripper, which you can rent, but great care must be taken in using it.

A LITTLE TIME SPENT PREPARING THE WALL SURFACE WILL BE MORE THAN REPAID IN TERMS OF A BETTER-LOOKING AND LONGER-LASTING PAPERED FINISH. VERTICAL STRIPES HELP TO GIVE THE ILLUSION OF GREATER HEIGHT IN A LOW-CEILINGED ROOM.

Treating bare plaster

NEW PLASTER NEEDS TIME to dry out, so should not be decorated with anything that is impervious to water vapor – that is, vinyl or washable wallcoverings – for three months. To prepare bare plaster, simply sand the surface smooth with sandpaper wrapped around a sanding block. Old bare plaster that is very porous and dusty to the touch should be treated with stabilizing primer.

Painted plaster

START BY WASHING THE SURFACE down with sugar soap or household detergent. Rinse this off with clean water and allow it to dry. Dry-scrape any areas that are flaking, and sand the edges of bare areas smooth; fill any large cracks and holes. Latex-painted walls need no further treatment. Sand gloss-painted walls with wet-and-dry abrasive paper to provide a key for the new decoration.

Dealing with distemper

YOU MAY FIND DISTEMPER beneath old wallpaper. The size-bound type will become soft as you wash it down, and must be thoroughly scrubbed away and rinsed off with warm water. Let the surface dry, then sand it smooth and apply stabilizing primer. The washable type will resist softening; simply sand it down and apply stabilizing primer directly to seal the surface.

Removing wallpaper

SPONGE OR SPRAY WARM WATER onto the wall and leave it for a time to soak in and soften the paste.

SCRAPE THE PAPER OFF, taking care not to gouge the plaster with your scraper or stripping knife. Finish by washing the wall down with clean water to remove nibs of paper and old paste. Then prepare the surface as described earlier, depending on what is revealed.

WASHABLE OR PAINTED WALLPAPERS will need help before water can penetrate the surface. You must either break it up with a serrated scraper before applying water, or use a steam wallpaper stripper (see page 118). This machine supplies steam to a metal plate which you hold over the surface to be stripped, forcing the steam into the paper to soften the paste. It is then a simple matter to scrape the paper off and complete the preparation as for ordinary wallpaper.

Vinyl wallcoverings require neither soaking nor scraping: you simply peel the outer vinyl layer off the dry wall. Lift a corner seam with your fingernail at baseboard level, peel across the width to free the bottom end of the length and then pull up to remove it completely. Repeat for other lengths. You can in theory leave the remaining backing paper in place so long as it is well stuck to the wall. In practice, however, it is best to remove it – it is easy to soak and scrape off – so there is no chance of it lifting and spoiling your new decorations.

Making good

ONCE YOU HAVE REMOVED old wall-coverings and washed down the surface, attend to any minor faults. Use the edge of your putty knife to rake loose material out of cracks, and an old paintbrush to dust out larger hollows. Then wet the plaster to stop the repair from drying out too quickly, and apply putty or plaster with your filling knife. For cracks, draw the blade across and then along the crack to force the filler in; fill holes in layers no more than $\frac{1}{8}$in (3mm) thick to avoid slumping.

Mold growth on wall surfaces indicates that the room suffers from condensation due to inadequate insulation, heating and ventilation. Scrub the mold off thoroughly, then treat the affected surfaces with either a commercial mold killer or household bleach diluted 1:4 with water to kill off any remaining spores. Follow the manufacturer's instructions with branded products; if using bleach, wipe the solution onto the surface with a sponge or cloth and leave it overnight before rinsing it off with clean water.

WALLPAPERING TECHNIQUES

PAPERHANGING IS ONE OF THE MOST SATISFYING DECORATING JOBS because you get results so quickly: once the preparation is over, you can cover whole walls in next to no time. The only awkward part is coping with obstacles - window reveals, door architraves, light switches, radiators and so on - and you need to know how to cope with these as you go along. But first you must master the basic paperhanging techniques.

A SMALL DOWNSTAIRS CLOAKROOM IS A GOOD ROOM ON WHICH TO START WALLPAPERING, ESPECIALLY WHERE ONLY THE TOP HALF OF THE WALLS ARE PAPERED. MATCHING THE PATTERN IS EASIER TO ACHIEVE WHEN YOU DO NOT HAVE LONG DROPS TO CONTEND WITH. A VINYL OR WASHABLE WALLPAPER IS THE BEST SOLUTION IN A HALF-BATH.

The rules of paperhanging

THE VITAL RULE THAT YOU IGNORE at your peril when paperhanging is to hang each length to a true vertical. If you do not, you will get very odd results at corners, patterns will not match and, worst of all, any motifs in the design that are repeated horizontally will appear to be climbing up the wall when viewed against ceiling lines or baseboards. The solution is to mark a plumbed vertical line on the wall where you start hanging, about 1in (25mm) less than the width of the paper away from the room corner. This allows a narrow tongue of paper to turn onto the next wall and means that a joint between lengths cannot open up in the corner of the room.

You should mark a fresh plumb-line every time you turn a corner because few corners are perfectly plumb, and if you simply continue hanging lengths without checking the vertical, your work will soon begin to run out of true. This means that the first length on the next wall is hung so that it just overlaps the turned edge of the previous length and disguises any irregularity. Of course, if the room corner is true, you will be able to abut the next length as usual instead of overlapping it, but you still must check.

If you have never hung wallpaper before, it is a good idea to start with a vinyl wallcovering as it is more tolerant of rough, inexperienced handling. It will not tear and does not stretch much either, so accurate pattern matching is easier to achieve.

Pattern matching

IF THE PAPER YOU ARE HANGING has a pattern, you need to allow for this before marking and cutting your lengths. First check the pattern repeat – the distance between repeating motifs down the length of the paper.

If this is large, you may be forced to waste quite a bit of paper in cutting so that the pattern will match between adjacent lengths. Then check whether the pattern is a straight match – with the same design repeat on each side of the wallcovering – or a drop match, where the design at one side of the length is repeated half a drop below.

Preparing the first length

SET UP YOUR PASTING TABLE (see page 118) and mix the paste according to the manufacturer's instructions. Measure the height of the wall, add on about 4in (100mm) to allow for trimming, then cut the paper to length. Mark the back to indicate which end of the length is the top.

Now position the length so the top is just overlapping the right end of the pasting table (the left end if you are left-handed), and draw it towards you so that one edge of the paper is in line with the near edge of the table.

Start brushing the paste out onto the center part of the length, spreading it evenly and checking that you have not missed any areas. Then brush more paste towards the top and out to the edge nearest you. When you have pasted as much of the length as you can, push the paper away from you so the other edge is lined up with the far side of the table, and paste out to that edge too. This technique ensures good coverage, without getting any paste on the table and then onto the face of the paper; this may not matter with a vinyl, but it could spell disaster for ordinary wallpaper and for more exotic wallcoverings such as silk or grasscloth.

DRAW UP THE MIDDLE OF THE AREA you have pasted to form an accordion pleat, pasted side to pasted side, leaving the top 12in (300mm) or so uncovered: this will be the first part you stick to the wall. Move the fold to the end of the table so you can pull the rest of the length up onto it.

Carry on pasting and folding in this way until the length is completely pasted, and leave it for a few minutes to become supple. The soaking time varies from paper to paper; always check the wrapper for precise details.

Slide one hand underneath the folded paper and carry it to the wall, with the exposed top edge of the length towards you. Climb the ladder, making sure the paper can drop freely between the ladder and the wall.

Using ready-pasted paper

IT IS IMPORTANT TO SOAK ready-pasted papers for precisely the time recommended by the manufacturer, and always to use cold water. Many people think warm water will work better, but it washes off the paste instead of just wetting it. It is worth having a bowl of ordinary paste mixed up so you can re-paste any edges and seams that dry out before you get them stuck down.

Hanging the first length

WHEN YOU ARE IN POSITION, press the top edge of the length against the wall with your free hand, roughly aligning one edge with your plumbed line, and let the pasted folds drop downwards gently. Slide the paper up so that about 2in (50mm) laps onto the ceiling, then align it accurately with the plumbed line.

BRUSH THE TOP PART OF THE LENGTH firmly onto the wall with your paperhanging brush, working from the center of the length out towards the edges to eliminate air bubbles. Then open up the remaining folds and smooth the rest of the length into place, down to the baseboard.

YOU NOW HAVE TO TRIM THE TOP and bottom of the length, using long-bladed paperhanging scissors. First of all, draw the back of the blade along the angle with the ceiling to crease the paper; then peel the top away from the wall; cut along the crease-line and brush the flap back into place. Repeat the process at the bottom to trim the paper at the baseboard.

Hanging the second length

HAVING TAKEN ANY PATTERN REPEAT and type into account (see box, left), you can cut and paste the second length. Align the top edge to the wall as you did before, and slide it up to the ceiling and across to the edge of the first length. Match up the pattern carefully, then brush the length into place. You may find that uneven stretch makes pattern matching difficult all the way down; if this occurs, as it may with cheaper, thinner papers, aim for a good match at eye level to help minimize the problem. Finally, trim top and bottom as before; then proceed in this way with remaining lengths until you reach a corner.

Turning corners

SOONER OR LATER you will have to turn a corner, and it is important to do this correctly. Never try to turn more than about 2in (50mm) of paper onto the adjacent wall; it will almost certainly crease, and the turned edge will probably not be truly vertical. So when you have hung the last complete length on the first wall, measure the distance to the corner. Unless it is within 2in (50mm) of the roll width, add about 1in (25mm) to the measurement and cut the strip to this width. Save the other half of the strip, which you will then hang on the second wall.

Hang the strip, matching the pattern carefully, then brush the flap firmly into the corner. If it creases as you turn it, make small cuts at right angles to the edge of the flap to allow the paper to lie flat. The same technique is used for external corners, for example around a chimney.

Now you need that second plumbed line, to be sure that lengths hung on the second wall will be truly vertical. Draw it about ¼in (6mm) less than the width of the second strip away from the corner, and hang this cut-down strip so that it abuts the plumbed line and just overlaps the turned flap. With vinyls and washable papers, use a little overlap adhesive to stick the overlap down.

Once the corner is negotiated safely, you can carry on hanging full lengths as usual.

Window reveals

WHEN YOU REACH A WINDOW reveal, hang the first length that overlaps it as before and make horizontal cuts in line with the top and bottom of the reveal so you can turn the center flap of paper onto the side face of the reveal. Trim the vertical rear edge of the flap if it reaches back to the window frame.

CUT A SMALL PIECE of the wallcovering to go on the underside of the top of the reveal, turning it up for about 1in (25mm) onto the face of the wall above the reveal, then brushing the section that is already there down over it. Use some overlap adhesive if necessary.

You can employ a useful trick at this point if you are hanging an ordinary printed paper, or one which will be painted over. Instead of having a hard-edged overlap, carefully tear the edge of the overlapping piece to form a feathered edge which will lie completely flat and form an almost invisible seam when brushed in place. With patterned or embossed papers, you must position the patch so that the patterns match.

Hang short lengths above and below the window, maintaining the pattern match, until you can hang another complete length at the other side of the reveal. Trim this as before, and fill in with a patch on the reveal underside. Finish off the reveal with narrow strips at the sides if necessary.

Use the same technique for recessed door openings. Where there is an architrave molding around the opening, simply hang the paper so it overlaps the door opening, make a diagonal release cut up towards the top corner of the architrave, and mark and trim the paper to fit around it.

Switches and sockets

TO ACHIEVE A NEAT FINISH around switches and sockets, turn off the electricity and loosen the plate. Let the paper hang over the switch or socket, then pierce the paper in the middle of the plate and make four cuts out towards the corners. Cut off most of the tongues so formed, leaving about ¼in (6mm) of paper which you can then tuck neatly behind the plate. Tighten the screws and turn the power back on. The one situation where you should not do this is if you are hanging a metallic foil wallcovering, since these can conduct electricity.

Other obstacles

WITH EXISTING OBSTACLES, such as built-in furniture or a fire surround, you should mark and trim the paper so it fits neatly into the angle between feature and wall. With irregular shapes like an ornate mantleshelf, make cuts into the edge of the paper to mark and trim each tongue in turn, without creasing the paper unduly.

Finishing touches

A SEAM ROLLER WILL HELP YOU to achieve better results by ensuring that your seams lie flat. If seams persist in lifting, ease them away from the wall and brush a little more paste behind them before pressing them back in place.

IF YOUR WALL SUFFERS FROM A RASH of small blisters as the paste dries out, do not worry; they will flatten eventually. But one or two larger blisters usually indicate that you missed pasting that area. Make two cuts in the paper at right

angles, using a razor blade or sharp craft knife, then fold back the tongues and brush on some paste before bedding them back to the wall. The cuts will be almost invisible, especially if they follow elements of the pattern.

MOVABLE OBSTACLES

○ *It is best to unscrew and take down anything movable like shelving, wall lights and radiators. Mark the positions of the holes by inserting a headless matchstick in each one. This will burst through the paper as you hang it, enabling you to locate the positions easily when you replace them.*

○ *With wall lights, turn off the electricity and then unscrew and disconnect the fixture, taping any bare cables with insulating tape before restoring the power.*

○ *To remove steam radiators, shut off the valves at each end and open the vent. Undo one valve coupling and drain the radiator contents into a shallow container, then undo the other coupling and lift the radiator off its brackets. Remove these too, and mark the positions of the mounting holes.*

How many rolls for walls?

DISTANCE AROUND ROOM (INCLUDING WINDOWS AND DOORWAYS)

HEIGHT	30ft 9m	33ft 10m	40ft 12m	42ft 13m	46ft 14m	50ft 15m	52ft 16m	56ft 17m	62ft 19m	66ft 20m	69ft 21m	72ft 22m	75ft 23m	82ft 25m	85ft 26m	88ft 27m	92ft 28m	96ft 30m
7-7½ft/2.15-2.30m	4	5	5	6	6	7	7	8	8	9	9	10	10	11	12	12	13	13
7½–8ft/2.30–2-45m	5	5	6	6	7	7	8	8	9	9	10	10	11	11	12	13	13	14
8–8½ft/2.45–2.60m	5	5	6	7	7	8	9	9	10	10	11	12	12	13	14	14	15	15
8½–9ft/2.60–2.75m	5	5	6	7	7	8	9	9	10	10	11	12	12	13	14	14	15	15
9-9 1/2ft/2.75–2.90m	6	6	7	7	8	9	9	10	10	11	12	12	13	14	14	15	15	16
9½–10ft/2.90–3.05m	6	6	7	8	8	9	10	10	11	12	12	13	14	14	15	16	16	17
10–10½ft/3.05–3.20m	6	7	8	8	9	10	10	11	12	13	13	14	15	16	16	17	18	19

Numbers based on roll size of 33ft (10.05m) long and 20½in (520mm) wide.

WHERE TO START PAPERING

THE BASIC TECHNIQUES described in previous pages cover most of the situations you will encounter in decorating a typical room. But one important part of the procedure – where to start hanging – depends on the design of the wallcovering and the features of the room.

IF THE PAPER HAS A BOLD PATTERN or a strong motif and you are decorating a room with a chimney, it is best to center the design on the face of the chimney breast. The width of the breast itself will affect how the lengths turn onto its side walls; you can either hang one length centrally, or place two adjacent lengths on each side of its center line. You can then work around the room in both directions from this starting point, finishing up with the last lengths meeting in the least obtrusive place – in a corner or above a door opening, for example.

Whatever wallcovering you are hanging, it pays to check where seams will fall in relation to corners, doors and window openings before you decide on your precise starting point. By using a roll of wallcovering as a width gauge, you can mark the anticipated seam positions on the walls, and then adjust the position of your starting point slightly as necessary.

Dormers and arches

Your room may include one of two particularly awkward features which can be difficult to decorate – dormer windows and arched recesses or openings. With dormer windows, work outwards from a line drawn through the center of the window so that the pattern is the same at each side of the recess, where it runs down the sloping ceiling. Trim the edges of these two lengths so they just turn onto the vertical faces of the recess, then cover these last with triangular-shaped pieces cut to fit.

Where there is an arch, paper the flat walls on either side first, turning about 1in (25mm) of paper onto the arch surface after making small release cuts in the edges. If the paper has a random pattern, cut a long strip and use it to cover the arch surface in one continuous length. If the pattern is directional, use strips running from the head of the arch down to the floor on each side. Tackle an arched recess in a similar way, papering the face and back walls first and then treating the arch surface as described for a through arch.

Papering stairways

There are two main problems to overcome when paperhanging in a stairway. The first is reaching the top of the stairway walls without impeding access to the wall surfaces themselves, while the second is handling very long lengths of wallcovering.

Gaining safe access usually requires some improvisation, using stepladders, sections of ordinary ladders and sturdy scaffold boards to provide a working platform about 2ft (600mm) above the level of the landing floor. You may have to rearrange the various components during the course of the job to enable you to reach each wall easily; pad the tops of ladders well if they have to rest against the newly papered surfaces. Always clamp or tie boards to their supports for safety. An alternative is to rent a special, narrow slot-together platform tower designed for use in stairs. However, this may take up more space than ladders and boards, making access to the stairs themselves awkward.

Handling long lengths of wallcovering is tricky; the sheer weight of the length may cause it to stretch as you unroll it, making accurate pattern matching difficult. If possible, for stairwells choose wallcoverings that are strong – a heavy-duty vinyl, for example – and with a free pattern match. Always work with a helper who can take the weight of the lower end of each length as you hang the top end. Remove any wall-mounted handrails before you start work.

Hang the longest drops in the stairway first, working to a plumbed line on each wall. When measuring up each length, ensure that it will be long enough to take account of the sloping staircase. If you have a landing handrail that runs up to a wall, slit the length that overlaps it from the bottom up and make small release cuts in order to fit the paper around the wall end of the rail.

PAPERING CEILINGS

Many people are terrified of tackling the job of papering a ceiling. At first sight it seems a difficult proposition, involving wrestling with unmanageable lengths of pasty paper while trying to make it hang upside down on the ceiling surface. It is much better to view the ceiling (apart from the surface being horizontal instead of vertical) as a large flat wall, with far fewer obstructions to cope with than you will find when papering the walls of a typical room. All you have to master is the art of handling the paper while coaxing it into position.

You can use any type of wallcovering – plain, washable, vinyl, relief – to paper a ceiling. However, for your first attempt it is a good idea to choose a fairly heavy (and therefore strong) paper with a random pattern, so you do not have to worry about tearing it or matching a pattern as you work.

If you do decide on a pattern, think carefully about which way to hang it. The traditional rules for papering ceilings say that you should hang the lengths parallel with a window wall since this prevents the overlapped seams from casting noticeable shadows on the ceiling surface. But now that seams are abutted, there is no reason why you should not work at right angles to the window wall, especially in a long, thin room, so that you will be handling shorter and more manageable lengths of wallpaper. Consider too how many complete lengths you will get out of a roll; working in one direction rather than the other may mean considerably less wastage.

Preparation

Treat the ceiling surface as you would a plastered wall (see page 120). Wash down existing paintwork thoroughly with household detergent or sugar soap, especially if there are smokers in the family. Rinse with clean water.

If the ceiling has already been papered, strip the old paper off (using a steam stripper if it is washable or has been painted over). Fill any large cracks, but ignore hairline ones as these will be concealed by the new paper. If the ceiling is newly plastered, treat it with a coat of size (diluted wallpaper paste) first.

How many rolls for ceilings?

Estimate the number of rolls needed by measuring the perimeter of the room.

PERIMETER OF ROOM																				
(Ft)	33	36	40	43	46	50	53	56	59	63	66	69	73	76	79	82	86	89	92	95
(m)	10	11	12	13	14	15	16	17	18	19	20	21	22	23	24	25	26	27	28	29

NUMBER OF ROLLS																				
	2	2	2	3	3	4	4	4	5	5	6	6	7	7	8	8	9	10	10	11

Numbers based on roll size of 33ft (10.05m) long and 20½ (520mm) wide.

ALWAYS WORK FROM A LOW-LEVEL PLATFORM WHEN PAPERING CEILINGS: USE TRESTLES AND STAGING OR IMPROVISE WITH SCAFFOLD BOARDS SUPPORTED ON STEPLADDERS, LOCKED INTO POSITION. STRIPES ARE ESPECIALLY TRICKY ON A SLOPING CEILING, AND YOU WILL NEED A GOOD EYE AS WELL AS A STEADY HAND TO GET THEM TO LINE UP WITH THE STRIPES ON THE WALLS. ALWAYS DISCONNECT THE LIGHT FIXTURE BEFORE PAPERING A CEILING.

Gaining safe access

THE MOST AWKWARD PART about papering a ceiling is reaching it. Since you have to be able to move from one end of each length to the other as you hang it, it is no good trying to perch on chairs or small steps. You need a continuous low-level work platform which you can position directly beneath each length, allowing you to walk along its length with no obstructions.

Professionals use trestles and staging or the components of a slot-together scaffold tower for this. You can either rent these, or set up one or two scaffold boards supported on the treads of a small ladder or on small home-made hop-ups. To avoid accidents, make sure you secure the boards to the supports. Either use wood-working clamps, or drill holes in the boards and the supports and drop in a bolt to lock the two together (you do not need a nut). This arrangement makes it easy to dismantle and reposition the working platform as you tackle successive lengths of paper.

Disconnecting light fixtures

TAKE DOWN THE LIGHT FITTINGS, rather than trying to fit the wallpaper around them. Turn off the power at the fusebox, then either remove the lighting circuit fuse or switch off the miniature circuit breaker before unscrewing and disconnecting the light fixture. If you have a pendant light, simply unscrew the cover or baseplate and disconnect the pendant cord from it. Then restore the power to the other circuits in the house; if you need light in the room you are working in, provide it by means of table or standard lights plugged into wall sockets

Hanging the first length

PIN A CHALKED STRING LINE across the ceiling parallel with your chosen direction of hanging. Position it about 1in (25mm) less than the width of the wallpaper away from the wall, to allow the long edge to be trimmed once the length is hung. Snap the string against the ceiling surface to leave a clear guideline, and remove the string.

Measure the width of the room and cut your first length, allowing an extra 2in (50mm) at each end for trimming. If you are using a paper without a pattern match, you can use the first length as a guide and cut the others to length at this stage too.

Since you will be handling longer pieces than when papering a wall, it is important to paste and fold the lengths correctly. Start at one end, and paste an area almost as long as your pasting table. Then fold this up into a series of pleats, pasted side to pasted side, so that each fold is about 18in (450mm) wide; leave a short fold, pasted side uppermost, on top of the pile. Move the paper along so that the accordion section is at one end of the table. Paste further sections and form pleats as before. When you reach the far end of the length, take the last fold to meet the short one on top of the pile. The paper edges should meet without paste getting onto the front of the paper.

PICK UP THE FOLDED LENGTH carefully and slip a spare roll of paper underneath to support the pasted length as you carry it to the ceiling. Peel away the last fold you made and let it hang free, then position the pasted end of the first fold on the ceiling; brush it into place so it overlaps onto the wall at right angles to the direction of hanging. Slip it across as necessary so its long outer edge lines up with your chalk line, and brush the first yard (meter) of paper into place.

Now move back along your working platform, letting more paper unfold from the pile, and brush a further section into position. Check that it is still aligned with the chalk line, and that its other long edge is brushed well into the wall/ceiling angle as you proceed. Complete hanging the first length by brushing the other end into the angle between the ceiling and the opposite wall.

Trim the ends by creasing the paper into the wall/ceiling angle and peeling it carefully away so you can cut neatly along the creased line. Repeat the creasing process all down the long edge, then peel and trim this too before brushing it back into place.

Completing the ceiling

HANG SUBSEQUENT LENGTHS in the same way, abutting one long edge carefully up against the edge of the previous length (and with the pattern carefully matched, if there is one). The last length will probably not be a full-width strip; cut it down in width before pasting it, allowing about 1in (25mm) extra so that its long edge can be neatly trimmed against the side wall.

Once all the lengths are hung and trimmed, check that all the seams are well stuck down by running a seam roller along them. Do not use a roller on a relief wallcovering or one with an embossed pattern, however, or you will flatten the raised surface. Instead, use your paperhanging brush with a firm, stippling action to ensure that the seams are well stuck down.

Trimming around a ceiling light

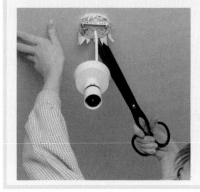

PIERCE THE WALLPAPER in line with the center of the light fixtures, then peel it away carefully, and make radial cuts from the hole outwards to just beyond the outline of the cover. Brush the length back into place, allowing the triangular tongues of paper to hang downwards. Trim each one off flush with the edge of the baseplate and brush it back against the ceiling surface. The cut edges will be concealed when the light cover is replaced.

CEILING TIPS

○ *Ceilings are often papered with a plain, unprinted lining paper which is then painted. This type of paper can stretch when pasted, so make sure you soak each length for exactly the same time.*

○ *Stick or stencil stars onto a plain ceiling in a bedroom so that you have something interesting to look at when lying in bed.*

○ *In attic or dormer rooms with sloping ceilings, it is a good idea to wallpaper the ceiling in the same way as the walls to unify the room and to draw attention away from the restricted height of the walls.*

SEE ALSO:

ACCESS EQUIPMENT	100
TYPES OF WALLCOVERING	114
PAPERHANGING TOOLS	118
WALLPAPERING TECHNIQUES	122

FRIEZES AND BORDERS

FRIEZES AND BORDERS ARE NARROW STRIPS OF PRINTED wallpaper or vinyl wallcovering which are used to add decorative detail to a room. This horizontal band of pattern running around the room is usually placed in line with an architectural feature such as coving, a picture rail or a dado, or it may be used to compensate for the absence of such a feature. It may equally highlight the junction between walls and ceiling, frame a door or window opening or create a feature panel on a plain wall or ceiling, perhaps breaking up a large surface expanse.

Creating a decorative panel

TO FORM NEAT MITERED CORNERS to a panel when hanging borders, overlap the two lengths at right angles. Then place a straight edge across the joint at 45 degrees and use a sharp knife to cut through both layers along the angled line. Peel off the two waste portions and carefully press the mitered ends down. Use a seam roller if necessary to ensure a good bond at each mitered corner.

A CO-ORDINATING FRIEZE HAS BEEN USED HERE BUT ITS EFFECT IS PERSONALIZED BY REPEATING THE MOTIFS ON THE DRAWER FRONTS OF A PAINTED CHEST AND VARNISHING OVER THEM.

Putting up the frieze

FRIEZES AND BORDERS ARE sold in rolls and range in width from around 3in (75mm) up to 12in (300mm); they can be used on plain painted walls as well as in conjunction with other wallcoverings. Many friezes and borders come in designs and colors that complement a selection of fabrics and wallcoverings from the same manufacturer, allowing a co-ordinated approach to the room's overall decor.

Most friezes and borders are intended to be pasted just like any wallcovering. However, ordinary paste will not stick well over washable wallpaper or a vinyl wallcovering, so you should use a self-adhesive frieze or border over these materials.

Before you start putting up a frieze or border, experiment with its position by sticking lengths in place using masking tape. When you have the ideal position, draw light pencil guidelines on the wall or ceiling, using a straight edge and carpenter's level. You do not need guidelines for friezes that follow a feature such as coving or a picture rail; simply butt the strips up against it.

CUT THE FIRST STRIP TO LENGTH. Brush paste onto the back of pasted friezes and borders and fold up the length, accordion-style. With the self-adhesive types, carefully peel away one end of the backing paper.

Position one end of the length on the pencil guideline and align it carefully. With pasted friezes and borders, simply brush the length into place with a paperhanging brush, checking its alignment as you proceed. Wipe away any paste that oozes out, using a damp cloth. Secure the end of self-adhesive borders, then carefully peel off the backing paper section by section as you stick the rest of the length into position.

WHEN HANGING A FRIEZE, try to cover each wall with a single continuous strip, forming neat seams in the room corners. If you have to use two pieces, overlap their ends and match up the pattern precisely. Then use a sharp knife and a straight edge to cut through both layers, peel away the offcuts and press the seam flat.

Découpage frieze

USE A COLOR PHOTOCOPIER to reproduce images which can then be cut out and stuck onto a wall with wallpaper paste to achieve the effect of a random frieze. The motifs can be reduced or enlarged to produce a more varied result. Animal motifs make a particularly appropriate border for a child's room. An alternative would be to stencil a repeating image around the walls (see page 110).

TYPES OF TILE

CERAMIC TILES ARE THIN SLABS OF FIRED CLAY decorated on one side with colored glazes and often with a printed or hand-painted pattern too. They are easy to handle, attaching them is simple and the resulting surface is waterproof, easy to keep clean, hardwearing and extremely long-lasting. The only drawback is their relatively high price.

Tiles for walls Ceramic wall tiles are generally just over ⅙in (about 4mm) thick, and come in a number of regular sizes. The most popular size used to be the 4in (100mm) square tile (**14**), but is now the larger 6in (150mm) square (**8**), which is quicker to mount – you need only 44 to cover a square yard (meter) of wall, compared with 86 of the smaller tiles, and there is less grouting to do as well.

The most common sizes of rectangular tile (**4**) are 8 x 4in (200 x 100mm) and 8 x 6in (200 x 150mm), with coverages of 33 and 50 to the square yard (meter) respectively. You can also buy tiles in interlocking shapes such as hexagons and curved Provencal styles. Some ranges include tile "slips" (**5, 7**): these are slim tiles 6in (150mm) long and 1in (25mm) wide, which can be used to create colored stripes or narrow borders on larger tiled areas.

Tile designs alter with changing fashions in interior design. Plain and small-patterned tiles, often with a simple border frame, can be interspersed with individual motif tiles (**14**) and mini motif tiles (**13**); these sometimes have a relief motif (**10**). There are also tiles which create a frieze effect when laid alongside one another and sets of tiles which build up into larger designs, known as feature panels (**12**), which can look striking when surrounded by an area of plain tiling. Border tiles (**15**) are available for finishing off the top edge

of a part-tiled area such as around a bath. Some tile ranges include "inserts" – tiles carrying molded bathroom accessories such as soap dishes and toilet-paper roll holders – and small quadrant-shaped tiles used for finishing off the junction between baths and tiled walls. These are available in only a limited range of colours now, since sealants and plastic trims have taken their place.

The surface of ceramic wall tiles was traditionally highly glazed, but you can now also choose semi-matte finishes, often with a slight surface texture that softens the somewhat harsh glare of a high-gloss surface.

Most tiles have square edges; these are sometimes glazed on one or two edges, sometimes not, so if you want an exposed glazed edge you should check the actual tiles before you buy. Otherwise, you must use some form of edge trim. Tiles which are glazed on all four edges are described as "universal".

Tiles for floors Floor tiles are a good choice for heavy traffic areas such as porches and hallways, as well as for kitchens and conservatories. They are generally thicker and harder fired than wall tiles, to enable them to stand up to heavy wear without cracking. They may be glazed (**3**), with a plain color or a printed design, or unglazed – more commonly known as quarry tiles (**6**) – and many have textured surfaces to make them less slippery underfoot.

Marble floor tiles (**9**) are also available. Most floor tiles are square-edged, so spacers have to be used to guarantee an even grouting gap; some selections (especially quarries) still include tiles with one or two rounded edges for finishing off part-tiled areas or forming tiled moldings.

Common sizes are 6in (150mm) and 8in (200mm) squares, and 8 x 4in (200 x100mm) rectangles; hexagons are also available in plain colors, and another variation is a plain octagonal tile (**2**), laid with small square colored inserts (**1**) at their intersections.

Frost-proof grades of floor tile are available for use outdoors, on steps, in passageways and so on; indoor grades will be damaged by frost.

Tiles for worktops You can of course use ordinary ceramic tiles as a kitchen work surface. Special shapes are available for finishing off the edges of a worktop: straight strips with an L cross-section, plus mitered lengths for internal corners, and square "caps" for external ones.

Mosaics (11) Mosaics are tiny tiles – usually plain in color, sometimes with a pattern – made up into sheets on a tough fabric backing. They are laid just like tiles in a bed of adhesive, and the gaps grouted afterwards. Square mosaics are most common, but discs, hexagons and other interlocking shapes are available. Sheets are usually 12in (300mm) square, and often sold in packs of 5 or 10; the best way of estimating quantities is to work out the area to be covered and to divide that by the coverage figure on the pack. Wall and floor types of mosaic tile are of different thicknesses, just like ordinary ceramic tiles.

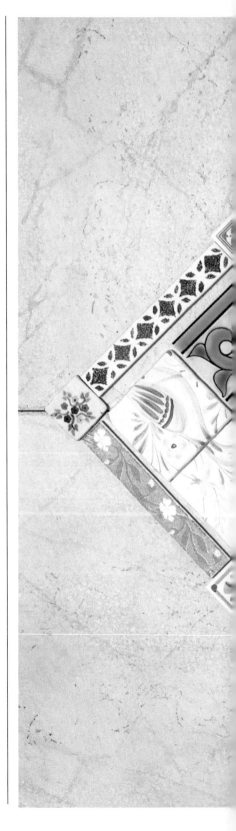

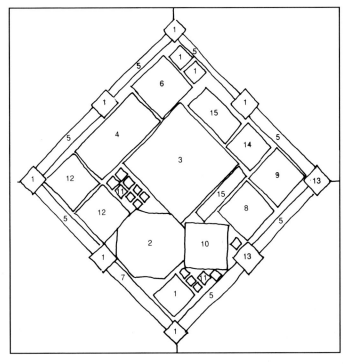

TILING TIPS

ESTIMATING QUANTITIES
The packaging of ceramic wall and floor tiles can vary a great deal, depending on the type of tile, the size and the manufacturer. There may be anything from 6 to 50 tiles per pack; larger packs can sometimes mean a lot of wastage but most retailers will split packs for you if buying whole packs would be uneconomical. It is best either to count up the exact number of tiles you need from a scale plan of the area to be tiled, or to use the figures per square yard (meter) given in the text as a guide.

○ The color of tiles can vary slightly, so make sure you buy all the tiles you need at the same time, to ensure they are from the same batch. Unpack and mix the tiles up a little before mounting them, to even out any color variations.

○ Always use waterproof grout on tiled worktops to maintain a hygienic work surface; ordinary grout will harbor germs.

○ Grout paint can be brushed on to brighten up old grouting that is beginning to look shabby.

WALL TILING TECHNIQUES

CERAMIC WALL TILES COME IN AN ALMOST ENDLESS VARIETY of patterns and colors, as well as in a range of different shapes and sizes, so it should not be difficult to find a design you like. Once the tiles are in place, you have a surface that is immensely hardwearing, easy to keep clean and totally immune to moisture and household stains.

EVEN A TILED SPLASHBACK TO A SINK CAN BE MADE INTO A DECORATIVE FEATURE IN ITSELF BY THE INNOVATIVE COMBINATION OF PLAIN COLORED TILES AND THE BORDER TO IT CREATED BY SMALL PATTERNED TILES ON THREE SIDES OF THE PANEL.

First thoughts

DO NOT BE TOO AMBITIOUS for your first tiling project. Plan to tackle just a small area, for example a splashback behind the wash basin in the bathroom, or the narrow strip of wall between your kitchen worktop and the wall cupboards above it (but beware if there are obstructions like electrical outlets which could call for some tricky tile cutting). You will then be able to get the feel of the technique without worrying about wasting a lot of tiles or having to master the intricacies of tiling a whole wall.

Check the surface you plan to tile. Paint can be left on, but wallpaper of any type – even if painted – must be removed. You can tile on plasterboard, but the surface should be latex-painted first. Never attempt to tile on hardboard. If the surface is tiled already, do not despair: you can simply stick your new tiles on top.

Think also about tile sizes, especially if you are planning to tile between fixed "boundaries" such as worktops and wall units. Choosing one size rather than another might avoid a lot of awkward cutting to fit. Remember that most suppliers will sell you a single tile to help you check a color match in the room.

Take accurate measurements of the area you are planning to tile, then work out exactly how many tiles will cover it. Count cut tiles as whole ones and buy an extra 10 per cent to allow for breakages.

Tiling a splashback

YOU CAN ENSURE THAT this uses only whole tiles. Mark the center of the wash basin on the wall; then check where the edges of the outer tiles will fall. If necessary, adjust this slightly by positioning the first tile either on the line or butted up against it. Where the tiled area runs out to the corner of the room, use the same trick to avoid cut pieces less than a third of a tile wide at the end of rows.

Checking the levels

IF YOU ARE TILING above a flat surface such as a kitchen worktop or vanity unit, the first row of tiles will sit flush with its rear edge. If your wash basin has a curved shape at the back, pin a slim strip of wood to the wall using masonry nails to act as a support for the first row of tiles. Cut tiles will fill the gap between this row and the basin when the batten is removed. Use a level to check that the batten is perfectly horizontal. Drive the nails only part-way into the wall, to make it easier to prise them out again later.

Prepare the wall by washing down any existing tiles and painted surfaces and scraping off any flaking paint. Strip off all old wallcoverings. If you are tiling just part of a papered wall, mark out and strip an area of paper 1in (25mm) less in each direction than the area of splashback. Brush latex paint over bare plaster or wallboard.

Spreading the adhesive

SCOOP SOME TILE ADHESIVE out of the tub with the notched spreader, and press it on to the wall. Draw the spreader across the wall surface so the teeth touch the plaster and ridge the adhesive to exactly the right thickness. Apply enough adhesive to allow you to position about six tiles in the first row. Make sure you can see your start line – scrape away a little adhesive if necessary.

Attaching the tiles

POSITION THE FIRST TILE. Rest the bottom edge of the tile on the worktop or supporting batten, holding the tile at an angle of about 45 degrees to the wall. Align one edge with your starting line, and press the tile firmly into the adhesive. Check with a level; if it is not level, twist it slightly until it is, and make sure that it is still accurately aligned.

Adding further tiles

ADD FURTHER TILES IN THE first horizontal row in exactly the same way, butting their edges closely together or fitting spacers according to the type of tile. Apply more tile adhesive to the wall if necessary to complete the row. If the row runs right up to a corner, leave any cut pieces until later (but scrape off the adhesive where they will go so it does not set). Check that all the tiles are sitting flush with one another, pressing in any standing out from their neighbors. Prise out any tiles that have sunk too deep into the adhesive, and put some more adhesive on the wall before re-bedding them.

Now add further rows of whole tiles, checking that the vertical rows are correctly aligned with each other; add spacers if necessary. If you are mixing patterned and plain tiles, check that you have maintained the correct proportions of each; this is the time to correct any mistakes.

Tiling equipment

FOR ALMOST ANY TILING JOB, large or small, you will need: tile adhesive and a notched spreader; some tile spacers (unless you are using universal tiles); lengths of tile edge trim (optional); grout and a flexible spreader; a steel ruler; some lengths of 1½ x ½in (38 x 12mm) softwood battening, plus masonry pins and hammer for large wall areas; a carpenter's level; a tile cutter or cutting jig; tile nibblers, pincers or tile saw; dowelling for shaping grout lines; a pencil and felt-tip pen; sponges and cloths for wiping and polishing. You may also need some silicone sealant for sealing joints where tiling abuts baths, basins and shower trays.

GROUT for wall tiling is usually sold ready-mixed in plastic tubs, complete with a notched plastic spreader. For areas that will get the occasional splash or may suffer from condensation, use a water-resistant grout, but for surfaces such as shower stalls, which have to withstand prolonged wetting, it is essential to use waterproof grout. Grout is generally white, but if you want to make a feature of the grout lines to brighten up an area, you can use colored grout or brush on special grout paint when the original white grouting has dried.

TILE ADHESIVE comes in both wall and floor types. It is widely available in powder form as well as ready-mixed, however the powder is generally more economical to use. You can use water-resistant adhesive for wall tiles in a kitchen splashback, for example, subject to occasional splashing, but you should use a waterproof type for areas such as shower walls. For floors, always use waterproof adhesive and waterproof grout. Check the coverage stated on the packet or container by the manufacturer when buying, so you do not buy too much or run out halfway through the job.

Finishing the edges

FOR A SPLASHBACK, you can finish off the edges of the tiled area with special plastic or metal tile trim. Bed the lengths of trim into the tile adhesive before fixing the last row of tiles in place, and adjust the trim as necessary once they have been positioned so that it fits snugly over the tile edges. This is a neat solution if the edges of your tiles are not completely glazed.

Cut the edge tiles. The most difficult part of the job is filling in any cut tiles needed to complete the area. The best way of getting pieces to fit accurately is to measure the width of each gap at top and bottom, and transfer the measurements to the tile to be cut using a felt-tipped pen. Then cut the tile, either using your cutting jig or by scoring along the line with a tile cutter (see box, page 138).

Test the fit of each piece of tile in its gap, then spread some tile adhesive onto the back of it and press it into place flush with its neighbor. Cut and fit other edge pieces in the same way to complete the area. If you fixed a wooden support below the first row, prise it away carefully in order to cut and fit the pieces of tile between it and the shaped edge underneath.

Grouting the tiles

LEAVE THE TILE ADHESIVE to set overnight, then use the plastic squeegee supplied to grout the tiles. Load a small amount of tub grout onto the squeegee and draw it across the gaps as when filling a crack in a wall. Wipe off any surplus as you complete an area of six or eight tiles, then draw the end of a slim length of dowel along each grout line to leave it slightly concave.

Allow the grout to dry for the recommended time, then complete the job by polishing the tile surface. Using a dry cloth, polish away the remains of the grout to leave the tiled surface clean and bright.

Decorating plain tiles

YOU CAN CREATE your own hand-painted tiles using ordinary solvent-based satin or gloss paint. First, make sure the tile is scrupulously clean by wiping it with a cloth moistened with mineral spirits. Then paint your design directly on the surface, using an artist's brush. If you are using more than one color, allow each color to dry before applying the next.

It is also possible to buy self-adhesive motifs for plain ceramic tiles to bring interest to a clinical bathroom wall.

TILING LARGE AREAS

TILING A LARGE AREA OF WALL IS NO MORE DIFFICULT than tackling a small one, since exactly the same techniques are used, but you do need to plan carefully. The main difference is the sheer scale of the job, which makes the preliminary setting-out so important. Unless you have absolutely plain walls, there will be a number of obstacles to tile around and you must decide how to achieve the best fit around them, without ending up cutting impossibly thin slivers of tile to fill in all the gaps.

THIS SHOWER STALL IS TILED FROM FLOOR TO CEILING IN HAND-FINISHED LARGE TILES FROM A SPECIALIST OUTLET. THE COMBINATION OF COLORS, ALL EARTH TONES, BRINGS INTEREST TO WHAT COULD OTHERWISE BE A VERY BLAND, CLINICAL AREA OF THE HOUSE.

IF YOU ARE PLANNING to tile a whole wall or room (or part of it – up to shoulder level, for example), you need to work out precisely where the tiles will fall. On a plain, uninterrupted wall, simply find its center line and plan your tiling to start from there. But if there are such obstacles as window reveals, door openings and built-in furniture in the room, you must work out the best "center point" while trying to avoid having any very thin-cut tile borders and edges anywhere.

Starting work

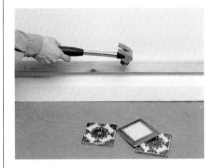

FIRST ATTACH A LINE OF BATTENS across the wall (or around the room), just above baseboard level, securing them with partly driven-in masonry nails to be removed later. The precise level will be dictated by your plan (see page 139), but will usually be between half and three-quarters of a tile's width above the baseboard. Do not rely on this being level. Draw the level out in pencil first, using a carpenter's level, then pin up the battens and check the level again.

If you are tiling over existing tiles, you will have to drill holes through them for the masonry pins. Drill nail holes in the batten, hold it up to the wall and drill through one hole into the tiling. Pin this end in place, swing the batten up to the horizontal and drill the others.

Laying the first row

REFER TO YOUR PLAN to see where your start point is; it may be a center line between the door and window, or a corner.

Apply a band of adhesive to the wall and fit the first row of whole tiles, adding tile spacers at the top corners. Carry on up the wall, fitting whole tiles until you reach an obstacle such as a window. Carry on tiling up the wall at each side of the window, to the top of the tiled area (if you are part-tiling) or the last whole row of tiles beneath the ceiling.

If you are using a plastic or metal tile trim to finish off a part tiled area, bed its rear flange in the adhesive before fitting the row of tiles that will butt up against it; then nudge it down against the tile edges for a neat finish.

Tiling around an opening

WHERE TILES ARE TO BE MOUNTED over a door or window opening, you need another support batten. Attach it to the wall over the opening, its top edge in line with the lower edge of the whole tiles you placed earlier at each side of the opening. Carry on tiling as before, placing whole tiles up to ceiling level. Leave all the battens in place for at least 24 hours, for the adhesive to set hard.

Fitting the cut tiles

THE NEXT DAY, USE A CLAW HAMMER to prise out the masonry nails and remove the battens. Take out the tile spacers at this stage too. Mark and cut tiles to fit between the base batten and the baseboard, and fix in position. Fit cut tiles at each side of the wall, and between the last row of whole tiles and the ceiling. It is easier to spread adhesive on the back of each cut piece than to apply it to the narrow section of wall left exposed.

If you have tiled more than one wall, fill in the cut pieces there too. Make sure there is a slight gap between adjacent cut corner pieces to allow for any slight movement in the house structure. If the pieces are a tight fit, a slight movement will crack them.

Cutting tiles

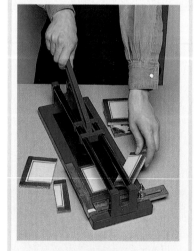

A HEAVY-DUTY TILE CUTTER scores and cuts in one go. Otherwise, you must score the glaze with a sharp-tipped tile cutter, then place a matchstick beneath the scored line and press firmly downwards on each side of the tile so that it snaps cleanly.

Tiling around obstacles

THE NEXT STEP is to tile around obstacles such as window recesses. Start by cutting tiles to fit the gap left on the wall between the last row of whole tiles and the edge of the recess. Then mount whole tiles on the sill, sides and head of the opening so that their glazed edges overlap the cut edges of the tiles you have just placed. (You may need to rig up a temporary support, such as a batten and prop wedged between head and sill, to support the tiles across the window head.) Fit cut pieces between these whole tiles and the window frame to complete the recess.

A SIMILAR OVERLAP to one around a window recess is formed at other external corners; the rule here is to have the tile with the exposed edge on the more prominent wall.

Making a tiling gauge

THIS DEVICE IS A BATTEN marked out in tile widths to help you work out the optimum starting point for tiling a large area. For the beginner, a paper plan (see page 139) is likely to be more accurate.

IF YOU ARE TILING THREE adjacent surfaces – on a fully tiled boxed-in bath surround, for example – the overlap at the external corner cannot be accommodated without a gap equal to the thickness of a tile being left somewhere. The only way to avoid this is to use cut rather than whole tiles on each external angle next to the corner, with the vertical edge finished with an overlap as before, then to cut down the top corner piece with its two glazed edges placed to fit over them.

Finishing the edges

ADD PLASTIC OR METAL EDGE trims to give a neat, rounded edge. Cut them to length with a fine-toothed hacksaw, mitering the corners if you are framing a window reveal or similar opening. Then bed them in the tile adhesive before placing the final row of tiles over the trim's back flange; tap the trim in carefully so that it sits flush with the tile edges.

If you are using wooden trims, simply pin them to the wall with slim masonry pins after tiling and grouting is completed, so they are not marked. These trims are particularly useful for concealing the edges of half-tiled areas which cover existing tiling.

Replacing fixtures

IF YOU HAVE ANY SCREW-mounted wall fixtures, such as mirrors and shelves, to replace, stick masking tape to the tile surface over the fixing position to prevent the drill bit skating away from the mark. Use a sharp masonry drill bit and a slow speed setting on the drill, pressing lightly until the bit bites through the tile glaze. Then drill the hole to the required depth, remove the tape, insert the wall plug and make the fixing. In a really wet area such as a shower stall, put a bead of silicone mastic around the screw shank as you drive it in, to prevent water from seeping in behind the tiles.

Fake tiles

A QUICK AND INNOVATIVE way to create a tiled look for a wall is to apply square blocks of paint using a mini roller. Leave gaps of approximately ¼ in (5mm) between each painted square to imitate grouting. Do not worry about uneven edges: they add to the effect of hand-made tiles. This is not, of course, a good solution in an area where a waterproof surface is essential, such as a bath or shower stall or a basin splashback.

Grouting

WITH ALL THE TILING COMPLETE, grout the gaps using a squeegee or other flexible spreader. Wipe off excess grout as you work, and round off the grout lines with a piece of dowel (see page 136). When the grout is dry, polish the tile surfaces with a clean, dry cloth to remove any smears.

Do not grout internal angles, since movement in the house structure could cause cracking. Instead, seal these angles with non-setting mastic (the silicone type is best in bathrooms or other wet areas).

Calculating where the tiles fall

YOU WILL NEED SQUARED graph paper (with ½in or 10mm squares) and some tracing paper – one sheet of each per wall to be tiled. Let each ½in/10mm square represent a tile (or half if using rectangular tiles), and use this scale to draw up a plan of the wall on the tracing paper, by laying it over the graph paper. Include all obstacles that will have to be tiled around, and ensure that your measurements are accurate. Then move the tracing-paper overlay backwards and forwards, up and down, over the graph paper to see where the tile edges will fall best; remember that you want to avoid cut pieces less than about a quarter of a tile wide. When you find the best alignment, tape the overlay to the graph paper and use this as your guide when tiling. Repeat the process for any other walls, starting from the same baseline on each wall.

TYPES OF FLOORCOVERING

MANY DIFFERENT FLOORCOVERINGS are readily available. The one you choose will depend on the look you want to achieve, the room it is intended for and how much wear and tear the floor is likely to have. Fitted carpets are many people's first choice for living areas, because they look good and feel luxurious to walk on, but wooden flooring with rugs is an attractive alternative. Cork and vinyl flooring are appropriate in rooms such as kitchens and bathrooms where easy cleaning is a high priority, while ceramic tiles are a good choice for areas of heavy traffic such as porches and hallways.

Carpet Carpets are made by weaving or bonding fiber tufts or loops to a durable backing. Woven carpets (**5, 9, 21**) are generally the most expensive type. Tufted carpets (**4, 14, 20**) are made by stitching tufts of fiber into a woven backing, secured by adhesive. Some cheaper types have a foam underlay bonded to the backing (**17**); others need separate underlay.

Many different types of fiber are used in carpet construction, including wool, nylon, acrylic, polypropylene and viscose rayon. Fiber blends can improve carpet performance: a mixture of 80 per cent wool and 20 per cent nylon provides a good combination of warmth, resilience, wear, low flammability and resistance to soiling.

The length and density of the carpet pile will affect its performance as well as its looks. The pile can be cut (**4, 5**); looped (**3**)(uncut and left long); corded (**11**) (uncut and pulled tight to the backing) or twisted (**14, 20**). A dense pile wears better than a loosely woven one; it should be difficult to see the backing when the pile is parted.

Carpet widths are usually described as broadloom (more than 6ft/1.8m wide) or body (up to 3ft/900mm wide). The former is used for large areas, the latter for corridors and stairs. Most broadloom carpet is in fact made in standard 12ft (3.66m) and metric 4m (13ft) widths; it is bought by the linear yard or meter.

Carpet tiles are small squares of carpet of various types, designed to be loose-laid. Common sizes are 12, 18, 20 and 24in (300, 450, 500 and 600mm) square.

Sisal (**15, 16**) and coir are one of the cheapest forms of floorcovering available and provide a good all-purpose surface. Available in a range of colors and textures, their disadvantage is they can be uncomfortable underfoot and dusty.

Sheet vinyl floorcovering Sheet vinyl comes unbacked and backed. Unbacked vinyls are made by sandwiching the vinyl pattern layer between a clear protective surface layer and a strong backing layer. The surface may be smooth, but is often textured to match the printed pattern – with imitation grout lines on a tiled pattern (**12**), or wood grain on a simulated timber one (**6, 8, 10**). Backed or cushioned vinyls (**7, 18**), have an additional layer of expanded foam between the patterned layer and the backing, making them softer and warmer underfoot. Some of the imitations of materials such as brick, cork and marble available in sheet vinyl look remarkably authentic, and cost a fraction of the real thing.

Sheet vinyl floorcoverings are usually sold in just two widths – 6ft 6in (2m) and 13ft (4m) – although you may find some brands sold in 9ft 10in (3m) widths. They are bought by the length. Choose a width that will allow you to cover the floor without seams if possible, though these will be unavoidable in rooms more than 13ft (4m) wide, and in L-shaped rooms. The best way of estimating your needs accurately (and minimizing unnecessary waste) is to draw a floor plan of the room to a scale of, say, 1:20, complete with alcoves, bays and other obstacles; mark on it all the relevant dimensions and take it with you to your supplier, who will then be able to advise you on the most economical choice of cut.

Cork and vinyl floor tiles Cork tiles come in a range of shades and textures, and the resulting surface is warm and resilient underfoot; it also has heat and sound insulation properties that are particularly useful in bathrooms, kitchens, halls and even children's bedrooms. Plain cork (**2**), once laid, has to be sealed to protect its surface, but there are also more expensive pre-sealed types that can be walked on as soon as they have been stuck down. Once laid, they only need an occasional wash and polish.

Vinyl tiles come in both plain and patterned varieties, and are harder-wearing than cork, if a little less gentle on the feet. You can lay a mixture of plain colors, or mix plain and patterned ones if you prefer. Some are self-adhesive, making the job of laying

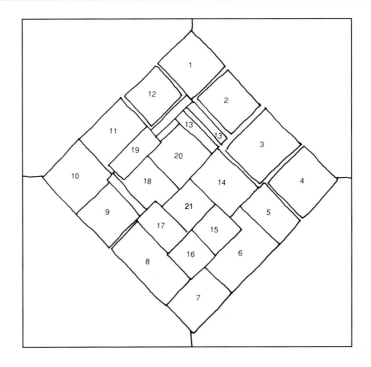

them even more simple. As with cork, little maintenance is needed once laid.

Cork and vinyl tiles generally come in 12in (300mm) squares, although larger squares and rectangles are available in some types.

Wood mosaic floor panels Mosaic floor panels (**1**) are square tiles made up from a number of small strips of decorative hardwood (**13**) mounted on a backing sheet. This may be felt, which acts as an underlay as well as bonding the strips together; the result is a sheet that will bend along the joint lines, and so can be easily cut to size if required. Alternatively, the strips may be wired or stuck together to produce a rigid tile. In either case, tiles are generally either 12in (300mm) or 18in (450mm) square.

The strips may be solid wood or veneer on a cheaper softwood backing; they are usually in a basketweave pattern, though other arrangements are also available. A wide range of wood types is used, including mahogany, teak, oak, iroko and merbau. Some tiles are supplied sealed, others have to be varnished.

Woodstrip flooring Woodstrip flooring (**13, 9**) is available in two main types: as solid planks, and as laminated strips (rather like plywood) with a decorative surface veneer. Lengths vary, from 16in (400mm) to 6ft (1800mm) and widths range from 2¾in (70mm) up to about 8in (200mm).

Solid planks are usually about ⅝in (15mm) thick, while laminated types are a little thinner. The latter may be manufactured to resemble one long plank, but more commonly the veneer is applied in shorter strips.

Both types are generally tongued-and-grooved on their long edges for easy fitting. Some are designed to be anchored to the sub-floor (wood only) by secret nailing, while others are loose-laid using ingenious metal clips to hold adjacent strips together. This means they can be lifted easily if access is needed under the floor.

A wide range of wooden varieties is available in each type, including elm, oak, ash, beech, maple, mahogany and tropical hardwoods such as iroko and merbau. Laminated types are generally prefinished; solid types may also be, but some will need sealing.

TILING FLOORS

CERAMIC FLOOR TILES ARE LESS WIDELY USED than wall tiles, but are a popular choice for areas of heavy use such as porches and halls, and for conservatories, where they have an appropriate indoors-out look.

A TILED FLOOR IS AN EXCELLENT SURFACE FOR HALLWAYS WHICH TAKE A LOT OF TRAFFIC. THESE ENCAUSTIC TILES, OFTEN LAID WITH A DECORATIVE BORDER, WERE TRADITIONALLY FOUND IN VICTORIAN AND EDWARDIAN HOUSES BUT GOOD REPRODUCTIONS ARE MADE TODAY. LAY THEM ON AN ADHESIVE BED AS SHOWN HERE FOR CERAMIC TILES.

Getting organized

WORK OUT THE NUMBER OF tiles you will need by accurately measuring the room size and calculating the number of rows, and the number of tiles per row, that will be required. Count part tiles as whole ones, then add an extra 5 per cent to allow for wastage.

You will need special floor tile adhesive (see page 135); there is a waterproof type for bathrooms, and a flexible type for use when tiling on a suspended wooden floor. You will also need waterproof grout, and a tile cutter; it is worthwhile investing in a tile file or saw if you anticipate a lot of fiddly cutting around pipes and similar obstacles.

Terracotta quarry tiles are generally laid in a mortar bed, although there is no reason why you should not use thick-bed tile adhesive instead, as described for laying ceramic tiles. Hire a heavy-duty cutting jig if you have a lot of quarries to cut; ordinary cutters are not usually strong enough for the job. Never lay quarry tiles on a suspended wooden floor, since the structure will probably not be strong enough to carry the extra weight. (If you are planning to lay ceramic tiles over such a floor, check whether there are any plumbing or heating pipes running beneath it first; it will be impossible to lift a tiled floor without wrecking it if pipework repairs are needed in the future.)

Planning the layout

FIND THE CENTER OF THE ROOM by linking the mid-points of opposite walls with string lines (see page 147). Dry-lay a row of tiles from this point out to each wall so you can see how wide the cut tiles for the borders will need to be, and adjust your starting point if necessary to avoid having a very narrow border strip which will be difficult to cut. When you are happy with the layout, mark your starting point clearly on the floor, ready for the tiles. Start laying whole tiles in the corner of the room furthest from the door, using battens pinned to the floor surface as guides, then work across the room in bays.

Preparing the floor surface

LIFT ANY EXISTING FLOORCOVERINGS. You can leave vinyl or cork tiles that are firmly stuck to a concrete sub-floor, but all traces of wax polish must be removed with a commercial cleaner and the tile surface should then be scored to improve the adhesion of the new tiles. Cover wood floors with a layer of ⅜in (10mm) thick exterior-grade plywood, fixed down with ring nails, to provide a stable surface that will not shift position with temperature and humidity changes, causing cracks in the new floor surface.

Seal the surface of a dusty concrete sub-floor by brushing on a solution of vinyl building adhesive. Check the clearance beneath the door of the room. If it will not clear the surface of the new tiles on their adhesive bed, take the door off before you start work and plane its bottom edge to achieve the necessary clearance.

Setting the battens

PIN TWO STRAIGHT WOODEN guide-battens to the floor surface to form a right angle at your corner starting point. Drive the fixing nails only part-way in, so you can prise them out easily without disturbing the tiles when you remove the battens. Use masonry nails on solid floors.

Cutting border tiles

PLACE A WHOLE TILE on top of the last whole tile in a row, then place another tile on top of this one, with its edge pressed against the baseboard. Mark a line on the middle tile, against the edge of the top one, and cut the tile along this line. The exposed part of the middle tile will then be an exact fit in the gap left around the outer border of the room.

Laying ceramic tiles

SPREAD ENOUGH TILE ADHESIVE in the angle between the guide-battens to cover about 10sq ft (1sq m), using a notched spreader or flooring trowel. Press the edge of the tool against the floor surface to leave the adhesive in ridges of equal height, guaranteeing an adhesive bed of even thickness.

BED THE FIRST WHOLE TILE in the adhesive, its edges against the guide-battens, and press it down firmly. Lay more tiles in a row against one of the battens, out to the edge of the adhesive-covered area. Use spacers to give a grout line of even width.

Lay a second row of tiles along the other batten, then fill in the L-shape with more tiles until you have completed a square. As you work, use a level to check that the tiles are level with each other and that rows and columns are perfectly aligned in both directions. Any discrepancies will show when the tiles are grouted.

Spread another area of adhesive and enlarge the tiled area by laying more rows. Extend the battens as necessary, and continue laying tiles until you reach the door. Leave the adhesive to set overnight.

When you restart work, lift the guide-battens first. Mark and cut the border tiles one by one (see box, left). Spread some adhesive on the back of each cut tile and bed it in place. Then repeat the marking and cutting sequence to set the other border tiles in place.

Where a border tile meets an irregular shape, such as a door architrave, the best way is to cut away the bottom of the architrave slightly and slip the tile underneath.

ALTERNATIVELY, USE A PROFILE gauge to form a template and mark the tile; then cut it to shape with a tile cutter or tile saw. Make U-shaped cutouts for tiles meeting pipes. Leave the border tiles to set overnight.

Grouting

STARTING IN THE ORIGINAL CORNER, use a rubber squeegee to force grout into the spaces between the tiles; scrape off excess grout as you work. Use a dowel rod to neaten all the grout lines. When the grout has set hard, polish the tiled surface with a damp cloth.

Laying quarry tiles in mortar

PIN THE GUIDE-BATTENS as for ceramic tiles. Then dry-lay a row of five or six tiles, complete with spacers, along one batten, and set a third guide-batten at right angles to it to form a bay. Lift the tiles.

Make a notched spreader that will run along the parallel battens and gauge the thickness of the mortar bed so the tiles will sit level with the top edges of the battens. Shovel in the mortar and use the spreader to level it out between the guide-battens.

Place the first tile against the two corner guide-battens, then lay the first row of the bay up to the third batten. Follow with further rows to complete this bay. Use a level as for ceramic tiles, to check that the quarries are level with the guide-battens and with each other.

Remove the third batten and reposition it parallel to the edge of the tiles to form another bay. Spread more mortar and lay the tiles in this bay, using the edges of the tiles in the first bay as one guide "batten". Continue repositioning the batten and filling in more bays until all the whole tiles have been placed. Leave the mortar to set overnight, then cut and fit the border tiles (as shown for ceramic tiles) on the mortar bed. Grout the tiles as described above.

If you prefer to lay quarry tiles using tile adhesive, you can follow the instructions given on the left for laying ceramic tiles.

SANDING WOODEN FLOORS

IF YOU HAVE FLOORBOARDS WHICH ARE IN REASONABLE condition, an alternative to laying floorcoverings is to leave the boards exposed and possibly cover them with rugs. All you need to do is to sand their surface to remove stains and blemishes and then seal it with several coats of varnish or floor sealer to protect it.

Tools and equipment

THE ONLY SPECIALIST TOOLS you need for this job are two powered sanding machines, which you can rent from a local firm. The larger machine, called a drum or floor sander, resembles a cylinder lawnmower and drives a belt of abrasive sandpaper around a large drum. It has a built-in dust extraction unit to suck up most of the sawdust as you work. The smaller machine is needed for sanding the areas of the room that are not accessible for the large machine, such as corners and edges. You may be offered a belt or a disc type: the belt type is preferable because it will not leave scratch marks across the grain.

When you collect the machines, make sure you are shown exactly how to operate them and are comfortable doing so. Pick up a generous supply of abrasive sanding sheets and belts in coarse, medium and fine grades. These are generally supplied on a sale-or-return basis.

Preparing the floor

CHECK THAT ALL NAIL HEADS are punched at least ⅛in (3mm) below the surface. Anchor loose boards by driving in cut flooring nails close to the existing nail positions, to minimize the risk of piercing hidden pipes or cables. If warped boards keep pulling the nails up, use deeply countersunk screws to keep them in place.

SEVERAL LAYERS OF VARNISH HAVE BEEN CAREFULLY APPLIED TO THESE FLOORBOARDS, SANDING IN BETWEEN COATS, TO GIVE THE FLOOR A GLOSSY SHEEN AND TO MAKE IT HARDWEARING. THE VARNISHED BOARDS MATCH THE RICH COLOR OF THE WOODEN PANELLING, DOORS AND WINDOW FRAMES IN THIS HANDSOME DINING ROOM.

Replace any split or otherwise damaged boards with new ones. To lift tongue-and-groove boards, first cut through the tongues along each edge with a circular saw. Then prise the board up from one end with a crowbar, using a scrap of wood to protect the end of the adjacent sound board. Cut the new board to fit and nail it firmly in place.

Sweep the floor, then close the door to the rest of the house and seal around it with wide masking tape. Open the windows of the room for ventilation and to help the dust to clear as you work.

Sanding the floor

ATTACH A COARSE ABRASIVE SHEET to the sander, then start sanding with the machine in one corner of the room. Work diagonally to begin with, to ensure that all the boards are sanded level with one another, so start by heading for the opposite corner of the room. Then turn around and run back over the first pass. Continue sanding each triangular half of the room in this way, taking care not to damage baseboards as you reach the end of each pass. Replace the abrasive sheets with new ones as they become worn.

Next, change to medium-grade abrasive sheets and sand the floor parallel with the direction of the boards, going back over each pass and working as close to the baseboards as you can without scoring them. Then switch to fine abrasive and repeat the whole process. From time to time, empty the dust bag and vacuum the floor to cut down on the amount of fine dust flying around.

Sanding the edges

NOW TACKLE THE EDGES, and any other parts that the drum sander could not reach, with your smaller belt or orbital sander. Once again, work through coarse, medium and fine grades of abrasive paper. Finish by hand-sanding or scraping any odd bits that the machines have missed.

When you are happy with the look of the floor, sweep and vacuum-clean it thoroughly, paying particular attention to the joints between the boards, and to the room corners and other crevices. Use a clean cloth soaked in mineral spirits to wipe over the surface of the boards to remove any remaining superficial dust.

Varnishing the floor

THIN THE FIRST COAT OF VARNISH with about 10 per cent mineral spirits. Wipe on this first priming coat with a cloth, rather than using a brush. Leave it to dry, then sand the surface lightly with fine abrasive on a sanding block to key the surface, ready for the next coat. Wipe it over with a cloth soaked in spirits to remove the dust. Apply two further coats of full-strength varnish with a brush, sanding after the second coat.

SEE ALSO:

STENCILING WOODEN FLOORS　　111

LAYING CORK AND VINYL TILES

UNLESS YOU ARE EXPERIENCED AT LAYING FLOORCOVERINGS, you will find it easier to use tiles rather than sheet materials. Their small size makes it simpler to get a good fit around obstacles, so there is less wastage involved in laying them. Cork and vinyl tiles can be laid on both solid and suspended wood floors, provided the surface is smooth and sound. If it is not, you will need to put down a hardboard underlay on wooden floors, or a self-smoothing concrete screed on solid ones.

CORK FLOOR TILES MAKE A WARM, PRACTICAL FLOORCOVERING FOR A KITCHEN. UNLESS YOU ARE USING VINYL-COATED CORK TILES, YOU MUST SEAL THE FLOOR WITH SEVERAL COATS OF MATTE VARNISH AFTER LAYING, TO MAKE IT MORE DURABLE.

What you need

ALL YOU REQUIRE to lay cork or vinyl tiles are a few simple tools plus tile adhesive, unless you are laying self-adhesive vinyl tiles.

Tile adhesive comes ready-mixed; a notched spreader is usually included in the tub. Choose water-based adhesive for cork tiles; for vinyl-coated cork tiles you need a vinyl acrylic adhesive. For vinyl tiles, an emulsion-type flooring adhesive is the best choice and this is applied with an old paintbrush.

Tile sealant is needed only if you are laying unsealed cork tiles. Use ordinary polyurethane varnish or a special floor sealant.

A chalked string line, pinned across the room between the baseboards, is useful for marking tiling guidelines on the floor.

A tape measure, a trimming knife and a steel straight edge are essential for marking and cutting border tiles.

A profile gauge makes it easy to cut tiles to fit around awkward obstacles such as architrave moldings and pipework. Or you can cut a cardboard or paper template.

Preparing the sub-floor

ON WOODEN FLOORS that are uneven or full of gaps, lay a hardboard underlay, smooth side uppermost, over the boards. Pin the board down with hardboard pins driven in at 6in (150mm) intervals along the edges and across the center of each board, leaving a ⅛in (3mm) gap for expansion at the edges and between boards.

On solid floors with a rough or uneven surface, fill any large cracks or holes with mortar, then lay a self-smoothing compound to make a screed. Compounds of this type are usually sold in powder form, ready to be mixed with water and poured on to the floor surface. The mixture is then trowelled out with a steel float to a thickness of about ⅛in (3mm) all over and left to harden.

Planning the layout

ANY TILED FLOOR looks best if the tile layout is centered, especially if you are using a pattern of different tiles. Planning a layout from the center outwards ensures an even border of cut tiles all around the room. Centre the layout, using chalked string lines as described in the box below. Then, having checked that you will not end up with awkward narrow strips in areas such as doorways and chimney breasts, lift the tiles, chalk each line and snap it against the floor to leave two guidelines to work to. Finally, remove the strings.

Centering your tile layout

IN A REGULARLY SHAPED ROOM, join the mid-points of opposite walls with string lines pinned to the baseboards, at floor level. Dry-lay a row of whole tiles from the room's center-point out towards the walls in each direction, to work out the number needed. If there is a narrow gap at the end of a row, move the string parallel to that wall half a tile's width nearer to it, remove one tile from the row and re-lay the others to fit. If the gap is more than half a tile wide, move the string further away from the wall and add a tile to the row instead.

Laying the tiles

START SPREADING the adhesive in one quarter of the room, next to the center point. Use a notched spreader with cork tile adhesive, or an old paintbrush with emulsion-type vinyl tile adhesive.

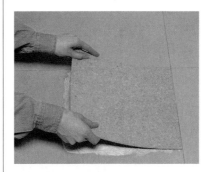

ALIGN THE FIRST TILE WITH the guidelines, then press it firmly down into position with the palm of your hand. Remember that unsealed cork tiles have one surface smoother than the other. Make sure you lay them with the rougher side down.

Continue adding tiles, working along the guidelines to the edge of the adhesive, building up the rectangle. Spread another area of adhesive and repeat the process until you complete the first quarter of the floor. Repeat this sequence in the other three-quarters of the room, working backwards towards the door. Kneel on an offcut of hardboard so you do not disturb tiles that have already been laid.

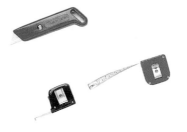

Finishing the borders

MARK THE PART-TILES that will fill the gaps next to the baseboards, as described for borders in ceramic tile floors (see page 142).

THEN CUT ALONG THE LINE with your knife and straight edge. Spread some tile adhesive on the floor and press the cut piece into place. Repeat the process to complete the border.

Pin slim quadrant beading to the baseboards to cover any gaps left at the edges. Fit a threshold strip across the door opening to cover the edge of the tiles.

LAYING SHEET VINYL

SHEET VINYL FLOORCOVERINGS ARE THE IDEAL CHOICE for kitchens and bathrooms, where spillages and splashes regularly occur. They can also be a low-cost flooring for areas of the home such as hallways and children's bedrooms. You need no special tools or equipment to lay sheet vinyl — just one gadget which you can make yourself.

SHEET VINYL COMES IN VARIOUS GRADES, AT THE TOP END RESEMBLING HIGH-QUALITY TILES OR WOOD BLOCKS BUT COSTING ALMOST AS MUCH TO BUY. ITS ADVANTAGES ARE THAT IT IS MUCH QUICKER TO LAY AND THERE ARE NO JOINTS THROUGH WHICH WATER CAN SEEP, MAKING THIS MATERIAL AN IDEAL FLOORING FOR A BATHROOM.

Preparing the floor

SHEET VINYL CAN BE LAID over both solid concrete and suspended wooden floors. Lift existing floor-coverings (although well-stuck tiles of all types can be left in place, as can sheet materials that have been stuck down all over). On boarded floors, drive in any nail heads to ensure a flat surface and put down a hardboard under-lay if the floor has gaps or is uneven. Dusty concrete floors should be sealed with a diluted vinyl bonding agent; uneven or pitted concrete floors will need a self-smoothing compound laid as a screed.

Laying out the sheet

UNROLL THE SHEET PARALLEL with the longest straight, unobstructed wall in the room, and push one edge up against the baseboard. (Let the other edges of the sheet lap up the other walls at this stage.) Then slide the length away from the baseboard by about 1in (25mm), and position your scribing block (see right) on it, with the end holding the ballpoint pen nearest to the baseboard. Keep this end pushed firmly against the molding, and draw the block towards you so the pen scribes the profile of the baseboard on the surface of the sheet.

Making a scribing block

THIS IS A DEVICE used to mark the longest straight edge of the sheet so that it is a good fit against the baseboard. All you need is a piece of scrap wood about 2 x 1in (50 x 25mm) in cross-section and around 4in (100mm) long. Drill a hole through it about 2in (50mm) from one end, large enough to accept a ballpoint pen. Put the pen through the hole and use the block to mark the longest straight edge of the sheet.

Cutting to fit

USE A SHARP KNIFE to cut along the scribed line, following it as closely as possible, and discard the offcut. Slide the sheet back against the wall to check its fit. Trim if needed.

Roughly trim off any excess of about 2in (50mm) riding up the baseboards along the other three walls, ready for the final trimming. Make sure you leave enough waste material across door openings to allow the floorcovering to reach to the threshold strip.

Dealing with corners

MAKE CUTS AT 45 DEGREES across all internal corners to allow the rest of the sheet to lie flat. Do this in stages, so that you do not risk cutting away too much material; you cannot put it back if you make a mistake.

Approach external corners with special care. At a chimney breast, for example, press the sheet into the angle across the face of the breast wall, fold the surplus back and mark the position of each external corner on the underside of the sheet. Then cut in from the waste edge of the sheet towards this mark at an angle of about 45 degrees, extending the cut a little at a time until the sheet lies flat round the corner, with the waste material lapping up the baseboard on each side of it.

The final trimming

START AT ONE END of the wall you scribed to fit earlier, and use your straight edge to press the sheet as far into the floor/baseboard angle as possible. Then push the knife blade through the sheet and draw it along the straight edge, holding it at a slight angle so that your knuckles are clear of the base-board. Continue trimming in the same way to remove the waste from the other edges of the sheet.

Sticking down the edges

USE EITHER FLOORING adhesive or double-sided tape for the edges. Lift back each edge in turn and spread adhesive or apply tape to the floor surface. Then press the edge down firmly all the way along. Do this for the doorway edge of the room first and fit a threshold strip across the room doorway. Then repeat the process for all the other edges of the room. (Sticking down the edges of the sheet is not necessary with some "lay-flat" brands: check with your supplier when you buy.)

Using a template

IN BATHROOMS you may be faced with the awkward problem of having to cut around basin and toilet pedestals. The best way to do this accurately is to make a paper template of the room's floor.

TAPE SHEETS OF PAPER to the floor and to each other, so that their edges are about 2in (50mm) in from the baseboard all round. Use scissors to cut the sheets to a similarly rough fit around pedestals and other obstacles. Then use your scribing block to draw the room outline (and the outline of any obstacles) onto the paper.

LIFT THE TEMPLATE, lay it on the unrolled floorcovering in another room and reverse the scribing procedure. Let the end of the block follow the line on the template, and the pen will trace out the room's outline on the vinyl. Cut along the outline with a knife or scissors (scissors are easier on curves) and discard the waste. When cutting around a pedestal base, make a straight cut in from the edge of the sheet, so the two "tongues" can be slid behind the pedestal.

TIPS

❍ At awkward obstacles such as door architraves, use a profile gauge to take an impression of the architrave's outline and use this to mark and cut the sheet to fit.

❍ Where pipes rise through the floor, make a short, right-angled cut in from the edge of the sheet in line with one side of the pipe, then cut out a circle to match the pipe's diameter.

❍ If you find you have seriously overcut the edges at any point, disguise the mistake by pinning lengths of beading to the bottom edge of the baseboard and painting them to match it.

❍ Leave new sheet vinyl in the room where it is to be laid for 48 hours to acclimatize; unroll it and either lay it out flat (with a fold or two across the width) or roll it up again loosely in the other direction and stand it on its end.

❍ Consider laying sheet vinyl in a playroom or young child's bedroom. It is practical, and softness can be added with fluffy rug islands.

❍ Vinyl flooring can stain, but any stains are less likely to show up on a textured finish.

❍ If you have an irregular-shaped room, consider using vinyl tiles instead of sheet vinyl, as they can be individually trimmed to shape. You can also lay a central block of sheet vinyl and make a border of vinyl tiles, perhaps in a checked or other geometric pattern.

❍ Always clear the room before you start, as you will not be able to work around any items of furniture.

SEE ALSO:

LAYING CORK AND VINYL TILES   146

LAYING CARPET

MOST CARPETS ARE BURLAP-BACKED AND ARE LAID over a separate underlay and tensioned with gripper strips which anchor the perimeter of the carpet all around the edge of the room. Foam-backed carpets have an underlay bonded to the backing and are effectively loose-laid, with the perimeter either stuck down with double-sided tape or secured with staples or tacks, making them easier to lay. Your first attempts at carpet-laying should ideally be in a small room, such as a bedroom, that is relatively free from obstructions, so that little intricate cutting and fitting is involved.

What you need

TO LAY FOAM-BACKED CARPET you will need a few basic hand tools – a tape measure and a sharp knife – and some special double-sided flooring tape or a staple gun. For burlapbacked carpet, you should hire a specialist tool called a knee kicker to help tension the carpet across the room, and buy gripper strips to pin the edges of the carpet. To cut and fit the gripper strips you need a tenon saw and a hammer (or panel adhesive on solid floors). Last, you may need a junior hacksaw to cut metal threshold strips to length.

Laying foam-backed carpet

LIFT ANY OLD FLOORCOVERINGS and prepare the floor surface in the usual way (see page 142), then put down an "undersheet" of stout brown paper or special glass-fiber matting. This stops dust from rising into the carpet from the floor below, and helps prevent the foam backing from sticking to the floor in areas of heavy traffic or underneath furniture. Lay down the undersheet to within about 2in (50mm) of the baseboards and tape or staple it down securely.

Lay the double-sided tape all around the perimeter of the room, leaving the top release paper in place for now.

PATTERNED COIR CARPET IS LAID IN EXACTLY THE SAME WAY AS A FITTED BURLAP-BACKED CARPET. HERE IT PROVIDES A HARDWEARING AND ORIGINAL FLOORCOVERING FOR THE STUDY AND THE STAIRS UP TO A BEDROOM, LINKING THE TWO AREAS VISUALLY.

Securing foam-backed carpet

ROLL THE CARPET OUT right side up, parallel to the longest wall in the room. Abut its edge up to the baseboard and let the excess ride up the long wall opposite and also up the two side walls. Then cut off all but about 3in (75mm) of the excess along the other three edges. Make triangular cuts across the two corners of the carpet next to the opposite long wall to allow the carpet to lie flat.

Secure to the floor the first edge you laid by peeling off the tape's release paper and pressing the carpet backing down onto it. Then stretch the carpet across the room to the opposite long wall by shuffling your feet across it, and trim off the excess carpet along that wall. To do this, press the carpet down into the angle between the wall and the baseboard and draw your knife along it.

Repeat the shuffling process from the room's center towards the two side walls, then trim off the excess carpet there. Finally, remove the release paper from the tape along the other three sides of the room and stick these edges down in the same way.

Laying burlap-backed carpet

NAIL OR GLUE GRIPPER strips to the floor all around the room, setting them about ⅜in (10mm) in from the baseboards.

Cut and lay the underlay so it fits right up to the gripper strip. Staple it down in position to stop it from rucking as you lay the carpet.

Securing burlap-backed carpet

UNROLL THE CARPET, allowing it to lap up the walls all around, and trim off all but about 3in (75mm) of the excess. Make triangular release cuts at internal corners, and cuts at right angles to the carpet edge at external corners, such as chimney breasts, to allow the carpet tongues to fall back into the alcoves. Remember to leave a tongue of carpet at doorways, long enough to reach the threshold strip between the rooms.

WITH THE CARPET LYING FLAT all around, trim one long edge with a sharp knife held at a 45-degree angle, cutting the carpet fractionally oversize.

USE A CLEAN BRICK BOLSTER CHISEL (or a proper carpet-laying bolster, which looks similar) to tuck the cut edge neatly into the gap between the wall and the gripper strips. Then use the knee kicker to tension the carpet along one adjacent side wall of the room towards the next corner. Trim and secure this edge in the same way.

Repeat the stretching process, working diagonally from the corner between the two edges you have just attached to the gripper strips, and secure the opposite corner of the carpet tightly to the grippers.

Finally, stretch the carpet out from the diagonal towards the remaining two walls and secure these two edges to their gripper strips. Then trim off the excess carpet and tuck the edge behind the strips.

LAYING WOOD-BLOCK FLOORS

MOSAIC WOODEN FLOOR BLOCKS — square sections made from a number of small strips of hardwood — make an attractive alternative to woodstrip floorboards, and the "stripped pine" look of sanded floors. They come in different decorative hardwoods and are simple to lay.

What you need

FOR LAYING MOSAIC OR PARQUET blocks you will need: flooring adhesive and a brush or spreader for applying it; chalked string lines; a retractable steel tape measure; a pencil or craft knife; a tenon saw or power jigsaw; a portable workbench; glasspaper and a sanding block or a power sander; varnish (for unsealed types) plus some lint-free cloth and a paintbrush.

Working out quantities

FIND OUT THE SIZE of the wooden blocks you intend to lay; most are either 12in (300mm) or 18in (450mm) square. Then draw a scale plan of the room so you can work out how many rows of blocks will be needed to cover the floor area, and how many blocks in each row. Multiply the two figures together and add 5 per cent extra to allow for wastage. Estimate the numbers needed to fill awkward areas such as bay windows by counting each cut block as a whole one.

Preparing the sub-floor

PREPARE THE SUB-FLOOR as for laying sheet vinyl flooring (see page 148). Decide whether to remove and refix the baseboards, or work with them in place; shave the bottom of any doors so they will clear the new raised floor level.

Find your starting point in the center of the room, in exactly the same way as for laying cork and vinyl floor tiles (see page 146). It is best to work in this way to ensure an even border of cut blocks at the perimeter of the room, although any variations will be less noticeable here than they would be with patterned vinyl tiles. If you are confident that the room is square, you could start laying in one corner instead, but it is difficult to guarantee a perfect result using this method.

THE PANELS IN MODERN WOOD-BLOCK FLOORING ARE USUALLY ARRANGED IN A HERRINGBONE OR A BASKETWEAVE DESIGN TO IMITATE OLDER PARQUET FLOORS. WHEREAS HARDWOOD PARQUET FLOORS LIKE THIS ONE WERE SOLID, TODAY'S WOOD-BLOCK FLOORING IS GENERALLY A VENEER AND IS THEREFORE EASIER TO LAY.

Laying the blocks

WHEN YOU ARE HAPPY with the setting out, spread some adhesive in the quarter of the room furthest from the door, and lay the first block to your guidelines. Press it down firmly with your hands, and then tap all over it with a hammer to ensure a really good bond, using an offcut of wood to protect the surface. Then lay further whole blocks out from the center point towards the perimeter of the room, filling each quarter of the floor area in turn. Make sure that the edges abut tightly and align squarely with each other; slight errors can easily accumulate into big ones at the end of a row. If you get any adhesive on the face of the blocks, wipe it off immediately. If it starts to dry, remove it with steel wool and mineral spirits.

Completing the borders

WHEN YOU HAVE LAID all the whole blocks, start filling in the cut pieces at the perimeter and around obstacles. For straight edge strips, measure the distance between the edge of the last whole block and the wall, and subtract ⅜in (10mm) for the essential expansion gap. Cut the block down to the required size and bed it in place.

Where you have to cut blocks around awkward shapes such as door architraves and pipes, either scribe the blocks directly (see page 148) or use an adjustable template device to transcribe the outline of the obstacle on to the block. Use a coping saw to make any intricate cutouts.

Finishing

REPLACE THE BASEBOARDS; if you left them in place, either fit cork expansion strips into the ⅜in (10mm) expansion gap or cover it with quadrant beading pinned to the lower face of the baseboard. It is best to paint the beading to match the baseboards before pinning it in place; you can touch up the pin holes afterwards to make them invisible. Pin an angled wooden filler at the door threshold.

SWEEP UP DUST AND debris, and polish sealed wooden blocks. With unsealed types, sand and vacuum clean the floor, then apply three coats of sealant.

TIPS

○ *Unpack the mosaic blocks and store them in the room where they will be laid for at least seven days, to allow them to acclimatize to the temperature and humidity levels. This will help minimize shrinkage when the blocks are laid.*

SEE ALSO:

TYPES OF FLOORCOVERING	140
LAYING CORK AND VINYL TILES	146
LAYING SHEET VINYL	148

LAYING WOODSTRIP FLOORS

IF YOU WANT A NATURAL WOOD-FLOOR FINISH, laying hardwood strip flooring is the perfect answer. You can lay it on both wooden and solid floors, provided you devote a little time to floor preparation first. If you do not, your expensive new floor surface will soon wear unevenly, and may shrink or sink.

THIS WOODSTRIP FLOOR HAS BEEN LAID OVER A HARDBOARD SUB-FLOOR TO ENSURE AN EVEN SURFACE. IT HAS BEEN SEALED WITH SEVERAL COATS OF A MATTE VARNISH TO MAKE IT HARDWEARING ENOUGH FOR USE IN A FAMILY KITCHEN.

What you need

TO LAY WOODSTRIP floorcovering, you should have: a retractable steel tape measure; a claw hammer; a tenon saw or an electric jigsaw; a portable workbench; a try square; a nail punch; a craft knife; a shape tracer (optional), plus some woodworking adhesive or brads (as recommended in the flooring instructions).

To prepare the sub-floor you will need hardboard plus pins for uneven wooden floors, floorboard nails or wood screws (plus awl and screwdriver) for anchoring loose boards, self-smoothing compound for uneven solid floors, and underlay if recommended by the flooring manufacturer.

Preparing the floor

A NEATER FINISH will be achieved if you prise off the baseboards all around the room and replace them once the flooring has been laid. This will then conceal the ⅜in (10mm) expansion gap around the perimeter of the room. You should also trim the bottom of door architraves to allow the flooring to fit beneath them. However, if this is impractical you can leave your expansion gap between the new flooring and the face of the baseboards instead, and either insert narrow strips of cork to fill the gap or conceal it with quadrant beading pinned to the baseboard.

Laying the woodstrips

PUT DOWN SPECIAL UNDERLAY (which may be plastic sheeting, glass fiber matting or foam), if recommended, and tape or staple the seams together so they do not ruck up as you work.

Bear in mind that your new flooring will raise the existing floor level noticeably, so doors opening over it will need to be shortened slightly. It is essential to do this before you lay the new flooring.

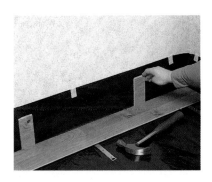

BEGIN LAYING ALONGSIDE a straight wall if possible; otherwise choose the one with the fewest obstructions. Offer up the first plank to the wall, with ⅜in (10mm) thick offcuts of wood positioned between the wall and the board edge to form the expansion gap. If there are obstacles along the wall, scribe and cut the planks in this first row to fit around them, using your tenon saw or jigsaw.

If the flooring you are using is pinned by secret nailing, always make sure that the grooved edge faces the wall. Then drive brads down through the tongues into the sub-floor.

IF YOU ARE USING CLIPS, tap them into the grooves in the underside of the first board at the recommended intervals, and lay the grooved edge of the board in place against the spacers.

Lay further planks end to end to complete the first row. Apply a little woodworking adhesive to one end of each plank before tapping it into position.

LAY THE SECOND (and subsequent) rows of planks by offering their grooved edges up to the tongues of the previous row, and use an offcut over their tongued edges to protect them while you tap the joints tightly closed. If using clips, tap the plank edges to make the clips engage in their grooves and lock the boards together.

Remember that an expansion gap is required at the ends of each row too, so insert spacers as required.

Laying the last row

THE PLANKS IN THE LAST ROW will probably have to be cut down in width to allow them to be fitted. Lay the last two whole rows dry (without clips or adhesive) so you can measure the width required minus the ⅜in (10mm) expansion gap. Then cut the planks down to the required width with your tenon saw or jigsaw.

With secret nailing, the last row of planks will have lost their tongued edges. If you have been gluing the long edges, you can rely on adhesive to hold the last row in place, but if you have just been nailing the tongues you will have to attach the last row with pins driven through the plank faces. Punch the pins in with your nail punch, and fill the holes with matching wood filler. With clips, it may be impossible to slip the last strip into place with the clips fitted. Here it is best simply to glue the final tongue-and-groove joint for a neat finish.

Finishing

REMOVE THE SPACERS all around the room and replace the baseboards so they cover the expansion gap. If you left the baseboards in place, cut and fit special cork strips (supplied by the flooring manufacturer) to fill the gap all round the perimeter, or else pin quadrant beading to the foot of the baseboard all around the room to cover the gap. Add a tapered wooden filler across the door threshold to disguise the change in floor level from one room to another.

TIPS

❍ *Always unpack the strips and leave them in the room where they will be laid for about a week to acclimatize to the temperature and humidity levels in your home. This will help to prevent undue buckling or shrinkage when they are laid.*

❍ *Where planks run up to awkwardly shaped obstacles such as architraves or pipes, either scribe the end of the plank to fit or use a shape tracer to transfer the outline of the obstacle on to it, ready for cutting. You may need a coping saw to make intricate cutouts.*

SEE ALSO:

TYPES OF FLOORCOVERING	140
LAYING SHEET VINYL	148

SWEEP UP SAWDUST and clear the room, ready for the floor to receive its final polish. If you have to varnish unsealed boards, vacuum-clean the floor thoroughly, then apply three coats of varnish.

SOFT FURNISHINGS

TEXTILES MAKE A HOME: they bring color, pattern, style and warmth into every room and give it individuality. Soft furnishing is the craft of using textiles to make curtains, blinds and shades, covers, cushions and all kinds of other fabric accessories that soften a room, make it more welcoming and give it a stamp of originality. Unlike ready-made soft furnishings, which are necessarily limited in color and design, those you make yourself will be a perfect match for your room scheme and can have all the designer details you would expect from professionally made furnishings. So take trouble over your choice of fabric, seek out ideal trimmings and spend a little time over the finishing touches: you will find that your efforts are well rewarded.

Over the following pages you will find instructions for making the most popular styles of soft furnishings together with tips and ideas to give them an individual look.

LEFT: SUMMERY YELLOW AND WHITE STRIPED AUSTRIAN BLINDS BRING A SUNNY ATMOSPHERE TO THIS BRIGHT LIVING ROOM. MADE IN THE USUAL WAY, THE TAILED EFFECT IS ACHIEVED SIMPLY BY OMITTING THE OUTERMOST LINES OF CORDING; A BIAS-CUT BORDER OF DIAGONAL STRIPES AVOIDS ANY HINT OF OSTENTATION. THE YELLOW IS PICKED UP IN THE BOLSTER AND CUSHION MADE FOR THE SOFA, COVERED IN NATURAL MUSLIN.

RIGHT: NATURAL FABRICS IN PALE, NEUTRAL COLORS ALWAYS LOOK COOL AND FRESH, AS THESE OXFORD PILLOWCASES TESTIFY. TO COPY THE EFFECT, USE A FABRIC PRINTED WITH DIAGONAL STRIPES — BIAS-CUT PILLOWCASES ARE DIFFICULT TO KEEP IN SHAPE.

CURTAINS: A STYLE TO SUIT YOUR ROOM

WINDOWS ARE THE EYES OF A ROOM and the curtains a focal point, so never underestimate their impact. A window treatment that harmonizes with its surroundings will always be the most successful; when deciding how to curtain a window, choose a style that — in addition to flattering the shape of the window — complements the architectural style of the room or other important elements within it, which may be the wallcoverings, the furniture or some of the accessories. However eclectic the assortment of furnishings and possessions in a room, there is almost always a strong stylistic theme connecting them that gives each room its character. Identify that essential character and you have the clue to the style of window treatment — and even the type of fabric the room needs.

The time you spend finding the right style of curtain is time well spent. Start by making a thumbnail sketch of your design theme for the room, then develop it into a more detailed picture by collecting illustrations from magazines, postcards from historic or modern houses, samples of fabrics and trimmings that capture the style you are aiming for, until your ideas begin to gel. If you are furnishing your home in period style, curtain design plays an important part: you may need to do a little research by visiting historic houses open to the public and this will help you to glean authentic ideas. The Victorians loved flamboyant, multi-layered heavy drapes in luxurious velvet and brocades, with valances, fringing and tiebacks. Turn-of-the-century style favored prints and chintzes in floral patterns to match the wallpaper; valances and pelmets were still in evidence but used with a lighter touch. From the 'thirties to the 'sixties, curtains became much simpler in style – if they were there at all – generally hanging straight down to the sill or floor from a track or pole.

To outline some popular design themes, consider the town house look. Decorated in classic style, it demands a rather formal window treatment with full-length drapes, neatly pleated with fabric or cord tiebacks and a shaped, stiffened valance. Contrasting edgings or linings give the arrangement a suitably tailored look. Silks, stripes, plain heavy cotton or velvet all give an impression of weight and substance.

Country-house curtains, though still traditional in style, can be less formal. Floral chintzes – particularly those reproduced using original printing blocks – faded-looking linen union and plain cotton figured with a tiny sprig pattern are all suitable fabrics. Make them up into long, full curtains falling from a gathered valance or swagged heading. Country cottage windows are treated in a more relaxed, informal way with short, cotton-print curtains, with or without a gathered valance. Hanging straight, or caught with tiebacks, they frame a view of open fields or garden flowers.

FAR LEFT: OVER-LONG, INTERLINED SILK CURTAINS AND A SWAGGED PELMET, BOTH IMMACULATELY PLEATED, FRAME THIS WINDOW IN FORMAL STYLE. FABRIC ROSETTES, TASSELS AND CORD TIEBACKS ARE APPROPRIATE DETAILS FOR THIS STYLE OF CURTAIN.

LEFT: THE EARLIEST CURTAINS WERE MADE OF FINE, TRANSLUCENT MATERIAL TO PROTECT FURNISHINGS FROM THE FADING EFFECTS OF THE SUN. THE WINDOW IN THIS PERIOD ROOM HAS BEEN SIMILARLY TREATED BUT WITH THE ADDITION OF A CHECKED WINDOW SHADE FOR PRIVACY.

A more contemporary rustic interior decorated with plain painted walls, colorwashed details, coir-covered floor and minimal furniture calls for a much simpler approach to window dressing. Here, unlined calico or canvas, checks or stripes make ideal fabrics for simply gathered curtains hung from a pole or almost flat panels held on by clip-on curtains rings. The look is unsophisticated, summery and spare. Natural rope tiebacks and undyed cotton fringing make appropriate trimmings. By contrast, contemporary-style rooms in urban houses and city apartments are generally furnished for style and comfort but with restraint. Their window treatments might feature full-length drapes in a silky slub, stripes or figured weaves, made up with regular pleated headings, either hanging straight or caught with a matching crescent tiebacks. Beautiful curtain poles with elaborate finials, cord trimmings and deep fringing are essential details.

BELOW: THESE GAUZY, CONTRAST-EDGED CURTAINS ARE JOINED AT THE CENTER AND LOOPED BACK AT A HIGH LEVEL TO EMPHASIZE THE HEIGHT OF THE MULLIONED WINDOWS AND FRAME THE WONDERFUL VIEW. THE TIEBACKS ARE MADE FROM THE SAME FABRIC, INTERLINED TO GIVE SUBSTANCE, THEN DECORATED WITH A SOFT, LONG-TAILED BOW.

A MINIMAL DRESSING SUITS THESE SMALL SASH WINDOWS IN A BEDROOM. LOUVERED SHUTTERS COVER THE LOWER PART OF THE WINDOW WHEN NECESSARY, AND A CHEERFUL GINGHAM SWAG CONCEALS A BLIND THAT COVERS THE UPPER PANE AT NIGHT.

Mood is sometimes more important than a particular style, and curtains can help to create it. In a bedroom, a romantic atmosphere might be conjured by dressing the bed and windows with generous swathes of gauze. The volume of fine, floating fabric will flatter the room like a soft-focus lens. In a dining room, theatrical decoration can lend a sense of drama to every dinner party. Here, multi-layered curtains, swags and tails, tassels, trimmings and rich fabrics are the very different ingredients required.

The way you curtain a window will be determined, to an extent, by its shape and by the character of the room. Small rooms will be overwhelmed by a grand, formal window treatment and a large room needs something more than a pair of straight hanging curtains to give it a focus. The fabric design, too, should be in keeping with its surroundings. Stripes and plain colors are always a safe choice, but ensure that patterns are in scale with the size of the windows.

Curtains can be a useful tool if you want to improve the proportions of a room visually. Too many patterns or colors will have an enclosing effect in a small room, so use curtains made from fabric in the same pattern or color as the walls to give continuity and a feeling of spaciousness. Light, bright rooms always seem larger and airier than they really are, so explore the possibility of curtaining with filmy sheer fabrics. If you need privacy or prefer a more solid window covering by night, fit a blind behind the curtains.

In rooms where the ceiling seems too low, ceiling-to-floor curtains will carry the eye upwards, giving an impression of height. This technique does not work in reverse, however – short curtains in a lofty room simply look penny-pinching. But wide, full curtains will draw attention away from the ceiling.

PROBLEM WINDOWS

Not all shapes and sizes of window are equally easy to curtain, but solutions can usually be found.

Bay windows can be treated in a number of ways, according to their size and design. Small bays with wide spaces between the panes need curtains which pull to the sides, leaving the glass uncovered. The track can be bent to follow the curve of the window

THE COUNTRY-HOUSE LOOK IS EPITOMIZED HERE BY THE JUXTAPOSITION OF HEAVY BROCADE DRAPES, THICK TASSELLED TIEBACKS AND CRISP TAFFETA SHEERS. THE VARIETY OF TEXTURES PROVIDES A WINNING COMBINATION OF AFFINITY AND CONTRAST.

or, if the bay is a shallow one, fitted straight across it. Large bays, however, can look bare with this treatment and benefit from having their width broken up by curtains stacked between the angles of the bay and in the middle. A valance or shaped pelmet designed to emphasize these divisions will serve to make the window more of a decorative feature. Where there is a radiator or window seat in the bay, the central curtains should be cut short to skim the sill or replaced by matching or contrasting blinds. Dress curtains at the sides, and a valance, will frame the window gracefully.

French windows present a problem only if they open inwards. The best way to deal with this is to extend the track or pole at the sides so the doors can open freely when the curtains are drawn back. Some French windows are flanked by smaller casements and these look best if they are treated as one window, with full-length curtains generously spanning the entire window area.

Patio doors are usually fitted in order to enjoy the sight of a beautiful garden or a spectacular view but, at night, the glass becomes a dark, reflective expanse which demands curtains. Because the windows are modern in style, it is more appropriate to opt for floor-length curtains, uncluttered with valances, pelmets and tiebacks, which pull back well clear of the opening panes. The large area of such windows offers great scope for using fabrics with large-scale designs.

Arched windows It would be a pity to conceal an arched window behind conventional curtains, but fixed curtains fitted around the arch can enhance its shape and tiebacks placed higher than usual will let in the maximum light. Alternatively, closing curtains might be hung from a track mounted well above the window and a pelmet or valance might be made to echo the curved shape.

Dormer windows and windows set into a deep recess are problematic because, when drawn back, the curtains block much of the light. Special dormer rods provide a good solution. Hinged at the corners and meeting in the middle, they swing the curtain away from the glass during the day. Another strategy is to continue the ends of the track along the return walls of the window recess, so the curtains can be pulled right back. Both these methods look much prettier if the curtains are caught with tiebacks. Full-length curtains can be slotted behind a pole set across the angle of the roof and wall.

STYLING IDEAS

○ *With recessed windows, decide whether to hang the curtains inside or outside the rabbet. Curtains hung close to the glass give a charming cottage effect but may block the light when open. Outside the rabbet you can hang long or short curtains and draw them back to clear the opening.*

○ *Change your curtains with the seasons: lightweight cotton curtains give a room a fresh, summery feel; heavier ones make it seem cozier for winter.*

○ *Curtains are not just window dressings: use them around a bathroom basin to hide ugly pipework and provide storage. Rediscover skirted dressing tables, with their feminine, country-house look. Draw them across doors to keep out drafts and hang them from a coronet above the bedhead.*

○ *When shopping for a boldly patterned fabric, gather it up in your hand to see how gathers will change the appearance of the design. Some patterned fabric works best as blinds or bedcovers, where the material is seen flat.*

○ *Use alternative textiles for window treatments: bedspreads, shawls, tablecloths and sheets make wonderful drapes.*

○ *Second-hand curtains are great value and can easily be altered to fit: find them at house sales, auctions and through classified ads in newspapers.*

FABRICS FOR CURTAINS

FABRICS SUITABLE FOR CURTAIN MAKING vary widely, depending on the window, the room and its décor, and the style of curtain. Materials as diverse as muslin and brocade, fibers as different as nylon and wool, plains, patterns, checks, stripes or florals, glazed or pile finishes, can all be used in the right context.

Woven stripe (1) A heavy jacquard fabric, usually made from a blend of natural and man-made fibers, with a multi-colored woven design. Suitable for full-length curtains at tall windows and for door curtains.

Printed moiré (2) A ribbed silky fabric with the characteristic watermark, overprinted with a design. This luxurious fabric is not washable and does not benefit from frequent cleaning, so use it only in areas where it will receive gentle handling.

Velvet (3) This heavy, rich pile fabric made from cotton, man-made fibers or a mixture of the two, drapes beautifully and creates wonderfully sumptuous drapes. Silky fringes, cords and tassels contrast beautifully with the matte surface.

Brocade (4) A rich, highly patterned woven fabric in which the pattern is additional to the basic weave. Expensive and luxurious, it looks best used in long drapes at large windows.

Mini print (5) A small, regular all-over print that is ideal for curtains at small windows or to make contrast linings for highly patterned curtains.

Cretonne (6) An unglazed printed cotton fabric suitable for curtains where a matte surface is required.

Gingham (7) Lightweight woven check fabric usually made from cotton, though polyester and cotton blends are available. The checks come in various sizes and colors, but are somewhat limited to primaries and pastels. Being washable, gingham is a good choice for kitchen curtains.

Peasant print (8, 17) Plain woven cotton, printed with bold folk motifs in earth colors.

Toile de Jouy (9) White or cream glazed cotton printed in a single color with finely detailed scenic designs, usually of pastoral life. Use as an alternative to floral chintz.

Crewel work (10) A heavyweight coarse-weave cotton embroidered with wool crewel embroidery in single or multi-colored designs. Patterns are ethnic in style and usually floral.

Damask (11) A traditional furnishing fabric with a woven design created by areas of satin and matte texture. In a wide range of colors and designs, it is used in classic decorating schemes.

Chintz (12, 13) Colorful, usually floral, designs printed on fine polished cotton. A favorite fabric for curtains, since it drapes well and comes in a vast choice of patterns and colors, often as part of a co-ordinated range.

Satin stripe (14) A medium-weight fabric with alternate matte and satin stripes. It comes in plain colors to give interest without pattern. Looks best when pleated with a regular pencil or goblet heading.

Woven check (15) A firm, medium-weight fabric with a check woven into it. This fabric is also suitable for upholsteryand would be an ideal choice where you want curtains to match a chair or sofa.

Printed cotton satin (16) A smooth, satin finish fabric that drapes well. Available in a variety of prints, including some with metallic highlights.

Dupion (18) A slubbed silky fabric, sometimes woven with warp and weft threads of contrasting colors for a shot effect. Drapes well and looks especially luxurious when trimmed with silky cord and fringing.

Madras lace (19) The pattern on this cotton lace is made by weaving extra weft threads into a fine, open weave cloth. Threads between areas of the design are cut away to leave an opaque design on an otherwise sheer background.

Polyester lace (20) An open, figured lace in white or cream with a slight sheen. It is easy to wash and dry.

Cotton lace (21) Sold either by length or as complete panels, this soft, easily draped cotton in floral, foliage or abstract design has a nostalgic look.

Flocked voile (22) A fine, sheer fabric with an all-over raised spot. Neat and pretty, it blends well with traditional and contemporary decorating schemes.

PAINTING PLAIN FABRIC

DECORATING WITH FABRIC acquires an extra dimension when you start by designing the cloth itself. Fabric paints come in a wide choice of colors and work best on natural fabrics like cotton and silk, with no special finishes. They can be used to embellish plain fabrics with a border, panel or all-over design. You can even treat the fabric as a canvas, completely covering it with paint – a method that works best on small areas such as tiebacks or a pelmet. Painting, stenciling and printing are simple techniques which can produce complex designs.

Painting *If you can use a paintbrush with confidence, painting on fabric is easy. Prepare the fabric by pressing it well; lay it on a flat surface, using masking tape or bulldog clips to hold it in place. Match the design to the type of fabric: for example, paint intricate designs on fine, smooth cotton or silk, make bolder strokes on coarser weaves. For a more graphic style, use fabric pens to draw, write or outline a shape.*

Stenciling *Wonderful effects can be achieved using the ready-cut stencil designs now available. Work out a stencil design on paper first and, if positioning is crucial, mark the fabric to ensure accuracy. Press the fabric and lay it out flat, then place the stencil in position and dab over it with a stencil brush or sponge dipped in fabric paint. Use sparingly, but paint layer upon layer to build up the depth of color.*

Printing *Hand-printed fabrics have a naive charm that complements rustic styles of décor. Potato printing gives very effective results, especially used with strong, earthy colors on a neutral or dark ground.*

CURTAIN POLES AND TRACKS

ALL CURTAINS AND SOME BLINDS ARE SUSPENDED FROM a track or pole. The kind you choose will depend on the style of the room and on the type and weight of the drapes. All tracks and poles sold in furnishing shops, do-it-yourself shops and department stores can be hung by an average-skilled person with a tool kit that includes a metal ruler, drill, screwdriver, carpenter's level and hacksaw. The hooks used to suspend the curtain on its track or pole are attached to the back of the heading tape at the top of the curtain, either by sewing them on or by inserting them into pockets in the tape.

CURTAIN TRACKS

Tracks are made from plastic or metal and come in varying lengths, widths, weights and colors. Most are pre-cut to standard lengths and are sold together with runners and brackets. Plastic track, usually in white and sometimes with gilt decoration, is inexpensive, pliable and easy to cut; it is most suitable for light and medium-weight curtains. Metal tracks are made from aluminum or steel. Aluminum track, in white, gold or grey metal finish, is reasonably priced and easy to cut; there are various thicknesses to hold light, medium-weight and heavy curtains. Steel track, in a white or grey metallic finish, is strong and rigid, suitable for all curtains, including heavy, interlined drapes. When buying track for a bay window, check that it can be curved by hand. Some tracks are only suitable for straight runs, some can only be bent professionally to order and others will not successfully make the double bend needed to carry curtains in and out of a bay.

Gliders, normally supplied with the track, may incorporate hooks that attach directly to the curtain heading tape. Overlap arms attached to the innermost gliders prevent any gap between the curtains when the pair is drawn together. Tracks with pull-cords help curtains last longer by reducing the amount of handling they receive. More expensive electronic curtain tracks, operated by remote control or a time switch, open curtains automatically. Curtains hung from non-corded track can still be opened and closed without touching

THESE THREE WINDOWS SPACED EVENLY ACROSS A WALL ARE TREATED IDENTICALLY, WITH A SINGLE CURTAIN HUNG BY CLIP-ON HOOKS FROM A METAL POLE. THE METHOD IS SIMPLE: A STRAIGHT, SHEER CURTAIN HUNG ON A TRACK IS COVERED WITH A PLAIN, UNPLEATED CURTAIN, DRAWN TO ONE SIDE. THE BLACK HOLDBACKS ADD AN ELEMENT OF SURPRISE.

HOW MUCH TRACK?

Measure the width of the window and add on about 8in (20cm) on each side to allow for stacking the curtains clear of the glass when they are opened. Adjust this allowance slightly if the curtain fabric is particularly bulky

the fabric, using a draw rod that hooks onto the inner-most runner and pulls it along the track.

Layered window treatments, combining curtains, blinds and a valance, require a multiple track system where two or more tracks are supported on the same brackets. Separate valance track is available to use together with a standard curtain rail, and purpose-made tracks can be bought to hang Austrian, festoon and Roman blinds. Extension brackets hold a track further out from the wall to hang curtains clear of a deep architrave or a window shade.

MOUNTING TRACKS AND POLES

Screw the curtain track directly to the wall or ceiling, or to the window frame, using the brackets supplied and appropriate sized screws. You may need to insert wall plugs (anchors) into a plastered wall first. Alternatively, screw the track to the underside of a valance board. For heavy curtains, anchor the track or pole brackets to a wooden batten screwed securely to the wall above the window. Tracks supporting heavy curtains should have more fixings, closely spaced. If the curtains have to clear a window sill or French-door handles, make sure the track or pole projects far enough forward.

CURTAIN POLES

Poles can look elegant, rustic, stately or simple, depending on their style, and since they are a decora-tive element they should not be covered with a valance or pelmet. Curtain poles consist of a wooden or metal rod, supported on brackets at each end and, for wide windows, in the center, too. Rings fitted with a screw eye are threaded onto the rod and the curtains hooked onto the screw eyes; depending on the position of the curtain hooks in the heading, they can either hang below or half-cover the rings. The ends of the pole are capped with finials to stop the outer ring from slipping off and to provide a decorative flourish. Poles vary in thickness from ½in (13mm) to 3in (7.5cm): choose a size in proportion to the window.

Curtains hung from poles have to be drawn by hand, using draw rods if the fabric is delicate. Corded "poles" are curtain tracks disguised to look like poles and the rings are half-rings attached to runners. Most have a polished brass finish, but wooden corded poles are available. Heavier and more substantial, they have a track running through the solid wooden pole.

Poles are most suitable for straight curtain runs but it is possible to fit them around bay windows, using

AN INLAID ORIENTAL CHEST AND PAINTED BASKET INSPIRED THE CHOICE OF AN INDIAN FABRIC TO CURTAIN THIS WINDOW. HUNG FROM A POLE, THE FABRIC IS CAUGHT BACK BY A CORD LOOPED AROUND ONE OF THE BRACKETS. WHEN RELEASED TO COVER THE WINDOW, ITS SCENIC DESIGN IS REVEALED.

angled corner pieces or corner brackets. You can buy double brackets supporting two rods for multi-layered window treatments. Other poles with special uses include slim café rods to support half-length curtains; dormer rods, hinged at one end, to swing away from small enclosed windows; and rise-and-fall portière rods to hold a door curtain and lift it clear when the door opens.

STYLING IDEA

○ *Transform a length of dowelling into a stylish curtain pole by painting it with a decorative technique such as marbling or verdigris, or apply a metallic finish with gold or silver paint. Buy finials to complete the effect.*

CURTAIN HEADINGS

THE HEADING IS THE PLEATED OR GATHERED TOP EDGE OF THE CURTAIN and its style determines the way the curtains hang, as well as affecting the quantity of fabric needed to make them. The traditional method of making headings was to stiffen the top edge of the curtain with buckram and pleat it by hand, stitching the pleats in position. Most people now use ready-made corded heading tape, which is sewn across the top of the curtain on the wrong side and the cords pulled up to form even pleats or gathers. The tape is sold by the yard or meter and comes in various widths and weights to create a range of different pleat styles.

TYPES OF HEADING

Standard heading

GIVES A SIMPLE, GATHERED HEADING suitable for lightweight curtains in a kitchen, bathroom or bedroom where an informal effect is wanted or where the heading will be hidden by a pelmet or valance. The tape is 1½ in (28mm) wide and requires fabric one and a half to two times the width of the track for gathering. There is only one row of pockets: to hide the track, set the tape at least 1in (2.5cm) down from the curtain's top edge.

Pencil pleat

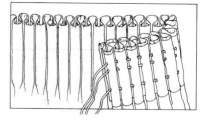

PRODUCES CLOSELY SPACED, slim pleats to give a neat, formal effect. The tape comes in several widths: select pleats in proportion to the curtain length. It requires fabric two to two and a half times the track width. Wider tapes have three rows of pockets – hang the curtain to cover or reveal the track.

GOBLET-PLEATED HEADINGS ARE SEEN AT THEIR BEST WHEN THESE CURTAINS MADE FROM TICKING ARE CLOSED, SO THESE DRAPES MEET IN THE CENTER THEN ARE LOOPED BACK TO ADMIT LIGHT. THE HEADINGS ARE WITTILY TRIMMED WITH MATTRESS TUFTS AT THE BASE OF THE PLEATS.

Triple pleat

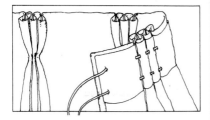

PULLS UP TO FORM PLEATS arranged in groups of three. Comes in a choice of widths and requires fabric twice the track width. Wider tapes have three rows of pockets to hang the curtain either to cover or reveal the track or pole.

Cartridge pleat

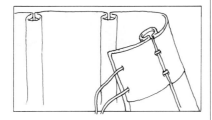

PRODUCES TALL, cylindrical pleats, held in shape with special hooks, and forms regular folds suitable for formal floor-length curtains. Requires fabric twice the track width. Where curtains meet, position the tape so the sequence of spaces and pleats continues across the width.

Goblet pleat

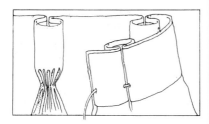

PRODUCES EVENLY SPACED cylindrical pleats with tapered stems. Requires fabric twice the track length.

Valances and fixed headings

Box pleat Produces large pleats that are then stitched down to form flat box pleats. Requires fabric three times the track width.

Smocked pleat Pulls up to give a decorative smocked effect, shown best on plain fabrics. Requires fabric twice track width.

Special-purpose tapes

Translucent tape Lightweight, unobtrusive tapes for net and sheer curtains. Requires fabric two to two and a half times the track width.

Press-on tapes These heading tapes, suitable for non-opening curtains and valances, work like touch-and-close fasteners, eliminating the need for hooks and track. The two-part system consists of a self-adhesive hooked strip that sticks to the window frame, wall or supporting batten, and a loop-pile heading tape. It comes in various widths and produces slim, regular pleats; it is stitched to the curtain, drawn up as usual, then pressed on to the hooked strip.

Fabric blind tapes These come in various designs to make Roman, Austrian and festoon blinds. The tapes incorporate loops for cording and, in the festoon blind tape, cords for drawing up the fabric.

Lining tape A narrow tape enabling loose linings to hook onto the main curtain heading tape, with a double-thickness or "skirted" lower edge. The lining's top edge is enclosed between the two thicknesses and stitched in place, then the cords pull up, gathering the lining to fit.

Curtain hooks

Curtain hooks are the essential link between curtain and pole or track; they come in a number of designs for different types of curtain. When using heading tapes, insert the hooks into the top, middle or lower row of pockets, depending on whether you want the heading to cover the track or hang beneath it. Space hooks close enough to hold the heading horizontally. You may need more hooks for very heavy curtains.

Single-prong hooks, made from plastic, nylon, aluminum or brass, are used with most heading tapes. Use plastic and nylon for light and medium-weight curtains and metal hooks for heavy drapes.

Double-prong hooks are specially designed for pinch pleat, cartridge pleat and box pleat heading tapes, where the two prongs are inserted through adjacent pockets in the tape behind each pleat to hold it firmly in place.

Deep-pleat hooks have long prongs to keep tall, pleated headings upright. The hooks can be short or long to hold the heading above or below the track or pole.

Pin hooks push into the back of each pleat for hand-sewn headings.

Sew-on hooks are stitched to hand-sewn headings.

Clip-on rings have a spring clip to grip the top of the curtain, eliminating the need for hooks. The ring slips onto the curtain pole.

CURTAINS: MEASURING AND CUTTING OUT

ACCURATE MEASUREMENTS ARE ESSENTIAL FOR calculating the amount of fabric, lining and heading tape needed to make curtains. Besides the dimensions of the window and the drop, the choice of track or pole and the style of heading affect the quantity of fabric required, so you should decide on these at an early stage, before shopping for material. Take all measurements with a metal ruler.

A CLEARLY DEFINED FABRIC DESIGN LIKE THIS SHOULD ALWAYS BE PERFECTLY MATCHED ACROSS BOTH CURTAINS AS EVEN THE SLIGHTEST DRIFT FROM THE HORIZONTAL WILL SHOW. TAKE EQUAL CARE TO MATCH UP LESS OBVIOUS PATTERNS BECAUSE THE REPEAT WILL BECOME VISIBLE WHEN VIEWED FROM A DISTANCE.

Measuring up

Before you start Hang the track or pole in position above the window, allowing enough on either side for stacking the opened curtains. Poles are placed a little higher than track so the curtain will totally cover the window frame or architrave.

For the length Decide on the length of curtain you want: sill and floor lengths are the most popular but you can choose any point between. Measure from the lower edge of the track or curtain ring to your chosen curtain hemline. Add extra for the heading (the distance from the hook pocket to the proposed top edge of the curtain, plus 1in/2.5cm for allowances) and 6in (15cm) for the hem.

For the width Measure the track or pole from end to end and multiply this by the factor recommended for your heading tape (see page 166); for example, multiply by 2 for a standard heading tape and by 2.5 for pencil pleats. Add a further 3¼in (8cm) per curtain for the side turnings. Divide the result by the fabric width – usually 48in (122cm) or 54in (137cm) – to

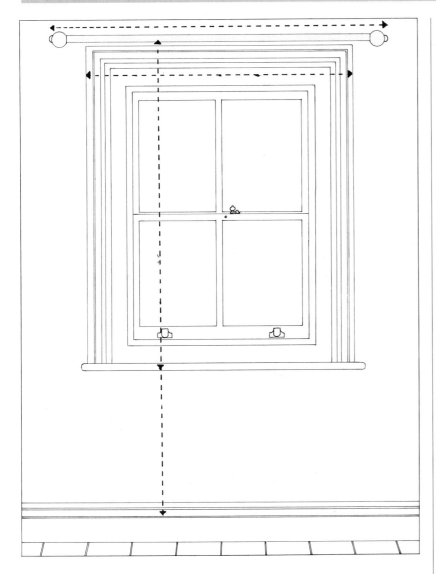

Cutting out

CHECK ALL MEASUREMENTS carefully before you cut as mistakes are difficult to put right afterwards.

You will need:
- metal ruler
- carpenter's square
- tailor's chalk
- sharp dressmaking scissors

Cutting a straight edge Most fabrics are cut along the grain to ensure they hang well. To find the straight grain on closely woven fabrics, snip through the selvage with scissors, then tear across the fabric width. On loosely woven fabrics, gently pull out one of the weft (crosswise) threads to leave a space in the fabric weave. Cut along this space.

Cutting out drops If the straight edge was cut along the grain, measure the length along the selvages from the straight edge; mark with pins. Rule a line between marked points and cut along it. Measure and cut the number of fabric widths needed for each curtain.

If a patterned fabric is printed out of true, cut so that the pattern appears straight: cut the straight edge 6in (15cm) below the lowest complete motif, then measure the length up both selvages and mark with pins. Rule a line to join the marked points, then cut along it. This method allows for a complete motif to be seen at the hem edge and any irregularity in the pattern to be hidden in the pleating at the top of the curtain. Cut the number of widths needed, using the first as a guide to ensure the pattern matches and remains straight when widths are joined.

find the number of fabric widths needed. If the measurement does not divide exactly but the remainder is more than half a fabric width, round it up to the next number of widths. If the remainder is less than half a width, disregard it.

If you are making a pair of curtains and an odd number of widths is needed, fold the fabric in half lengthwise, press and cut one width in half down its length.Unfold and cut along the crease.

Total fabric required To calculate the final amount of both curtain and lining fabric you need to buy, simply multiply the length by the number of full widths required.

STYLING IDEAS

✔ *Never cut down on the width of fabric: voluminous curtains in a cheaper material will look far better than skimpy ones made from expensive fabric.*

✔ *Choose a fabric design in scale with the room. Large patterns swamp a small room and mini-prints appear plain in large areas.*

✔ *Colored lining fabric lends drama to a color scheme; fold the curtains back so the color can be seen when the curtains are open.*

✔ *Patterned linings give added interest and look good from the outside: use co-ordinating fabrics or a harmonizing stripe or mini-print.*

✔ *In bright rooms, hang a blind behind the curtains to protect the fabric from the bleaching effect of strong sunlight.*

✔ *If you move to a house with taller windows, lengthen your curtains by sewing bands of co-ordinating or contrasting fabric at the hem. Use the same material to make tiebacks and a valance for a co-ordinated effect.*

✔ *Dress curtains are decorative drapes that hang at the sides of the window and are never drawn: use them at large windows where full curtains would be too expensive, and add blinds for privacy.*

✔ *If you are using fabric with a definite pattern, you will need to allow extra for matching the pattern repeat across the width. Fabric manufacturers often indicate the length of pattern repeat but you can calculate it yourself by measuring from the top of the pattern to where it starts again. Add the length of one pattern repeat per fabric width to the total length of fabric required.*

MAKING UNLINED CURTAINS

UNLINED CURTAINS FILTER LIGHT WITHOUT EXCLUDING it and have an airy, informal look that suits kitchen, bathroom and other windows where a simple, unstudied treatment is required. They can be machine-washed, if made from pre-shrunk fabric. Easy to sew, unlined curtains are an ideal first project if you are new to curtain making; the only skills required are accurate measuring and the ability to sew a straight seam. Standard or pencil pleat headings are the most appropriate for unlined curtains.

THESE NATURAL COTTON CURTAINS HAVE BEEN GIVEN A PRETTY GATHERED HEADING IN KEEPING WITH THEIR RELAXED STYLE BY MAKING A DEEP TURNING AT THE TOP EDGE AND SEWING STANDARD HEADING TAPE ABOUT 4IN (10CM) DOWN FROM THE FOLD. THIS CRISP FABRIC HOLDS THE GATHERS BEAUTIFULLY.

Making curtains

CUT THE NUMBER OF FABRIC widths needed (see page 168). Trim off the selvages or snip into them at 2in (5cm) intervals to prevent the seams from puckering.

Pin, baste and join widths with french or flat fell seams (see page 220), placing half widths to the outside edges and matching the pattern if necessary.

Mitering the corners

FOR THE HEM, TURN IN AND PRESS 3in (7.5cm) along the lower edge; then turn in and press ¾in (2cm) along both side edges. Fold in and press a further 3in (7.5cm) along the lower edge, and unfold; then turn in and press a further ¾in (2cm) along the side edges, and unfold. Fold in the corner so the diagonal crosses the point where side and hem creases intersect. Refold and slip-stitch the sides and the hem, then slip-stitch the edges of the miter (see page 220).

Making the heading

TURN DOWN 1IN (2.5CM) along the top raw edge, then check curtain length and adjust the turning if necessary. Cut a length of heading tape to the curtain width, adding 2in (5cm) for allowances. Pin the tape in position on the wrong side of the curtain to cover the raw edge, leaving edges loose.

At the leading edge of the curtain, where the pair of curtains will meet, pull out the cord ends and knot them together. Turn in and pin the raw edge of tape level with the leading edge so the knot is hidden. At the outer edge of the curtain, pull out the cords and leave them loose. Turn under the raw edge of tape level with the outer edge. Baste, then machine stitch the heading tape in place, stitching both long edges in the same direction to avoid puckering. Machine stitch across the short ends, catching the cords in the stitching at the leading edge and leaving them free at the outer edge. Pull threads through to the wrong side and darn in neatly.

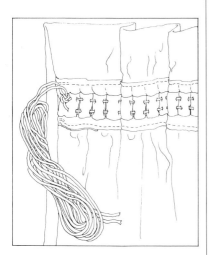

DRAW UP BOTH CORDS together from the outer edge of each curtain to form evenly spaced gathers or pleats, until the heading measures half the track width. Secure the cords with a slip knot, then wind them neatly into a hank or onto a cord holder. Do not cut off the cords or it will be impossible to pull the headings flat for washing. Insert hooks in the tape pockets; place one at each end and space the others approximately 3in (7.5cm) apart.

Edgings and Borders

DECORATIVE EDGINGS SET HAND-MADE CURTAINS apart from their ready-made counterparts, and plain curtains especially benefit from discreet trimming. Some edgings can be added to the finished curtains but others must be planned before you start sewing. Choose an edging to suit the style and proportion of the curtains: large, heavy drapes need a more imposing decoration than lightweight curtains for small windows, which require more delicate trimming. Embellish the leading edges to emphasize the curve of tied-back curtains or the regimented folds of straight hanging ones; continue the border or edging along the hem for a sumptuous effect.

Bobble edging is a dainty trimming suitable for sheers and lightweight unlined curtains. Bought by length, it has tiny pompons spaced along a narrow braid. Pin, then slip-stitch or machine stitch along the edge of the finished curtain on the right side.

Braid is a decorative band that comes in a wide range of widths, colors and designs; it is suitable for lined and unlined curtains. Stitch it to the curtain before making up. If you want the braid to run close to the edge of the curtain, fold and press the side turning, then place the braid against the fold and machine stitch in place. If you want a space between the braid and the curtain edge, fold in and press side turnings, then mark with tailor's chalk a line parallel with the fold down the curtain's length.

Contrast borders consist of a band of fabric joined to the leading edge of curtains. The width of the border should be in proportion to the size of the curtain and is added when joining fabric widths. Cut a strip of fabric, twice the desired width of the border plus 1¼in (3cm) for seams, and the length of the curtain before turnings.

Pin, then machine stitch the strip along the leading edge with right sides together and edges matching, taking a ⅝in (1.5cm) seam. Press the seam open, then fold back the border to the required width. For unlined curtains, turn in and slip-stitch the raw edges along the seam line; for lined curtains, baste the border fold-back in place and complete.

Ruffled edging gives lined curtains an unsophisticated, pretty look. Ruffle the leading edge only unless the windows are small, in which case the ruffle can be continued around the hem and side edges. To calculate the length of the ruffle, measure the curtain edge and double it. For the width, double the desired frill width and add 1¼in (3cm) for seams. Fold the strip in half lengthwise, right side out, then run a gathering thread along the raw edges. Draw up until the ruffle fits the curtain edge. Spacing the gathers evenly, pin, baste and machine stitch the ruffle in place on the right side of the fabric, with raw edges level. Place main fabric and lining right sides together, with the ruffle between, and machine along the seam line.

STYLING IDEAS

✔ *Hang curtains on glazed doors for prettiness and privacy. Stitch channels at the top and bottom of each curtain and slot through a plastic-covered wire or slim curtain rod, then attach wire or rod at the top and bottom of the glazed area.*

✔ *Check out cheap fabrics: canvas, ticking, sheeting and gingham look great for unlined curtains and will not cost a fortune. Jazz up plain fabrics with braid, fringing or a contrasting bound edge.*

✔ *Dress fabric can look effective made up into curtains but is best at small windows where the fine weave billows gently in the breeze.*

✔ *Unlined, informal curtains look pretty when they are cinched with a sash tie, but without being caught back to the window frame.*

✔ *Pleated edging gives a soft yet sophisticated finish. Cut a fabric strip as for the ruffled edging and pleat it to fit the curtain's leading edge. Pin, baste and machine stitch close to the edge of the strip to hold the pleats in place, then attach it to the curtain edge as for ruffled edging.*

✔ *Fringe is bought by length: slip-stitch it along the leading edge of finished curtains, or enclose the braided edge in the side seam when attaching the lining.*

✔ *Piping neatly outlines lined curtains or can be combined with a ruffled edging. Make a length of piping (see page 209) to fit along the leading edge before turnings; attach it, with raw edges together, before attaching the lining.*

MAKING LINED AND INTERLINED CURTAINS

LINED CURTAINS HAVE A WEIGHT AND SUBSTANCE that makes them hang well. They exclude light, stop drafts and insulate against heat loss better than unlined ones; the lining protects the main fabric from the damaging effects of sunlight and dirt. Traditional lining fabric is buff or white cotton sateen but the material comes in a whole spectrum of colors, too. Interlining is a thick, fleecy fabric which can be sandwiched between the lining and main fabric. Special blackout and insulating linings are also available.

MAKING LINED CURTAINS is not in itself difficult. The trickiest part is handling the quantity of fabric required and this becomes much easier if you have a large table or floor space on which to work. You will also need enough surface around the sewing machine to support the fabric while you sew.

Because of the volume of fabric and the possibility that the lining and the main fabric will shrink at different rates, professional cleaning is recommended for most lined curtains. The need for cleaning will be less frequent if the windows, frames and tracks are kept clean and the curtain fabric is lightly vacuumed with a dusting brush attachment from time to time. If you prefer to wash curtains, use detachable linings and launder them separately.

Making curtains

MEASURE AND CUT OUT THE FABRIC widths as for unlined curtains. Join the widths with flat seams, matching the pattern if necessary. Trim or clip the seams and press them open. Measure, cut out and join widths of lining fabric in the same way.

A LENGTH OF FABRIC TACKED TO A BOARD BECOMES A STYLISH PELMET THANKS TO THE INSPIRED USE OF A DARKLY CONTRASTING SILK BORDER TO MATCH THOSE OF THE LINED CURTAINS. NOTE HOW THE BORDER STRIPES RUN VERTICALLY TO MATCH THE CURTAINS AND THE PELMET IS CINCHED AT THE CENTER TO GIVE A MORE SHAPELY PROFILE.

Weighting the hem

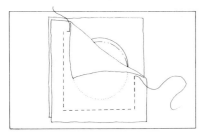

WEIGHTS HELP THE CURTAINS TO HANG better: prepare a curtain weight for the lower corners of each curtain by placing it between two small squares of lining fabric and stitching all around. When in place, these bags will not be seen.

Preparing the lining

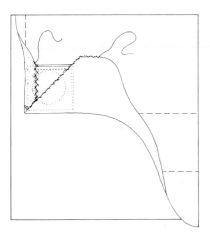

LAY THE MAIN FABRIC FACE DOWN, then fold in and press a 1½in (4cm) allowance along the side edges. For the hem, turn in and press a double 3in (7.5cm) turning along the lower edge. Unfold the side allowance and the second fold of the hem, then miter the corners (see page 170). Place a bagged weight inside each corner, stitching it in place through the hem on the wrong side. Refold the side allowance and herringbone-stitch them in place. Refold the hem and slip-stitch to finish.

Lay the lining over the wrong side of the curtain, with top edges matching. Trim the side edges of the lining level with the hemmed sides of the main fabric and trim 1in (2.5cm) off the lower edge. Turn in a double 3in (7.5cm) hem along the lower edge; pin, baste and machine stitch in place. Turn in, pin and baste 1in (2.5cm) along both side edges.

Locking in the lining

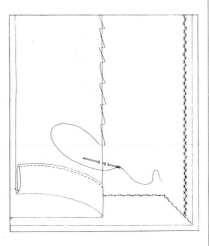

LAY THE PREPARED LINING centrally over the curtain fabric, with wrong sides together and top edges matching. Pin the two together down the center length. Fold back the lining to the line of pins, then lockstitch the lining to the curtain down the fold, ending about 2in (5cm) from the hem. Working out from the center in both directions, lockstitch along every seamline and half-width in the same way. Slip-stitch the side edges of the lining in place, continuing about 3in (7.5cm) along the hem edge.

Making sure the top edges of the lining and curtain are straight, treat the two thicknesses as one and attach your heading tape as for unlined curtains. Draw up the pleats, insert the hooks and hang.

Interlined curtains

INTERLINING IMPROVES THE WAY lined curtains drape, lengthens their life and gives them a full and heavy look. In addition to the main fabric and the lining, you will need flannel or domette interlining cut to the finished length of the curtains; add 3in (8cm) to the width measurement for allowances.

Making

CUT OUT THE WIDTHS of the main fabric, lining and interlining; join fabric and lining widths as for lined curtains. To join interlining widths, overlap their edges by ¾in (2cm); herringbone-stitch in place.

Lay the main fabric face down and lay the interlining over it, with margins all around for hems. Pin the two together down the center length; then fold back interlining to the row of pins and lockstitch down the fold as for lined curtains. Repeat at half-width intervals across the curtain, making the last line of stitches 1½in (4cm) from the side edges. Complete as for lined curtains.

STYLING IDEAS

✂ *Line curtains that are hung across archways with matching fabric, so that they look the same from both sides.*

✂ *Curtains at bay windows can be stacked at the sides, clear of the glass, or in the angles of the window to emphasize its shape. Where there is a window seat, hang either short curtains or blinds, with full-length dress curtains at the sides.*

✂ *If there is a radiator under the window, hang sill-length curtains. Full-length drapes would prevent heat from entering the room and would waste energy.*

✂ *Hem sill-length curtains so they end ½in (1cm) above a protruding sill or cover a flush one.*

Bagged Linings

Bagged linings are almost entirely machine stitched and are a great time saver. Though they are not as professional as the hand-sewn method described here, the results are good enough for many needs.

Cut and join widths of curtain fabric and lining as above, but make the lining 8in (20cm) less wide than the main fabric. Mark the center length of both pieces with a row of basting stitches. Place main fabric and lining right sides together, matching the side edges; pin, baste and machine stitch the edges, taking a ¾in (2cm) seam. Trim or clip seams, press open, then turn right side out.

Press the curtain flat, matching up the central lines of basting, then fold down the top edges and attach the heading tape as described. Hang the curtains and mark the desired hemline, then trim the hem allowance to 6in (15cm). Hem the main fabric, taking a double 3in (7.5cm) turning; you may have to unpick the lower end of the side seams. Turn up and hem the lower edge of the lining so that it is 1in (2.5cm) shorter than the main curtain fabric.

VALANCES AND PELMETS

VALANCES AND PELMETS ORIGINALLY DESIGNED to hide the curtain track and heading in an attractive way and to stop light and drafts from coming up behind the curtain, are often referred to only as valances. In recent years they have become more of a decorative feature, often more distinctive than the curtains which hang below them. In some cases, an elaborate example is the window's only adornment.

THOUGH THEY PERFORM the same role, pelmets and valances look unlike each other and are made in quite different ways. Pelmets are rigid, smooth and formal. They are made from plywood, buckram or a purpose-made, self-adhesive stiffened material, usually with a shaped lower edge; they are then covered with fabric and mounted on a pelmet board above the window. Valances, however, give a much softer effect. Made like a gathered or pleated frill, they can be mounted onto a board or hung from a track screwed to the wall above the window.

Choosing a pelmet

PELMETS COMPLEMENT CURTAINS of various styles, from grand, floor-length drapes to short, gathered curtains. The pelmet's shaping gives it its character. Purpose-made pelmet stiffener comes printed with scalloped edgings in various configurations: you simply cut along your preferred outline. Alternatively, you can choose a classic castellated, vandyked (zig-zag) or serpentine shaping, or follow a flowing shape in the fabric design. A pelmet may echo the pretty shape of an arched or gothic window, or it may disguise awkward proportions. A curved

THE DEEPLY CUT ZIG-ZAG PELMET BASED ON A LIGHTLY UPHOLSTERED BOARD IS THE MAIN DECORATIVE FEATURE OF THIS PLAIN WINDOW. DISCREETLY TRIMMED WITH DIAGONALLY STRIPED PIPING, THE POINTS ARE TIPPED WITH TINY BELLS.

pelmet, deeper at the sides than the center, can suggest greater height; a narrow pelmet, with an evenly waved or scalloped edge, gives an impression of increased width. Experiment with paper cutouts until you find a design you like, then use the paper as a template, folding it in half to get a perfectly symmetrical shape.

Cover the pelmet with fabric, making sure any pattern aligns with the curtains or blind, and trim it with braid, contrasting edging or cord to match the curtains.

Mounting a board

FOR THE BOARD, you need a piece of wood 4in (10cm) wide and 4in (10cm) longer than the curtain track. Cut end pieces of wood 4in (10cm) square and glue and nail them to the ends of the board. If the pelmet is a deep one, an additional board glued and nailed across the front will provide extra support.

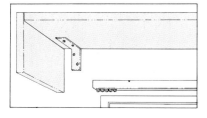

USING A WOODEN RULER and carpenter's level, mark the pelmet position on the wall about 5cm (2in) above the curtain track. Screw angle brackets to the wall, with one at each end and others spaced about 30cm (12in) apart, then screw the board to the brackets.

Making a simple pelmet

You will need:
✂ fabric
✂ lining
✂ buckram, self-adhesive pelmet stiffener or plywood
✂ touch-and-close fastener

MEASURE THE TOTAL LENGTH of the sides and front of the pelmet board and decide on its depth. Cut a strip of buckram or stiffener to this size. Using a paper template or printed edging outlines, and placing the design centrally, cut the lower edge of the stiffener to shape and crease it at the corner positions. For a plywood pelmet, cut the front and side pieces separately, then join them with strips of glued fabric to form hinges at the corners.

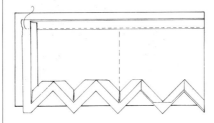

CUT ENOUGH FABRIC WIDTHS to make a piece long enough to cover the board. Join the widths, matching any pattern and making sure you have a complete fabric width at the center and part-widths at the sides. Make a lining piece in the same way. Lay the stiffener over the fabric and lining and cut both to shape, allowing ¾in (2cm) all around to turn under. Cut a strip of touch-and-close fastener to fit along the length.

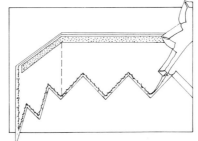

FOR A SELF-ADHESIVE STIFFENED pelmet, peel off the backing paper and smooth the stiffener onto the fabric. Turn raw edges to the wrong side and baste or stick in place, clipping into the curves. Machine stitch the pile half of the touch-and-close fastener across the lining on the right side, ¾in (2cm) in from the top edge. If the stiffener is adhesive on only one side, place lining on the wrong side, turn in raw edges, then baste and slip-stitch in place. If it is adhesive on both sides, peel off the backing and smooth it onto the lining, turning in the raw edges.

FOR A BUCKRAM-STIFFENED pelmet, place the fabric and lining right sides together; stitch along the top edge. Turn right side out, then stitch the pile half of the fastener along the lining, close to the seam. Place the buckram on the wrong side of the fabric, its top edge level with the seam; turn in and bond the raw edges to the back of the buckram with a hot iron. Fold the lining over the back of the pelmet; turn in and slip-stitch raw edges.

FOR A PLYWOOD PELMET, cover the shape with thin batting, then cover with fabric as above, glueing or stapling the fabric at the back.

FOR ALL PELMETS, glue or staple the hooked half of the fastener around the board's edge ; press in place.

A GATHERED VALANCE IS THE ONLY FABRIC TREATMENT NEEDED AT THIS SHUTTERED WINDOW. MADE FROM STRIPED COTTON DRESS FABRIC, UNLINED AND SIMPLY GATHERED WITH STANDARD CURTAIN HEADING TAPE, IT IS PERFECTLY IN KEEPING WITH ITS INFORMAL SURROUNDINGS.

STYLING IDEAS

✔ **Make a billowing valance like a short festoon or ruched blind: make it in the same way as a fabric blind (see pages 190-193), but finish by knotting the cord to hold the valance folds in place.**

✔ **Create free-form valances by draping lengths of fabric around a curtain pole hung above the track.**

✔ **Hold draped valances in place with staples, adhesive tabs or self-stick touch-and-close fastener. Hide the fixings with folds of fabric.**

✔ **If you like the look of a valance but prefer curtain poles to tracks, make curtains with an integral valance: sew a deep, lined ruffle of matching fabric along the top edge of the curtain so that it hangs down on the right side.**

✔ **Decorative edgings are an important part of valance design and the addition of frills, pleats, fringing and tassels can give an otherwise simple window treatment a designer look.**

Choosing a valance

VALANCES ARE TECHNICALLY part of a pretty, informal window treatment but, with the right combination of fabric, pleating and trimming, they work just as well in a sophisticated setting. A valance can be straight or shaped like a pelmet, with a scalloped, zig-zag or curved edge.

Valances are made in the same way as curtains, using heading tape to produce ruffles or pleats. Because the top of the curtains will be hidden, you can economize by using a simpler heading tape for the curtains themselves and concentrate your resources on creating a decorative valance.

Make the fabric valance the same weight as the curtains, lining and interlining it in the same way. To allow for gathering, the valance width will be two to two and a half times the width of the board or track, so when drawing out a pattern for a shaped edging, elongate the design accordingly.

Making a simple valance

You will need:
- ✂ fabric
- ✂ lining and interlining if used for the curtains
- ✂ curtain heading tape
- ✂ touch-and-close fastener (if using a board)

MEASURE THE WIDTH OF the board (for mounting, see page 174) or valance track, including the sides. Multiply this by the fullness needed for the style of heading tape being used (see page 166). Decide on the valance depth; add 1¼in (3cm) for a hem, 1½in (4cm) for a turning at the top. Cut the fabric and lining to this size: join widths if necessary. Cut the tape to the same length.

Line the valance, following the method described for lined curtains (see page 172), then turn down the raw edge at the top and attach the heading tape. Pull up the gathers or pleats until the valance fits the board or track; secure the cords. If you are using a board, cut a strip of lining fabric 1¼in (3cm) wider than the heading tape and 1¼in (3cm) longer, then fold in and press ⅝in (1.5cm) all around.

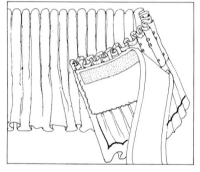

STITCH THE PILE HALF of the fastener strip close to one long edge. Slip-stitch the lining strip to cover the heading tape on the wrong side, with the strip of fastener close to the top edge.

Stick or staple the hooked half of the fastener strip around the edge of the pelmet board and press the valance in place. If you are using a valance track, insert hooks in the heading tape at 4in (10cm) intervals and hang from the gliders.

SWAGS AND TAILS

SWAGS AND TAILS ARE NORMALLY PART OF A GRAND WINDOW TREATMENT, but the simple version given here is easy to make and frames a plain window well, alone or with curtains. Choose a contrasting fabric for the lining, which will be visible in the fluted folds of the tails.

CLASSIC SWAGS AND TAILS ARE SUPPORTED ON FABRIC-COVERED POLES, DECORATING THE WINDOWS OF THIS FORMAL DRAWING ROOM WITH PERFECT SYMMETRY. ON A PRACTICAL NOTE, A ROLL OF MATCHING FABRIC CUTS OUT DRAFTS BETWEEN THE SASHES.

Making a Swag and Tails

You will need:
- curtain fabric
- contrasting lining
- touch-and-close fastener
- a 1x2in (2.5 x 5cm) wooden batten, 6-8in (15-20cm) longer than the window width
- a pair of angle brackets
- 2 decorative hooks

Mount the batten on angle brackets above the window frame.

Calculating measurements

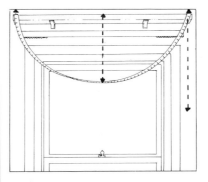

FOR THE TOP EDGE, measure from the end of the batten to the lowest point the tails will reach and double it. Add to the width of the batten. FOR THE LOWER EDGE, measure the proposed curve of the swag across the top of the window; add 12in (30cm) for draping around hooks. FOR THE DEPTH, measure from the center of the batten to the lowest point of the swag curve; double it.

Use these measurements to draw a pattern: the top and lower edges are parallel and centered; the space between them is the swag's depth.

Making

CUT FABRIC AND LINING ¾in (2cm) larger than the pattern all around. Place the fabric and lining with right sides together and join with a ¾in (2cm) seam, leaving a gap for turning. Trim the seam, turn right side out and press. Turn in the raw edges at the opening and slip-stitch together.

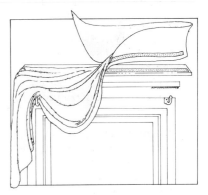

CUT A STRIP OF TOUCH-AND-CLOSE fastener the length of the batten. Machine stitch the pile side of the fastener centrally along the top edge of the swag, on the wrong side. Then staple or stick the corresponding hooked side along the top of the batten.

Press the swag onto the batten, matching the strips of fastener. Screw decorative hooks into the window frame, close to the upper corners. Loop the tails over the hooks and arrange them into attractive folds.

TIEBACKS AND TRIMS

TIEBACKS HOLD CURTAINS AWAY FROM THE WINDOW to let in the maximum daylight, at the same time as cinching them to form an attractive curved frame. Various devices exist to do the job, including brass or wooden holdbacks and cords, but fabric tiebacks offer the greatest scope for creativity. They can be made from the same material as the curtains in a wide range of styles and you can pipe or edge them to match the valance and drapes for a totally co-ordinated window treatment. Brass rings stitched to the ends of the tiebacks loop onto a hook screwed into the wall or the window frame at each side of the window.

IN THIS SOPHISTICATED GREEN AND WHITE BATHROOM, SIMPLE CRESCENT TIEBACKS MATCH THE CURTAIN FABRIC. THE CAST IRON CURTAIN RODS PROVIDE A STARK CONTRAST AND DEFINITION FOR THE DECORATING SCHEME.

Classic crescent tieback

WIDE AT THE CENTER and tapering towards the ends, this traditional style of tieback can be customized by piping or frilling the edges.

To find the length of the tieback, loop a fabric tape measure around the curtain at the desired height (usually about two-thirds of the way down from the top of the curtain) and draw it back until it holds the curtain firmly but without crushing the folds. Add 2in (5cm) to allow for the rings to be hidden. Decide on the center width in proportion to the curtains: an average is 3-4in (7.5-10cm). Then make a crescent-shaped paper pattern this size, rounding off the ends.

For each tieback, cut out one piece each of fabric and lining ⅝in (1.5cm) larger all around than the pattern itself; one piece of interlining, if required, ⅜in (1cm) larger all around, and a piece of buckram or self-adhesive pelmet stiffener the size of the pattern.

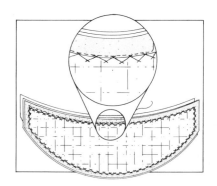

LAY THE FABRIC FACE DOWN and place the interlining, then the buckram, centrally on top. Herringbone-stitch the buckram in place, then place the stiffened fabric and lining pieces with right sides together. Machine stitch close to the edge of the buckram, leaving the upper edge open. Trim the seam and clip into the curves, then turn right side out. Turn in the remaining raw edges and slip-stitch together to complete.

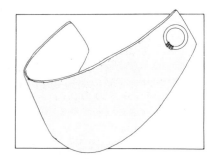

STITCH A BRASS CURTAIN RING firmly to each end of the tieback on the wrong side. Screw a brass hook to the wall at the appropriate height and hang the tieback from it.

Plaited tieback

THESE PADDED TIEBACKS have a pleasing texture against smooth curtain folds. Make them from one or from three contrasting fabrics.

Calculate the finished length as for the Classic Crescent Tieback. For each tieback, cut three strips of fabric and three of medium-weight synthetic batting to one and a half times this length and 4¾in (12cm) wide.

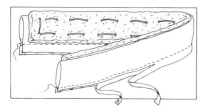

TAKING EACH FABRIC STRIP in turn, baste a strip of batting to the wrong side then fold in half, with the long edges level. Keeping the batting clear, join the edges with a ⅜in (1cm) seam to form a tube. Trim the seam and turn right side out. Fold in the raw edges at one end and slip-stitch.

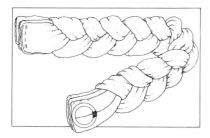

FLATTEN THE TUBES so the seams lie underneath, then place the slip-stitched ends one on top of another and sew together. Plait the three tubes evenly, then trim to the required length if necessary. Turn in and slip-stitch remaining raw ends of each tube, then stitch the three together to secure. Sew a brass ring firmly to each end.

Bow tieback

THIS INFORMAL STYLE OF TIEBACK, with its trailing, tapered tails, is a pretty finishing touch for ruffled curtains.

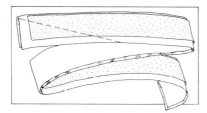

FOR EACH TIEBACK CUT TWO STRIPS of fabric 9½ x 51in (24 x 130cm) and two strips of medium-weight iron-on interfacing 4¼ x 50in (10.5 x 127cm). Fold each fabric strip in half lengthwise; press, then open out. Pin a strip of interfacing on the wrong side, one edge level with the center crease, leaving a ⅝in (1.5cm) margin of fabric at the short ends; bond in place following the manufacturer's instructions.

Taking one strip at a time, refold lengthwise and pin the two thicknesses together, then draw a diagonal stitching line from the end of the fold to a point 6in (15cm) up the open edge for the tail. Trim the fabric ⅝in (1.5cm) from the line. Join the open edges with a ⅝in (1.5cm) seam, leaving a gap in the long edge for turning. Trim the seam and turn right side out. Turn in, then slip-stitch the raw edges to close; press.

Sew a brass curtain ring to the square short edge on the wrong side. Hang the brass rings on the tieback hook, then tie the strips in a bow around the curtain. Arrange the loops and tails of the bow until you are happy with its shape, then hand stitch the bow in place to secure it permanently.

Trims and Finishing Touches

ROSETTES, CHOUX PUFFS AND BOWS can be stitched to blinds, curtain headings, valances, pelmets and tiebacks to give the final flourish to a window treatment; they can also help to disguise seams.

Rosettes

ROSETTES MAY BE PLACED at the corner of a heading or the top of a pair of tails; they can decorate the front of a tieback or the top of a blind. They should look dainty.

You will need:
- ✂ 2 strips of polished cotton, pinked on one long edge: one 24 x 2½in (60 x 6cm); the other 18 x 1½in (45 x 4cm)
- ✂ a fabric-covered button

Join the short edges of each strip with a ¼in (5mm) seam to form two rings of fabric. Make a row of gathering stitches along the straight edges of each ring, then pull up tightly and fasten off.

Place the smaller rosette over the larger one and stitch them together at the center. Stitch on the button to cover the raw edges.

Cheap Chic Tiebacks

The more decorative and elaborate of the ready-made rope and tasselled tiebacks are expensive to buy, but there is no reason why you should not add your own touches to plain, inexpensive tiebacks. Gold or silver fabric paint lightly brushed onto the tassels adds a sumptuous note to an undistinguished trimming. Other colors could be used to co-ordinate or contrast with the fabric of curtains or other furnishings featured elsewhere in the room.

SHEERS AND CAFÉ CURTAINS

AS A FAMILY OF FABRICS, SHEERS EMBRACE LACE, gauze, net, voile, fine synthetics and many more delicate, translucent materials. They can be coarse-textured or gossamer fine, plain, patterned, printed or embroidered. With such variety, it is possible to find a sheer to complement any window and every style of décor. Sheers are used mainly to provide privacy without obscuring the view, but they have many other benefits too: filtering bright sunlight, softening the outline of a window and expanding the possibilities for decorative window treatments. Use them as part of an elaborate, multi-layered design or alone for a cool, simple effect. Hang lace panels smooth and flat, the better to appreciate their intricate design, or bunch generous swags of gauze over a pole as a romantic heading for a bare or plainly curtained window. Café curtains usually cover the lower half of a window, to give privacy without excluding daylight. They hang ungathered from a slim pole, hung in line with the central bar, and often remain closed.

SHEER FABRICS are often bought with a pre-stitched channel at the top to take a slim curtain pole or plastic-covered wire. These slot-headed curtains are intended to hang in front of the window or be looped back with tiebacks. If you prefer curtains that hang from a track, make them in the same way as unlined curtains (see page 170) but use a translucent heading tape designed for sheer fabrics. When measuring for sheers, never skimp on the width: whether you want a billowing or strictly pleated effect, generously cut curtains look best. A fine lead-weighted tape threaded through a hem improves the fall.

Sewing sheers

CHOOSE WIDE FABRICS to keep seams to a minimum. Seams in sheer curtains are very noticeable. Join widths with french seams to avoid fraying and to give a neat finish.

Where possible, avoid taking turnings. Some sheers have ready-finished side and hem edges that need no further neatening. When turnings are necessary, make double hems of equal depth to avoid uneven show-through; press all turnings before sewing. Machine stitch using a long, loose stitch. If your machining puckers the fabric sew all turnings by hand.

FILMY SHEER CURTAINS MAKE AN APPROPRIATE TREATMENT FOR THIS LOFTY WINDOW. THE SWAG OF MIDNIGHT BLUE GAUZE DRAWS THE EYE TO THE WINDOW'S GRACEFUL ARCH.

Edging sheers

TRIM SHEERS WITH only lightweight edgings. Bobble edging, picot trim or lightweight fringing can be hand-stitched carefully in place to define the curve of a looped-back curtain or the edge of a blind.

Ruffled edges give cotton voile or silk curtains a more feminine look. To make, cut a 4in (10cm) strip of matching fabric twice the length of the edge to be trimmed. Make a double ³⁄₁₆in (5mm) hem all around, then run a row of gathering stitches along the length, ¾in (2cm) from one edge. Pull the gathers until the ruffle fits the edge and fasten off. Spread the gathers evenly, then pin and baste the ruffle to the curtain, the gathering close to the edge, so the widest part of the ruffle extends beyond it. Stitch along the gathering line.

Bound edges emphasize the outline of a draped and looped curtain. Bind the edges when making the curtains. For a ¾in (2cm) wide edging, cut bias strips 3¼in (8cm) wide from lightweight cotton; join them to make the required length. Fold and press the long edges to the center, then fold and press the strip in half, right side out. Open out the strip and place it along the curtain edge, right sides together and raw edges level; machine stitch on the first crease. Re-fold the strip to enclose the curtain edge and slip-stitch the remaining folded edge on the wrong side.

Café Curtains

MEASURE THE CURTAINED area: add 3¼in (8cm) to the width for side turnings and 7in (18cm) to the length for hem and heading.

Scalloped heading

FIRST MAKE A PAPER PATTERN for the shaping. Cut a strip of paper 3¼in (8cm) deep, the width of the finished curtain. Using a wine glass or small cup as a template, draw 2in (5cm) deep scallops along one long edge; space them about 1¼in (3cm) apart, leaving 1¼in (3cm) at each end. Adjust spacing to fit curtain width. Cut out.

Cut a 2¾in (7cm) strip of iron-on interfacing the width of the curtain fabric and bond it to the wrong side, ⅜in (1cm) down from the top edge. Fold the raw edge of fabric over the interfacing and machine stitch in place.

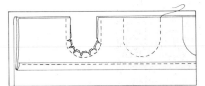

FOLD THE INTERFACED EDGE of the curtain to the right side and pin the paper pattern over it, 1½in (4cm) from the side edges so the top edges of the scallops are level with the fold in the fabric. Draw around the scallops with tailor's chalk, then machine stitch along the lines. Trim ¼in (5mm) from stitching lines and clip into the curves. Turn right side out; press.

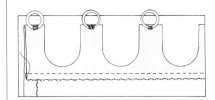

Turn and slip-stitch a ¾in (2cm) double hem along both side edges and at the lower edge. Slip-stitch the open ends of the scalloped heading. Stitch a brass ring at each end and between all the scallops.

Tab heading

CUT OUT THE CURTAIN FABRIC 2½in (6.5cm) shorter than before. Cut a 3¼in (8cm) strip of matching fabric and iron-on interlining, the width of the curtain. Bond the interlining to the wrong side of the fabric strip. Calculate the number of tabs needed by marking the curtain's top edge with pins spaced 5in (12.5cm) apart; start and end 2½in (6.5cm) from the sides.

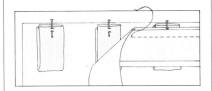

FOR EACH TAB, cut two 7 x 3¼in (18 x 8cm) strips of fabric and one of interfacing. Trim off ⅝in (1.5cm) all around the interfacing, then bond it centrally on the wrong side of one fabric strip. Place the fabric strips with right sides together and edges matching, then join the long edges with ⅝in (1.5cm) seams. Trim close to stitching; turn and press.

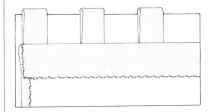

FOLD TABS IN HALF, then place on right side of curtain with raw edges level, centering on marked points. Pin, then baste in position. Place stiffened interfacing over the tabs, with right sides together and upper raw edges level, then machine stitch in place, taking a ¾in (2cm) seam. Trim seam, turn right side out and press. Finish as before.

BLINDS: IDEAS AND INSPIRATION

BLINDS AND SHADES ARE THE MOST VERSATILE FORM of window dressing. They can be used alone or with drapes in a layered treatment; they can be functional or decorative and, since they frequently require less fabric than conventional curtains, they offer a stylish, low-cost option for decorators on a limited budget. The most popular types are roller window shades, Roman, Austrian and festoons, but there are countless variations.

WINDOW SHADES (ROLLER BLINDS)

These are the simplest blinds of all, consisting of a flat panel of fabric stretching down from a spring-loaded roller at the top of the window. Though they are often regarded primarily as kitchen and bathroom they are hugely versatile and combine well with almost any kind of fabric blind or drape at windows throughout the house.

The most basic type, made from plain, stiffened cotton with a straight edge and a cord pull, has the right minimalist appeal for a spare modern interior but patterned examples are often used as part of a co-ordinated window treatment in traditional settings. Because of their firm, cartridge-paper texture, plain blinds lend themselves to painted decoration. This can be done freehand, using fabric paints, or with stencils (see page 163). The lower edge of the blind is often all that is visible by day as it hangs like a valance at the top of the window and, for this reason, the edge is often cut into a scalloped, zig-zag or castellated shape. The roller itself is not visually appealing and may be neatly hidden by a box or a more elaborate valance of fabric swagged around a curtain pole.

A SIMPLE TREATMENT FOR A COUNTRY KITCHEN WINDOW, THIS PANEL OF BRIGHT PROVENCAL PRINT HUNG FROM A SLIM BRASS ROD TAKES ON THE APPEARANCE OF A RUCHED BLIND WHEN TIED UP WITH MATCHING TAPES. THE AMOUNT OF SEWING REQUIRED IS MINIMAL. HEMMED ALONG ALL SIDES WITH A CHANNEL FOR THE ROD, THE TAPES ARE ATTACHED IN PAIRS, FRONT AND BACK, AT THE TOP EDGE OF THE PANEL.

ROMAN BLINDS

Though softer than a roller, a Roman blind is more structured and architectural in appearance. It too drops as a flat panel of fabric over the window but, being lined, it offers a degree of insulation and a more elegant feel. Pulled up, the blinds fold into deep pleats stacked one above the other. Roman blinds work best in plain fabric but can be made in patterned materials where it is more appropriate to the scheme. Choose small-scale patterns that will not be broken up by the pleats when the blind is raised, and beware of stripes or checks unless your cutting and sewing skills are such that you can keep the lines absolutely straight. Roman blinds can be made more sophisticated by the addition of contrasting borders down the sides.

AUSTRIAN AND FESTOON BLINDS

More glamorous and extravagant than plain blinds, these ruched and often ruffled blinds are found at windows of all shapes and sizes in every room, including the bathroom. Made from fabric wider and longer than the window they cover, they pull up into a billowing, scalloped heading. Closed, festoon blinds retain their ruched appearance, but Austrian blinds hang like an ordinary curtain.

Both types can be made in a wide variety of fabrics, from lace to calico, printed cotton to silk, as long as the material has enough body to hold the shape of the scallops without sagging. Smaller prints, plain fabrics, weaves and stripes are most suitable for the complicated construction of these blinds; large patterns will distort in the folds.

You can alter the character of a festoon or Austrian blind by your choice of fabric and trimming. A blind made from crisp white cotton with no trimming will look quite different from one made in a floral print with frilled edging, or a heavy silk version bedecked with a cord-trimmed heading and tassels hanging between the scallops. If you hang these luxurious fabric blinds together with curtains, a pelmet or valance, exercise restraint: plainly made curtains and a simple valance make the most complementary kind of frame for their opulence.

STRIPES ARE A FAVORITE FABRIC FOR AUSTRIAN BLINDS, SIMPLIFYING THE BUSINESS OF SPACING THE SCALLOPS BY DICTATING THE POSITIONS OF THE CORDS. THIS ONE FOLLOWS A SHALLOW BAY AND SOLVES THE DIFFICULTY OF HANGING CURTAINS ABOVE A WINDOW SEAT.

FABRICS FOR BLINDS

THE WAY A BLIND IS CONSTRUCTED influences the type of fabric from which it can be made. Roller shades need firm, closely woven cloths, which are treated with a fabric stiffener first. Roman blinds may be made in softer, medium-weight materials, and Austrian and festoon blinds can be created in a variety of fabrics from crisp cotton to luxurious velours and lace.

Ikat print cotton (1) Plain cotton printed to imitate an ethnic weave pattern. Suitable for Roman or Austrian blinds.

Plain cotton (2) Firm, evenly woven cotton fabric suitable for roller or Roman blinds.

Madras cotton (3, 4) Lightweight Indian cotton with a woven check. Inexpensive, colorful and suitable for roller, Austrian and festoon blinds.

Ticking (5) Firm, strong woven twill fabric traditionally made in black and white for mattresses and pillows. Now available in a choice of colors with white or cream. Suitable for roller, Roman and Austrian blinds.

Chintz (6, 7, 10) A light to medium-weight printed cotton with a glazed finish, suitable for all types of blind. Available in colorful florals (**6**), sophisticated stripes (**7**) and neat, regular prints (**10**).

Muslin(calico) (8) An inexpensive natural woven cotton. Available bleached or unbleached, it can be used to make blinds of all kinds.

Toile de Jouy (11) Closely woven cotton decorated with finely detailed scenes printed from engraved copper plates. Typically, these are printed in a single color on a cream or off-white ground. Use as for chintz.

Woven stripe (9, 12) Coarse cotton with a stripe woven into it. Ideal for roller and Roman blinds.

Twill check (13) Strong cotton with woven checks and a fine herringbone texture. An alternative to ticking.

Lawn (14) This finely woven sheer cotton may be plain, printed or woven to give a striped or checked effect.

Printed voile (15) A fine, almost transparent, printed woven fabric. Designs sometimes match or co-ordinate with a printed cotton fabric.

Slubbed sheer (16) Made of cotton, polyester or a mixture of the two fibers, this sheer fabric has a delicately slubbed weave and may be printed to give added interest at a large window.

Cotton lace (17) Heavy woven lace with a large-scale open design. Traditional floral patterns abound; many of them have an integral border along the side edges.

MAKING ROLLER WINDOW SHADES

SIMPLE TO MAKE, ROLLER SHADES consist of a piece of stiffened fabric suspended from a spring-operated roller fixed at the top of the window. A slim lath slotted through a channel at the lower edge adds weight and holds the fabric straight. A shade pulls down to cover the window completely or it can be stopped at any level to give the right balance of privacy and light. Fully open, the shade rolls tightly around the roller above the window glass to allow in maximum light.

ANY MEDIUM-WEIGHT, closely woven fabric would be suitable for making a shade but first it must be stiffened using a special spray-on stiffening solution available from furnishing-fabric shops and department stores. Ready-stiffened shade fabric, known as holland, can be bought but it is not widely available. Wherever possible, avoid joining widths of fabric as the seams may be too bulky to roll smoothly around the roller. No side seams are needed, as the stiffening process also prevents fraying. Hardware – the roller, the spring fitting, brackets, lath, cord pull and, sometimes, fabric stiffening solution – are sold in kit form. Buy a kit to fit the width of your window exactly or one slightly longer that can be cut to size.

You will need:
- ✂ a roller shade kit
- ✂ closely woven furnishing fabric and fabric stiffener
- ✂ a steel ruler, carpenter's square and soft pencil
- ✂ maskingtape
- ✂ a heavy-duty staple gun or a hammer and tacks

ROLLER SHADES HAVE BEEN USED SINCE THE MID-EIGHTEENTH CENTURY, SO THEY FORM AN AUTHENTIC PART OF A TRADITIONAL WINDOW TREATMENT. HERE, FRINGING HAS BEEN ADDED TO THE HEM OF THE SHADE TO MATCH THE DECORATIVE EDGES OF THE CURTAINS.

Measuring

FIRST MEASURE THE WINDOW size accurately (see page 168). If the shade is to fit inside the window recess, measure the width of the recess and deduct 1¼in (3cm) to allow clearance at the sides. If the window is not recessed, or if you want the shade to hang in front of the recess, measure the width of the window frame or recess and add 1½in (4cm) to exclude more light. Cut the roller to this length.

For the fabric width, measure the roller, excluding fixtures. For the fabric length, measure from the top of the roller to the sill (or longer if you prefer), and add 12in (30cm) for attaching to the roller, making a channel and any shaping at the lower edge.

Mounting the brackets

FIT THE END CAP onto the roller and hammer the pin into the roller through the central hole. Screw the brackets in place on the wall or the window frame, with the square socketed one to the left; use the roller and a level to check that they are the correct distance apart and will hold the roller perfectly level. In a recessed window, the brackets should be set about 1¼in (3cm) down from the top of the recess to allow for the thickness of the rolled-up shade. For a shade hung in front of the recess or over an unrecessed window, position the brackets about 2in (5cm) above the window frame or the recess.

Preparing the fabric

TREAT THE FABRIC with fabric stiffener, following the manufacturer's instructions, and press. Cut the fabric to size using a carpenter's square and ruler to make sure all sides are straight and square.

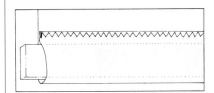

TURN UP AND PRESS a 1½in (4cm) hem along the lower edge and machine zigzag-stitch in place to form a channel for the lath. Cut the lath 1in (2.5cm) shorter than the width of the shade and slot it through the channel, then slip-stitch the ends to close.

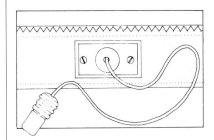

SCREW THE WOODEN KNOB (ACORN), with the cord attached, to the center of the lath on the wrong side of the shade.

Attaching the fabric

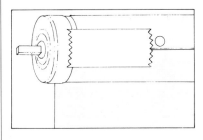

IF THE ROLLER IS NOT MARKED with a guideline for positioning the fabric, draw a straight line along it from end to end, using a pencil. Lay the fabric right side up and place the roller across it, close to the top edge, with the square pin to the left. Stick the fabric to the roller with masking tape, placing the top edge level with the guideline. Then fix the fabric to the roller with tacks or staples, spaced about 1in (2.5cm) apart.

Roll up the shade and insert the roller in the brackets. Pull the shade down and allow it to spring back as far as it will go. Remove the roller from the brackets and rewind, then replace it in the brackets and pull down again. When released, the blind should roll up completely.

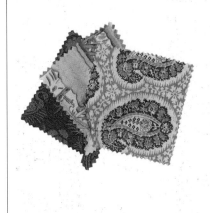

STYLING IDEAS

✔ Wide shades do not work as smoothly as narrow ones, so cover extra-wide windows with two or three matching ones.

✔ Trim the lower edge of a shade with lace, braid, contrasting binding or a decorative border, or appliqué it with shapes such as flowers and leaves or seashells.

✔ For visual interest at a small kitchen or bathroom window, hide the roller mechanism behind a stiffened valance shaped to match the lower edge of the shade.

✔ Continue a stencilled border on the walls across a plain shade.

✔ At semi-basement windows, shades can be trimmed to a deep point from the center of the window and left pulled down; this will give privacy where it is needed at the top of the window and still admit light at the bottom.

✔ Roller shades hung at the bottom of the window and pulled up halfway to catch on hooks at the sides will give privacy and allow light into street-level rooms.

MAKING ROMAN BLINDS

SOFT YET SIMPLE, ELEGANT AND ECONOMICAL, Roman blinds drop down to form a flat panel covering the window but when open, they pull up into tailored pleats. The pleats are formed by a series of laths encased in channels stitched in the lining, with cords running through rings attached to the channels to operate the blind. The blind is supported on a batten hung across the top of the window, and the cords are carried to one side, where they are secured on a cleat.

Closely woven fabric that holds its shape well is the best choice for Roman blinds. Striped or checked blinds look stunning but lines that are not absolutely straight will be immediately obvious.

You will need:
- ✄ medium-weight, closely woven furnishing fabric
- ✄ curtain lining fabric
- ✄ square, ruler and pencil
- ✄ thin wooden laths, about ½in (12mm) wide – one for each pleat plus one for the lower edge
- ✄ a wooden batten 2 x 1in (5 x 2.5cm) to fit across the window
- ✄ angle brackets and screws
- ✄ ½in (12mm) plastic rings: these are spaced 12in (30cm) apart along each casing – with one at each end
- ✄ nylon cord
- ✄ screw eyes for cording rings
- ✄ a heavy-duty staple gun or hammer and tacks
- ✄ a cleat and screws

Measuring

MEASURE THE HEIGHT and width of the window recess or frame. Add 2½in (6cm) to the width for turnings and 4in (10cm) to the length for the hem and hanging. Cut a piece of fabric to this size. Cut a piece of lining fabric the same width, but add an extra 2in (5cm) to the length for each channel (see right).

A ROMAN BLIND, IDENTICAL TO THOSE AT THE WINDOWS, HANGS ABOVE THE HALF-GLAZED DOOR IN THIS COOL DINING ROOM TO GIVE THE IMPRESSION, AFTER DARK, OF A ROW OF MATCHING WINDOWS. THE BLINDS ARE MADE WITH NARROW PLEATS.

To calculate the spacing between channels

DECIDE HOW MANY PLEATS you want the blind to form. Deduct 4in (10cm) from the fabric length for turnings, then divide the result by the desired number of pleats. The depth of pleats should be in proportion to the length of the window but, as a guide, 6in (15cm) is an average depth.

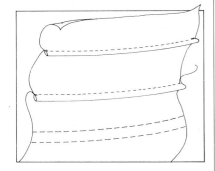

To form 6IN (15CM) PLEATS, the channels will be spaced 12in (30cm) apart. If your calculations show that the pleats will be much narrower or deeper than this, adjust the number accordingly. There will be one channel for each pleat.

Preparing the lining

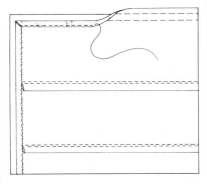

ON THE RIGHT SIDE OF THE LINING, draw a line 1¼in (4cm) up from the lower edge for the hem, and another line, 2in (5cm) down from the top, to indicate the batten position. Turn in and press a 1½in (4cm) turning along both long edges. Turn in and press a 1¼in (3cm) turning along the long edges of the fabric piece.

Mark the lining on the right side with pairs of parallel lines spaced 2½in (6cm) apart to indicate the channel positions. Draw the first pair of lines 6in (15cm) or half a pleat depth up from the hem line, then mark the next pair 12in (30cm), or a full pleat depth above that. Continue, spacing the channel positions a full pleat depth apart, to the top of the lining. To form the channels, bring the marked lines together in pairs, then pin and machine stitch along them.

Assembling the blind

PLACE THE LINING AND BLIND FABRIC with right sides together and lower edges matching; pin, baste and stitch the lower edges together, taking a ⅝in (1.5cm) seam. Turn right side out, with the seam at the lower edge, and press. Machine stitch across the blind along the marked hem line.

Lay the fabric and lining flat, lining uppermost, and pin, then baste together all around. Pin, baste, then machine stitch along the channel positions through both thicknesses of fabric to hold the lining to the blind. Slip-stitch the lining to the blind along the sides, leaving the channels free. Then turn in and stitch the raw top edges of the blind and the lining together.

Fitting the laths and cords

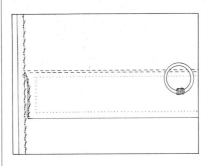

CUT THE LATHS ¾IN (2CM) SHORTER than the width of the lining and slot one into each channel. Slip-stitch the ends to close. Stitch nylon rings firmly to the lining, 4in (10cm) in from the ends of each lath and 12in (30cm) apart.

Cut a length of cord twice the blind length plus its width, for each vertical row of rings. Thread through each row separately, tying the end of the cord to the lowest ring, then passing it up through the row of rings; leave the cord hanging loose.

Hanging the blind

MOUNT ANGLE BRACKETS to support the batten at the required height above the window. Remove the batten and fold the top edge of the fabric over it so that the marked line matches the top front edge.

Attach the fabric to the batten with tacks or staples, spacing them at regular intervals along the length. Fix screw eyes into the underside of the batten, one above each row of rings. Screw the batten onto the angle brackets.

Thread the loose end of each cord through the screw eye above it, then through each screw eye in turn to the right hand side of the window. Trim the cords level, thread them through a decorative pull and knot together. Screw a cleat to the side of the window to secure the cords.

With the blind lowered, slot the remaining lath through the hem at the lower edge, then slip-stitch the open ends to enclose it.

STYLING IDEAS

✔ *A border, which can be sewn along the side edges or all around, gives a note of distinction to a plain Roman blind.*

✔ *Make unlined Roman blinds from fine cotton fabric for a stylish, translucent screen. Estimate the fabric and sew the channels as for the lining, but hem the edges to the reverse side.*

✔ *Roman blinds look stunning hung alone at a window but if your furnishing style demands a softer touch, drape a simple pleated swag across the top.*

MAKING AUSTRIAN BLINDS

THESE OPULENT BLINDS pull up to form deep swags at the top of a window. Let down, they resemble a generously gathered curtain, slightly ruched at the hem. To emphasize their feminine character, they are usually ruffled around the sides and base.

THIS AUSTRIAN BLIND HAS A SLOT HEADING INSTEAD OF THE USUAL CURTAIN HEADING TAPE. ITS UNFUSSY CONSTRUCTION, WITH NO FRILLS OR TRIMMINGS, ALLOWS ATTENTION TO FOCUS ON ITS BRILLIANT COLORS.

THE BLIND IS SUSPENDED from a wooden batten or a specially designed track and operated by cords threaded through rings or loops attached to vertical tapes spaced across the back of the blind. The cords are carried across the underside of the supporting batten through screw eyes and secured at the side of the window on a cleat. The blinds may be lined for extra weight and volume or left unlined for an airier effect.

You will need:
- medium-weight, closely woven furnishing fabric
- curtain lining fabric
- pencil pleat heading tape
- curtain lining tape plus small brass split rings or purpose-made Austrian blind tape
- nylon cord

Then either:
- a wooden batten 2 x 1in (5 x 2.5cm) to fit across the width of the window
- angle brackets and screws
- screw eyes
- a heavy-duty staple gun or a hammer and tacks
- touch-and-close fastener

Or:
- Austrian blind track to fit across window, plus hooks
- cleat and screws (for both)

Measuring and cutting out

HANG THE BATTEN OR TRACK over the window, then measure its width and multiply by two and a half. Measure the length of the window from the top of the batten or track to the sill and add 19¾in (50cm). Cut blind fabric and lining to these measurements, joining widths with a flat seam if necessary. For the ruffle strip, join enough 6in (15cm) wide strips cut from the width of the fabric to fit twice around the side and base edges of the main blind piece.

Decide how many scallops you want across the width of the blind and cut one more strip of lining tape or Austrian blind tape than the number of scallops, making each the same length as the blind fabric. Cut a length of heading tape 2in (5cm) longer than the width of the blind fabric.

Making the ruffle

FOLD THE CONTINUOUS FABRIC STRIP in half lengthwise, with right sides together, and stitch across the short ends. Trim seams and turn right side out. Fold the strip in half with right sides out and long edges level, then divide it into three sections to correspond with the ruffled edges of the blind; mark the divisions with soft pencil or tailor's chalk. Each section should be twice the length of the side to which it corresponds.

Gather each section separately, running two rows of stitches along the raw edges through both thicknesses. Pull up the gathers to fit around the sides and lower edge of the blind. Lay the ruffle around the main fabric piece on the right side, the ends positioned ⅝in (1.5cm) down from the top; have the raw edges level and match the division marks in the frill to the corners of the blind. Spreading the gathers evenly, pin and baste in place.

Attaching the ruffle

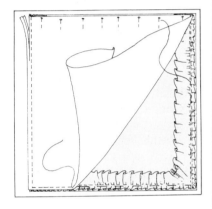

LAY THE LINING OVER THE BLIND with right sides together, raw edges level and ruffle sandwiched between. Pin, baste and machine stitch around the side and lower edges with a ⅝in (1.5cm) seam. Trim the seam, turn right side out and press. Pin and baste top raw edges together.

Attaching the tapes

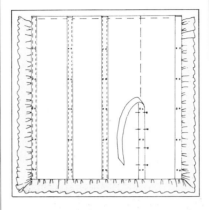

DIVIDE THE BLIND WIDTH, not including the ruffle, by the number of scallops required and, on the wrong side, mark vertical divisions down the length of the blind with a soft pencil. Pin a strip of lining tape or Austrian blind tape down each side edge, alongside the ruffle seam, folding the end level with the lower ruffle seam. The first loop on the Austrian blind tape should be about 2in (5cm) up from the lower seam line. Pin further strips of tape over the division lines in the same way, making sure the pockets of the lining tape and the loops of the Austrian blind tape align across the width. Machine stitch the tapes in place.

Attaching the cords

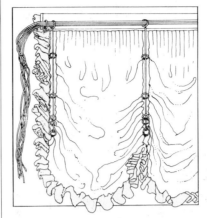

CUT A LENGTH OF CORD twice the blind length plus its width, for each vertical tape. If you are using lining tape, insert split rings through the pockets, placing the first one 2in (5cm) up from the lower end, then spacing them 12in (30cm) apart, with the last one 10-12in (25-30cm) below the heading tape. Make sure the rings align horizontally. Thread cord along each tape by tying the end of the cord to the lowest ring, then passing it up through each ring in the row, right up to the top.

Hanging the blind

PULL UP THE HEADING TAPE cords until the top of the blind fits the track or batten, then fasten off and spread the pleats evenly. If you are using an Austrian blind track, insert curtain hooks in the heading and attach the blind to the track by means of the hooks. If you are attaching the blind to a batten, tack or staple the heading along the batten so the tacks are hidden between pleats.

If you are using touch-and-close fastener, place the lining strip over the pleated heading tape on the wrong side and hand stitch in place all around. Staple or tack the hooked part of the fastener along the batten, then press the blind in place so the two halves of the fastener connect.

With Austrian blind track, lock the cord holders above the vertical tapes. For a batten mount, insert screw eyes into the underside of the batten, above each tape, with an extra one close to the batten's right hand edge. Place the batten on the brackets and screw in place. Pass the end of each cord through the screw eye or holder immediately above it, then through each one in turn to the right hand side of the window. With the blind let right down, knot the cords together close to the track or batten; plait the ends together, knot and trim.

Screw a cleat to the wall or window frame on the right-hand side. Pull up the blind and twist the cord around the cleat to secure it.

Making the heading

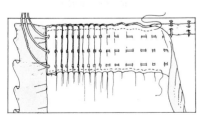

TURN IN THE TOP RAW EDGE by ⅝in (1.5cm) then place the pencil

pleat tape along it, covering the turning; pin in place. Knot cords together at one end of the heading tape and pull them free at the other, then turn in the cut ends level with the side seams; pin in place. Machine stitch the tape in place all around.

If you are attaching the blind to the batten with touch-and-close fastener, make a backing strip for

the heading tape as follows: cut a strip of lining fabric 1¼in (3cm) deeper than the heading tape and 1¼in (3cm) longer than the batten. Cut a strip of touch-and-close fastener to the same length. Pin, then machine stitch the pile half of the fastener along the lining strip, 1in (2.5cm) down from one long edge. Turn in and press ⅝in (1.5cm) all around the lining strip.

MAKING FESTOON BLINDS

WHEN PULLED UP, A FESTOON BLIND LOOKS SIMILAR TO AN AUSTRIAN BLIND, the difference only becoming apparent when it is dropped down. Where Austrian blinds hang in straight folds, festoon blinds retain a ruched appearance down their entire length. The construction of the blind produces a frilly effect at the sides, so if a ruffled edging is required, it should be added at the lower edge only.

THIS CO-ORDINATING FESTOON BLIND IN A SEMI-SHEER FABRIC FILTERS THE LIGHT THROUGH THE WINDOW. IT REMAINS RUCHED WHEN PULLED UP, AN ORNATE EFFECT WHICH SUITS THE ELABORATE WINDOW TREATMENT FOR THIS GRAND ROOM, WITH ITS DRESS CURTAINS, SWAGS AND TAILS. THE HEM OF THE BLIND IS TRIMMED WITH FRINGED TUFTS TO MATCH THE TRIMMING ON THE CURTAINS.

THOUGH THE METHOD OF MAKING is similar to that for Austrian blinds, festoons require more fabric to allow for the ruching. Because of their volume, festoon blinds are best made from a lightweight fabric that drapes well and left unlined. To make the workings less obtrusive, use curtain heading tape for sheer fabrics.

You will need:
- lightweight, sheer or semi-sheer cotton or silk fabric
- pencil pleat heading tape for sheers, and curtain hooks
- translucent narrow standard curtain tape plus small brass split rings, or purpose-made festoon blind tape
- nylon cord

Then either:
- a wooden batten 2 x 1in (5 x 2.5cm) to fit across the width of the window
- touch-and-close fastener the same length
- screw eyes, angle brackets and hanging screws

Or:
- Austrian blind track to fit across the window
- cleat and screws (for both)

Measuring and cutting out

HANG THE BATTEN OR Austrian blind track above the window. Measure its width, multiply this by two and a half, then add 4in (10cm) for turnings. Measure the length of the window from the top of the batten or track down to the sill: multiply by one and a half. Cut out fabric to these measurements, joining widths with a flat seam. For the ruffle, join enough 6in (15cm) wide fabric strips to total twice the blind width.

Decide how many swags you want across the blind. Cut one more strip of lining tape or festoon blind tape than the number of swags, making each the same length as the blind fabric. Cut heading tape 2in (5cm) longer than the width of the blind fabric.

Making the ruffle

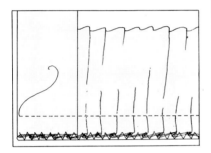

FOLD THE STRIP IN HALF lengthwise, right sides together; stitch across the short ends and trim the seams. Re-fold the strip with right sides out and long edges level; gather along the raw edges through both thicknesses. Pull up gathers until the ruffle measures 4in (10cm) less than the width of the blind.

Lay the ruffle along the lower edge of the blind on right side of fabric, 2in (5cm) in from each side, with raw edges level. Spread the gathers evenly, pin and baste in place. Turn in and press 2in (5cm) along both side edges of the blind, enclosing the ends of the ruffle. Machine stitch along the lower edge, taking a ⅝in (1.5cm) seam. Trim the turnings and oversew raw edges with a machine zigzag stitch. Fold side turnings to the wrong side and press. Press the ruffle seam towards the main blind piece.

Attaching the tapes

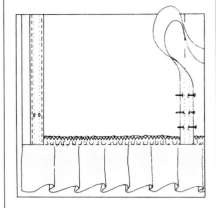

PIN A LENGTH OF CURTAIN TAPE or festoon blind tape down each side turning to cover the raw edge. The first loop on the festoon blind tape should be about 2½in (6.5cm) up from the ruffle seam. Measure the space between the tapes and divide by the number of swags required, then mark vertical divisions down the wrong side of the blind with a soft pencil. Pin further strips of tape over the division lines in the same way, making sure the pockets of curtain tape and loops of festoon blind tape align across the width.

Turn under the lower ends of the tape level with the ruffle seam, then stitch the tapes in place. Pull the cord free of the tape about 2½in (6.5cm) from the top edge to prevent them from catching in the heading tape. Attach the heading tape and pull up pleats as for the Austrian blind.

Attaching the cords

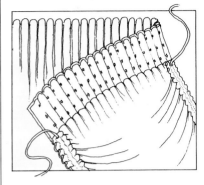

PULL UP THE CORDS in the vertical tapes from the top, until the blind is the required length. Wind up and knot the surplus cord to secure. Spread the gathers down the length of the cords until the blind is evenly ruched. Insert split rings if required, and thread the cording as for the Austrian blind.

Hanging the blind

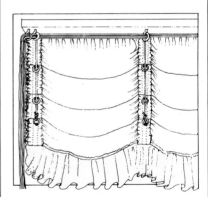

ATTACH THE BLIND TO THE TRACK or batten and complete the cording as for the Austrian blind. Screw a cleat to the wall or window frame on the right-hand side. Pull up the blind and twist the cord around the cleat to secure.

STYLING IDEAS

✂ For a truly glamorous effect, use ballgown fabrics like satin or taffeta for pull-up blinds.

✂ If a ruched blind forms part of a multi-layer window treatment, make sure the curtain track projects far enough forward to pull up the blind without crushing its folds.

✂ Heavy lace trimming along the lower edge of an Austrian blind gives it a pretty, cottagey look.

✂ Emulate high Victoriana by trimming a brocade or silk Austrian blind with heavy fringing.

✂ For a less voluminous Austrian blind, use a narrow-width fabric and, instead of pencil pleats, make pinch or box pleats above each vertical tape position. For box pleats, place the tape centrally down the back of the pleat. These blinds have fewer scallops and are more restrained.

✂ Omit the outermost tapes on an Austrian blind, so that when the blind is pulled up, the sides drop down to form tails.

✂ To create a virtually no-sew ruched blind, hang a flat panel of fabric at the window, with two or three pairs of ribbons or tapes attached front and back, at the top edge. Gather up the lower edge of the fabric and hold in place by tying each pair of tapes together in a bow. The fabric between the ties will hang in scallops.

STYLES AND SHAPES OF CUSHION

THE SIMPLEST AND MOST VERSATILE OF SOFT FURNISHINGS, cushions soften a hard seat, provide support where it is lacking and comfort wherever you need it. Apart from their practical benefits, cushions are also an important decorative asset. They can pull together a decorating theme, enliven a color scheme by introducing splashes of contrast or brilliance, act as a showcase for your needlework skills or emphasize a particular furnishing style.

ABOVE: CUSHIONS IN ASSORTED SHAPES AND SIZES ADD COMFORT AND COLOR TO A SEVERE DAYBED. THE HAPHAZARD COLLECTION OF PROVENCAL PRINTS, DAMASK AND CONTRASTING PLAIN FABRICS IS BROUGHT TOGETHER BY COMPLEMENTARY FRINGED TRIMMING.

LEFT: THE WHITE CUSHIONS IN THIS GROUP ARE MADE WITH AN INNER FLAP LIKE A PILLOWCASE AND SECURED WITH FABRIC TIES. THE OTHER CUSHIONS RELY ON COLOR AND PATTERN FOR INTEREST, SHOWING HOW, WITH A DEFT TOUCH, PATTERNS CAN BE MIXED SUCCESSFULLY.

THE BRAID BORDERING THESE SQUARE PILLOWS AND ENCIRCLING THE ENDS OF THE BOLSTERS LINKS TOGETHER CUSHIONS OF DIFFERENT SHAPES. ARRANGED SYMMETRICALLY, THE CUSHIONS EMPHASIZE THE SHAPE OF THE ELEGANT SOFA AND CONTRAST WITH THE QUIET DAMASK UPHOLSTERY.

STYLING IDEAS

✂ *For a quick make-over, wrap a cushion in a silk scarf, knotting the points at the center.*

✂ *For a contemporary look, mix square, circular and triangular boxed cushions in plain covers.*

✂ *Combine ruffles and piping, or braid and cord, for edgings which have more impact.*

✂ *Edge plain cushions with thick cord, knotting it or twisting it into a loop or trefoil at the corners for more interest.*

✂ *Quicker than hemming, trim single ruffles on cushions with pinking shears.*

✂ *Make a simple bolster cover by rolling it in a piece of fabric about 20in (50cm) wider than the pad and tying the ends with tasselled cords like a Christmas cracker.*

✂ *Emphasize the shape of rectangular cushions by adding fringing to the short ends only.*

✂ *Make border-printed cushions by sewing together two table napkins.*

You can buy cushion pads in all shapes and sizes – rectangular, circular and even triangular – and a collection of different forms, variously covered, makes an attractive display. Small, square cushions with frilled embroidery or lace covers look pretty in a bedroom, while large cushions break up the expanse of a roomy sofa. Bolsters are part-cushion, part-upholstery: firmer than conventional cushions, they give shape and support to a straight-sided sofa or divan and achieve a more formal effect than soft scatter cushions. Boxed cushions, another hybrid type, are often found on hard wooden seats where more resilient padding is needed; they regain their square shape when no one is sitting on them.

Covering cushions is easy and, once you have mastered the basic methods, you can trim and decorate them to complement the style of a room. Piped or pleated-edge cushions are the popular choice for a classic room: made from patterned or plain fabric to match or accent the curtains or slipcovers, they complete the scheme, giving it a seamless continuity. A sophisticated country-house look can be achieved by making cushions from scraps of antique textiles, damasks, brocades and tapestry, edged and trimmed with cord, braid, fringing and tassels. If you prefer a more relaxed, rustic look, use printed, striped or checked cotton, linen or even wool weaves for a country air. Choose a style and trimming to complement other furnishings in the room: ruffled, floral print cushions look appropriate in pretty, country style rooms decorated with dried flowers and bric-à-brac, but plain, square cushions in checks or stripes would be more in keeping in a simpler room setting.

Unless the decor is minimal, cushions can be a valuable accessory in contemporary rooms too. Plain-colored glazed chintz or robust weaves edged with contrasting piping look stylish on modern upholstered furniture, especially when the colors are bold and bright. In quieter surroundings, large, flat-bordered cushions made from textured natural fabrics in neutral shades, or uncomplicated colors like navy, terracotta, duck-egg blue and sage green, all look wonderful against the muted paintwork and uncluttered lines of American country furniture.

Bedroom cushions can afford to be a little more fussy and feminine in style. Old embroidered napkins, tray cloths and other secondhand finds can be converted into cushion covers which have a nostalgic charm, while plain covers embroidered with either a monogram, a verse or a personal message lend an air of intimacy. In a bedroom where chintz is used for the curtains and bed cover, make matching cushions from the same fabric but give them a softer look by outline-quilting the design.

FABRICS FOR CUSHIONS

ALMOST ANY FABRIC, PLAIN OR PATTERNED, textured or smooth, can be used to cover scatter cushions as long as it is robust enough to withstand the level of wear it will receive. Decorative bedroom cushions can be made from delicate, luxurious fabrics, but the cushions on the sofa in a family room will last longer if they are made from a tapestry weave, twill or some other strong cloth. Between the two extremes, any chintz, cotton print or weave would be suitable. If you choose a pattern, the motif should be small enough to appear complete on the cover.

Printed cotton (1, 8) Plain, medium to lightweight woven cotton with a printed design. Usually the scale of the pattern matches the fabric, so detailed designs are found on finely woven cloths and exuberant patterns on slightly coarser materials.

Twill stripe (2) A firmly woven cloth with a distinctive herringbone weave. This one is striped in the manner of ticking but with a more sophisticated effect.

Chintz (3) Finely woven, printed and polished cotton. The traditional designs were realistic floral motifs, but the pattern range now varies widely.

Printed moiré (4) The basic fabric is a finely ribbed silky material with a shimmering watermark. This example is overprinted with a bamboo lattice design and foliage tracery. Very much a luxury fabric, moiré is unsuitable for washing.

Damask (5) Originally made from silk, this jacquard-weave fabric now comes in cotton, wool, linen and synthetic fibers. Patterns are formed by a combination of satin and sateen weave; the design appears in reverse on the wrong side.

Velvet stripe (6) A decorative fabric alternating stripes of velvet pile with smooth woven cotton.

Dobby weave (7) This plain woven fabric with a regular geometric design is useful where discreet pattern is needed, such as a companion to a flamboyant print.

Dupion (9) A lustrous, slubbed fabric made from silk or synthetic fibers. It is most often used for curtains, valances and cushions in classic, traditional schemes.

Tapestry weave (10) A tough, textured cloth in designs influenced by traditional needlework, tapestries or kelims. Because of its thickness, cushions made from this cloth should preferably be edged with cord or fringing rather than piping.

Satin weave (11) The warp, or vertical, threads of this fabric are carried over several weft threads and under one to give a smooth, lustrous surface. Sometimes stripes of satin and matte finish are produced by reversing the process in alternate bands.

USING BOUGHT TRIMMINGS

Cording
This smart edging can be added to ready-made as well as hand-sewn cushions. First measure the circumference of the finished cushion and buy cord 4in (10cm) longer. Hand stitch the cord neatly around the edge of the cover to hide the seam. Twist and stitch the ends of the cord together and tuck into a small opening in the seam. Re-sew the opening to close it.

Fringe
Ready-made fringe gives a professional finish to plain, home-made cushions. Buy fringe 4in (10cm) longer than the cushion's circumference. Pin, baste and sew the fringe around the cover front before it is made up, as for ruffled edging (see page 199). Complete the cushion in the same way.

Indian cotton (12) A coarse, inexpensive cotton with an attractive, slightly uneven weave. Often woven in checks for a colorful plaid design.

Jacquard weave (13) This fabric is woven on a Jacquard loom which is programmed to raise the weft threads; the design produced emphasizes the positive/negative effect of the technique.

Tartan (14) A wool fabric with a checked design produced by interweaving groups of colored warp and weft threads. Designs may be authentic Scottish clan tartans or more freely colored plaids.

MAKING SQUARE AND ROUND CUSHIONS

ARRANGED INVITINGLY ON A SOFA, stacked against the bedhead or tossed carelessly into an armchair, cushions add comfort and color exactly where you need them. Ready-made cushion pads come in square, rectangular and round shapes in standard sizes and some shops also sell bolsters. They can be stuffed with feather or synthetic fillings: feather cushions plump up beautifully but synthetic fillings have the advantage of being washable. Avoid pads filled with foam chips: they always feel lumpy and quickly lose their shape. Solid blocks of foam, however, are ideal for seat cushions and bolsters.

Making Square Covers

SQUARE COVERS ARE THE SIMPLEST of all cushion covers to make. You can use exactly the same method to cover rectangular cushions.

MEASURE THE CUSHION PAD both ways, from seam to seam; add a 1¼in (3cm) seam allowance to each measurement. Cut two pieces of fabric this size.

Place fabric pieces right sides together, with edges matching. Pin, baste, then machine stitch all around, ⅝in (1.5cm) from the edge; leave a central opening in one side large enough for the cushion pad to go through. Trim the seam allowances, snipping off the corners. Remove basting, then turn cover right side out; press.

Insert the cushion pad. Turn in the raw edges of the opening in line with the seam; slip-stitch the edges together.

Side-seam zipped fastening

PLACE THE FABRIC PIECES together as before and baste along one side. Measure the opening part of the zipper and mark its position centrally on the seam. Machine stitch along the seam from each corner to the marked points, then reverse for about 1¼in (3cm) to strengthen

THESE CUSHIONS ARE GIVEN A CONTEMPORARY LOOK BY USING CONTRASTING VELVETS FOR THE FRONT AND BACK AND ARRANGING THEM SO THE COLOR CHANGE SHOWS. CORD, FRINGING OR EVEN PIPING WOULD DETRACT FROM THE EFFECT, SO THEY ARE LEFT UNTRIMMED.

the ends of the opening. Leaving basting stitches in place, press the seam open. On the wrong side, place the zipper, face down, centrally over the seam and pin, then baste in place. Use a zipper foot on the sewing machine to stitch all around the zipper, about ¼in (5mm) from the teeth.

Remove the basting stitches and finish off the sewing threads neatly on the wrong side. Leaving the zipper slightly open, place the two sides of the cushion cover with right sides together; complete the cover as before.

Center-seam zipper fastening

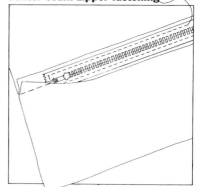

CUT THE THE CUSHION COVER front as before. Cut the back the same width but 1¼in (3cm) longer; cut it in half across the length. Place the two cover-back pieces with right sides together and pin, then baste, along one long edge. Insert the zipper as above, then open out the back piece and make the cushion cover as before.

Making Round Covers

MEASURE THE DIAMETER of the pad, add a 1¼in (3cm) seam allowance, then make a paper pattern to that size (see page 206). Using the paper pattern, cut out two pieces of fabric.

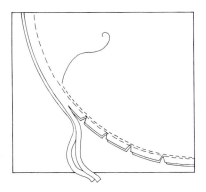

PLACE THE FABRIC PIECES RIGHT SIDES together, with edges matching. Pin, baste, then machine stitch all around, ⅝in (1.5cm) from the edge, leaving an opening in the seam for inserting the cushion pad. Trim the seam, cutting notches into the allowance at intervals to help the seam lie smoothly. Remove basting stitches, turn right side out and press.

Insert the cushion pad, turn in the raw edges of the opening in line with the seam; slip-stitch the opening to close.

Decorative Edgings

EDGINGS GIVE A PROFESSIONAL finish to cushions and can be as simple or elaborate as you like. Use ready-made cord or fringing (see page 197), or make piping or ruffles to match or contrast with the cover.

Piped edge

A PIPED EDGING gives cushions a sharp, tailored finish. Plain piping works well on patterned cushions; for plain cushions, you should choose a contrasting color or a deeper tone of the main fabric.

Before assembling a cushion, make enough piping to go around its edge, plus 3in (7.5cm) (see page 209 for method). Pin, then baste the piping around the cushion front on the right side, with raw edges level. To turn corners smoothly on a square or rectangular cushion, snip into the piping from the raw edges to the stitching. To curve piping around circular cushions, snip into it at intervals along its length.

Join the piping ends neatly. On square and rectangular cushions, place the seam at the center of the lower edge. Complete the cushion as before, using a piping foot on the sewing machine and stitching as close as possible to the piping cord.

Ruffled edge

CUSHIONS FOR A BEDROOM or country-style living room look pretty with a ruffled edge. The width should be in proportion to the size of the cushion but most are 1¾-3in (4-7.5cm) wide. Decide on the width and add 1¼in (3cm) for seam allowances and hems. The length should be about twice the circumference of the cushion. Cut strips of fabric across

its width, joining them end to end with french seams to achieve the desired length, then join the ends to form a ring.

To hem the outer edge of the ruffle, fold and press a ¼in (5mm) turning to the wrong side, then fold and press a further ⅜in (1cm) turning. Machine stitch in place, stitching close to the edge.

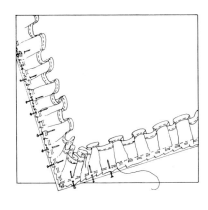

RUN TWO ROWS OF gathering stitches along the remaining raw edge. Pull up the gathers to fit, then pin the ruffle around the cushion front, with right sides together and raw edges level; place the pins at right angles to the edge to keep the gathers straight. Spread the gathers evenly, allowing more fullness at the corners.

Stitch the ruffle to the cushion front about ⅜in (1cm) from the edge; complete as before.

Double-sided ruffle

THIS SHOWS THE RIGHT SIDE of the fabric on front and back. Cut the frill strip twice the desired width plus a 1¼in (3cm) seam allowance. Join the short ends with plain seams to form a ring. Fold the strip in half, right side out, with raw edges level; continue as before.

Pleated ruffle

A PLEATED EDGING gives living room cushions a more formal effect. Make the strip as for a double-sided ruffle, joining the ends to form a ring; fold in half with right side out. Divide the ring into four equal sections and mark the divisions with pins or chalk. These will correspond with the corners of a square cushion.

Make an equal number of pleats in each section, with two smaller, closely spaced pleats on either side of the marked points to give extra fullness at the corners. Pin the pleated strip around the cushion front as for the ruffled edging, adjusting the pleats to fit. Baste, then machine stitch in place. Complete as before.

Flat border

AN INTEGRAL FLAT BORDER looks good especially on medium to large square cushions.

Measure the cushion both ways and add 5in (13cm) to each measurement for the borders and seam allowances. Cut the cover front to this size. Cut the back an extra 1¼in (3cm) long to allow for a center-back zipper. Join the two back pieces and insert the zipper centrally (see page 198).

Place the cushion front and back with right sides together and edges matching. Pin, baste and stitch all around, ⅝in (1.5cm) from the edge. Trim seam, turn right side out and press.

With chalk or basting stitches, mark a square centrally on the cover the size of the cushion pad. Machine stitch around the square through both thicknesses of fabric. To finish, work machine satin stitch over the stitching line.

MAKING BOXED CUSHIONS AND BOLSTERS

BOXED CUSHIONS MAKE WINDOW SEATS, PEWS, WICKER CHAIRS and other unpadded seats more comfortable to sit on. The square, boxy shape is achieved by inserting a gusset between the front and back cover pieces; piped seams give the shape even more definition. For the filling, use gussetted feather-filled cushion pads or blocks of foam cut to size.

BOXED CUSHIONS PROVIDE A FIRM SEAT AND BACK REST FOR THIS WINDOW SEAT. THE SEAT CUSHION COVERS ARE MITERED TO FIT AROUND THE SEAT, WHILE THE BACK CUSHIONS ARE HELD UPRIGHT WITH FABRIC LOOPS ATTACHED TO DRAWER KNOBS SCREWED INTO THE WOODWORK.

Square and Rectangular Boxed Cushions

MEASURE THE CUSHION both ways and add 1¼in (3cm) to each measurement for seam allowances. Cut two fabric pieces this size. Measure the length and depth of each side of the cushion and add 1¼in (3cm) to each measurement for seam allowances. Cut one gusset strip for each side.

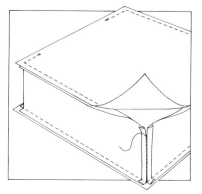

PIN, BASTE, THEN STITCH the gusset strips end to end with right sides together and edges level, taking ⅝in (1.5cm) allowances, to form a ring. For rectangular cushions, make sure the same size strips are opposite each other. Pin, then baste the gusset around one cover piece, matching the gusset seams to the corners. Unpick a few stitches at both ends of each seam to avoid puckering. Stitch all around, ⅝in (1.5cm) from edge.

Join remaining cover piece to the other edge of the gusset; leave an opening in one side, stitching in a zipper if wished (see page 198). Trim seams; turn right side out.

Round Boxed Cushions

MEASURE THE DIAMETER of the pad or foam block; add 1¼in (3cm) for seam allowances, then make a paper pattern to that size (see page 207). Using the pattern, cut out the cushion back and front. Measure the circumference and depth of the pad and add 1¼in (3cm) to both measurements for seam allowances. Cut a strip of fabric this size for the gusset.

Pin, then stitch the short ends of the gusset strip together to form a ring. Machine stitch a line of ½in (1.2cm) from each raw edge, then snip into seam allowances at intervals so the gusset fits around the front and back smoothly.

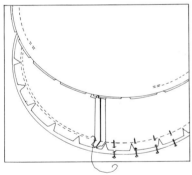

PIN, THEN BASTE THE GUSSET around one cushion piece, right sides together and raw edges level. Machine stitch all around, inside the first row of stitches. Join the remaining cushion piece to the other edge of the gusset in the same way, leaving a gap in the seam. Insert a zipper if required (see page 198). Trim seams, turn right side out and press. Insert the cushion pad. If there is no zipper, turn in the raw edges neatly in line with the seam and slip-stitch the opening to close.

Bolsters

THESE FIRM, CYLINDRICAL cushions come in various sizes, from small neck cushions to double-bed-width pillows. Between these extremes are bolsters to tuck in at the sides of a sofa for more arm support or along the back of a divan that doubles as a sofa. Their covers can be either smoothly fitted or gathered.

Fitted bolster cover

THIS TAILORED COVER has flat end pieces; it may be piped or edged with cord to emphasize its shape.

Measure the length and the circumference of the bolster; add 1¼in (3cm) to the measurements for seam allowances. Cut a piece of fabric this size. Measure across the end of the bolster and make a circular paper pattern this size (see page 207); use it to cut out two pieces of fabric.

Fold the main fabric piece in half lengthwise with right sides together and edges level. Pin, baste and machine stitch, inserting a zip centrally in the seam (see page 198). Make a row of stitching ½in (1.2cm) in from both raw edges, then snip into the seam allowances at intervals; this makes it easier to fit the circular end pieces.

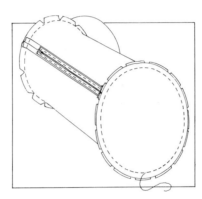

WITH RIGHT SIDES TOGETHER, pin, then baste a circular end piece into one open end of the cover. Then machine stitch all around, inside the first row of stitching. Insert the other end piece in the same way. Trim seams, turn right side out and insert bolster pad.

Gathered bolster cover

FOR THIS COVER, the fabric is simply gathered to fit at the ends and a button or tassel trimming usually added to cover the gathers.

Measure the length of the bolster plus the diameter of one end, adding 1¼in (3cm) for the seam allowances. Measure the circumference and add 1¼in (3cm) for seams. Cut out a fabric piece to these dimensions.

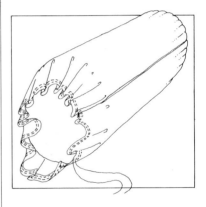

JOIN THE LONG EDGES and insert a zipper as for the fitted cover. Turn right side out. Turn in and hem ⅝in (1.5cm) at the open ends, then make two rows of gathering stitches close to the edge. Pull up the gathers firmly at one end and fasten off. Insert the bolster pad, then pull up and fasten off the gathers at the remaining open end to give a good fit.

Remove the bolster pad, then sew on fabric-covered buttons or tassels to cover the center of each gathered end. Replace the pad.

SLIPCOVERS: STYLES AND SHAPES

SLIPCOVERS CAN GIVE NEW LIFE TO SHABBY FURNITURE, transform a collection of mismatched seats and play a major part in revamping a jaded color scheme. Unlike upholstered coverings, which are permanent and best made and fitted by a specialized craftsperson, slipcovers can be removed for washing or simply when you want a change. Often thought of in the context of armchairs and sofas, removable covers can actually improve the appearance of all kinds of seats. Use them to give bedroom chairs a more casual character, to bring unappetizing dining chairs up to date, to make a simple stool into a significant piece of furniture and to link window seats visually with curtains or other seating.

CHANGING THE IMAGE

You can use slipcovers as image changers. Wicker or Lloyd loom chairs with floor-length slip-on covers and a matching seat cushion look more like club chairs than garden furniture as they move into the living room. Kitchen chairs and an odd collection of dining chairs covered in pull-on cotton covers become a matching set smart enough to gather around a dinner-party table. Upholstered furniture, which is often bought in matching sets of a sofa and two chairs, or a pair of sofas plus a chair, can sometimes seem a bland arrangement. By the simple device of covering one chair in a toning plain fabric or a co-ordinating patterned material, you can bring the group to life.

The style of cover will be determined largely by the shape of the seat, but minor adjustments can be made by changing details. For example, an uphol-stered wing chair with exposed legs looks less formal clad in easy-fit covers with a valance that reaches to the ground. And a squashy armchair can be smartened up with neatly tailored covers piped at every seam, especially if a firm new cushion is put on the seat. As with all soft furnishings, it is the details that count, and the valance or edging can do much to reinforce the style of slipcovers. A gathered valance round the lower edge of an armchair gives it a country look, while box pleats, or a flat valance with kick pleats at the corners, indicates a smart, urban style and a skirt of long bullion fringing, formality.

THE BEST FABRIC

The choice of fabric is another major influence on the style of loose slipcovers. Chairs of the same design covered in printed cotton, damask, ticking or a figured weave will assume completely different personalities to complement a diverse range of interiors. There are no rules for what design and type of fabric suits which style of seat, but when choosing the fabric, always

SLIPCOVERS UNITE A DISPARATE COLLECTION OF SEATS IN THIS ROOM. TOUGH, INEXPENSIVE FABRICS LIKE CANVAS OR COTTON DUCK ARE AN EXCELLENT CHOICE WHEN WORKING TO A BUDGET; IN THIS PALE SCHEME, THEY OFFER NO VISUAL COMPETITION TO THE BRILLIANT RUGS.

consider its suitability in practical terms. Ask yourself how it will stand up to wear, will it crush easily, must it be washable? There is great scope for variety, however, since every seat in the household need not be covered in the same way. A seldom-used occasional chair in a bedroom or hall can be covered in a delicate chintz, but a robust linen union or a heavy cotton weave would stand up better to the hard wear imposed on a family sitting room.

Since one important function of removable covers is to extend the life of the upholstery and protect it from wear and dirt, you can prolong the life of the covers by having two sets and changing them over from time to time. By making one in a light, bright fabric for summer and the other in a heavier fabric and a warmer color for winter, you can change the mood of your room with the seasons. Off-white cotton duck, for example, which is both tough and inexpensive, can be stitched into simple, unstructured covers to transform a room for summer.

Fabrics with large-scale patterns look wonderful on over-sized chairs and sofas, but plain materials, or those with a small, regular design that requires no pattern matching, are the easiest to make and involve little wastage. If you are new to cover making, think carefully before using stripes or checks. Both require absolutely accurate cutting to keep the lines perfectly horizontal and vertical.

STYLISH STRIPED COVERS IN BLUE AND WHITE COTTON DUCK TRANSFORM THESE DIRECTOR'S CHAIRS FROM GARDEN TO INDOOR FURNITURE. TOUGH AND INEXPENSIVE, THIS FABRIC CAN BE READILY LAUNDERED AT HOME.

STYLING IDEAS

☛ New covers can of course revitalize junk-shop furniture – but never waste money and effort covering seats that are uncomfortable to sit in.

☛ Make sleeves in matching fabric to cover the arms of chairs and sofas where they get most wear.

☛ Define the shape of furniture with contrasting piping. Bold combinations like green and red, blue and yellow, and yellow and red have a contemporary freshness.

☛ Give plain covers a luxury look with ruched piping. Make the bias strip slightly wider and about twice as long as for standard piping, then thread the cord through it, ruching as you go.

☛ Save time by buying ready-made piping, which comes in plain colors and is sold by the length.

☛ Do not put removable covers on top of velvet upholstery: the movement of the pile when you sit down shifts the fabric, making it ruck and crease.

☛ For a swift make-over, cover a chair or sofa with a sheet, bedspread or large tablecloth, smoothing over the seat and tucking it down at the sides. A thick rope tied around below the seat will hold it in place.

☛ Give any sofa a country look by tucking a patchwork quilt over the seat and back rest.

☛ Tartan-plaid throws draped over a chair or sofa give a warm, cozy look for winter. Use three or four different plaids for a really luxurious effect.

☛ Integrate a newly covered chair or sofa into an existing room scheme by adding cushions covered in fabrics to match other furnishings.

SLIPCOVER FABRICS

DURABILITY, FADE RESISTANCE AND CLOSELY WOVEN TEXTURE are the most important qualities in any upholstery fabric. For slipcovers, bulk is also a consideration since you will sometimes sew through four or more thicknesses at once. Make sewing thick fabrics easier by piping with a strong but lightweight fabric, or trim the seams with cord or fringing instead. Most upholstery fabrics are now treated for flame resistance, but check the label carefully before buying.

Plain weave cotton (1, 3, 12, 14) Closely woven cotton is a robust cover fabric. Easy to sew, and with no pattern matching, it looks best when piped using similar fabric in a contrasting color. A plain colored sofa or chair is an excellent foil for highly patterned curtains or wallcoverings and an ideal background for decorative cushions.

Ticking (2) Inexpensive, stylish and easy to work with, this durable fabric is an excellent choice for those on a limited budget. The smooth surface wears well and the fabric is washable, though the volume of fabric may make dry cleaning more practical.

Dobby weave (4, 5, 7, 11, 13) Woven on a loom that produces a small, repeating design in the weave, dobby cottons introduce discreet patterning to complement more exuberant prints. Designs produced by the dobby technique are varied, but all have a neat, regular, all-over appearance.

Brocade (6) This distinctive fabric has a raised pattern against a woven background. It is particularly suitable for covers in traditional interiors.

Rep (8) A strong ribbed cloth made by alternating thick and thin weft yarns.

This example has a bird's-eye dot made by an additional weft thread. The robust nature of the weave demands chunky trimmings.

Linen union (9) A traditional woven upholstery cloth made from a blend of linen, cotton and sometimes a small amount of nylon, too. It is available in plain colors and prints and may form part of a co-ordinated range of fabrics and wallcoverings.

Damask (10) The distinctive self-colored design in this fabric is produced by combining areas of satin and sateen weave to give a contrast of textures. The fabric is both elegant and durable and blends well with other patterned furnishings.

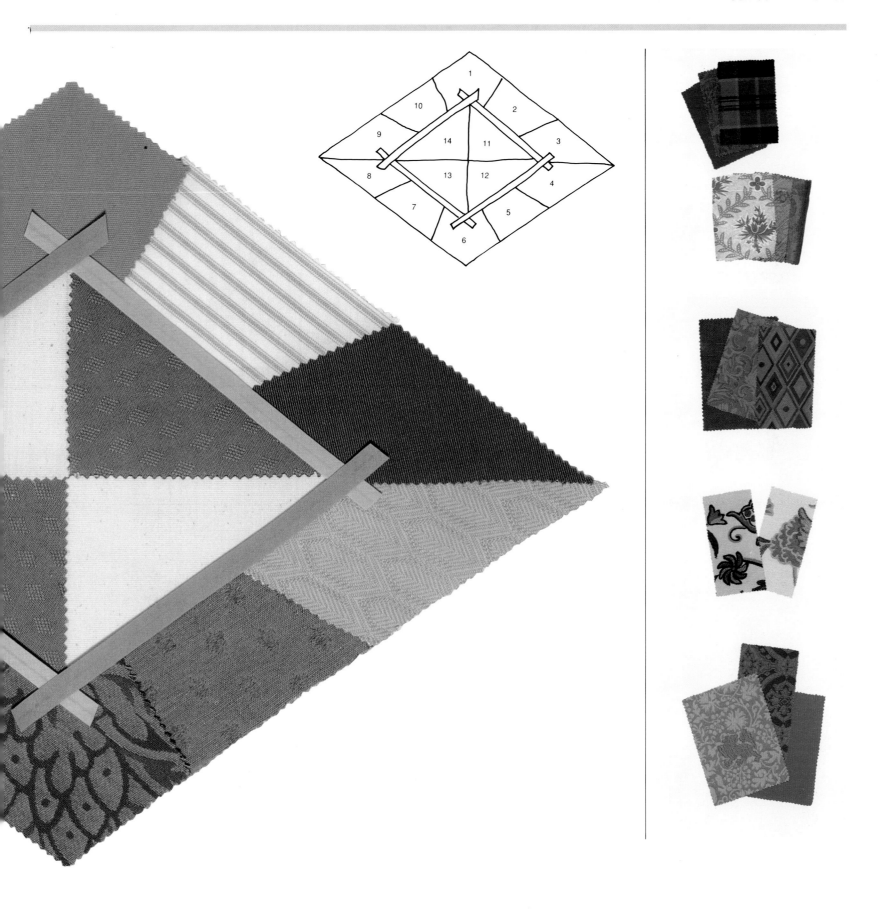

SLIPCOVERS: MEASURING AND CUTTING

THE MOST RELIABLE WAY TO ESTIMATE THE QUANTITY OF FABRIC needed for chairs and sofas is to work it out using squared graph paper. On average, it takes about 6½ yards (6m) of fabric, 48in (122cm) wide, to cover an armchair and 11 yards (10m) for a three-seater sofa, with an extra 1⅛ yards (1m) for each seat cushion. The fabric quantity will vary according to the size of pattern repeat and the style of furniture, so always measure individual pieces and work out the most economical way of cutting out, before buying the cover material. The method of taking measurements is the same for armchairs and sofas.

THE BRIGHTLY COLORED COVERS FOR THIS WIDE SOFA ARE MADE FROM A ROBUST COTTON/LINEN UNION BLEND. THE SEAT COVERS ARE PIPED AROUND THE EDGES FOR GREATER DEFINITION AND A MORE TAILORED LOOK. A STRAIGHT VALANCE TAKES THE SLIPCOVERS DOWN TO THE FLOOR.

Taking measurements

REMOVE EXISTING CUSHIONS and measure:
The length and width of:
○ the outside back;
○ the inside back;
○ the seat;
○ the inside arm from the seat, over the curve of the arm;
○ the outside arm from the curve of the arm to the floor;
○ the front panel from the edge of the seat to the floor (the arm front panels can often be cut from spare fabric but if they are very wide, include their measurements, too).

Add 1½in(4cm) to each measurement for seam allowances. Add 6in (15cm), for tuck-ins, to the lower edge of the inside back and inside arm pieces; to the back edge of the inside arms; and to the back and side edges of the seat.

The valance is made up of four separate strips – one to fit each side. Measure along the lower edge of each side: double the measurements for a gathered or box-pleated valance, or add 12in (30cm) to each side measurement for a straight valance with corner pleats. The valance depth should be in proportion to the size of furniture: 4-6in (10-15cm) is average. Add 1½in (4cm) to both measurements for allowances.

Measure seat cushions as for boxed cushion covers.

Calculating the fabric

TO WORK OUT THE AMOUNT of 48in (122cm) wide fabric needed, draw the cover pieces to scale on graph paper; remember to draw two each of the inside and outside arm pieces. Label each piece, mark the top edge and cut out. Draw parallel

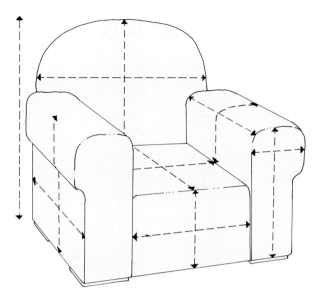

lines representing the fabric to the same scale, marking any pattern repeat. Lay the pieces between the lines in an arrangement that allows for any pattern matching, and economical use of fabric. For sofas measuring more than 45in (115cm) across the back, you will need to join fabric widths for the back and seat pieces, so allow extra fabric for this. Add 1⅛ yards (1m) for making matching piping. Calculate the fabric needed for any seat cushions and add to the total.

When positioning the pieces, place them so a pattern is seen the right way up: on the inside arm, it runs upward from the seat; on the outside arm, it runs upward

from the floor. All pieces should match across each join. If the fabric has a large pattern, cut out the pieces so a complete motif shows centrally on the inside back, outside back and seat.

Cutting out

LAY THE FABRIC RIGHT SIDE UP, then following the scale layout, mark the cover pieces to size with tailor's chalk and cut them out. At this stage, all the pieces are rectangular; they will be trimmed to shape during fitting. Cut the arm pieces in pairs, so that the pattern corresponds on both sides of the furniture. Label each piece and mark its top edge with chalk.

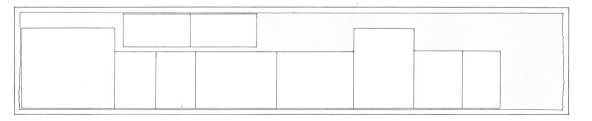

FITTING A SOFA COVER

THE COVER FABRIC has now been cut into approximate rectangles to fit each part of the sofa. The pieces will be pinned on the sofa and cut to shape, leaving seam allowances and a tuck-in allowance where indicated. Since upholstery is never quite symmetrical, this is done with the fabric right side out, to ensure a perfect fit. Remove any existing covers before you start.

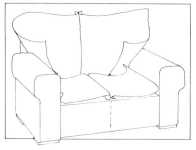

JOIN FABRIC WIDTHS if necessary. For a two-seater sofa, place the seam centrally; for wider sofas, place a complete width of fabric in the middle, joining part-widths at both sides. Cover the piping cord (see opposite).

Mark the center back, inside back and seat with a row of pins or a chalk line. With the fabric right side out, pin the pieces in position on the chair or sofa, matching centers, so they lie smoothly, with the pattern straight. Position the inside back, seat and inside arm pieces so the 6in (15cm) tuck-in allowance is at the back and sides of the seat and the back of the arm. Mark the exact shape of each piece with a line of closely spaced pins or tailor's chalk.

Remove the pieces and trim to shape, leaving a tuck-in allowance of 6in (15cm) along the lower edge of the inside back, the back and side edges of the seat and the back edge of the inside arms. Leave a seam allowance of ¾in (2cm) on the remaining sides. Trim the tuck-in allowance at the back of the inside arm, tapering it from 6in (15cm) at the inner edge to ¾in (2cm) at the outer edge.

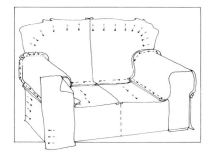

REPLACE THE PIECES on the furniture, right side out, and pin them together along the marked lines in the following order:
❍ outside back to inside back;
❍ inside back to seat, along the edge of the tuck-in;
❍ seat to seat front;
❍ inside arm to outside arm;
❍ inside arm to inside back and seat tuck-in edge.

Pin the arm fronts to the joined arm pieces and seat front. Adjust pinning for a smooth fit and trim seam allowances to exactly ¾in (2cm). Do not trim tuck-ins.

Gather or pleat to fit any curved edges, such as the top of an arm or the top corners of the inside back. Snip notches in the seam allowances through both thicknesses to facilitate matching adjoining pieces later. Unpin the cover pieces.

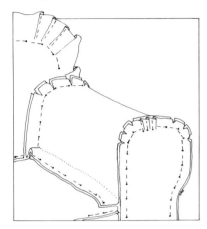

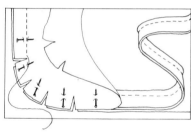

PIN AND BASTE THE PIECES together in the same order as for pinning, matching notches and adding piping where required. Machine stitch, taking ¾in (2cm) seams. The back edges will be unsewn at this stage.

Fit the cover over the chair or sofa and pin the back edges together, leaving one of them open from about midway down to allow for removing the cover. Take off the cover and machine stitch the pinned edges together.

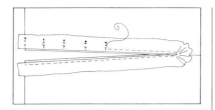

TO MAKE A PLACKET for the opening, cut a 3¼in (8cm) wide strip of fabric twice the length of the opening plus 1½in (4cm) for seams. With right sides together, pin, then stitch the strip along both raw edges of the opening in a continuous seam. Trim the seams, machine stitch a narrow hem along the remaining raw edge and turn the placket to the inside. Press towards the cover back and slip-stitch in place.

Place the cover on the sofa or chair and mark the valance position all around with tailor's chalk or a row of pins. Trim the lower edge of the cover, leaving a ¾in (2cm) seam allowance below the marked line. Join the valance strips, with right sides together and the short edges matching, in the sequence: back, side, front, side. Leave the ends open to correspond with the opening in the cover. Hem the lower edge and short ends so the valance will clear the floor when attached.

Gather, box pleat or corner pleat the valance (see page 211), so that the seams match the cover's corner seams.

Pin the valance around the lower edge of the cover, matching corner seams and adding piping if desired, then machine stitch in place. Trim and finish the seam. Stitch hooks and eyes along the cover opening, sewing them to the valance in such a way that it meets edge to edge.

Piped edges

PIPING CONSISTS OF cotton cord covered with a strip of fabric cut on the bias to curve smoothly. It is placed between the two layers of fabric when seams are sewn.

Cutting bias strips

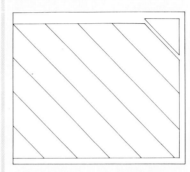

TO DECIDE THE WIDTH of the bias strip, measure around the cord and add twice the seam allowance. For small projects such as cushions or dining chairs, the simplest method is to cut and join strips of fabric. But for a large amount of piping, it is better to make a continuous fabric length first.

Cut and join

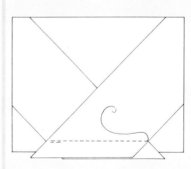

FIND THE STRAIGHT GRAIN of the fabric by pulling out a weft (crossways) thread. Cut along the gap left. Fold the fabric diagonally so the straightened edge is level with the selvage; press and cut along the fold. Cut strips parallel with this diagonal cut and join them by placing the short ends right sides together, with the strips at right

angles; machine stitch across. Press seams open and trim allowances.

Continuous strip

STRAIGHTEN THE FABRIC as before and cut a square, using the full width of the fabric. Mark opposite sides of the square with colored threads, then fold the fabric diagonally as before and cut along the fold to produce two triangles. Join triangles along one pair of matching sides, with right sides together and taking 1cm (⅜in) seams. Press seams open. Join the other pair of matching sides to form a tube, but stagger them so one edge projects by the bias-strip width at both ends. Start at one projecting end and cut around the tube in a spiral to produce a continuous fabric strip.

Covering the cord

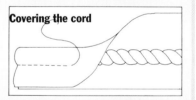

CUT THE CORD 4IN (10 cm) longer than required and cut a bias strip to the same length. Fold the strip over the cord, right side out, with long edges level. Pin, then baste close to cord.

Piping the edges

PIN, THEN BASTE PIPING along edge to be piped on right side of fabric with raw edges level. To join the ends, cut cord to fit exactly and bind ends together with thread. Trim covering strip so one end is ¾in (2cm) longer. Turn in ⅜in (1cm) on the longer end: overlap the other to cover raw edge; slip-stitch in place. Ease around corners and curves. Complete basting piping in place, lay the other fabric piece face down over piped piece and stitch close to the cord.

MAKING A DINING CHAIR COVER

A SLIPCOVER TRANSFORMS SHABBY or mis-matched dining chairs and gives them a stylish look. The cover fits over the chair back and has a floor-length skirt with corner pleats. The back is made in a single piece and the inside back, seat and three remaining skirt panels are cut separately. Use any hardwearing, closely woven fabric for this type of chair cover. If the chair has a hard seat, cut a piece of 2in (5cm) thick foam to fit it exactly and glue it in place first.

Alternative styles of valance

For armchairs and sofas	For dining chairs
Gathered-edge valance	*Corner-pleated valance*
Bound gathered valance	*Gathered skirt*
Box-pleated valance	*Short skirt*
Contrast pleated valance	*Inverted pleat at back*

LONG, UNBLEACHED COTTON COVERS CHANGE UPHOLSTERED DINING CHAIRS INTO SOMETHING LESS FORMAL. MADE IN SECTIONS, THEY ARE SEWN TOGETHER TO FIT OVER THE CHAIR SMOOTHLY BUT NOT TOO CLOSELY, OR THEY WILL PUCKER. ACCURATE MEASURING IS ESSENTIAL.

Taking measurements

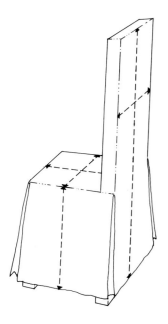

MEASURE THE MAXIMUM width and height of the outside chair back, the height and width of the inside back, the width and depth of the seat and the distance from the seat to the floor. Add 1½in (4cm) to each measurement for seams. The skirt is made up of separate panels to fit the front and sides of the chair from seat to floor. Add a further ¾in (2cm) to the length on the outside back and skirt panels for the hem.

To calculate the amount of 122cm (48in) fabric needed, draw the pieces to scale on graph paper and cut out shapes to represent the outside back, inside back, seat, skirt front and the two skirt sides. Draw parallel lines representing the fabric to the same scale and lay the pieces between them (see the instructions for measuring and cutting out fabric for a sofa, page 207), so that the pattern matches horizontally around the skirt and vertically down the inside back, seat and skirt front. Allow extra for matching piping and four corner pleats, each measuring 13½in (34cm) wide, and the length of the skirt.

Cutting out

CUT OUT AND LABEL the pieces as for sofa covers (page 207). If preferred, you may cut the piping strip and corner pleats from contrasting fabric.

Making

PIN THE INSIDE AND OUTSIDE back pieces together along the top edge, with right sides out. Place on the chair, then pin the sides together to fit. Trim to shape, ¾in (2cm) outside the line of pins. Do not make the cover too tight or it will be difficult to remove for cleaning. Cut the seat cover piece to shape, allowing ¾in (2cm) seams all around.

Pin and baste the piping around the side and front edges of the seat piece and around the side and top edges of the inside back. Join the skirt panels and pleat strips along their side edges in the following sequence: pleat; skirt side; pleat; skirt front; pleat; skirt side; pleat.

Mark the center top of each pleat with a pin, then fold the skirt along the seam lines and bring them together at the pleat center. Baste in place. With right sides together, matching pleat centers to the corners, pin, baste, then machine stitch the skirt around the sides and front of the seat. A half-pleat will be left free at both ends.

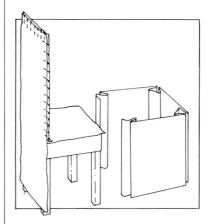

JOIN THE SEAT TO THE INSIDE BACK, then pin, baste and machine stitch the outside back to the inside back and rear pleat. Fold and press the rear pleats to shape and slip-stitch in place.

Fit the cover over the chair and turn up the lower edge so that it clears the floor by ⅜in (1cm). Remove the cover once again and machine stitch a double hem.

Forming Corner Pleats

Measure the length of the lower edge of the cover on one side of the chair and divide by two. Find the center of the corresponding valance strip and measure this distance from the center on both sides; mark with pins. Bring the marked points level with the seam so that the raw edges are level, pin and baste in place. This will form a half-pleat. Repeat on all sides.

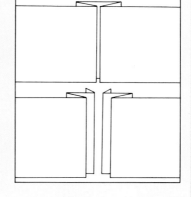

STYLING IDEAS

✔ Make close-fitting tie-on covers for chairs with exposed legs by omitting the valance and instead sewing a flap of fabric along the lower edge of each side. Stitch tapes to the ends of the flaps and tie them together under the seat.

✔ For ease of fitting, make a dining chair cover in two parts: a skirted seat cover and a slip-over cover for the back rest.

✔ Trim box-pleated valances by stitching a plain fabric-covered button at the top of each pleat.

✔ Trim off deep integral borders from print fabrics and use them for the valance and for the seat-cushion gussets.

✔ Decorate the outside back of a dining chair cover with a bow tied like a sash. If the ends are stitched into the side seams, it can be tied more tightly to give the cover a waisted appearance.

✔ For a pretty, feminine look, make a narrow ruffle from a double thickness of fabric and use it to trim the seams joining the inside and outside back pieces, the seat and skirt of a dining chair cover.

✔ An alternative way to make a gathered valance is to hem both long edges of the valance strip and make a line of gathering stitches ¾in (2cm) from the top edge. Pull up the gathers to fit, then overlap the lower edge of the cover with the top edge of the valance. Stitch in place along the gathering line, so the top edge of the valance makes an upstanding ruffle. Slip-stitch silky cord over the stitching line.

LINEN IN THE HOME

HOUSEHOLD LINEN ENCOMPASSES SUCH EVERYDAY FABRIC furnishings as tablecloths, napkins, sheets, pillowcases, valances and other bedding, but although these items are primarily functional, household linens can also be extremely decorative. Cleverly chosen bed linen can alter the way a bedroom looks in the time it takes to change the sheets, and the right tablecloth will turn the family table into a luxurious and special setting for a festive dinner.

When there is so much well-designed linen available to buy, it may seem unnecessary to go to the trouble of making your own, but there are many occasions when it is the only appropriate option. For example, if you own a non-standard bed, it is possible to have linen made to fit, but the chances are that it will be expensive and the choice of color and design restricted. If you make the bed linen yourself, you can choose the size, style, fabric and trimmings, ensuring that the design will be right in every detail. As the focus of the room, the bed and its covering are central to the bedroom décor and their style can contribute greatly to the atmosphere you wish to create.

Fabric is the first consideration. White linen, floral prints, checks, pastel and deep shades all suggest different moods, but just as important is the way in which they are used. Take plain white cotton, for example. Unadorned, it has an aesthetic purity; add a black and white check border along the top edge and it becomes sophisticated; substitute a frill of ribbon-threaded lace for femininity or an embroidered motif for a nostalgic look. It is this combination of fabric, trimmings and design that gives bed linen its decorative value, but practical considerations are important too. Your budget may determine the type of fabric and trimmings used, but your lifestyle could well be the deciding factor when it comes to choosing between pure cotton or linen, which need careful laundering, and good-natured cotton blends which you can simply wash and use.

The main function of a tablecloth is to protect a polished dining table at mealtimes and provide an attractive background against which to display china. In recent years, however, tablecloths have been rediscovered as a way of protecting and transforming all

THE RICH MIX OF COMPLEMENTARY COLORS AND PATTERNS WHICH BRINGS THIS BEDROOM TO LIFE CAN ONLY BE ACHIEVED BY MAKING YOUR OWN BED LINEN. AN ASSORTMENT OF PLAIN, FLORAL, PLAID AND PAISLEY LINEN FOCUSES ATTENTION ON THE BED IN THIS PLAINLY DECORATED ROOM. ALL STYLES OF PILLOWCASE — OXFORD, RUFFLED AND BUTTON-FASTENED — ARE PILED HIGH, BESIDE THE LACE-TRIMMED, EMBROIDERED SQUARE PILLOWCASE IN THE CENTER OF THE BED.

kinds of table, including desks and occasional tables. The Victorians primly covered most tables with floor-length cloths of chenille or velvet to conceal their legs, but decorative cloths nowadays are used to convert cheap chipboard surfaces into elegant bedside tables, to protect precious writing tables and to hide unfashionable yet serviceable dressing tables.

Tablecloths may be made from fabrics as diverse as plastic-coated cotton and brocade; they can be designed to complement any style of furnishing. A short, provençal-print cloth for a patio table, an embroidered linen cloth for a dinner table and a chintz cover for a circular display table are all made following the same basic method, but they differ widely in character. A cloth for a living room lamp table, lined, interlined and edged with bullion fringing, will involve several sewing techniques, while making a cloth for an informal dining table can be a simple matter of fraying the edges on a rectangle of coarse-woven Indian cotton. Both are equally effective in the appropriate setting, proving that customized furnishings are within the reach of everybody.

THE DELICATE PINK AND WHITE THEME OF THIS CHILD'S ROOM IS EXTENDED TO THE BED LINEN FOR THE CRIB AS WELL AS THE RUCHED BLIND, THE TABLECLOTH AND THE CHAIR SEAT COVER. MAKING YOUR OWN FABRIC FURNISHINGS IS THE ONLY WAY TO CO-ORDINATE DIFFERENT FABRICS IN EXACTLY THE RIGHT SHADES.

STYLING TIPS

✔ **When making a set of matching bed linen, experiment with the cutting layout to make the most economical use of the fabric.**

✔ **Buttoned closures give pillowcases a neat finish. Make buttonholes along the open edge of the front and stitch mother-of-pearl or large, fabric-covered buttons to the inside flap.**

✔ **Lace-edged pillowcases will stay looking crisp if there is a fabric ruffle to support the lace.**

✔ **For a tailored look, make a flat valance, with kick pleats at the corners, to match the bedspread, headboard or curtains. Stiffen or interline the fabric to give it body.**

✔ **Valances for cast-iron bedsteads must be split at the lower corners to fit around the legs.**

✔ **Choose a gathered or pleated valance to go around a bed with storage drawers underneath.**

✔ **Valances come in for a good deal of wear and tear from feet, vacuum cleaners, dirt and dust, so choose a fairly robust fabric that can be washed or cleaned easily.**

HOUSEHOLD LINEN FABRICS

THE REQUIREMENTS OF TABLE LINEN AND BED LINEN are similar in that they should both be washable, durable and easy to care for. Cotton and linen are the classic choice for both, but fabrics containing a mixture of cotton and polyester need less ironing and, for that reason, are sometimes the preferred choice for bed linen. Synthetics are sometimes more susceptible to greasy stains, so pure, natural fibers are the most practical option for the table.

Pure cotton sheeting (1) Smooth, unglazed cotton comes in wide widths to match bed sizes. Mainly available in plain colors.

Gingham (2) Traditional woven check fabric using yarns in white and one other color. Typically used for café tablecloths and popular for table linen in kitchens and family dining rooms.

Flanelette (3) A warm-to-the-touch cotton fabric, brushed to give it a light pile. Popular for winter bed linen, especially with infants and the elderly. Available in plain colors and stripes as well as prints.

Eyelet lace (4) Embroidered fine cotton, usually with a cut-out design. The uncut type, shown here, is suitable for bed linen and the cut version for trimmings and for decorative pillowcases.

Polyester cotton sheeting (5, 8) Wide, finely woven fabric, usually in a 50:50 blend of synthetic and natural fibers. It comes in a choice of pastel and plain colors as well as prints suitable for the nursery and adult bedrooms. It is washable and needs little or no ironing.

Striped cotton (6) Plain cotton printed with stripes. No pattern matching is necessary so it is easy to join widths. Good for table linen and bed linen too, if a suitable width can be found.

Linen (7) A strong fabric usually found in white, cream or plain colors. It is washable but creases easily and requires careful ironing. Expensive to buy, it is available as sheeting and in narrower widths for table linen.

Seersucker (9) The warp (vertical) threads of this fabric are arranged in groups alternately tight and loose to give the slightly puckered finish. Usually made from cotton, it comes in plain colors, stripes or checks. Seersucker bed linen needs minimal ironing, and table linen made from this fabric has a relaxed charm.

Madras cotton (10, 16) Fine Indian cotton with a woven check design, perfect for table linen.

Provençal prints (11, 13, 14, 15, 18) Fine cotton printed with distinctive designs from the Provence region of France, such as regular lozenge patterns, paisley, stripes and all-over florals. The colors are usually strong and bright, and the background may be white or colored.

Indian prints (12, 17) Woven cottons printed with paisley, stylized flowers, checks and stripes, using traditional vegetable dyes or modern dyes that emulate the traditional colors.

STYLING TIPS

✔ A pillow sham is a decorative daytime cover for a pillow, usually made from the same material as the bedspread. When the bed is made, lay the pillows on top of the bedspread for a streamlined look.

✔ For a less uniform look, make the pillowcases and valance from a fabric that co-ordinates with, rather than matches, the duvet: plain with checks, sprigs with florals, floral and fine lines with broad stripes are some combinations to try.

✔ Make a reversible duvet cover by cutting the back and front pieces from different, complementary colors or patterns.

✔ Fabrics other than purpose-made sheeting can be used for bed linen. Some dress fabrics and cottons are suitable, but check first that they are washable, easy to iron and come in suitably wide widths.

✔ Raised decorations such as cross stitch, lace or ribbon trimming may be uncomfortable to sleep on, so apply it around the edges of a pillowcase only, leaving a smooth surface in the middle.

✔ Table linen must be easy to care for, so check that all fabrics are color-fast, pre-shrunk, machine washable and iron well.

✔ Scour antique stores for hand-embroidered cloths which were popular in the 'forties and 'fifties, to give your table a nostalgic look.

✔ Decorate pillowcases with embroidery, or with appliqué or a stencilled design using fabric paints (see page 163).

MAKING BED LINEN

TWO POPULAR STYLES OF DECORATIVE PILLOWCASE are the plain "housewife" type and the Oxford with its flat border. The instructions given here are for a standard 30 x 20in (75 x 50cm) pillowcase but the measurements can be adapted to fit various other sizes. Add machine embroidery, ribbon, lace or braid for a more decorative effect. A valance covers the base and feet of the bed to give it a co-ordinated look. It can be frilled, pleated or straight, with inverted pleats at the corners. Soft valances are made from sheeting, but more tailored styles may be made from the same fabric as the curtains or headboard.

THIS IRON-FRAMED DAY BED HAS BEEN SOFTENED BY THE ADDITION OF A GATHERED VALANCE AND A COLLECTION OF BLUE AND WHITE PILLOWS AND CUSHIONS. THE CONTRAST EDGING AROUND THE BASE OF THE VALANCE ECHOES THAT OF THE OVER-BED DRAPES AND THE BORDER ON THE CURTAINS TO GIVE A TOTALLY CO-ORDINATED LOOK TO THE ROOM.

Making a "housewife" pillowcase

CUT A PIECE OF FABRIC 68½ x 21¼in (174 x 54cm). Make a double ⅜in (1cm) hem at one short end. At the other end, fold and press ¾in (2cm), then 2in (5cm) to the right side and machine stitch close to the folded edge.

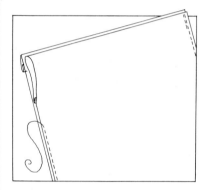

FOLD THE NARROW, HEMMED edge down 6in (15cm), wrong sides together, to form the pillow flap and pin it in place. Fold the fabric piece in half, wrong sides together, so the wide hemmed edge is level with the pillow-flap fold.

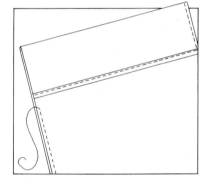

PIN, THEN MACHINE STITCH the side edges, taking ⅜in (1cm) seams, and trim close to the stitching. Turn the pillowcase wrong side out so that the flap covers the wide hemmed edge. Press, then machine stitch along the sides, ⅜in (1cm) from the edge, to complete the french seams. Turn right side out and press.

Making an Oxford pillowcase

CUT OUT A PILLOWCASE FRONT 40 x 31in (103 x 78cm); a back piece 31 x 21¼in (79 x 54cm); and a flap 21¼ x 8 in (54 x 20cm). For the border, turn in and press ¾in (2cm) then 2½in (6cm) all around the front piece, then unfold.

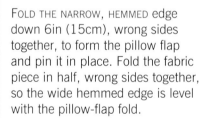

To miter the corners, mark the fabric edge with a pin 5½in (14cm) from the corner in both directions, then chalk a straight line between the points on the wrong side of the fabric. Fold the corner diagonally, with right sides together, adjacent edges level and marker pins matching, and then machine stitch along the chalk line from the inner crease line to the outer one. Trim close to the stitching and press the seam flat. Miter the remaining corners in the same way, then turn the border right side out, fold under the raw edges of the border along the crease lines and press.

Turn in and machine stitch a double ⅜in (1cm) hem along one long edge of the pillowcase flap and lay it across the front piece with wrong sides together. Tuck the raw edge of the flap under the border by ¾in (2cm) and pin in place. Machine stitch along the edge of the border, enclosing the long edge of the flap.

Turn in ⅜in (1cm), then 1¼in (3cm) along one short edge of the pillowcase back, and machine stitch. Lay the back over the front piece, wrong sides together, with the hemmed edge of the back level with the stitched-down edge of the flap. Tuck the raw edges of the back piece under the folded edges of the border and pin.

Starting and finishing at the ends of the stitched-down border, machine stitch around the three remaining border edges so that the border stitching appears to be continuous around all four sides.

Making Valances

Conventionally, valances fit over the bed base, under the mattress, but they can alternatively be attached to the bottom sheet. A valance sheet is a fitted bottom sheet with the valance attached, making it more easily removed for laundering.

Making a bed valance

REMOVE THE MATTRESS and measure the length and width of the bed base. Add 1½in (4cm) to both measurements, then cut out the fabric this size, joining widths if necessary. For the ruffle depth, measure from the top edge of the base to the floor and add 2¾in (7cm) for seams and hems. For its length, add the length of the bed base, multiplied by four, to its width, multiplied by two. Cut enough ruffle strips from the width of the fabric to make up the required length, joining them with french seams to make up a long, continuous piece.

Round off all four corners of valance top by placing a saucer in the corner and drawing around it with tailor's chalk. Cut along the chalk line.

Using pins as markers, divide the strip into three sections, for the side and lower edges of the valance. Each section should be twice the length of the side it is to fit. Gather each section separately by running two rows of gathering stitches along the edge.

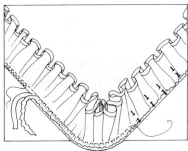

PIN THE RUFFLE AROUND THE SIDE and lower edges of the valance top with right sides together, matching the marker pins to the lower corners and pulling up the gathers to fit. Machine stitch in place, taking a ¾in (2cm) seam. Trim the seam, then machine zig-zag stitch over the raw edges to finish them.

Turn in and machine stitch a double ⅜in (1cm) hem along the top edge of the valance and the raw ends of the ruffle. Turn in and machine stitch a double 1in (2.5cm) hem all around the lower edge.

Making a valance sheet

MEASURE THE LENGTH and width of the mattress. To each measurement add twice the mattress depth, plus 1½in (4cm) for allowances. Cut fabric this size for the sheet. For the ruffle, measure the depth from the lower edge of the mattress to the floor and add 2¾in (7cm) for hem

and allowances. Calculate the length as for the bed valance (see left) and add 24in (60cm). Cut enough ruffle strips across the fabric width to make up the required length; join them with french seams to form a continuous piece. Turn in and machine stitch a double ⅜in (1cm) hem along the short edges.

Shape all four corners in this way. Measure the mattress depth plus ¾in (2cm) along the fabric edge from the corner in both directions; mark the point with a pin. Using a carpenter's square, chalk a line at right angles to the edge at each marked point. With wrong sides together, make a diagonal fold from the corner to the point where the chalked lines meet, matching up the marker pins; machine stitch along the chalk line. Trim close to the stitching, refold with right sides together and machine stitch ⅜in (1cm) from the folded edge to complete the french seam.

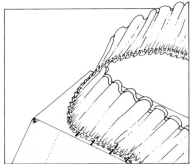

GATHER THE RUFFLE AND PIN it around the edge of the sheet, as for the valance, but continue it along the top edge of the sheet for 6in (15cm) from the corners. Machine stitch, trim seams and finish as before. Turn in and machine stitch a double ⅜in (1cm) hem along remaining raw top edge of sheet. Hem ruffle as described for the valance.

MAKING TABLE LINEN

TABLECLOTHS FOR DINING TABLES CAN BE MADE FROM VIRTUALLY ANY WASHABLE FABRIC, from seersucker to damask, and should overhang the table by approximately 8in (20cm) all around. Circular tables, which have become familiar as pieces of living room furniture in place of occasional or lamp tables, are usually covered with a floor-length cloth made from furnishing fabric and topped with a square cloth of much lighter material. Napkins are always made from washable material – preferably cotton – and can be simply embellished by decorating them with hemstitching, a border of contrasting fabric, lace edging, fringing or embroidery.

Joining fabric widths

WHEN MAKING A CLOTH for a large table, you may need to join fabric widths. Do this by cutting two widths of fabric to the required length, then fold one width in half with selvages matching, and cut along the fold. Place one half-width on each side of the full width, selvage to selvage, matching any pattern. Join the pieces with flat fell seams (see page 220).

THE ROUND TABLES IN THIS COZY LIVING ROOM ARE AN INTEGRAL PART OF THE SYMMETRICAL SCHEME. THE LONG, CIRCULAR CLOTHS ARE OVERLAID WITH SQUARE ONES, ARRANGED SO THE POINTS FALL IN A STAR SHAPE. NOTE HOW THE FABRIC MATCHES THE BOLSTER CUSHIONS ON THE SOFA AND REPEATS THE STRONG, SPICY COLORS OF THE KELIM-COVERED STOOL.

Making Tablecloths

CHOOSE WIDE FABRICS to avoid seaming. But if widths must be joined to cover a large table, place a complete fabric width at the center, with half- or part-widths at the sides. If possible, arrange the seams so they run along the edges of a rectangular table.

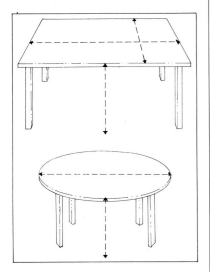

Square or rectangular cloth

MEASURE THE LENGTH and width of the table top then, to each measurement, add 16in (40cm) for overhang and 3¼in (8cm) for hems. Cut fabric to this size.

Turn in and press ⅜in (1cm), then 1¼in (3cm), mitering the corners neatly, and machine stitch in place.

Circular tablecloth

MEASURE THE DIAMETER of the table top and then add 16in (40cm) overhang, plus 1½in (4cm) for hems. Cut a circle of fabric to this diameter (see page 220). Machine stitch around the cloth, ¾in (2cm) from the edge, then fold in and press the hem along the stitching line. Turn in the raw edge by ¼in (5mm); pin, baste, then machine stitch in place.

Full-length circular cloth

MADE FROM FURNISHING FABRIC, these cloths are often interlined and lined for a more luxurious drape, then trimmed with braid or heavy fringing at the hem.

Measure the height and the diameter of the table. Add twice the height measurement to the diameter, plus 1½in (4cm) for hems. Cut a circle of fabric, plus interlining and lining, with this total diameter; join widths together if necessary.

Trim ¾in (2cm) from the edge of the interlining, then lay it centrally on the wrong side of the piece of fabric. Lockstitch the two together down the center and along any seam lines (see page 172). Baste together around the edge of the interlining.

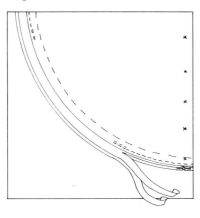

PLACE THE LINING AND FABRIC pieces with right sides together, matching seams, then pin, baste and machine stitch all round, ¾in (2cm) from the edge. Leave a gap in the stitching, trim the seam allowance, then turn right side out. Fold in the raw edges at the opening, in line with the hem edge, and slip-stitch.

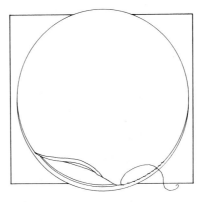

CATCH-STITCH THE LINING to the interlining and fabric along the seam lines, to hold the three thicknesses together. Hand or machine stitch braid or fringing around the hem if desired, turning in the raw edges neatly.

Making napkins

NAPKINS FOR THE LUNCHEON or tea table measure about 8in (20cm) square, but dinner napkins should be a more generous 16-20in (40-50cm).

Cut each napkin to the required size plus 1½in (3.5cm) all around for hems. Turn in and press ¼in (5mm), then 1¼in (3cm), mitering the corners as for the rectangular tablecloth, then machine stitch the hem in place all around.

SEWING GUIDE

Making Seams

Plain seam

THE SIMPLEST OF SEAMS, this is used to join widths of fabric and may be finished by pinking or oversewing the raw edges of the seam allowances.

Place the fabric pieces with right sides together and raw edges matching, then pin. If necessary, baste inside the seam line. Machine stitch along the seam line – this is usually done ⅝-¾in (1.5-2cm) from the raw edge; make a few reverse stitches at both ends of the seam to secure the threads. Remove the pins and basting, then press the seam open.

French seam

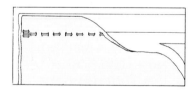

THIS SEAM ENCLOSES the raw edges to prevent fraying. It is best for lightweight fabrics.

Place the fabric pieces with wrong sides together and raw edges matching and pin. Machine stitch ¼in (5mm) from the raw edge, then press the seam flat and trim the

allowances to ⅛in (3mm). Turn the fabric with right sides together, and machine stitch ⅜in (1cm) from the edge.

Flat fell seam

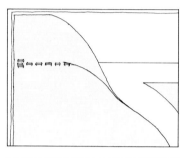

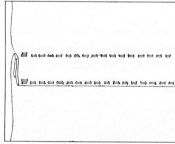

THIS SEAM ENCLOSES the raw edges and is double-stitched for strength. It is particularly useful for fabrics that are seen from both sides or frequently laundered.

Place fabric pieces right sides together and make a plain seam. Trim one seam allowance to ¼in (5mm) from the stitching line, then open out the fabric and press the allowances to one side with the wider one uppermost. Fold under the raw edge of the wider turning, then pin flat to enclose the trimmed seam. Machine stitch along the turning, close to the fold.

Hand Sewing Techniques

Basting stitch

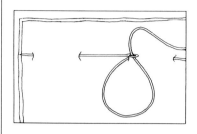

A LONG STITCH USED TO HOLD LAYERS of fabric in place for machine stitching. Use contrasting-color thread to make removal easier.

Knot the end of the thread, then make a line of stitches about ⅝-¾in (1.5-2cm) long, just inside the seam line. The stitches should be the same length as the spaces between them. Finish by knotting the thread again. To remove, cut off the knot at one end of the basting thread and pull out from the other end.

Slip-stitch

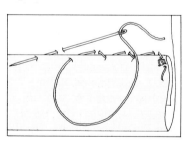

USE THIS TO JOIN TWO folded edges or to join a folded edge to flat fabric.

Bring the needle out through the folded edge, then pick up a few threads of the adjoining fabric and pull the thread through. Make a small stitch through the fold of fabric, then bring the needle out through the fold, ready for the next stitch.

Gathering stitch

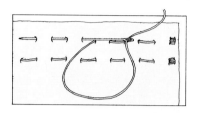

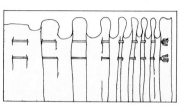

USE THIS TO MAKE a ruffled edging or for easing fabric around a curve. Gathering can be done by hand or machine. When gathering long lengths such as a ruffled bed valance, a sequence of shorter gathering threads is more manageable than one long one.

By hand: Secure the thread with a few stitches worked in the same spot, then sew a line of small stitches, passing the needle in and out of the fabric, making the stitches and the spaces between them the same length. Make two parallel rows of gathering stitches, one on each side of the seam line. To gather, gently pull up both threads with one hand while sliding the fabric along the threads with the other. Insert a pin at the end of the gathering line, at right angles to the fabric edge, and secure the gathering threads by winding them around the pin in a figure-eight.

By machine: Set the machine to a long stitch length and slightly loose tension. Make one row of stitching on each side of the seam line. Knot the threads together at one end of the row and draw up the gathers by pulling up the threads on the underside of the fabric. Space the gathers evenly and secure the threads on a pin.

Remove gathering threads after stitching by cutting off the knotted ends and pulling them out.

Hemming stitch

USE ORDINARY HEMMING stitch for lightweight fabrics and herringbone stitch for heavy materials.

Knot the thread and pull it through the hem so it is hidden in the fold. Bring the needle out through the folded top edge of the hem and pick up a few threads of the flat fabric just below the line of the fold. Bring the needle through the hem again and continue in this way. The stitches should be virtually invisible on the right side.

Herringbone stitch

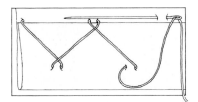

WORKING FROM LEFT TO RIGHT, secure the thread with a few stitches worked in the same spot on the hem, then make a long diagonal stitch from left to right, taking the needle through the flat fabric about ¼in (5mm) above the hem edge. Bring the needle out again slightly to the left of where it went in, then make a second diagonal stitch from left to right, crossing the first, passing the needle through the hem. Bring the needle out slightly to the left and repeat.

Lockstitch

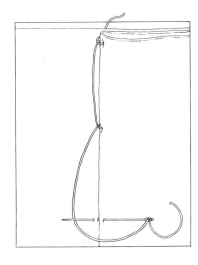

USE THIS STITCH TO HOLD interlining to the back of the curtain fabric.

Lay the curtain right side down and lay the interlining over it. Pin the two together down the center length, then fold the interlining back along the pinned line. Use a thread to match the curtain fabric and start from the top edge. Knot the thread and secure it in the interlining, then make a small stitch at right angles to the fold, picking up threads from the interlining and the curtain fabric. Make the next stitch about 3in (7.5cm) below the first, keeping the needle over the thread. Work down the fold, keeping the stitches loose and finishing with a few small stitches.

Cutting a circle of fabric

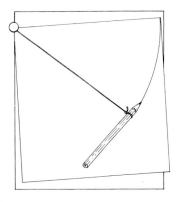

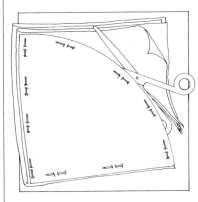

USE THIS METHOD TO CUT a fabric circle of any size. Take a square of fabric, each side measuring slightly more than the diameter of the circle you need. Fold the fabric in quarters, matching edges and any seams. Attach a length of string to a thumbtack, then tie it close to the tip of a soft pencil, so the distance between thumbtack and string equals the radius (half the diameter) of the circle you want. Push the pin into the fabric at the folded corner; then, keeping the string taut, mark a quarter circle. Keeping the fabric folded, cut along the pencil line; open out.

Alternatively, use the same method to make a quarter circle pattern from paper. Pin the pattern to the fabric and cut out.

Mitering a corner

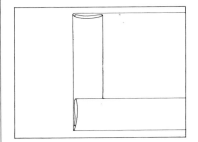

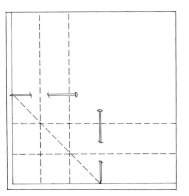

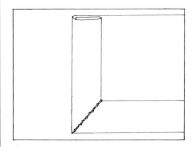

FINISH THE HEMS of a tablecloth or curtain by mitering the corners.

Turn in and press the side and hem allowances. Mark the lower raw edge of fabric with a pin at the top of the side turning and mark the raw side edge where the top of the hem falls. Unfold the allowances, then fold in the corner, making a diagonal crease from pin to pin. Refold the turnings so the folded edges meet at the corner in a neat miter. Slip-stitch the edges together.

FINISHING TOUCHES

THE FINISHING TOUCHES WE PUT TO OUR HOMES — *including wall decorations such as pictures, mirrors and wallhangings, as well as ornaments, collections and flowers — are often, ironically, the first to be noticed. They allow us to say something about ourselves, our preferences and taste, and they are the aspect of decorating an interior that enables us to give full rein to our creative side. Limitations may beset us elsewhere — not least financial ones — but the effectiveness of finishing touches is largely a matter of imagination, personality and flair.*

Lighting and storage, although they are fundamental components of a room, are generally put in place after working out how you will use the room and deciding where all the furniture will be positioned. The type of lighting will influence a room's ambience or, indeed, help to create a choice of different moods. Both task and background lighting must be planned in relation to the way the room is used; your room plan will help you to organize practical switching points.

There are many ways of providing storage for all that has to be hidden from view. It makes sense to use any natural features such as alcoves for built-in storage in the form of tailor-made cupboards, units and shelves. Or storage can come in the shape of freestanding furniture like chests of drawers, cupboards and dressers. Using a mixture of freestanding pieces and built-in furniture will create the most flexible storage system.

LEFT: THIS ENTRANCE HALL IS MADE ALL THE MORE WELCOMING BY FINISHING TOUCHES SUCH AS THE INFORMAL ARRANGEMENT OF FRESH FLOWERS ON THE TABLE AND THE ARTISTICALLY PLACED DISPLAY WHICH EMBELLISHES ITS WALLS. THE INNOVATIVELY HUNG WALL CLOCK AND DECORATIVE PLATE ARE FRAMED ON EITHER SIDE BY A SYMMETRICAL ARRANGEMENT OF PRINTS. AN UMBRELLA STAND IS USED TO HOUSE SPORTS EQUIPMENT AS WELL AS UMBRELLAS.

RIGHT: MAKE A FEATURE OF YOUR STORAGE WHENEVER YOU CAN. THESE TALL GLASS STORAGE JARS ARE USED FOR DECORATIVE SWEETMEATS TO PROVIDE A COLORFUL DISPLAY ON A KITCHEN SHELF.

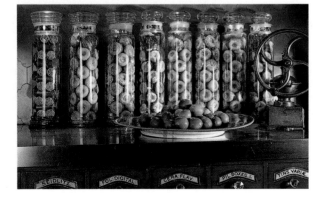

PLANNING THE LIGHTING

ELECTRICITY IS ONE OF THE ESSENTIAL SERVICES, along with water and natural gas, which you have to consider at the outset when designing a room. It must be in the right place to provide power and to illuminate different surfaces adequately, according to the way each room, and individual areas of it, are used. Lighting is, however, much more than a utilitarian service which allows you to see after dark. It is a great asset in creating the mood and atmosphere of a room, enabling you to relax, to entertain or to work. You can play "tricks of the light" to improve the shape and proportion of a room, to highlight an interesting feature dramatically or to detract from an ugly one.

TYPES OF LIGHTING

There are two main categories of lighting. The functional type needs to relate to the way the room is used: it is usually unobtrusive and is selected for the way it lights a surface or object, not for the type of fixture. Functional lighting is often built into the structure of the property (ceiling-recessed downlighters and wall-washers; wall- and floor-mounted uplighters; some spotlights; track lighting) or, as display lighting, it may be an integral part of furniture and equipment (hidden behind a batten or a wall-mounted cupboard; as part of a ventilation hood; as strip lighting in cabinets).

Decorative lighting on the other hand is usually chosen as an integral and visible part of the room scheme and the style of fittings chosen to suit it (table and standard lamps, wall lights, pendants and chandeliers). Many styles are available, from heavy black iron Gothic-style wall lights and candelabras to graceful Art Deco table and wall lamps.

LIGHTING EFFECTS

Artificial lighting can significantly change the way a color looks under natural daylight. Lighting should ideally be installed at the outset, before a decorating scheme is planned, so proposed fabrics, paint colors and carpet can be checked before ordering.

LIGHTING FALLS INTO THREE TYPES — BACKGROUND, TASK AND ACCENT OR DISPLAY, AND MOST ROOMS NEED TWO, IF NOT ALL THREE DIFFERENT TYPES, INSTALLED ON SEPARATE CIRCUITS FOR GREATER CONTROL. BACKGROUND LIGHTING IN THIS LIVING AREA IS PROVIDED BY THE CENTRAL HANGING CHANDELIERS, AND IN THE DINING AREA BY DOWNLIGHTERS; TASK LIGHTING IS ADDED WITH TABLE LAMPS FOR READING AND SPOTLIGHTS OVER THE DINING TABLE; PICTURES ARE ACCENTED BY SPECIAL PICTURE LIGHTS.

Light also reacts with the texture of a surface: a shiny surface (ceramic, silky wallcoverings, highly polished wood, metal, glazed chintz) will reflect light, making the color of the surface look brighter, or in some cases paler, and can also cause glare. A soft, matte or textured surface (such as rough brick, unpolished wood, tweedy fabrics, velvet, looped-pile carpet) will absorb light, making the color look deeper, darker or more subtle, but it can also make both surface and color seem dull and lifeless. Light-filtering textures, like lace, slatted or cane blinds, will diffuse light, softening and lightening the colors, and reduce glare.

LIGHTING A ROOM

Most rooms require a flexible lighting plan, so the light can relate to the way you use the room, and the position of furniture and equipment: several different sources are often necessary. This should be worked out at an early stage so that any structural work, such as cutting holes for downlighters or concealing wires in walls, can be done before decorating starts. Always plan for optimum needs: to provide as many light sources as the room will eventually require, on different circuits. Install twice as many plug-in points as you first thought of, and always use double sockets, so that all the wiring can be done at the outset.

Background lighting gives the overall brightness which enables you to see, walk around safely, clean and so on. This can be provided in a number of different ways, such as ceiling pendant lights, wall lights, downlighters, wall-washers or uplighters, and should be switched on and off from the door of the room. The degree of light can be controlled by dimmer switch for greater flexibility.

Task lighting is clear, direct (but not glaring) light which bathes a surface and materials in a pool of light to allow specific tasks to be performed, including reading, desk work, food preparation, cooking, washing dishes, sewing, shaving or putting on make-up. This type of light is often provided by lamps specifically designed for the purpose: by shaded fluorescent tubes and strips; by individual spotlights or by track lighting combined with spotlights which can be angled towards the necessary surface.

Accent or display lighting is used to highlight features such as architectural details, plants, pictures, special collections. Display lighting may be provided by spotlights, wall-washers (better than conventional clip-on lights for pictures, as it illuminates the whole surface); fluorescent and other lights concealed in alcoves and cabinets, under pelmets and battens, uplighters (especially effective for lighting plants) or carefully sited downlighters. Low-voltage lighting comes into its own as accent lighting because of the clarity of the light, the nature of the fixtures (neater and more discreet) and the more tightly controlled light beam.

MAKING A LIGHTING PLAN

The only way to get the lighting right is to make a separate lighting circuit plan; this will also help you to instruct the electrician. Once you have prepared a room plan (see page 36) and decided where furniture, fixtures and appliances will be positioned, you must work out exactly what needs to be illuminated. The best way to see whether the lighting plan works is to make it on a tracing paper overlay, which you can position on top of the master room plan. Each circuit should be color-coded to show what lights what:

❍ Mark the proposed positions of any ceiling and wall fixtures accurately and of any outlets that are intended to be centrally switched.

❍ Join up the groups of fixtures which will be operated together with a colored line (this may be only one central fixture), following it back to the switch.

❍ Show other circuits in different colors and indicate the exact positions of power sockets in yet another color. You can use symbols for the various fittings.

❍ It is possible to install several on/off switches in one room, overriding each other, but it may be more practical to have the main switch (usually just inside the main door) on a dimmer control and to have the other lights on the same circuit individually switched.

Low-voltage Lighting

THE ADVANTAGES OF THIS FORM OF LIGHTING are that it is discreet and unobtrusive, gives a truer color rendition and has a more tightly controlled beam. The light stays physically cool, making it ideal for banks of spotlights or task lighting where normal fixtures become hot in use. Low-voltage lighting involves the use of a transformer to bring the voltage down to 6, 12 or 24 volts: most fixtures run at 12 volts, like a car battery. Many fittings have a built-in transformer and are both slim and neat; otherwise the transformer has to be connected to the circuit. Low-voltage lighting must be used in conjunction with special bulbs, such as tungsten halogen bulbs, which are smaller and neater than conventional light bulbs.

STYLES OF LIGHTING

THE COLORS YOU CHOOSE, AND THE PATTERNS AND TEXTURES you select for a room will help you to achieve the style and atmosphere you want, as will the furniture and window dressings. The lighting is an equally significant factor in creating ambience and will help you to play some visual tricks, such as adding height or lowering a ceiling. It can also add a romantic touch by creating a cozy glow in a large area.

Consider any features you want highlighted – an interesting architectural detail, a specific surface texture, a carefully arranged collection, paintings and wallhangings, a dramatic plant or a piece of statuary. Choose whether, for best effect, to illuminate them from a direct light source, by integral fittings in cabinets, niches and display shelves, with strategically positioned uplighters or by softer wall-washers. Decide what might be better side- or back-lit, to throw interesting shadows on to the ceiling, wall or floor.

MOOD LIGHTING

In most rooms you may well wish to vary the moods by flicking a switch; this will mean installing several different circuits and possibly incorporating dimmer controls. Be selective in your choice of light fixtures, since some functional lighting and modern fixtures may not suit the character of a room with original features like decorative ceilings or panelled walls. Such architectural features should be lit from an unobtrusive source. Friezes, cornices and covings can be effectively lit from below, using small, low-voltage spots, concealed behind old beams. Wall-washers or recessed downlighters (set in the ceiling) will draw attention to a fireplace or attractive wall treatment.

Decorative fixtures – for example lamps, wall lights and some pendant fittings – can emphasize the overall style of a room. Black wrought iron or *verdigris* finishes will fit well in a medieval, Tudor or Victorian Gothic scheme; glittering chandeliers can enhance a classical interior; candle-type pendants and wall sconces are appropriate in Georgian or colonial rooms; converted oil or gas lamps suit a Victorian or Edwardian setting. Specialized light fixtures range from colorful Tiffany glass and graceful Art Deco lamps to streamlined hi-tech fixtures.

HALL LIGHTING SHOULD BE WELCOMING AND PRACTICAL ENOUGH TO LIGHT STAIR TREADS CLEARLY; IT SHOULD BE CONTROLLED FROM BOTH HALL AND LANDING. HERE TABLE LAMPS PROVIDE A WARM GLOW, LIGHTING THE HALL TABLE AND ITS FLORAL DISPLAY. WALL BRACKETS, CHOSEN TO COMPLEMENT THE ARCHITECTURAL STYLE OF THE HOUSE, LIGHT THE STAIRS WITHOUT DAZZLING PEOPLE ASCENDING OR DESCENDING THEM.

TRICKS OF THE LIGHT

Many rooms are less than perfectly proportioned; others are square and box-like or bland and characterless; some are dark and dismal. Clever lighting can help to correct some of these defects.

To make a ceiling look taller or to flatten out a slope, throw light up onto the ceiling using floor or wall-mounted uplighters, or conceal lighting behind a cornice or coving or a batten or "pelmet" mounted high on the walls to run around the perimeter of the room. In a kitchen this can be placed above wall-mounted cupboards, provided, of course, that there is enough space between the top of the cupboards and the ceiling to avoid scorching.

To make a room look less tall, keep the light away from the ceiling. If you use a pendant lamp, choose one with an enclosed top and install it on a rise-and-fall system so the height can be easily adjusted. Site wall lights fairly low and use a type with an enclosed top to prevent light from being thrown up onto the ceiling. Draw attention to pictures or wallhangings positioned low on the wall, or groups of accessories placed on a low surface, by lighting them from above, to the side, or with a lamp standing on the surface. Create "pools"

of light with table or standard lamps which give a warm glow to the area immediately beneath them.

To make a long, narrow space look wider, focus attention on one of the end walls by lighting the curtains with pelmet- or spotlights or by focusing on an attractive feature; wash the other walls with an even light.

To make a space look larger, take the eye through to the area beyond by lighting a feature dramatically. "Wash" opposite walls with light to make them seem further apart. Combine lighting with mirrors and reflective surfaces to double the apparent size: use ceiling-recessed downlighters or track-mounted spotlights above a mirror or panel of mirror glass (make sure it is glare-free); position lamps or candles so they are reflected in a freestanding or wall-mounted mirror. Plants or objects which look as though they are floating will help to create an impression of space: use glass shelves or a glass-topped table and light it from below with uplighters, or from above so the light travels through the shelves.

To create a more intimate atmosphere in a large room, use candlelight when feasible, but always make sure this will be safe. Have lots of table lamps to create a cozy glow. Consider warm-colored shades or bulbs (test them lit for effect); use downlighters with gold, rather than silver, reflectors. Use wall-washers to bathe a wall in comforting color: you could use different colored filters so the color can easily be changed at the flick of a switch.

Create theatrical effects in a large room. Throw interesting shadows on floors, walls and ceilings (this can be equally effective with daylight as artificial light) by using stained glass panels, open-work screens, shutters and blinds, sheer fabrics, plants or other interestingly shaped items at the window, or placed just in front of it. Try to combine this with night lighting so the effect is magnified. Round light bulbs set into a frame around a mirror epitomize the theatrical dressing-room image (not necessarily good to make up by, as they tend to light the wall rather than the face!); they can be copied in a bedroom, hall or bathroom. Similarly, lengths of flexible, clear plastic tubing containing small, low-voltage light bulbs can be used to outline mirrors and other features; they are particularly effective when used to define stair treads and risers.

An intimate atmosphere is created in this library-style living room: reading lamps and the wall-mounted candle brackets provide a warm glow. By keeping the fixtures and lighting level low, the height of the room is reduced visually.

LIGHTING ROOM BY ROOM

EACH ROOM HAS TO BE CONSIDERED IN TERMS OF ITS FUNCTION when it comes to lighting decisions. The main influencing factor will be how the room, and even different parts of it, are used, but you should also think carefully about the ambience you wish to create, particularly in living rooms and bedrooms.

Living areas Aim to create several moods with differently sourced lighting on separate circuits. Choose the background lighting to create a warm, inviting glow, supplied by lamps, wall-washers, uplighters, pelmet lighting and softly lit display cabinets and alcoves. In a room which may be used for many different activities, aim for maximum flexibility: for dining, reading, studying and sewing, plan any task lighting accordingly. This can be provided by separate lamps: pull-down pendants over a table, downlighters and spots.

Use display lighting to enhance plants, an attractive piece of furniture or an architectural feature. In a dining area, apart from lighting the dining table (keep the light low so it does not shine into the eyes of diners), illuminate any food serving area clearly but not too brightly – put this on a separate circuit so it can be switched off once the food is served. Provide subtle lighting to create a relaxing atmosphere for watching television and make sure light fixtures are not reflected in the screen.

Kitchens The food preparation and cooking areas will need to be clearly lit, as will the sink (if it is placed under a window, it may be poorly illuminated at night). Strip lighting may be concealed under wall-mounted cupboards or can be an integral part of a ventilation hood; more gentle light might be provided by downlighters, strategically positioned in the ceiling, or from ceiling-mounted track carrying several spotlights which can be angled towards the work surfaces. Other parts of the room which may need to be task lit are any utility areas (washing or ironing) or the telephone. Light a breakfast bar or dining table separately (see above). Light the inside of deep cupboards

and larders, preferably with door-jamb switches which operate as the door is opened – this is helpful when your hands are covered in flour! Display lighting can be used to highlight a shelf or cupboard filled with decorative china.

Bedrooms A degree of mood or soft background light is usually required in a bedroom, with some functional lighting to see to dress or make up by, and clear, easily controlled bedside lighting which illuminates the pages of a book when reading in bed. In bedrooms which are dual-purpose, provide task, general and accent lighting similar to that in the living room. Individual lamps, wall lights, downlighters and even uplighters can provide an adequate source, on a separate circuit from the general lighting. The insides of deep closets and cupboards should always be well lit. Accent any interesting features or drapes with light. Some bedrooms, such as a child's room, will need task lighting for changing a baby, for playtime or for homework; a child may also require a low-level light which can be left on all night. A special night-light can be used, or you can fit the background lighting with a dimmer switch. For safety, use shuttered sockets or dummy plugs and choose unbreakable lamps.

Bathrooms Here lighting must above all be SAFE (no portable lamps or fixtures) and preferably controlled by a pull-cord or switched from outside the bathroom door so that wet hands do not come in contact with the switch; any ceiling or wall lights must be enclosed. Aim for good color rendition: any fluorescent lights should not be too harsh; tungsten-halogen downlighters will give a crisp, clear light. Light the bathtub and shower clearly from above so that no

LEFT: IN THIS LARGE KITCHEN THE WORK AREA IS ILLUMINATED BY DOWNLIGHTERS; SPOTLIGHTS ON A TRACK CAN BE ANGLED TOWARDS THE DINING TABLE AND USED TO EMPHASIZE THE BOTANICAL PRINTS; CONCEALED LIGHTING UNDER WALL-MOUNTED CUPBOARDS AND IN ALCOVES ILLUMINATES THE WORK SURFACES AND COOKER HOB CLEARLY.

RIGHT: PLAN TASK LIGHTING IN THE BATHROOM TO ILLUMINATE FACES IN MIRRORS WITHOUT DAZZLE; HERE A SERIES OF CEILING-RECESSED DOWNLIGHTERS DO THIS WELL AND LIGHT THE REST OF THE ROOM FOR CLEAR VIEWING WHEN BATHING OR SHOWERING. BATHROOM FITTINGS SHOULD ALWAYS BE PROPERLY ENCLOSED SO THEY ARE DAMP- AND CONDENSATION-PROOF, AND SWITCHED EITHER WITH A PULL-CORD OR FROM OUTSIDE THE BATHROOM DOOR, SO THAT THE FITTINGS ARE NEVER TOUCHED WITH WET HANDS.

shadows are thrown. Lights above showers must be sealed: special low-voltage models are available. Fully-recessed spill-ring downlighters will prevent the light from bouncing off tiled surfaces; gold reflectors add warmth to a chilly bathroom. Make sure that mirrors for shaving and make up are well-lit so that the face, rather than the mirror, is illuminated, without glare or dazzle. In a small, cold bathroom combine a wall- or ceiling-mounted infrared heater with a light: install it on a separate circuit and control it with a pull-cord.

Halls, stairs and landings Illuminate the front door or at least the house name and number so that people can see it clearly from the road or pathway. Provide warm, background lighting so that the hall looks inviting. Make sure the stair treads and risers are clearly lit, so the edge of each step is defined. If you have lights stepped up the wall at the side of the stairs, avoid the escalator look, and make sure the bulbs are not seen when ascending or descending the staircase. Light the landing clearly but without dazzle – a dimmer switch might be fitted if there are children in the house who are afraid of the dark. Control the main lighting so it is dual-switched from both hall and landing. Light a hall mirror with a glare-free fixtures.

STYLING IDEAS

☞ *To work out the correct height of bedside lamps, place them on the bedside table, make up the bed with the usual complement of pillows, sit against them and open a book or magazine – check whether the light from the lamp falls onto the page. Do the same test with wall-mounted lights.*

☞ *Make sure bedside lamps are well shaded so they do not disturb a sleeping partner on the other side.*

☞ *Use an enclosed shade for pendant lamps in bedrooms, to avoid glare and so that the bulb cannot be seen from the bed.*

☞ *Install lights inside deep cupboards and larders: position them so they do not present a fire hazard to clothes and other stored items; if the switch is fixed to the door jamb, the light automatically comes on when you open the door.*

☞ *For a desk, the best choice may be a flexible desk lamp or a fixed one concealed behind a batten. Make sure there is no glare.*

☞ *If you fancy a theatre-dressing-room arrangement of naked bulbs around a mirror in the bathroom, these must be placed behind a plexiglass or glass panel for safety.*

☞ *Light a dining table with a pendant on a rise-and-fall system to pull down centrally over the table, so it will not dazzle diners: with a long table you may need two lights.*

☞ *In a dual-purpose living/dining room, have several lighting circuits; plan the dining room lighting so this area of the room can be plunged into darkness when the meal is over – that way, you do not sit looking at the debris on the table. Do the same in dining areas in a kitchen: make sure the working end of the kitchen can be darkened while you sit around the table.*

A PLACE FOR EVERYTHING

WE ALL NEED SOMEWHERE TO STORE THE NECESSITIES OF LIFE — clothes; hobbies and sports equipment; cosmetics, jewellery and medicines; luggage, wellington boots and umbrellas; toys, books, games and papers; tapes, compact discs and records; towels and household linens; food and kitchen utensils; gardening equipment; cleaning materials and so on: the list is endless. Many modern houses and apartments have very little space in which to install shelves, drawers and cupboards so it is essential that the storage you provide can be utilized efficiently.

IN THE KITCHEN, MORE THAN IN ANY OTHER AREA OF THE HOME, YOU CAN MAKE A DECORATIVE FEATURE OF YOUR STORAGE. IN THIS TRADITIONALLY STYLED KITCHEN, THE ORIGINAL SHELVING HAS BEEN RESTORED AND THE STORAGE SHELVES ARE INDIVIDUALLY ILLUMINATED FROM INSIDE TO CREATE A DESIGN FEATURE. DISPLAY LIGHTING CAN GIVE A WARM BACKGROUND GLOW TO A ROOM, GREATLY ENHANCING ITS MOOD.

There are several ways of providing built-in storage, including tailor-made cupboards, units, window seats and shelves. Or storage can come in the form of free-standing furniture such as cabinets, dressers, wardrobes, bookcases, chests of drawers, under-bed storage drawers, tallboys, ottomans and toy boxes. There are many companies specializing in fully fitted kitchens, bedrooms and bathrooms, or you can call in a local carpenter to create items to your individual requirements – otherwise you can make your own. Adjustable shelving is fairly simple to install (see page 238), and there are home-assembly built-in storage units, as well as ready-made doors and sets of drawers available which facilitate doing it yourself.

Freestanding pieces can be bought new or second-hand, in which case consideration will have to be given to the wood or other finish as well as their style, size and shape; bear in mind that all-matching pieces tend to make the room look like a furniture showroom. Older pieces might be refurbished by using a special finish or painting technique to make them an integral part of the room scheme, or to contrast with it as a special feature.

CREATING SPACE

In most homes, where there are many disparate items to be stored, the ideal answer is to use a mixture of built-in and freestanding furniture, and to create as flexible a system as possible. Make the most of adjustable shelves, pull-out rails, racks and drawers where these are installed inside cupboards, closets and built-in units.

Measuring In order to maximize the available space and to plan a really functional system, storage should be planned from the inside out. This means measuring exactly what you need to store, and then relating these figures to the width, depth, height and strength of drawers (runners and bases are particularly important), shelves and cupboards. Remember to measure the height and depth of stacks of plates, bottles and glasses, the size of large serving dishes; the vital statistics of books, boxes of games, record sleeves, tapes and cassettes; the length of dresses, coats, skirts and trousers and the width of such items, including the coat hanger; the width, depth and height of suitcases; the sizes of the many different pieces of sports equipment, items needed for hobbies, cleaning or cooking; the size and shape of stacks of canned foods, packets of dried goods and so on.

Making a plan Measure the space you have available for storage, room by room, and make a scale plan (see page 36); it may also be necessary to draw up the wall elevations to the same scale, so you can see what will fit in on the vertical plane. You can then work out the insides of built-in cupboards and units.

When measuring, allow for the depth and width of baseboards, door architraves and window frames as well as the recesses into which you may be considering installing cupboards or shelves. Recesses should be checked at several different levels, since walls are rarely perfectly true – mis-measuring can result in shelves and their supports, hanging rails or pull-out baskets not slipping in and out smoothly, or lift-up tops banging against sills. Make sure you get the true vertical and horizontal by using a plumbline and carpenter's level. If you are having custom-built items, insist that the carpenter measures, so you will not be held liable for any mistakes.

Always allow for the opening of doors and drawers of any storage; work out door swings on the scale plan, so these do not knock into other items of furniture, or make it impossible to circulate comfortably. Where space is tight, sliding, bi-fold or folding doors may be a solution, or the tambour type which roll up; stable-doors, sectioned horizontally, can be practical in some situations. Mirrored or glazed doors create an illusion of greater space and light in a small room. For less permanent storage, a curtain, roller or louvered blinds make a softer alternative to doors.

Never discount the backs of cupboard doors, which can often be fitted with narrow racks and shelves to store small items for cooking, cleaning or ironing, or used to hang accessories such as belts, ties or scarves. To store heavy items on the back of a door, you may need to strengthen the hinges.

Lighting Relate lighting to your storage at the planning stage: the interiors of deep cupboards can be lit with door-jamb control so they automatically switch on as the door is opened; if the doors are mirrored, down-lighters recessed in the ceiling above the run of doors will give good light for dressing; any cosmetic or bathroom storage might include an illuminated mirror as an integral part of it. Bookshelves, filing drawers and workroom storage should be well lit, so you can see titles, papers and tools at a glance. Display shelving can incorporate accent lighting; this is particularly effective with glass shelves, illuminated from above, so the light travels through them.

FACELIFT IDEAS

☛ *If you have to make do with some temporary storage, there are plastic stacking crates (these can be covered with a fabric "skirt"), folding cardboard boxes and drawers, soft storage to slip under a bed or hang behind doors.*

☛ *For more permanent solutions, look for items to refurbish in auction sales and junk or thrift shops, or at rummage sales.*

☛ *A set of new handles and hinges, the addition of some molding or other decorative trim, even a change of doors (these can be bought separately with some ranges of cupboards – or you can cover existing doors with a special self-adhesive or laminate) will give old cupboards a new lease of life.*

☛ *You can completely transform a tired old chest, cupboard or set of drawers with a decorative treatment, for example by stencilling, or using a trompe l'oeil paint technique such as marbling, graining or découpage (see page 112).*

☛ *Find out whether a second-hand item is solid wood or veneered: if it is veneered and has been painted, you will not be able to strip it, as caustic strippers remove the veneer as well as the paint – but you can always repaint it.*

MAXIMUM USE HAS BEEN MADE OF THE RECESSES TO EACH SIDE OF THE CHIMNEY BREAST IN THIS DINING ROOM. UNOBTRUSIVE WHITE-PAINTED SHELVES HAVE BEEN INSTALLED, WHICH ARE USED TO STORE AND DISPLAY A VAST ASSORTMENT OF DECORATIVE BLUE AND WHITE CHINA.

NATURAL STORAGE SOLUTIONS

In any room, always try to make the most of a natural space which already exists, so that any built-in units can be fairly unobtrusive and not project too far into the room. Storage can be most easily tucked into any alcove or recess, or low units and window seats with lift-up tops may be positioned under a bay or dormer window. A projecting window is also a good place for a desk or a play area: two units or cupboards can be placed side by side under the window with a space left between them, and linked with a countertop; shelves can be mounted above this, to each side of the window. Small awkward corners between a window and a return wall can also be fitted with slim shelves or cupboards (any curtain treatment will have to be carefully considered). Wall space above doors, above existing low furniture or below wall-mounted items may also be the obvious place for some extra shelves, cupboards or sets of drawers. The triangular spaces under sloping eaves provide the perfect place for custom-made built-in units. And the area under the stairs, which often contains a cupboard full of clutter, can always be opened out and re-designed.

Fitting out a recess One of the most practical places to install cupboards and shelving is in a natural recess or alcove to each side of a projecting chimney breast, often found in a living room or bedroom. You will need to do some careful measuring – the bedroom recess, for example, may not be deep enough to hang garments sideways. It may be possible to extend cupboards in the recess forward into the room, and if there is no fireplace set into the breast, they can be linked by shelves for a tailored look. Or you could use a slim cupboard and hang the garments flat rather than sideways. Where one recess abuts a window, it may be necessary to chamfer cupboard or shelves slightly into the corner to avoid cutting out any light.

There may be a chimney breast in a dining room or kitchen where an old range used to be; if a new oven or fireplace is not to be sited here, you can open up the breast to form an alcove (make sure the chimney is closed off at the top or fitted with a cowl); fill it with dramatically lit shelves or storage cupboards. In a living room, this unused space can be covered with doors to house the television set (positioned on a turntable so that it pulls out and swivels around for easy viewing), or for the music center, video, storage of tapes, compact discs and cassettes, or it can be converted to store bottles and glasses.

ROOM BY ROOM STORAGE

APART FROM GENERAL STORAGE, MOST ROOMS HAVE SPECIFIC REQUIREMENTS: it usually makes sense to store clothes and personal effects in a bedroom or dressing room; outdoor clothes and umbrellas near the front door; items for cooking, ironing and cleaning in the kitchen or utility area; glasses, utensils and table linen as close to the dining table as possible. This means drawing up a practical plan for each room, working out what you need to store, then fitting the two together.

THE LIVING AREA

Storage here will depend on the way you use the room, but provision will probably be needed for books, records, video tapes and cassettes, and you may wish to store glasses for serving drinks. In a dual-purpose living room, china and table linen may have to be housed, as well as hobby equipment, games and toys. Some storage can be provided by built-in units, the rest by modular units or freestanding furniture: a mixture of pieces will add character to the room and provide visual variety. Painting built-in units will make them fade easily into the background.

Utilize any natural recesses for shelves, low units and cupboards, with a place for the television, music center and desk close at hand. Recesses can also be an ideal place for drawers, cupboards or shelves for the storage of drinks, glasses and china. A window seat with lift-up top, set into a bay or bow window, can hide children's toys at the end of the day.

A complete storage wall can be an alternative solution in a room with no natural recesses. In a multipurpose living room, storage units and shelving can be used as a room divider. Chests or waist-high cupboards can be placed back-to-back, one set facing the living space, the other with access from the dining area. The top can double as a food serving surface (illuminate this clearly on a separate circuit). If you

FOR ROOMS WITHOUT ALCOVES OR RECESSES, A COMPLETE STORAGE WALL IS A PRACTICAL SOLUTION. IN THIS LIVING ROOM, A WALL IS FILLED WITH BOOKSHELVES WHICH PROVIDE STORAGE SPACE AND ARE ALSO USED FOR DISPLAY PURPOSES, ILLUMINATED FROM ABOVE BY SPOTLIGHTS MOUNTED ON TRACK. MAXIMUM USE HAS ALSO BEEN MADE OF THE SPACE ABOVE THE DOORS — A SHELF CONTINUES AROUND THE WALL TO UNIFY THE TOP OF THE BOOKSHELVES WITH THE DOOR ARCHITRAVES.

BUILT-IN STORAGE LINES THE WALLS OF THIS NARROW HALL. ALL THE CUPBOARDS AND DRAWERS ARE PAINTED TO BLEND IN WITH THE REST OF THE SURFACES SO THE OVERALL IMPRESSION IS NOT CLAUSTROPHOBIC. MIRRORS COULD ALSO BE USED TO GREAT EFFECT HERE.

STYLING IDEAS

☛ *In a living area also used as a playroom by a toddler, store toys out of sight at the end of the day in an ottoman, a large, decorative box, or even a theater trunk. Or a seat with a lift-up top can be installed in a bay or bow window.*

☛ *In a long corridor or hall, there may be space for floor-to-ceiling bookshelves or a run of cupboards – mirror the doors or decorate them with a trompe l'oeil treatment to stop them from making the area look even more long and narrow.*

☛ *A freestanding or built-in cupboard for outdoor clothes, with mirrored doors or fronts, can help to create an illusion of greater size and width in a hall.*

☛ *Even in a narrow hall, there is usually space for a large pot or umbrella stand close to the door, for walking sticks or racquets as well as umbrellas.*

have to provide desk or study facilities in a dual-purpose dining or sitting area, you might use one fireplace recess for this, with shelves above for books and files; this could be balanced in the other recess with a storage cupboard to hold videos, cassettes, compact discs, bottles and glasses, with matching shelves above to provide a visual link. In a limited space, the dining table may have to double as a desk top, and provision will have to be made to store files, keyboard or typewriter – a sideboard might be adapted.

THE ENTRANCE HALL AND LANDING

This area is usually short on space, but you will need to be able to hang visitors' coats; keep umbrellas and walking sticks; leave keys, letters, clothes brush and so on. In a narrow hall, wall-mounted shelves, a pin-up notice or peg board, hooks and a mirror may be all you have room for; corner shelves are often space-saving. In a wider hall, a hat stand or refurbished hallstand may be an ideal solution; otherwise try free-standing units or a chest of drawers. There may be space for a built-in desk with shelves above it, which is practical if the telephone is sited in the hall.

On the landing, if there is space, a linen cupboard, a chest of drawers or an armoire will provide deep storage for spare bed and bathroom linen. In a larger area, a full-height cupboard or wardrobe can be used to store cleaning materials. If there is a window on the landing or half-landing, this may be a good place to site a window seat with lift-up-top for some practical between-floors storage. See that it does not project too far onto the landing and create circulation problems.

In many houses there is wasted space under the stairs; if there is an understairs cupboard, it usually becomes filled with clutter. It is sometimes possible to open out this area completely and fill it with purpose-built storage, providing, perhaps, a desk with shelves or a cocktail cupboard and bottle storage, complete with serving top, furnishing an extension to living room or kitchen storage. If you still need to house the vacuum cleaner and the ironing board, as well as outdoor coats here, and it contains the utilities meters too, it may be possible to box these in with a slimline cupboard and combine it with pull-out racks and drawers. If the cupboard itself is to remain, at least organize it well, with hooks and racks designed to hold brooms, brushes and cleaning materials as neatly as possible.

THE BEDROOM

Bedrooms are the obvious place to store clothes, personal items, luggage and possibly sports and hobbies equipment. One of the most practical ways of providing adequate storage is by a run of built-in cupboards along one wall or sited in recesses to each side of a chimney breast. Such arrangements can be continued into corners or under a window to make a dressing table and/or desk area – or to form a window seat with doors or a lift-up top. Freestanding furniture and wardrobes can be used if there is enough space. Whatever type of clothes storage you decide on, you will need to measure all that you want to store carefully: work out the width and length of bulky coats and long dresses (on their hangers); the width, depth and height of cases and holdalls; the vital statistics of sports equipment like golf clubs, skis and racquets. The interiors can then be tailored to fit, with rails, shelves, pull-out drawers and racks.

An inexpensive, and usually temporary, means of providing hanging space is to use a portable (collapsible) clothes rod, which can fit into a recess or positioned along a wall and hidden behind curtains, screens or blinds. Use the area left underneath long hanging space for shoe racks and under short hang-

IN A ROOM WITH SLOPING CEILINGS, BUILT-IN CUPBOARDS ARE A PRACTICAL STORAGE SOLUTION: THEY ARE MORE PRACTICAL THAN FREESTANDING FURNITURE AS THEY CAN BE CARRIED UP IN PIECES AND CONSTRUCTED ON SITE. IN THIS MAGICAL PLAYROOM, THE STORAGE CUPBOARDS HAVE BEEN PAINTED TO ECHO THE UNDERWATER AQUARIUM THEME, WHICH HELPS THEM TO BLEND INTO THE BACKGROUND.

ing space for pull-out wire baskets or shelves for sweaters, underwear or accessories. The shelves above a clothes rod can be used for hats, luggage or handbags. The backs of doors can be fitted with narrow shelves or used to hang small items.

The space underneath the bed is often overlooked as storage; some beds already have storage drawers built in, really intended for spare bedding, but there is no reason why you should not use it for other items. You can add pull-out drawers on castors; use special soft plastic storage containers or stacking crates – these can all be hidden by a fabric valance.

In children's and teenagers' rooms, storage requirements may be more like that needed for dual-purpose rooms. When you are planning a child's room, aim to choose furniture which can be added to and which will grow with the child. Older children will require more of a teenage den: this can be accommo-dated with adapted industrial shelving or with special metal tubing (like scaffolding) which slots together. Spray-painted metal filing cabinets, old kitchen cup-boards or second-hand furniture, painted up, can all make ideal budget solutions.

THE KITCHEN

The amount of storage needed will depend to a large extent on the cook, but also on whether all dining items, as well as laundry equipment, have to be accommodated in this area. Figure out exactly what you need to store and measure it all, including dry goods, tins, jars and bottles, before you decide on a particular choice of kitchen cupboards.

The majority of kitchen storage is usually provided by the base units and cabinets as well as the wall-mounted cupboards and tall cupboards which form part of a built-in kitchen, linked by continuous work-tops. There are many interior fittings available, which help to expand the use of these units and cupboards, including revolving shelves or carousels which make the most of a corner; pull-out wire racks and drawers; adjustable shelves; built-in chopping boards. Many of these can be supplied as an integral part of the units and others can be installed later.

In some ways the unfitted kitchen (see page 40) can provide more flexible storage than the built-in kitchen, with shelf units, larder cupboards and freestanding chests. Many can be fitted with racks or can incorporate built-in baskets and pull-out sections. If you opt for this style, you may be able to use old pieces of furniture which you can refurbish, creating continuity with a painted or stained technique, with stencils or another decorative treatment.

There is often room in existing cupboards and units to store more if the space is properly organized. The backs of doors can be fitted with shelves or racks to hold small items or, in tall cupboards, with special fittings to hang brooms and baskets. Drawers and shelves can be fitted out with compartmentalized storage for saucepans, lids, china, plates, glasses and mugs. Drawers can have segmented insets for utensils, or to keep bottles and cleaning materials upright.

Existing shelves, or the underside of wall-mounted cupboards, can be fitted with speciality racks, which hold glasses by their bases or stems, or spice jars by their lids. An even simpler method is to screw cup hooks into the edge of a shelf, or under the bottom of a wall-mounted cupboard on which to hang cups, mugs, jugs or small cooking implements.

Glass-fronted cupboards and open shelves can be used to store as well as display china or attractive storage jars. A Delft rack, or wide shelf, placed fairly high up around the perimeter of the room, can be similarly used. Pots, pans and cooking utensils can be hung up neatly, either on special hanging racks or on steel bars with clip-on hooks, magnetic racks, wire grids for wall-mounting, shelves with movable hooks, pegboards or heavy metal chains which can be slung from ceiling- or wall-mounted hooks. All these items are heavy so the fixings must be firm, and it is practical to position them as close as possible to the oven or food-preparation countertop.

THE BATHROOM

Some of the kitchen ideas above can be adapted to the bathroom, and indeed several kitchen manufacturers have adapted their cupboards, etc, for bathrooms. You may want to store items as diverse as cosmetics, rolls of paper, towels and facecloths, soaps, shaving equipment, bath foams and a collection of medicines in the bathroom. It may be possible to create space for bathroom storage from almost nowhere – there is often a place to the side or under the bath (concealed by a panel), or as an integral part of the panel itself: some

panels come ready adapted, others can be simply converted with doors. A small cupboard can be made underneath a wall-hung wash basin or there may be space to fit wall-mounted shelves above the basin, bath or toilet; ensure that they are high enough up to prevent knocked heads. Corner shelves may be a more practical alternative.

In some places, an airing cupboard in the bathroom, containing the water tank (which may also be on the landing or in a bedroom), is an ideal place to air linen and to store dry goods on slatted shelves, so the warm air can circulate. However, do not store linen continually in a warm atmosphere or it will discolor and eventually rot. Allow for the bulk of folded sheets, towels, pillowcases, bedcovers and blankets for single, double and any king-sized beds; measure the height, depth and length of folded piles.

In a generous-sized bathroom, there may be space for a chest or freestanding cupboard, a washstand or a vanitory unit to enclose the plumbing for the basin. For the budget-conscious, shelves, stacking crates or wire drawers can be concealed behind a fabric skirt.

KITCHEN STORAGE CAN ADD ATMOSPHERE AND STYLE TO A FUNCTIONAL ROOM. IN THIS SMALL AREA, MAXIMUM IMPACT IS CREATED BY MAKING A VIRTUE OF NECESSITY. AN OPEN-SHELVED CABINET IS USED TO STORE BEANS, HERBS, SPICES AND OILS WITH WEBBING STRETCHED ACROSS THE FRONT TO PREVENT SMALL JARS FROM TOPPLING FORWARDS. THE PLATE RACK DRAINS AND STORES CHINA AND JUGS AND TEAPOTS HANG FROM A CEILING-MOUNTED RACK ON SPECIAL HOOKS.

SHELVING SYSTEMS

THERE ARE MANY DIFFERENT SORTS OF SHELVING, from permanently fixed, purpose-built wooden shelves to simple clip-on systems for small corners. Some systems, mostly used in recesses, are entirely flexible — slotted struts are screwed to the wall and brackets of different types and sizes are slipped into the slots in the angle to hold the shelf: the brackets can be moved up and down the length of the struts to change their relative heights. Other systems are made on the modular principle, with bases and end struts, and these are more suitable for a freestanding situation.

TYPES OF SHELVING

Shelving systems can be utilitarian or highly decorative. The brackets may also be ornamental and, if used in conjunction with glass shelves (lit from above or below, so the light travels through them), the effect can be magical. Glass shelves can be placed across a window that doesn't open and used to display a collection of colored glass, china or plants.

At the other end of the scale there is industrial shelving, where the supports are made from slotted metal angle which bolts together using corner plates, nuts and bolts to form freestanding sections; these may be combined with wood, laminate or metal shelves. This can be a practical solution for garage, garden shed and workshop storage, where it can be used for do-it-yourself equipment and tools, as it will take heavy loads. It can also look stylish in teenage bed-sitting rooms, painted in bold primary colors. A bonus of this system is that it may be unbolted and reassembled elsewhere, making it very flexible; the angle can be cut with a hacksaw, or overlapped.

MAKING SHELVES

Putting up shelves is one of the simplest do-it-yourself jobs, and also one of the most popular – probably for that very reason. Even if you prefer your furniture to be freestanding rather than built-in, you are sure to need some wall-mounted shelves somewhere – in the kitchen, a child's bedroom, a living room alcove, a cupboard, even in the garage. The only skill you need is the ability to make a firm mounting on your walls, so that your new shelves stay where you put them. Since shelves are often required to carry very heavy loads, such as books, records and hi-fi equipment, the consequences of a collapse could be disastrous. Sound fixtures mean safe shelving.

READY-MADE SHELVING SYSTEMS CAN OFTEN BE A QUICK AND EASY SOLUTION TO STORAGE PROBLEMS. HERE A RANGE OF SELF-LEVELLING SHELVES CAN BE SWIFTLY INSTALLED AND THE SHELVES USED FOR DISPLAY PURPOSES. ALWAYS ENSURE FIXINGS ARE TRULY LEVEL (BY USING A CARPENTER'S LEVEL) AND PROVIDE ENOUGH SUPPORT.

WALL-MOUNTED SHELVING

Wall-mounted shelves fall into one of two basic types: adjustable or fixed. With fixed shelving, each shelf is supported independently of the others, using two or more shelf brackets which are attached to the wall and to the underside of the shelf itself. With adjustable shelving, the shelves are carried on brackets slotted or clipped into vertical support strips; these are in turn screwed to the wall.

Fixed brackets are ideal for putting up a single shelf, over a radiator for example. However, if a bank of shelves is required, each shelf has to be mounted individually on the wall and it can be difficult to align subsequent shelves accurately with the first one. Once the shelves are in place, you are stuck with the shelf spacing – a potential nuisance if you decide at any time to rearrange your storage. Fixed brackets come in a choice of styles, shapes and colors. Metal brackets are most common, but wooden ones complement shelves of natural or veneered wood.

Adjustable systems are more flexible. There is only one set of fixtures to be hung, to secure the supporting channels to the wall, no matter how many shelves are being used. Then the shelves themselves can be positioned at whatever level – and spacing – is required, and can also be moved up or down easily at any future time.

Adjustable systems are mostly all-metal, with colored or metallic finishes, although one or two wooden versions are available. Some have channels with closely spaced slots, while others have a continuous channel into which the brackets can be locked at any desired level. The channels are sold in a range of standard lengths, and two or more lengths can be butted together to form wall-to-ceiling shelving.

The shelves can be of natural wood or any man-made boards. Ready-made shelves are widely available; they are usually made from veneered or plastic-coated chipboard. The latter traditionally have either a white or an imitation woodgrain finish, but subtle pastel shades and bold primary colors are more widely available. If you prefer to cut your own shelves from full-sized boards, chipboard, plywood and block-board are all suitable.

PLANNING SHELF STORAGE

It is a good idea to make a rough sketch of your storage plans so you can take account of the height of your books and other items which you know you want to store or display. Where several shelves are being installed, aim to keep everyday items within easy reach – in practice, between about 2ft 6in (750mm) and 5ft (1.5m) above the floor. Position the deeper shelves near the bottom so you can see and reach the back easily. Allow 1-2in (25-50mm) of clearance on top of the highest objects to be stored, so that you can take them down and put them back easily.

Think about weight too. If you plan to store heavy objects, choose your shelving material with care, since thin shelves will sag if heavily laden unless they are adequately supported.

SHELVES USING FIXED BRACKETS

There is a huge range of bracket types to choose from and the installation sequence is straightforward. When you are choosing the material for your shelf, remember that if you are cutting your own shelves using man-made boards, you will have to fill the cut edge in order to disguise the board's core, or lip the edge by adding decorative beading.

Decide on the number of brackets you will need to support the load (see box below). Then mark the positions of the brackets on the shelf underside and attach them with short screws. Use a carpenter's level to mark a horizontal line on the wall to indicate the shelf position.

Hold the shelf up to the line (you may need a helper for this) and mark the fixing screw positions. Drill holes in the wall at the marked positions and insert the appropriate firm fixing device (see the panel on the opposite page). Get a helper to hold the shelf steadily in place while you insert and tighten up the fixing screws.

Making shelves in alcoves

ALCOVES BESIDE CHIMNEY BREASTS or other obstructions make a perfect site for shelves, since you can make use of the back and side walls as supports. There is nothing to stop you from using either fixed brackets or an adjustable shelving system to support the shelves in this situation, but it is very simple, and cheaper, to mount slim battens directly to the alcove walls and rest the shelves on these.

You simply need to mark the shelf level on the alcove walls, cut battens to the required lengths and screw them in position. Then cut your shelf to size: the only difficult part is in getting the shelf to be a good fit, since the alcove walls may not be truly square, so careful measuring of the width at front and back is the only answer. Slip the shelf into place, resting it on the battens. You can also pin, screw or glue it on later if you wish.

MARK THE SHELF POSITION using a level. Extend the marks right around the alcove. Measure, cut and mount the back wall batten first, screwing it to the wall. Mount the side battens in the same way. Cut their front ends back at an angle to make them less obtrusive. Measure the alcove dimensions. Cut and fit in the shelf.

Making adjustable shelving

THE MANY DIFFERENT TYPES of adjustable shelving on the market all operate on broadly the same principle. Decide first on the position and spacing of the uprights; this will depend on the shelf material you will be using and the load you will be putting on it (see box, page 238). Then you hang the uprights, making sure that they are perfectly vertical and set level with each other; finally, you clip in the brackets and then fit on the shelves.

DRAW A HORIZONTAL LINE with which to align the tops of the uprights, and mark off their spacing. Hold each upright in place with its top aligned, and mark the top fixing screw position. Drill the holes and fit the appropriate fixing devices. Then drive the top screws in partway only, so that the uprights can swing freely.

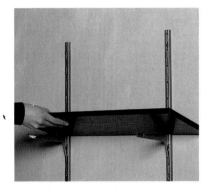

USE A CARPENTER'S LEVEL to check that each upright is truly vertical and mark the other screw positions. Swing each upright aside on its top screw so you can drill other holes where marked. Insert appropriate fixing devices and tighten up all the fixing screws, including the top ones.

Insert the brackets, lay on the shelves and mark the bracket positions on them. Screw the brackets to the shelves. Try out the shelves plus their attached brackets on the channels and slot them in where required. If you want the shelves to fit flush with the wall surface, cut small notches in their rear edges.

Using shelf support strips

THERE ARE SEVERAL INGENIOUS supports for single shelves. They consist of a specially shaped channel which is screwed to the wall at the required position, ensuring that it is horizontally level; then the shelf is simply knocked into place with a soft mallet. The channel grips the shelf securely and can support surprisingly heavy loads. Various lengths are available, and there are special types for hanging glass shelves and corner shelves.

Making Firm Fixings

Solid masonry walls
Choose the right length of screw; for shelves you need them at least 2in (50mm) long; 2½in (65mm) is better for heavy loads. Insert a wall anchor of the right type and size to grip the screw securely: drill a neat, parallel-sided hole a little deeper than the screw length and at right angles to the wall surface to take it. Mark screw hole positions on the wall, using masking tape on tiled surfaces. Use a masonry drill bit to match the screw and anchor size; tape the bit to mark the hole depth. Insert a wall anchor, then thread the fixing screw through whatever you are mounting, and try it out in the anchor. Drive the fixing screw home fully. If the anchor rotates, fit a larger one.

Wood-framed (stud) walls
○ *Mount heavy shelf supports by screwing directly into the wall's wooden framework.*

○ *For lighter-duty fixings, use a device such as a toggle or an anchor, designed for hollow stud partition walls (see below). All work by gripping the rear face of the plasterboard when the fixing screw is tightened.*

○ *To fit spring-loaded toggles, drill a hole in the plasterboard. Feed the toggle screw through whatever you are mounting, folding up its wings; the wings spring open to grip the plasterboard.*

○ *Fit gravity toggles similarly. Allow them to drop to a vertical position after pushing them in, then tighten the fixing screws.*

○ *Push in expanding anchors, then tighten the fixing screws.*

ADDING THE PERSONAL TOUCH

ACHIEVING A CERTAIN LOOK CAN SEEM A RATHER ELUSIVE EXERCISE when you first design a room — but knowing the impression you want to create is halfway to achieving it: Do you want cozy, homespun clutter, with lots of knickknacks everywhere or, at the opposite end of the scale, cool minimalism, with perhaps one large, carefully selected image adorning a wall? To create a room that you can really live with, you must choose images and objects that you love: they will endure and delight long after the latest fashion has passed. But always keep your eyes open for ideas and inspiration: look in shop windows, browse through home interest magazines and look around when visiting other people's homes. Develop your eye for detail so that you can attempt to recreate a particular effect at home.

DISPLAYING PICTURES

An unadorned wall is somehow incomplete. Without pictures, wallhangings, mirrors, or displays of collectables, however humble, a wall is an unused canvas. Although embarking on its embellishment can at times seem daunting, it should be seen as a wonderful opportunity to express your taste, to experiment and to be adventurous.

At all times bear in mind scale and balance. Symmetrical arrangements are always pleasing to the eye, whether in the positioning of pictures or in the placing of furniture or houseplants, but asymmetrical displays can be made to work just as well and are often more exciting. Be prepared to experiment, moving things around for a better balance or changing the juxtaposition of one element to another, until you are happy with the result.

If you have a number of pictures to display, they will make most impact if they are grouped together, rather than being dotted around the room. The simplest display to create is where you have a series of related images – prints, for example – all of a similar size, uniformly framed in wood or metal. Depending on the space, they can be hung in a single vertical or horizontal line (this in turn will help to make a room look longer or wider).

Alternatively, they can be grouped in rows, again with a vertical or horizontal emphasis. For example, six prints can be hung in two rows of three or in three rows of two. Such symmetrical arrangements are also possible with disparate images and sizes: a large picture could be placed centrally, with smaller sized images flanking it on either side.

Asymmetrical arrangements such as an L shape or a cross offer an interesting alternative to the symmetrical theme, and are slightly less predictable. Arrange the images carefully to follow the axes of your chosen shape. If you are working with a variety of sizes and shapes, you will need to think carefully about the positioning of the dominant (in other words, the largest) picture. Although it might seem the obvious place for it, avoid positioning the largest image in the center and then trying to fit everything else around it. You will find the arrangement looks much more effective if the dominant picture is positioned in one corner of the display or slightly off-center.

Images for walls are not limited to drawings, prints and paintings. Also choose from posters, post cards, photographs, framed embroidery or tapestry. A small piece of special fabric or hand-printed wallpaper also looks wonderful framed. Silhouettes look effective in a frame too: you can always make your own "antique" silhouette by copying an original from the eighteenth or nineteenth century and cutting it out of black cardboard.

LEFT: BY AVOIDING A RIGIDLY SYMMETRICAL DISPLAY, AN AIR OF OLD-FASHIONED INFORMALITY IS LENT TO THIS ECLECTIC ARRANGEMENT OF IMAGES. THE SLIGHTLY ECCENTRIC PLACING OF THE PIECES, WHICH BEGINS WITH A PROMISE OF HARMONY IN THE LEFT-HAND AND CENTRAL PANELS, ONLY TO BE BROKEN IN THE RIGHT-HAND PANEL BY AN IRREVERENT ASYMMETRY, SERVES ONLY TO DRAW MORE ATTENTION TO THE MIXTURE OF PERIODS AND STYLES.

RIGHT: ADDING SOME FORM OF RIBBON AND BOW ARRANGEMENT TO PICTURES WAS POPULAR IN THE EIGHTEENTH CENTURY, AND IT IS A DECORATIVE TREATMENT PARTICULARLY SUITED TO TRADITIONAL INTERIORS AND IMAGES. IT IS ALSO A USEFUL WAY TO BRING TOGETHER A DISPARATE COLLECTION OF ITEMS. HANG THE IMAGES IN A LINE ON THE WALL FIRST, THEN GLUE OR NAIL LINKING LENGTHS OF RIBBON. TOP WITH A BOW, OR A SERIES OF BOWS AS SHOWN HERE.

When it comes to displaying a picture collection of all different sizes and images, such as photographs, drawings, paintings, postcards and prints, or combining these with decorative objects such as plates or plaster reliefs, first decide on the final shape of the arrangement – for example, a triangle, rectangle or circle. If you want to be precise – and this is recommended when making holes in your walls! – try one of two different methods to establish the layout. One is to trace around the images on, say, shelf paper, then cut them out and use a removable wall adhesive to stick them to the wall. When you have a pleasing arrangement, mark the position of each image and start hammering. Or cut your shape out of paper, lay it on the floor, place the various images on top and start playing around with them, rather like a jigsaw puzzle, until you are satisfied.

Large single pictures look best hung over the mantelpiece or over a significant piece of furniture such as a sofa or sideboard, centered within its space. Make sure the picture is no wider than the item it is being hung over, and beware of hanging it too low over a sofa, in case people bang their heads.

STYLING IDEAS

☞ Do not hang pictures too high, or too far apart. Try to hang them at about eye level, taking into account the height from which they are usually viewed – when sitting or when standing.

☞ When arranging a grouping, aim for an overall balance of shapes: you might, for example, match a large image on one side with two smaller ones on the other side. Try to keep the gap between pictures roughly the same – about half the width of the smallest image being hung is about right.

☞ Picture frames come in many guises, from glass with clip-on mountings to ornate antique frames. Keep an eye out for old framed pictures in junk shops; you can discard the image inside and use the frame for your own picture.

☞ Plain flat wooden frames can be stained or painted as a cheap and effective way to achieve a co-ordinated look for your pictures.

☞ Photographs look best in plain black or chrome frames.

☞ A miscellaneous series of prints can be linked together by using the same colored mounts.

☞ Bring a disparate range of images together by using similar picture frames.

☞ On a limited budget, posters offer excellent value for money. Mount them on stiff cardboard with spray mount, or frame them simply under glass with clip-on mountings.

☞ The idea of a print room, first made popular in Europe in the eighteenth century, is enjoying a revival. Ready-made print room packs, complete with paper trompe l'oeil frames and decorative borders, are now available.

AN ASSORTMENT OF BLUE AND WHITE CHINA PLATES AND BOWLS FROM VERY DIFFERENT PERIODS AND STYLES ARE GIVEN COHESION AND STATUS WHEN THEY ARE PLACED TOGETHER IN A PAINTED DISPLAY CABINET. THIS IS THE SORT OF COLLECTION THAT IS VERY EASY AND ENJOYABLE TO BUILD UP, SIFTING THROUGH PILES OF THE AFFORDABLE CHINAWARE IN ANTIQUE AND SECOND-HAND SHOPS FOR ANY DESIGNS THAT TAKE YOUR FANCY. THE SUCCESS OF THIS DISPLAY LIES IN STICKING TO A SINGLE COLOR THEME, WHICH GIVES THE COLLECTION SOME SEMBLANCE OF UNIFORMITY, AND IN PROVIDING THE RIGHT VEHICLE FOR PUTTING IT ON SHOW. HERE, A CUPBOARD DECORATED IN STRONG, WARM PEACH WITH DUSTY YELLOW BOTH HIGHLIGHTS AND COMPLEMENTS THE BLUES IN THE COLLECTION.

DISPLAYING OTHER WORKS OF ART

Wallhangings Fabric wallhangings are the ideal solution for covering large areas decoratively – and they will hide a multitude of blemishes or eyesores on the wall too. Antique quilts and ethnic rugs make popular wallhangings but these sought-after items can be pricey. If you are on a limited budget, substitute modern ethnic rugs, many of whose designs are still traditional, and contemporary fabrics. There is a vast range of materials to choose from, to suit every style of room, from sumptuous damasks and silks to colorful Indian cotton weaves and pretty provencal prints. With the cheaper fabrics, you can change the hanging to suit the season – something warm, heavy and rich for the winter months, and an airy, light fabric for summertime.

Mirrors Mirrors are very versatile. With an attractive wooden or gilded frame, they are most decorative; they reflect light and can help to create the illusion of more space. A large mirror placed at the end of a dark, narrow passageway will open up the area dramatically, especially if you play a spotlight or two onto the glass. In a small room, a mirror placed opposite a window or windows will create a feeling of greater space and airiness; with pairs of windows, a smaller mirror also positioned between them provides an added dimension. If the mirror faces an outdoor view, it will reflect the verdant scene, and may well dictate the decor for the rest of the room. A large mirror or "pier glass" is traditional over a mantelpiece or bigger pieces of furniture such as a sofa, and often provides a useful focal point in a room. Pairs of ornate mirrors are always stylish, while a single mirror functions much like a picture and can be framed and hung in the same way.

Displaying collections

Whatever we choose to put on display – whether it is a prized china ornament, a pottery vase, a piece of ephemera, or a lovingly accumulated specialized collection – is an important signal to others of our taste and interests and it is important that they are displayed to greatest advantage.

The best way to draw attention to larger pieces of sculpture or wooden carvings is to present them on their own. Stand them on the floor, mount them on a pedestal, or display them on a small table or at one end of a mantelpiece.

To make the most of a thematic collection – anything from china and glassware to collectables such as perfume bottles, snuff boxes or toy models – always try to group them together, whether in a glass-fronted cabinet, on wall-mounted shelves or on a low table. Even inexpensive objects such as a selection of seashells, earthenware or tinware, can be made interesting if they are assembled into a still life and combined with a few other objects, such as a piece of driftwood. Collections can be more idiosyncratic and comprise a magpie assortment of memorabilia, provided they are put together with care, enthusiasm and some unifying link. Any arrangement looks better if the grouped items have a common factor, be it shape, color or texture; otherwise, the display will risk looking like clutter.

Screens Screens are very adaptable. They may be used instead of drawn curtains at a window, can disguise an ugly or functional corner, provide a useful decorative barrier behind which to store things, or serve as a room divider. You may be able to pick up a screen cheaply in a junk shop, otherwise you can make your own out of lengths of wood to form two or three simple rectangular frames. Attach these together with a series of screw hinges. Cover the frames with wallpaper or stretch and staple calico over them using a staple gun (hide the staples with braid), or gather or pleat a suitable piece of fabric and attach it to the frames, again using a staple gun to hold the material in place. Alternatively, for total flexibility, simply drape lengths of fabric over the frames, changing them as required.

Using clip-on curtain rings

ONE OF THE EASIEST WAYS TO MAKE A FEATURE of a wall is to introduce a wallhanging. Use the almost no-sew method shown here, and you have a simple way to create a hanging out of almost any large piece of material. Turn under and hem the top and bottom of the fabric. Attach clip-on curtain rings, spacing them evenly along the top of the fabric. Then slide the rings onto a pole fixed at the required height to the wall. This method is suitable for all but the heaviest of fabrics, including cotton, silk, wool, quilts and tapestries. The semi-sheer Indian cotton madras illustrated will give a soft, billowy effect suitable for a bedroom or bathroom, softening the wall without being over-pretty.

ALMOST ANYTHING CAN BE COLLECTED AND DISPLAYED EFFECTIVELY, AS THIS FINE ASSORTMENT OF ANTIQUE BRASS CANDLESTICKS ASSEMBLED TOGETHER ON A SMALL SIDE TABLE IN A HALLWAY DEMONSTRATES. SYMMETRY PLAYS AN IMPORTANT ROLE HERE: THE CANDLESTICKS ARE ARRANGED IN ORDER OF HEIGHT, STARTING WITH THE TALLEST; THE SMALLEST CANDLE HOLDER IS PLACED IN THE CENTER OF THE COMPOSITION, WHICH ALSO SERVES TO EMPHASIZE ITS VERY DIFFERENT SHAPE AND STYLE. A HANDSOME ANTIQUE PAINTED BOX IN A SUBDUED RED-BROWN ADDS A FURTHER DIMENSION, TONING WITH THE WARM, DULL GLOW OF THE METAL.

STYLING IDEAS

☛ To make the most of ornaments displayed on shelving in a small area, back the shelves with a large mirror to reflect the objects.

☛ Old printers' type-drawers are perfect for displaying all manner of small objects of interest, from tiny shells to miniature dolls.

☛ A length of Thai silk stretched over a frame like a canvas looks superb hung in a hallway or dining room.

☛ Make a wall display of decorative plates, hats, baskets, traditional kitchen utensils or old tools.

☛ Hang dried flowers and herbs from the ceiling in a kitchen or breakfast room. Tie the small bunches of herbs on long pieces of string first.

☛ Hang heavy-weight fabrics from curtain rings on a decorative pole or sew a row of small rings to the back of the fabric and hook these to corresponding nails hammered into a batten of wood screwed to the wall.

☛ For lighter-weight materials, an alternative to clip-on curtain rings is to sew a series of tabs made from fabric in a complementary color to the top of the wallhanging and thread a narrow rod through them. Another option is to glue one strip of touch-and-close fastener to a batten of wood mounted on the wall and stitch the other strip to the reverse of the fabric.

DECORATING WITH FRESH FLOWERS

FLOWERS BRING COLOR AND JOY TO A ROOM LIKE NOTHING ELSE DOES. Their natural appearance softens hard lines and they can when required make a stunning focal point for a room. Flowers may be arranged either formally or informally, depending on both the room setting and the occasion.

FORMAL FLOWER ARRANGEMENTS

Even if you do not generally have formal flower displays in your home, they are a welcome addition at special times of the year such as Christmas, anniversaries and celebrations. These are occasions when you want an arrangement that is bold, festive and striking. But formal arrangements need not be confined to those times when you are expecting guests – a thoughtfully put together composition gracing a table in the hallway or living room always adds a special quality. With formal displays, some prior thought needs to be given to the materials that will make up the finished arrangement – the container, the flowers, the foliage, accessories such as ribbons or bows – as well as how the components will be put together.

With a formal arrangement, the best place to start is the location of the finished display: whether in the hallway, in the empty hearth of a living room, or perhaps on the main table in a dining area. From there, you can establish the scale of the arrangement, and whether it is front-facing only or it will be viewed from all sides. Next consider your color scheme. It is a good idea to choose a main color that contrasts with the surrounding decor, as this will be more eye-catching. For example, if you have a green hallway, aim for an arrangement with a red or pink theme. If your living room is predominantly apricot, lean towards blues. This will suggest ideas for flowers and foliage, depending on the time of year. The container is an important consideration in enabling you to create a particular look. If you want to achieve height, go for a tall, square or cylindrical container; if you want a more spreading arrangement, choose a wide, shallow bowl.

UNDERSTATED ELEGANCE IS THE KEYNOTE TO THIS SERIES OF MORE FORMAL FLOWER ARRANGEMENTS. A MASS OF HYDRANGEA HEADS IN THE MAIN ARRANGEMENT IS COUNTER-BALANCED BY AIRY SPRAYS OF DELICATE BAMBOO STEMS, THE COLORS CAREFULLY CHOSEN TO ECHO THE NATURAL TONES THAT DISTINGUISH THIS INTERIOR. ON THE MANTELPIECE THE TWO MATCHING DISPLAYS OF LILIES IN TALL, FLUTE-SHAPED VASES INTRODUCE A WELCOME SPLASH OF COLOR, ALL THE MORE STARTLING AND EFFECTIVE FOR BEING PLACED IN A ROOM THAT DRAWS ON SUCH A RESTRAINED PALETTE.

There are three classical forms used in formal flower arranging that meet most requirements: the triangle, the circle (or dome) and an attractive S shape known as a Hogarth curve. Before starting work, you may well need to insert some chicken wire or wet oasis into the bottom of your container to enable you to tame and manipulate stems: this will hold them firmly in place and allow you a certain amount of flexibility. It helps to position some stems of foliage first, to establish the basic structure, or bones, of the arrangement. Then place the largest flowers, followed by medium and smaller sized blooms. As a general rule, a composition that is one and two-thirds the height and width of the container gives a pleasing ratio – but do not let that stop you from experimenting. Keep standing back to check how everything is working together, and adjust as necessary. Be prepared to do some further tweeking once the arrangement is in position.

Making Cut Flowers Last

THE KEY TO LONG-LASTING FLOWERS starts at the florist. Always choose healthy-looking flowers with plenty of buds, and get them home as quickly as possible. Treat the ends of the stems depending on the plant type (see right), remove any leaves that fall below the water line and place the plants in a bucket of tepid water to have a good long drink before you arrange them. If the flowers come with a commercial cut-flower feed, do use it in the final water – it will make all the difference to the lifespan of the plant material.

○ Most stems, including woody and hard stems, should be treated simply by cutting the end of the stems at an angle. Do not hammer the ends of woody stems or split the ends of hard stems, such as those of chrysanthemums and roses – research has shown that such treatment does nothing to assist water uptake.

○ The hollow stems of plants such as delphiniums, amaryllis and lupins should be filled with water and the ends plugged with a small piece of absorbent cotton.

○ Sappy stems like poppies and euphorbias benefit from having the end of their stems burnt; clematis may also receive this treatment.

○ A few plants, such as geum, valerian, lavatera, hollyhock and buddleia will benefit from having their stems plunged into boiling water for 5-10 seconds.

Tulips are notorious for their tendency to droop down. Some arrangers find this an attractive fault and choose low containers to encourage and emphasize the curved stems and bowed heads. Others prefer to ensure an upright display that brings the attractive heart of the flower into view. A tall container, as used here, will support the stems and heads, confining the arrangement firmly to the color and shape of the blooms. The most important thing is to condition the flowers before they are arranged by standing them in a bucket of water first (see above). Adding a commercial plant food to the water will make tulips last longer.

DECORATING WITH INFORMAL FLOWERS

WHEN MAKING UP AN INFORMAL FLOWER ARRANGEMENT, aim for a look that is artless and uncontrived. Even if you do not live in the country and have wayside flowers at your disposal, no matter — casual, rustic compositions can just as easily be created using florists' and garden flowers to bring a sense of the country and all its homespun associations into the most urban of settings.

The key to achieving an informal look lies in choosing both appropriate flowers and the right container. Select traditional country-style or garden blooms such as narcissi, poppies, larkspur, snapdragons, cornflowers, ranunculus, thistles, love-in-a-mist, stocks, bachelor's buttons, scabious and, of course, roses (the more "cabbagey" in shape the better). Most of these are available from good florists during the spring and summer months — at the height of the growing season — and they can be supplemented with flowers and foliage from the garden if you have one. If not, bunches of fresh herbs can be found locally and some of them, including lavender and dill, are very decorative and will provide welcome color and foliage in an informal display. Containers made from wickerwork, wood, stone, metal and earthenware, including baskets, bowls, tinware, jugs and cups, will continue the country theme.

Fresh flowers may sometimes seem rather like a luxury, but there are economical ways to get the most from purchased material. Flowers in season are always the most reasonably priced — in spring, for example, two or three bunches of daffodils cost very little. If you have a garden or access to plant material, use garden flowers and foliage to supplement your arrangements. If you use a vase with a narrow neck, you only need a few flowerheads to make an impact — such as miniature sunflowers, gerberas, or roses. If you place an arrangement in front of a mirror, you get twice the value from it.

Informal arrangements may range from a tiny posy of violets or pansies in a small, delicate cup to generously bunched flowers in a large, exuberantly patterned jug. The displays can either be put together in your hand or arranged one stem at a time. Apparently

AN INFORMAL DISPLAY RELIES ON THE QUALITY AND VOLUME OF FLOWERS USED. HERE, TWO GENEROUS BUNCHES OF PEONIES ARE ARRANGED SIDE BY SIDE IN MATCHING CONTAINERS. THE BOLD COMBINATION OF PINK PETALS AND YELLOW CENTERS PROVIDES A STRIKING AND EYE-CATCHING FOCAL POINT IN THIS QUIET, COOL INTERIOR. A SMALLER, ALTOGETHER MORE SUBDUED FLORAL DISPLAY WOULD HAVE BEEN LOST IN SUCH ELEGANT AND SPACIOUS SURROUNDINGS.

STYLING IDEAS

✔ **The simplest arrangements are often the most effective. Whatever the time of year, a row of quaint jars or a collection of roughly blown colored glass can be filled with a bunch of seasonal flowers or foliage, either all of the same kind or each vessel containing a different variety.**

✔ **Arrangements made up of all the same type of flower invariably work well – a generous bunch of daffodils, a posy of snowdrops or masses of old-fashioned roses, for example.**

✔ **During late autumn and winter, when it is more of a challenge finding material for making up country-style displays, try arrangements of autumn-hued or evergreen foliage and berries. Make up a still-life of colorful seasonal vegetables, such as pumpkins, sweet peppers and gourds.**

✔ **Trailing plants, such as ivy, and creepers, particularly Virginia creeper, are very valuable in informal arrangements. Use them to soften lines and to extend the arrangement beyond the confines of the container. They can also be wound round and round to cover the container itself, turning an indifferent vase into a sculpted piece of vegetation.**

✔ **Use double-sided tape on a container to attach moss, twigs and other dried materials.**

SWEET PEAS AND ANEMONES ARE AN EXCELLENT CHOICE FOR A DISPLAY THAT TAKES PINKS AND PURPLES AS ITS COLOR THEME. CHOOSING ONLY TWO COLORS THAT ARE CLOSELY RELATED — OTHER EXAMPLES ARE GREEN AND YELLOW, YELLOW AND ORANGE, AND ORANGE AND RED — PRACTICALLY GUARANTEES SUCCESS, AND CONFINING YOURSELF TO JUST ONE OR TWO SPECIES KEEPS EVERYTHING SIMPLE AND STRONG. AN EXTRA TOUCH HERE IS THE INTRODUCTION OF A VARIETY OF CONTAINERS IN BRILLIANT TURQUOISE BLUES, A DARING NOTE WHICH HEIGHTENS THE MAIN COLOR THEME.

casual arrangements on a larger scale and containing a wide range of plant material sometimes require some help, however. A piece of crumpled chicken wire placed in the bottom of your chosen vessel will enable you to control wayward stems without sacrificing a natural appearance. You can still apply the basic principles of formal flower arranging (see page 244) and put in some foliage first to give the arrangement form, followed by your selection of flowers.

When you are striving for a spontaneous-looking result, there is no need to fight the natural inclination of the plants – let heavy-headed roses gently bow, sheafs of grass stand to attention, love-lies-bleeding swoop downwards, delphiniums spiral skywards and so on. The formal principle where the arrangement should be one and two-thirds the height of the container, can be eased on country-style displays. An arrangement where all the flowerheads open just above the lip of the vessel, or alternatively where the material generously spills out over the edges, almost touching the surface on which the container is placed, can look simply wonderful. Do not completely forsake all notions of balance when putting together an informal arrangement, however. It should still retain some shape, but without being too rigid. Always allow some material, such as leaves, twigs and buds, to break the outline of the arrangement.

DECORATING WITH DRIED FLOWERS

Dried plant material offers the same creative scope as when working with fresh produce, with the added bonus that your efforts will last and be appreciated for much longer. Dried flowers are especially welcome when fresh material is scarce. The excellent range of dried materials to choose from includes not only flowers but leaves, grasses and cereals, berries and hips, gourds and seedheads.

Dried flowers, leaves and berries can be used to make flower arrangements large and small, as well as wreaths, garlands, even dried "trees". Dried florist's foam is a boon when arranging dried materials, or you can use crumpled chicken wire to hold everything in place. The best plants for drying include immortelles, yarrow, sea lavender, sea holly, honesty, roses, helichrysums (everlasting flowers), Chinese lanterns, heather, bachelor's buttons, thistles, golden rod, delphinium, baby's breath, larkspur and hydrangea.

DRYING FLOWERS

Most plant material can be dried by hanging it in small bunches in any dry, airy place. Once the plants have dried out, arrange them or suspend them decoratively on view in a kitchen, bedroom or living room.

Fragile flowers can be dried in desiccants. Use either silica gel crystals or borax and alum (all available from pharmacies), mixed together in equal quantities. Place a layer of desiccant about 1½in (3.5cm) deep in the bottom of an airtight container. Put the flowers in, their stems cut to about 1in (2.5cm) below the head (these can then be wired later), and cover with more desiccant. Place round-faced flowerheads downwards; for multi-petalled blooms, place a piece of chicken wire cut to the size of the container on the first layer of desiccant and use this to support the flowerheads. Put on the lid and leave until the petals feel papery – this will take anything from a day to two weeks.

AIR DRYING IS AN EFFECTIVE AND VISUALLY PLEASING WAY TO DRY FLOWERS. ANYWHERE DRY AND AIRY IS SUITABLE FOR THIS PROCESS, WHICH MEANS THAT MOST ROOMS IN THE HOME CAN BE USED, APART FROM KITCHENS AND BATHROOMS. (IF YOU WANT DRIED FLOWER ARRANGEMENTS IN THESE ROOMS, DRY THE FLOWERS ELSEWHERE FIRST, AND THEN TRANSFER THEM TO THEIR FINAL POSITION). ARRANGING THE FLOWERS INTO ASSORTED BUNCHES ALWAYS LOOKS ATTRACTIVE, AND A SERIES OF DISPLAYS HUNG CLOSE TOGETHER MAKES A CONSIDERABLE IMPACT.

Making a dried wreath

A wreath of dried flowers provides an attractive, long-lasting decoration for a wall or shelf and it is easy to make your own. This wreath is based on memories of a summer holiday island, and includes suitable seaside plants and fruits of the sea. The inspiration could just as easily be a favorite garden or some other spot that brings back fond memories. Include aromatic plants, particularly dried herbs with evocative scents such as lavender, thyme and rosemary.

The beauty of this wreath is that you do not need to wire up any of the plant material individually – a time-consuming job at the best of times. Because it is so densely packed with moss and plants, it is possible simply to push short stems into the basic wreath and they will stay in place.

You will need
- ✔ 14 in (37 cm) florist's double wire ring
- ✔ small bag of sphagnum moss
- ✔ florist's wire
- ✔ raffia
- ✔ small bunch each of marjoram, oregano, sea lavender, Timothy grass, yarrow, sneezewort, bachelor's buttons, poppies, scabious, everlasting flowers, sea holly
- ✔ small bag reindeer moss
- ✔ 1 sea fan
- ✔ 3 small starfish
- ✔ 3 small scallop shells

If you cannot get hold of a ready-made ring as shown, shape a strip of chicken wire into a curved circle; electrical wire can be used instead of florist's wire.

Attach the sphagnum moss to the ring by packing small handfuls at a time into the frame, then wind around florist's wire to hold it in place. Continue working in this way until the whole ring is covered in moss.

Mix together handfuls of the marjoram and sea lavender and bind it onto the mossy frame using raffia. Do not worry if the result looks rather untidy, as this will soon be covered with other plant material.

Now add the rest of the plant material, beginning with the outer edge: use Timothy grass here to define and soften the line of the wreath. Make sure the flowers and seedheads are evenly distributed; use short stems of the sea holly to fill in any gaps around the edge.

Break the sea fan into pieces and push them into the wreath, then position the starfish and scallops. Wind raffia around two opposite arms of each starfish and tie them into position at the back of the wreath. The scallops will stay in place by simply wedging them into the position, or you could tie raffia crosswise for a more secure hold.

DECORATING WITH PLANTS

HOUSEPLANTS CAN READILY BE CONSIDERED AS LIVING ORNAMENTS and there is almost no empty space in a room which will not be enhanced by a plant of some sort. They give year-round pleasure for very little outlay, they change in subtle ways as they grow, and they are invaluable for softening hard lines or extreme formality.

In choosing plants for the home there are several important considerations. First, your style of decor: if you have a fairly traditional or classic scheme, then bold, architectural plants, such as a yucca, dracena or a bromeliad, may look out of place, whereas they would complement perfectly a modern interior, with simple, clean lines. Where do you want the plants to go? If they are meant to pep up a dim corner, choose a shade-tolerant plant such as a fern or one of the philodendrons. In a bathroom, choose a plant which enjoys humidity. Do you want your plants to serve any other function apart from a decorative one? You may want to use them to divide a room in some way, for example between dining and sitting areas, in which case you must choose tall, upright-growing plants such as a palm, or indoor trees such as a weeping fig. If you have little spare time or if in the past you have experienced a series of houseplant mishaps, avoid plants that need constant nurturing and go for the more robust survivors such as palms, small-leaved ivies, grape ivy or spider plants.

Large, mature plants with magnificent sculptural forms like the Kentia palm, the Swiss cheese plant or

THE COMBINATION OF A LARGE, GRACEFUL PALM AND A STURDY WEEPING FIG CREATE A REFRESHING AND DRAMATIC EFFECT IN THIS DIMINUTIVE BATHROOM. ALTHOUGH THE ATMOSPHERE IN A BATHROOM — SUDDEN BLASTS OF STEAM AND THE AIR FILLED WITH SCENTS AND SPRAYS — AND THE OFTEN DIM LIGHTING MAKE IT OUT OF BOUNDS FOR MANY HOUSEPLANTS, THE WEEPING FIG AND THE PALM ARE TOLERANT ENOUGH TO WITHSTAND A CERTAIN DEGREE OF ADVERSE CONDITIONS. HOWEVER, THE FIG MUST RECEIVE A GOOD SOURCE OF NATURAL LIGHT IF IT IS TO THRIVE; HENCE IT IS GIVEN THE WINDOW POSITION HERE.

Buying and Caring for Houseplants

✔ *Always buy houseplants from a florist that cares for its plant material – they should be housed in a draft-free and well-lit area. Check that they are healthy looking, and reject anything that is wilting, yellowing or which has leaves dropping off.*

✔ *Follow the care instructions which come with your plants. To survive, houseplants need an environment that approximates to their natural habitat, although many will tolerate a consistently lower temperature than that recommended. However, this may not tally with an electricity time-clock, which has the heating off during the greater part of the day, with a burst of heat first thing in the morning and again during the evening.*

✔ *Drafts are the downfall of many healthy houseplants, as is too sunny a position. Most plants like a well-lit position, but not right against the glass unless they are true sun lovers.*

✔ *For watering, check the soil every other day. Feed with a commercial plant food during the growing season.*

✔ *Repot houseplants every spring, and prune back any straggly or unsightly growth. Deadhead all flowering plants as soon as the blooms wither.*

✔ *Check regularly for pests and diseases and take remedial action at the first sight of a problem.*

a castor oil plant make an instant impact in a room. Pairs of plants are always stylish in formal settings: for example, two indoor trees standing either side of a door, or two plants standing sentinel at either end of a mantelpiece or on an occasional table. Put a selection of pot plants in a metal *jardinière* stand on legs in front of a window or a single plant on a pedestal for more impact. Small and medium-sized plants always look better grouped together in twos or threes, or very small ones massed together in a larger grouping. Exploit the natural habit of different houseplants: climbing plants look pretty trained around a recessed window or along a shelf or ledge, while trailing plants are happy spilling attractively from an indoor hanging basket or wall planter. A group of three flowering plants, such as primulas or busy lizzies, placed in a basket will bring seasonal color and impact to a room.

When using plants for more practical purposes, such as room dividers, either use tall-growing plants or indoor trees, or place a selection of medium-sized self-supporting plants in a planter trough. Alternatively, you can train climbers up some kind of support, such as trellis (even inexpensive garden trellis, smartened up with some paint). This is particularly suitable in a conservatory or solarium, where you may wish to use trailing and climbing greenery as the "furnishings".

Painting a Terracotta Flower Pot

TRADITIONAL TERRACOTTA FLOWER POTS are not only more attractive to look at than the modern plastic varieties, but they are also easy to decorate with water-based paints. Special paint effects such as sponging (shown here with a deep terracotta base coat and sponged top coat of pale tangerine), stippling, spattering and ragging are striking finishes. Or try simple contrasting stripes (shown here, with a lemon base coat and white stripes), or spots and wavy bands. Choose color combinations that will complement the plants the containers are to hold – soft green arching ferns need equally soft colors, while a strident yucca can take strong, hot colors. Do not forget to paint the outer and inner rim of the drip tray to match. If you are concerned about the effect of water drips and spills on your work, brush on one or two coats of clear matte varnish.

✔ *Use seasonal flowering houseplants to supplement more permanent displays of plants grown for their foliage. Flowering pot plants are usually short-lived, but they bring a welcome touch of color into the home and are often better value than a bunch of fresh flowers.*

✔ *Bowls massed with the same type of bulb bring a sense of spring to a room and often smell delicious too. Early in the growing season, try hyacinths, grape hyacinths or narcissi.*

✔ *Traditional terracotta clay pots are prettier than the plastic pots in which most houseplants are bought, so it is worth repotting them immediately.*

✔ *Or try a more unusual container such as a wicker basket, a wastepaper basket, a birdcage, a galvanized bucket or china and earthenware bowls. If the container is not waterproof, either line it with plastic before repotting, or place another, smaller container inside the decorative one. If there is no drainage, water little and often.*

✔ *Grow pots of herbs on a kitchen windowsill for an attractive display that is also handy when cooking.*

✔ *Use plants to hide an ugly outlook: fix a narrow shelf across the window and place on it trailing plants such as ivies and spider plants which will grow down to screen the view.*

✔ *A grouping of cacti and succulents looks striking: place them together on a tray for impact and for easy care.*

✔ *If you wish to grow plants in a bathroom with no natural light, you can buy light bulbs which will simulate daylight.*

INDEX

GLOSSARY OF TERMS FOR UK READERS

absorbent cotton - cotton wool
awl - bradawl
baby's breath - gypsophila
bachelor's buttons - cornflowers
baste (ing) (ed) - tack (ing) (ed)
batting - wadding
blockboard - chipboard
brad - panel pin, fixing pin
burlap - hessian
burner - hob
carpenter's level - spirit level
clothes rod - hanging rail, dress rail
cord(electric) - lead, flex
downspout - downpipe, drainpipe
eyelet lace - broderie anglaise
faucet - tap
flanellette - wincyette
flashlight - torch
hutch - kitchen dresser
latex - emulsion
liquid detergent - washing-up liquid
mineral spirits - white spirit
mullioned - leaded, part-glazed
paint bucket - paint kettle
pickled (wood finish) - limed
polished cotton - glazed cotton
putty - filler
ruffle - frill
sheers - net curtains
slipcover - loose cover
stove - cooker

ACKNOWLEDGMENTS

The publisher wishes to thank the following suppliers who kindly lent materials for photography (for addresses, see Suppliers, page 254).

Art materials: Daler-Rowney Ltd
Bathroom basin: C.P. Hart
Brushes and paint equipment:: L.G. Harris & Co Ltd (thanks also to Hamilton Acorn Ltd)
Dried Flowers: The Hop Shop
Chair: Paperchase
Clothing for models: Bhs (additional clothing, stylist's own)
Cork tiling: Wicanders
Ethnic artefacts (furniture, glass and pottery): Nice Irma's Ltd
Flooring: Oak hardwood flooring from Junckers Ltd; carpet from The Carpet Studio and Heal's
Floor and tile adhesives: Evode Ltd
Paints: Crown Berger (thanks also to FADS and Dulux)
Poles and accessories: Harrison Drape Ltd (thanks also to Chesil Court Studios for the loan of finials and accessories)
Power tools: Black and Decker
Shaker peg rail: The Shaker Shop
Shelving: Sainsbury's Homebase
Tiles: Corres Tiles (thanks also to Walton Ceramics of Knightsbridge)
Tiling equipment: Cintride Ltd
Tools: Stanley Tools
Vinyl and cushioned floorings: Forbo-Nairn Ltd
Wallpaper: Osborne & Little plc
Wood panels: Wicanders

Models: P.M. Glarvey, Caroline Jones, Jennifer Jones, Stewart Walton, Susie Hedley-Smith

Special thanks to Joanna Gilbert, P.M. Glarvey, Miles Newby and Top Layer for their advice and assistance, and also to D.R. Hayes.

Fabric and wallpaper samples: Grateful thanks are due to the following fabric and wallpaper houses, whose samples appear throughout this book:

Brunschwig & Fils; Nina Campbell; Jane Churchill; Colefax & Fowler; Cooks Mills; The Design Archives; Designers Guild; Donghia; Firifiss Contemporary Textiles; Christian Fischbacher (London) Ltd; Forbo Lancaster; Pierre Frey; G.S.W. Co. Ltd; Anya Larkin Ltd at Donghia (UK) Ltd; Harlequin Wallcoverings; Liberty Retail Ltd; John Lewis; Ian Mankin; Andrew Martin; Monkwell Fabrics & Wallpaper; Mulberry Company (Design) Ltd; Nice Irma's Ltd; The Nursery Window; Les Olivades (UK) Ltd; Osborne & Little plc; Percheron; Peter Jones; Ramm, Son & Crocker Ltd; Arthur Sanderson & Sons Ltd; Ian Sanderson (Textiles) Ltd; John Stefanidis; Titley & Marr; Today Interiors; Vymura plc; Warner Fabrics; Watts & Co Furnishings Ltd; Zoffany.

Picture Credits: The publisher thanks the following photographers and organisations for their permission to reproduce the photographs in this book: names in italics are designers or suppliers.
The English Stamp Company 35; Explorer 12; P Roy 11 top; Loirat 12; J B Laffitte 101; Fired Earth 134; Michael Freeman 18; Robert Harding Syndication/IPC Magazines 52, 64, 69, 100, 178; Insight Picture Library/ Michelle Garrett 247&245; The Interior World/ Simon Brown 27; The Interior World/Fritz Von Der Schulenburg 8, 9 left, 16 *Rupert Cavendish* 36, *Osborne & Little* 37, *Mimmi O'Connell* 38, *Bingham Land* 41, *Janet Fitch* 42, *Osborne & Little* 46, *Miani d'Angoris* 53left, *Sissi* *Edmiston* right *Bingham Land* 54-5, *Julia Boston* 57top, 60, *Osborne & Little* 62top *Jill de Brand* 66, *Moltons* 67, *Bingham Land* 73, *Mimmi O'Connell* 75, 80, *Cristabel Bielenberg* 81, *John Stefanidis* 87&88, *Mimmi O'Connell* 96, *Richard Mudditt* 90, 109, *Mimmi O'Connell* 110, *Janet Fitch* 128, *Anna Fendi* 151, *David Milnaric* 158left, *Monika Apponyi* 164, *Kelly Hoppen* 165, *Osborne & Little* 170, *Michael Cooper* 171, *Mimmi O'Connell* 172, *Osborne & Little* 177, *Fee Tussling* 186, *Christophe Gollut* 190, 192, 194right, *Vicky Rothco* 195, *Stephen Ryan* 200, *Monika Apponyi* 202, *Cristabel Bielenberg* 206, *John Stefanidis* 212, *Mimmi O'Connell* 213, *Conrad Jameson* 216, *Mimmi O'Connell* 223, *Anouska Hempel* 224, 226, *Meltons* 227, *Monika Apponyi* 228, *Meltons* 229, 232, *Mimmi O'Connell* 236, *Juliette Mole* 240, *Jeannie Chesterton* 242, *Barry Ferguson* 244, *Jeremiah Goodman* 246, *Jeannie Chesterton* 250, *Ken Turner/ Peter Wolozynski* 22, 47, 49, 56, 61, right, 68, 82, 84, 89, 120, 126-7, 157, 161, 176, 203, 210, 222; Erica Lennard/ Roberto Bergero 198; Marianne Majerus 15, 78, 86, 112left, 234, 235; Marston & Langinger Conservatories, 192 Ebury St, London, SW1W 8UP 0171 823 6829 79; Mike Newton 13left, 97, 102below, 105below, 118right, 129below, 135below, 130below, 145top right, 147below right, 149top right, 153top right, 154, 155top right; Hugh Palmer 70; Parkertex(Key Largo) 184left; David Parmiter 20, 32, 44, 57right, 104, 113, 116, 130, 142, 156;166, 168, 248; Ianthe Ruthven 13right, 19, 21left, 24, 30, 31, 33, 40, 102, 159, 160, 243left; Paul Ryan/ International Interiors 7, 14 Sasha Waddell, 17, 23right, 26, 45 Charles Rutherford, 48 Jan des Bouvrie, 59, 61left, 62right Charles Rutherford, 71 Sasha Waddell, 72, 76, 83, 137 Kirstina Ratia, 158right, 174, 180, 183, 208, 210, 233; Christian Sarramon 6, 10, 11right, 21right, 23left, 28 Margaret Behrers, 29 Paul de Lusonet, 74 N Robbins, 144, 148 C Bataille, 152, 182 N Wotternck, 183, 230 Maison Lang, 241; Wicanders Cork 146.

All special photography: John Freeman.

First published in the United States of America in 1995 by
RIZZOLI INTERNATIONAL PUBLICATIONS, INC.
300 Park Avenue South, New York, NY 10010

First published in Great Britain in 1995
by Collins & Brown Ltd.

Library of Congress Cataloging-in-Publication Data

Walton, Stewart.
    The Complete Home Decorator / Stewart Walton.
        p. cm.
    ISBN 0-8478-1898-5
    1. Interior decoration—Handbooks, manuals, etc. I. Title.
    NK2115.W155   1995
    747—dc20   95-1234
                                                              CIP

This book created by Amazon Publishing Ltd.

Color reproduction by J. Film Process, Singapore
Printed in Italy by New Interlitho, SpA, Milan